I0804512

Nietzsche and the Becoming of Life

John D. Caputo, *series editor*

PERSPECTIVES IN
CONTINENTAL
PHILOSOPHY

Edited by VANESSA LEMM

Nietzsche and the Becoming of Life

FORDHAM UNIVERSITY PRESS
New York ▪ 2015

Fordham University Press also publishes its books in a variety of electronic formats. Some content that appears in print may not be available in electronic books.

Library of Congress Cataloging-in-Publication Data is available from the publisher.

Printed in the United States of America

17 16 15 5 4 3 2 1

First edition

Contents

Abbreviations

References to Nietzsche's unpublished writings are standardized, whenever possible, to refer the most accessible edition of Nietzsche's notebooks and publications, *Nietzsche, Sämtliche Werke: Kritische Studienausgabe*, compiled under the general editorship of Giorgio Colli and Mazzino Montinari, are cited as *KSA*. References to the edition of the *Nietzsche, Werke: Kritische Gesamtausgabe Werke,* compiled under the general editorship of Giorgio Colli and Mazzino Montinari, are cited as *KGW*. References to the editions of letters, *Nietzsche, Sämtliche Briefe: Kritische Studienausgabe Briefe*, compiled under the general editorship of Giorgio Colli and Mazzino Montinari, are cited as *KSB*. In the cases in which the *KSA* are cited, references provide the volume number followed by the relevant fragment number and any relevant aphorism (e.g., KSA 10:12[1].37 refers to volume 10, fragment 12[1], aphorism 37). In the cases in which the *KSB* is cited, references provide the number of the letter, followed by the volume and the page number (e.g. Letter Nr. 648, *KSB* 5:271). In the cases in which the *KGW* are cited, references provide the volume number followed by the section number followed by the fragment and in some cases the page number. The following abbreviations are used for citations of Nietzsche's writings:

A	*The Antichrist*
AOM	*Assorted Opinions and Maxims* (*HH*, vol. II, part 1)
BGE	*Beyond Good and Evil*
BT	*The Birth of Tragedy*

CW	*The Case of Wagner*
D	*Daybreak* (alternately: *Dawn*)
DS	"David Strauss, the Writer and the Confessor" (*UM* I)
EH	*Ecce Homo* (sections abbreviated "Wise," "Clever," "Books," "Destiny"; abbreviations for titles discussed in "Books" are indicated instead of "Books" where relevant)
FEI	"On the Future of Our Educational Institutions" (*KSA* 1)
GM	*On the Genealogy of Morals*
GMD	*Greek Music Drama* (Das Griechische Musikdrama, *KSA* 1)
GS	*The Gay Science*
GSt	"The Greek State" (*KSA* 1)
HC	"Homer's Contest" (alternately: "Homer on Competition")
HH	*Human, All Too Human* (two volumes, I and II)
HL	"On the Use and Disadvantage of History for Life" (*UM I)* (alternately: "Use and Misuse of History for Life"; *Vom Nutzen und Nachtheil der Historie für das Leben*)
KSA	*Sämtliche Schriften: Kritische Studienausgabe*
KSB	*Sämtliche Briefe: Kritische Studienausgabe Briefe*
KGW	*Werke: Kritische Studienausgabe Werke*
NCW	*Nietzsche contra Wagner*
P	"The Philosopher. Reflections on the Struggle between Art and Knowledge"
PPP	*The Pre-Platonic Philosophers* (followed by section and page number)
PT	*Philosophy and Truth*
PTA	*Philosophy in the Tragic Age of the Greeks* (*KSA* 1)
PW	"On the Pathos of Truth" (*KSA* 1)
SE	"Schopenhauer as Educator" (*UM* III)
ST	"Socrates und die Tragödie" (*KSA* 1)
TI	*Twilight of the Idols* (sections abbreviated "Maxims," "Socrates," "Reason," "World," "Morality," "Errors," "Improvers," "Germans," "Skirmishes," "Ancients," "Hammer")
TL	"On Truth and Lies in an Extra-Moral Sense" (*KSA* 1)
TSK	"Teleology Since Kant" (*Die Teleologie seit Kant*) (*KGW* I/4, NF 62[1–58], p. 548–578)
UM	*Untimely Meditations* (Volumes I–IV) (alternately: *Untimely Considerations*; *Unmodern Observations*)
WP	*The Will to Power*
WS	*The Wanderer and His Shadow* (*HH*, vol. II, part 2)
Z	*Thus Spoke Zarathustra* (references to *Z* list the part number and the chapter title followed by the relevant section number when applicable)

Acknowledgments

This collection of essays is in great part based on conference papers given at the International Conference "Nietzsche and the Becoming of Life," which took place in November 2009 at the Institute of Humanities, Diego Portales University. I am grateful to the Diego Portales University, Chile, the Goethe-Institute Santiago, Chile, and the German Embassy, Santiago de Chile for their indispensable financial support without which the realization of this event would have been impossible. I thank all the contributors of this volume for their participation.

A draft translation from Spanish to English of the chapters by Virginia Cano, Mónica Cragnolini, and Mariana Cruz has been provided by Jennifer Croft. I thank Miguel Vatter, Matías Bascuñan, and Benedict Storck for their help with the revision of the translations as well as the text by Eduardo Nasser. I also thank Nicolás del Valle and Tabita Galleguillos for their support. Finally, I thank Michigan State University Press for their permission to reprint my article "History, Life and Justice in Friedrich Nietzsche's *Vom Nutzen und Nachtheil der Historie für das Leben*" © 2011 Michigan State University. This article originally appeared in *CR: The New Centennial Review* Vol. 10, Iss. 3, 2011, pages 167–188.

Spanish versions of the essays by Tracy B. Strong, Lawrence J. Hatab, Herman W. Siemens, Daniel Conway, Debra Bergoffen, Keith Ansell-Pearson, Dieter Thomä, Mónica Cragnolini, and Gary Shapiro are also available in *Nietzsche y el devenir de la vida*, ed. Vanessa Lemm, Santiago de Chile: Fondo de cultura económica, 2014.

Nietzsche and the Becoming of Life

Introduction

VANESSA LEMM

Throughout his writing career, Nietzsche advocates the affirmation of earthly life as a way to counteract the nihilism and the asceticism he believes are inevitable once human beings begin to orient their lives toward a transcendent source of truth and value. But what Nietzsche means by life on earth, and what the affirmation of such a life entails, is still very much up for discussion. This is in great part due to the fact that the concept of life in Nietzsche's work takes on a variety of different but not unrelated meanings, which largely correspond to the different periods of his writing career. Mapping out this variety of meanings of the concept of life in any detail would, by far, exceed the purpose of this introduction. However, the reader may find it useful to have a sense of the different concerns that animate Nietzsche's discussion of the concept of life throughout his works.

In the belated preface to *The Birth of Tragedy*, Nietzsche claims that his task as a philosopher was from the very beginning to "*look at science through the optic of the artist, but also to look at art through the optic of life*" (*BT* "Preface" 2). In *The Birth of Tragedy* Nietzsche reconsiders the various dimensions of human culture: science, history, morality, politics, philosophy, and so on, from the perspective of life. The "optic of life" becomes the privileged starting point of Nietzsche's critical philosophical undertakings. But what does it mean to consider human culture from the perspective of life?

In his early writings, in particular in *The Birth of Tragedy*, Nietzsche articulates what could be called a cosmic or poetic-metaphysical conception of life. Its highest expression is the tragic vision of the world as Dionysian chaos according to which the best thing is "not to have been born, not to *be*, to be *nothing*," and the second best thing is "to die soon" (*BT* 3). From the standpoint of the Greeks in the age of tragedy, life is unbearable suffering that stands in need of art to make it possible and worthwhile to go on living. Only art has the power to overcome "the terrors and horrors of existence" (*BT* 3), the "absurdity of life" (*BT* 7), and hence Nietzsche concludes that "all life rests on illusion [*Schein*], art, deception, optic, the necessity of perspectivism and error" (*BT* "Preface" 5).

The insight into the intimate relation between art and life has important implications for Nietzsche's understanding of morality: it reveals life as "something that is essentially immoral" and morality as inherently "hostile to life" (*BT* "Preface" 5). Whereas Nietzsche further problematizes the relation between life and morality in *Dawn,* and then in *On the Genealogy of Morals*, in *Twilight of the Idols*, and in *The Antichrist* where he calls out for a "naturalism in morality" (*TI* "Morality" 4), in his early writings he seems to be primarily interested in the relation between art, science, and life.

In *Untimely Considerations* Nietzsche adopts the perspective of life to advance a radical critique of Western civilization, questioning its so-called cultural and scientific achievements. In particular, in "On the Disadvantage and Use of History for Life," he directs his critique against the scientific value of historical knowledge and concludes that "it is possible to value the study of history to such a degree that life becomes stunted and degenerate" (*HL* "Preface"). While he acknowledges that life needs history, he warns against an overdose of historical knowledge that destroys life (*HL* 1). Furthermore, in "On the Disadvantage and Use of History for Life," we find the idea of life as a cultural force exemplified in the cry of youth: "Only give me life, and then I will create a culture for you out of it!" (*HL* 10). In line with Rousseau, Nietzsche "returns to nature" in view of unsettling our traditional understanding of what it means to be human. Unlike Rousseau, however, Nietzsche does not construct the natural human being as an ideal. For Nietzsche, the return to nature reveals human life to be inseparable from the totality of life. The continuity between human life and the life of all organic and inorganic matter unsettles our anthropocentric conception of the world and shows that human culture and civilization must be understood as part and parcel of the greater order of the totality of life. It is in this sense that Nietzsche understands culture as an improved *physis* (*HL* 10).

Already in *Untimely Considerations*, but then more important in *Human, All Too Human*, Nietzsche begins to thematize the relationship between life and justice. In these texts we find what could be called a moral-epistemic conception of life, which draws on a direct analogy between life and injustice. In Nietzsche's account of critical history, as a form of historical knowledge in the service of life, life is featured as a "dark, driving power that insatiably thirsts for itself" and whose sentence over the past is "always unmerciful, always unjust" (*HL* 3). Nietzsche further pursues this idea in *Human, All Too Human*, where he puts forth the claim that life is conditioned by the perspectival and hence is inherently unjust (*HH* "Preface" 6). In both texts, what stands in the foreground is an epistemological problem: the injustice of life, as the example of critical history shows, arises from the impossibility of pure knowledge. This insight leads in *Human, All Too Human* to the claim that "the whole of human life is deeply sunk in untruth" (*HH* 34). For Nietzsche, the nature of human knowledge, that is, its inherent erroneousness, has important moral consequences. For him, to live means to constantly value, measure, and judge. In other words, as human beings we cannot but value, measure, and judge—this is how we keep ourselves alive—but all our judgments are false, interested, and hence also necessarily unjust. Nietzsche sees in this necessity of injustice "the greatest disharmony of life" (*HH* 32).

As early as in "Schopenhauer as Educator," Nietzsche advocates the meaning of life as freedom and responsibility: "to live according to your own standard and law" (*SE* 1). This existentialist conception of life *avant la lettre* is centered on the problem of the liberation of life (*SE* 1). Nietzsche introduces the great figures of human culture, notably Goethe, Schopenhauer, and the pre-Socratic philosophers as "examples of life and thought" (*SE* 3) that may guide us in the overcoming of social conformism and public opinion toward a freer and more authentic life. This existentialist approach to life culminates in Nietzsche's *Ecce Homo* where he recounts his own life, providing the reader with an example of how one becomes who one is.

Nietzsche further develops the intimate relation between life and philosophy in his conception of the philosopher and her pathos for truth in *The Gay Science* where he claims that "what was at stake in all philosophizing hitherto was not at all 'truth' but rather something else—let us say health, future, growth, power, life . . . ." (*GS* "Preface" 2). The inseparability of life and thought, body and soul, means that philosophy can no longer be understood as an abstract search for truth but rather as an "art of transfiguration": "Life—to us, that means constantly transforming all that we are into light and flame, and also all that wounds us; we simply *can do* no other" (*GS* "Preface" 3). For the philosopher as Nietzsche imagines her, "life itself has become *a problem*" (*GS* "Preface" 3); "life becomes an experiment for the knowledge-seeker" (*GS* 324). Given the entanglement of life and thought, the question of truth can no longer be abstracted from the question of life. Nietzsche observes that life and truth contradict each other to such a degree that "it seemed that one was unable to live with it [truth]" (*GS* 110). Nietzsche thus reformulates the question of truth in terms of an experiment: "to what extent can truth stand to be incorporated?" (*GS* 110). The experiment of incorporating truth reveals, on the one hand, that "the conditions of life might include error" and that "we have arranged ourselves a world in which we are able to live—by positing bodies, lines, planes, causes and effects, motion and rest, form and content; without these articles of faith, no one could endure living!" (*GS* 121). On the other hand, the experiment of the incorporation of truth shows us that "life is a woman" (*GS* 339): life is always a riddle, inaccessible and at a distance: affirming and appreciating it means becoming Greek, that is "superficial—out of profundity" (*GS* "Preface" 4).

Beginning with *Thus Spoke Zarathustra*, Nietzsche increasingly understands life as something structured by power relations, from life as self-overcoming defined through relationships of command and obedience (*Z* II "On Self-Overcoming") to the straightforward definition of life as will to power in *Beyond Good and Evil* and *On the Genealogy of Morals*. Nietzsche's conception of life as will to power allows him to articulate a series of concerns reaching from moral, legal, and political considerations to biological and physiological ones. The latter entail Nietzsche's critique and rejection of Darwinian evolutionary theory, which understands life as self-preservation and assimilation motivated by the so-called struggle for the survival of the fittest. Against the Darwinian idea of life as self-preservation and assimilation, Nietzsche holds that "[a] living thing seeks above all to *discharge* its strength—life itself is *will to power*; self-preservation is only one of the indirect and most frequent *results*" (*BGE* 13). Furthermore, he holds the idea that "life itself is essentially appropriation, injury, overpowering of what is alien and weaker; suppression, hardness, imposition of one's own form, incorporation and at least, at its mildest, exploitation [. . .]" (*BGE* 259). Life is not something that adapts or assimilates itself to the outside world. Rather, life is something that stands in a relation of active form-giving to the outside to such an extent that it can no longer be conceived as something that actually has an inside, which stands in need of preservation (*GM* II: 12). Instead, for Nietzsche, life is radical exteriority and always in becoming. As such, life is fullness and overabundance: "the general aspect of life is *not* hunger and distress, but rather wealth, luxury, even absurd prodigality—where there is a struggle it is a struggle for *power* . . ." (*TI* "Expeditions" 14). The overabundance of life, exemplified in the strong type of human being, makes the latter more fragile and vulnerable. Hence Nietzsche concludes that supposing something like the "struggle for life" existed, it would be characterized by the general and repeated "defeat of the stronger": "the weaker dominate the strong again and again—the reason being they are the great majority, and they are also *cleverer* . . ." (*TI* "Expeditions" 14).

Apart from Nietzsche's biological and physiological concerns around the conception of life as will to power, in *Beyond Good and Evil* and in *On the Genealogy of Morals*, Nietzsche is particularly interested in the moral, legal, and political implications of his understanding of life as a value, norm, and law-giving force. Nietzsche's investigation of the value of values from the perspective of life reveals, first, that there are no such things as moral facts and, second, that values are not absolute standards that transcend human history. On the contrary, every value judgment reflects a struggle between different and often contradictory life forces that cannot be traced back to something like an origin. This aspect of life as will to power has come to be known as the agonistic dimension of Nietzsche's conception of life. The priority of struggle or agonism takes the form of a "law of life" defined as the "law of the necessity of 'self-overcoming' in the essence of life" (*GM* III: 27). The latter implies that "all great things bring about their own destruction through an act of self-overcoming" and hence "the law of life" stands in tension with the institution of a stable and durable rule of law (*GM* III: 27). Nietzsche confirms that legal conditions can never be other than "*exceptional conditions*," since they constitute "a partial restriction of the will to life" (*GM* II: 13). From this point of view of agonism, there can be no such thing as a sovereign and universal legal order. Rather, in view of the preservation and enhancement of life, the challenge is to maintain a plurality of values as well as their productive engagement for and against each other alive (*GM* II: 11).

Nietzsche distinguishes between those values that are life-enhancing and life-affirming, such as the values advanced by noble morality, and those that are life-diminishing and life-denying, such as those values found in slave morality. However, from the perspective of agonism, both these types of moralities describe different aspects of life, which are irreducible to each other and mutually depend on each other. The struggle between these two types of moral judgments—noble and slave morality—comes to full fruition in Nietzsche's analysis of the ascetic ideal. Although the ascetic ideal is distinctly life-negating and life-diminishing, this very self-contradiction of life is in the interest of life, namely, in the interest of the weak and sick life. Weak and sick life is a kind of life that keeps itself alive at a minimum thanks to the life-conserving and ultimately life-affirming power of the ascetic ideal: "*the ascetic ideal springs from the protective instincts of a degenerating life*" (*GM* III: 13). As such the ascetic priest, the "apparent enemy of life" and "denier of the body" must be counted among "the greatest *conserving* and yes-creating forces of life" (*GM* III: 13). In the end, the problem of the ascetic ideal confirms that everything is will to power and that the human being "would rather will *nothingness* than *not* will" (*GM* III: 28). This enigmatic formulation, while overcoming a simplistic opposition between vitalism and spiritualism, seems to open up new and yet to be explored possibilities for a productive unfolding of the mutual involvement of nihilism and life.

The various meanings and multilayered dimensions of the term "life" in Nietzsche's writings have also been taken up differently in the reception of Nietzsche's work during a great part of the twentieth century. First of all, Nietzsche's affirmation of life's becoming was understood as an early form of "existentialism." Existentialist readings of Nietzsche's conception of life take as their starting point his tragic vision of the world as chaos confronting the human being with the challenging task of having to give life a meaning that it inherently lacks while at the same time assuming full responsibility for their life and that of others. This approach has gradually been replaced over the course of the last couple of decades by two other interpretative tendencies. The first and most prevalent approach to Nietzsche's conception of life's becoming is understood as a function of his adoption and reaction against the Darwinian evolutionary paradigm change. The second approach is linked to post-existentialist French thought, mainly Foucault and Deleuze, characterized on one side by a theory of power and resistance, and on the other side by a theory of radical immanence. The scholarship on Nietzsche remains divided among these three approaches, often setting them up against one another without mediation. In reality, Nietzsche's conception of life is so influential precisely because it tracks the becoming of life along a plurality of planes: from the biological to the existential, from the scientific to the moral, from the human to the animal and overhuman, from the earthly to the cosmological. The intention of this volume, taken as a whole, is to take stock of the complexities and wide-ranging perspectives that Nietzsche brings to bear on the problem of life's becoming on earth by intentionally engaging all three interpretative paradigms and measuring their continued importance against the standards of the latest advances of scholarship on Nietzsche and on his reception.

Since Hobbes and Spinoza, modern philosophy and social sciences have sought to model their theories on the objectivity and lawfulness attained by the experimental natural sciences. The goal was to find for the human sciences an equivalent set of "laws of nature." Since the relatively recent acceptance of evolutionary biology into the realm of the so-called hard sciences, we are witnessing an increasing biologization of the social sciences and of philosophy, as these disciplines work out the implications for their own fields of the Darwinian revolution. Although this application of life sciences to human sciences seems to follow the previous pattern of modeling human sciences on natural sciences, in reality it is arguable that the opposite is the case, and that the revolution consists in the discovery of a normativity intrinsic to the becoming of life, and allowing human norms to be patterned on biological normativity. If life develops its own norms, if it is capable of "knowing" what is good or bad for it, what is health and sickness, and can restore itself from an abnormal to a normal condition, then this opens the possibility that our own concepts and norms should be modeled after life and not life after our concepts and norms. In modern times, such a hypothesis was first proposed by Nietzsche, whose thought begins and ends with the insight that normative validity is dependent upon the affirmation of life's becoming. The essays composing this volume, then, address how Nietzsche arrives to the insight that the becoming of biological life is of normative significance to human beings, and they draw out the implications of this thought with regard to the ongoing shift toward life in the human sciences and philosophy.

Part I, "Contesting Nietzsche's Naturalism," addresses the character of Nietzsche's naturalism. Against the recent trend in Nietzsche studies that emphasize his adherence to modern scientific naturalism, these essays argue that Nietzsche advocates a return to the Greek conception of nature, in which science, art, and life are not seen as separate and irreconcilable spheres. Part II, "Evolution, Teleology, and the Laws of Nature," treats Nietzsche's engagement with Darwin and with the state of biology at the end of the nineteenth century. Here the fundamental question is the degree to which life can be captured from the perspective of causality (especially teleology), whether and how life can come under "laws of nature." It is against the crisis of teleological explanation that Nietzsche begins to understand life as what gives laws to itself, and attempts to clarify why the becoming of life cannot be subsumed under the "laws of nature" as if life were a mere object of the natural sciences. In order to understand this normative power of life, Nietzsche thematizes the question of the justice of life: this is the theme of Part III, "Justice and the Law of Life." Part IV, "The Becoming of a New Body and Sensibility," deals with the importance of the body and of species-life in Nietzsche's conception of the human being, once the "law of life" or life's becoming is assumed to be normative. In Part V, "Purification and the Freedom of Death," a return to "existentialist" themes is made from within the horizon of this new approach to Nietzsche's conception of life: what is the significance of death if one accepts the continuum between life and death, organic and inorganic nature? The book concludes with Part VI, "The Becoming of the Soul: Nomadism and Self-Experiment," in which the constitution of the knowing subject is discussed in light of Nietzsche's call for a love and self-experimentation with life itself, or the modeling of the subject on life's own experimentalism.

While it is widely accepted that Nietzsche advocates a return to life and nature, the meaning of this return remains an open question. What kind of "naturalism" did Nietzsche advocate? Is it a conception of nature determined by modern natural science, as recent studies have argued? In the opening essay of this collection, "The Optics of Science, Art, and Life," Tracy B. Strong suggests that Nietzsche's naturalism is "scientific" only if "science" itself is understood from the perspective disclosed by *The Birth of Tragedy*. According to this Greek conception, science is viewed "through the optic of the artist" and art, in turn, is viewed "through the optic of life." Thus art needs to be understood from the point of view of life, which simply means, from out of the condition of perspectivism. Perspectivism is understood by Strong under two registers: first of all, it is indicative of an unsurpassable condition of immanence; there is no possibility of radical doubt or of absolute knowledge (the "view from nowhere") because every perspective on something is always a perspective from somewhere on earth. But, second, this condition of immanence is ultimately "tragic," primarily because there is no way to bring an external judgment as to which perspective is correct: each perspective is equally "natural," although each perspective expresses a different kind of life or nature and leaves room for self-decision. In this sense, Strong's understanding of Nietzsche's naturalism is also existential.

In "Nietzsche, Nature, and the Affirmation of Life," Lawrence J. Hatab also defends the idea that Nietzsche's naturalism is an "existential naturalism" rather than a scientific or metaphysical naturalism. In order to understand the sense in which nature can have an existential significance, Hatab reaches back to ancient Greek philosophy of nature, in particular the Aristotelian conception of nature as *phusis* or self-manifesting movement. Hatab argues that Nietzsche's understanding of nature as will to power is a radicalization of Aristotelian *phusis* where, for Nietzsche, dynamic power is no longer kept in check by pre-given actualities or forms that provide the finality for this power's actualization. For Hatab, the "death of God" essentially means that potentiality is no longer determined teleologically by actuality. Hatab also believes that nature as will to power contains what he calls "a presumption of immanence" in the sense that everything that appears does so in a contest or *agon* of opposing forces and resistances. From this perspective, "scientific" honesty calls for the acceptance of all such oppositions. Compared to this Greek conception of scientific naturalism, Hatab argues that for Nietzsche the modern scientific naturalism is a species of the ascetic ideal, which has more in common with Judeo-Christian religion than with Greek philosophy. Despite having defeated Christian beliefs, modern scientific naturalism shares with religion the structure of being a perspective that wishes to eliminate the contest of perspectives or interpretations. In so doing, Hatab argues that modern scientific naturalism deepens the problem of nihilism and meaninglessness in the face of a mechanized physical understanding of nature bequeathed to us after the demise of the Aristotelian idea of nature.

While the first part of the book shows the debt of Nietzsche's naturalism to the Greek philosophical understanding of life's becoming, this was not the only significant context for Nietzsche's thinking about life. The essays of the second part, "Evolution, Teleology, and the Laws of Nature," thematize Nietzsche's active consideration and exchange with the new biological sciences of the nineteenth century, in particular Darwin's theory of evolution and its effects on German philosophy and the return of teleology within the context of the Kantian critical system. Whereas Strong and Hatab emphasize Nietzsche's critique of the modern scientific world view, Virginia Cano's essay "Is Evolution Blind? On Nietzsche's Reception of Darwin" situates Nietzsche's conception of life in the scientific debates of the nineteenth century, in particular for and against Darwin's conception of evolutionary biology. At issue for Nietzsche was not Darwin's discovery of evolution, or a becoming of life that is not teleological: on this point he agrees with Darwin. Rather, Cano argues that for Nietzsche the real question was whether Darwin's theory rendered this becoming too mechanical and did not emphasize sufficiently its creative potential, its normative dimension. While Cano stresses the importance of Darwin's evolutionary theory and its underlying idea of mechanics for an understanding of Nietzsche's conception of life and its becoming, Mariana A. Cruz's "Nietzsche and the Nineteenth-Century Debate on Teleology" confronts Nietzsche's conceptions with eighteenth- and nineteenth-century theories of teleological causality. Strong and Hatab both point out the Aristotelian inheritance of Nietzsche's understanding of nature. Cruz's essay attempts to reconstruct Nietzsche's early confrontation with natural teleology, as this was reproposed by Trendelenburg and his attempt to reject German idealism and "return to Kant" together with proposing a revaluation of Aristotelian teleology. Trendelenburg, on this reading, was seeking to give a philosophical foundation for the emergent science of biology. Nietzsche was very interested in these debates because they essentially turn around the problem of what is a law, what is lawful or normative, when we consider the phenomenon of life. He was clearly looking for arguments that would allow him to switch from the problem of the kind of causality exhibited by life (the observable regularities of living phenomena) to the problem of life's normativity (life as a source of legitimacy). In order to do so, as Cano discusses, he formulates his critique of natural teleology (Trendelenburg's neo-Aristotelianism) in the form of a recovery of pre-Socratic philosophies of nature. This recovery turns on understanding nature's creativity as a function of a game between forces that lacks entirely a planning intellect behind it. Nietzsche connects this idea with the biology of his lesser known contemporaries who attempt to rule out the idea of organic unity and its preformism in order to introduce time and evolutionary considerations into the formation of so-called organic unities. Cano's and Cruz's contributions, therefore, highlight the fact that Nietzsche's disagreement with Darwin ultimately boils down to their different ideas of temporal becoming. Finally, Herman W. Siemens, in "Nietzsche's Conception of 'Necessity' and Its Relation to 'Laws of Nature,'" investigates Nietzsche's conception of necessity in terms of his critical engagement with the scientific (mechanistic) conceptions of laws of nature. Siemens argues that what motivates Nietzsche's critical engagement are primarily moral concerns around questions of self-legislation and artistic concerns around questions of self-creation, which become crystallized around a conception of the "law of life." In contrast to the traditional view according to which laws of nature, and in particular the concept of necessity, are understood to stand in direct opposition to ideas of moral and creative freedom, Siemens claims that Nietzsche's conception of necessity must be read as a transvaluation and reinterpretation of this view and hence oriented toward the reconciliation of the laws of nature with the supposedly human idea of normativity. In his approach to the problem of transvaluation of the meaning of necessity in Nietzsche, Siemens follows the Nietzsche dictionary methodology and accordingly bases his analysis on a careful distinction between the various meanings of the term "necessity" in Nietzsche's work.

These moral or normative concerns with respect to life's becoming are the focus of the essays in Part III, "Justice and the Law of Life." Nietzsche famously claimed that life is "unjust" through and through when one compares it to "anthropomorphic" conceptions of justice. Hence the question arises as to whether a form of morality or ethics that returns to life and nature would be possible at all, or, as has often been assumed, whether Nietzsche's naturalism is doomed to remain an immoralism. Vanessa Lemm's essay, "Life and Justice in Nietzsche's Conception of History," explores this paradox of life and justice in an analysis of how historical knowledge that is, according to Nietzsche, inherently unjust can nonetheless provide the material for the constitution of a just order of life. While Lemm investigates this question primarily in relation to Nietzsche's early work, Scott Jenkins in "Life, Injustice, and Recurrence" pursues the problem of justice and its relation to life in a reading of Nietzsche's early work but also its repercussions in Nietzsche's vision of the eternal return of the same put forth in *Thus Spoke Zarathustra*. According to Jenkins, it is the insight into the injustice of life rather than the eternal return of the same that reflects Zarathustra's most abysmal thought. Finally, Daniel Conway in his essay, "Heeding the Law of Life: Receptivity, Submission, Hospitality," offers a reading of the final section of Nietzsche's *On the Genealogy of Morals* where Nietzsche enigmatically invokes "the law of life" (*GM* II: 27). Conway is particularly interested in exploring the effect Nietzsche hopes to have on his readers when he evokes the law of life against the backdrop of the overcoming of Christian morality. According to Conway, Nietzsche encourages his readers to overcome Christian morality, calling out for the adoption of a new law of life where the virtues of submission, receptivity, and hospitality play a central role.

The overcoming of Christian asceticism brings with it the task of creating a new relationship to the body and to sensibility. But this turn toward the body and sensibility is also a reflection of Nietzsche's standpoint that life has become norm-setting for human beings. In the fourth part of the collection, "The Becoming of a New Body and Sensibility," the essays explore how Nietzsche thinks through the normativity of life by offering new accounts of the body with regard to the constitution of spirit or soul, of sensibility with regard to the constitution of knowledge or experience; of the species-life with regard to the constitution of individuality; and, last but not least, a new account of animality in the constitution of humanity. In her essay, "Toward the Body of the Overman," Debra Bergoffen examines two bodies: first, the body of the last man representative of the embodiment of the ascetic ideal of Christianity and Platonism. Bergoffen puts forth the hypothesis that the new body Nietzsche envisages under the name *Übermensch* is the body of a woman divested of its stigma. Bergoffen expands on her hypothesis by putting Nietzsche in conversation with post-existentialist French feminists, such as Luce Irigaray and Julia Kristeva. Rainer J. Hanshe in "Nietzsche's Synaesthetic Epistemology and the Restitution of the Holistic Human" argues that the becoming of a new body requires, before all, the cultivation of a synaesthetic conception of sense experience. He shows that synaesthetics was for Nietzsche not a merely metaphysical endeavor but part and parcel of the restitution of a holistic human being. According to Hanshe, Nietzsche encourages us to develop our synaesthetic potentiality. This means advancing a sense-oriented epistemology, which requires us to change our modes of obtaining knowledge. According to this new conception of epistemology, becoming overhuman means activating our synaesthetic capacity, thus overcoming the division between reason and the senses as well as the hierarchization of the senses, thus returning the human being to a Greek idea of the whole that was lost with the functional differentiation of modernity.

Whereas Bergoffen and Hanshe are both drawing on Nietzsche's vision of a new humanity and human body, Donovan Miyasaki in "Nietzsche's Naturalist Morality of Breeding: A Critique of Eugenics as Taming" questions whether the way in which Nietzsche advances the "breeding" of such a new (human) type is compatible with ethically dangerous forms of eugenics and hence with the historically associated practices of discrimination, racisms, and genocide. Unlike Bergoffen and Hanshe, Miyasaki is not interested in the question of what kind of human type Nietzsche wishes to promote but in what way he wishes to accomplish that promotion. Miyasaki argues that Nietzsche's morality of breeding is directly opposed to both positive and negative forms of comparative eugenics, that is, both the genetic promotion of beneficial traits as well as the elimination of harmful ones. The question of life and the becoming of culture on the level of the human kind as well as on the level of the human body inevitably leads to the question of the human self and the task of becoming who one is. Mónica Cragnolini in her essay, "An 'Other Way of Being': The Nietzschean 'Animal': Contributions to the Question of Biopolitics," seeks to pursue Nietzsche's thoughts on animality as a "rest" or "remainder" that is left over from the process of humanization that was discussed by Miyaski among others, and also that is importantly different from corporeality as a source of resistance to the ascetic ideal as discussed by Bergoffen and Hanshe.

As mentioned earlier, Nietzsche's philosophy of life was interpreted in the second half of the twentieth century, following Jaspers, Heidegger, and Sartre, mainly as a precursor of existentialism. In the existentialist reading, the perspective of biological life was made secondary to the human capacity for being-for-death, for confronting the "nothingness" of existence by way of a decisionism that was thought to lift the human being over and above the continuity of life with other species and inorganic matter. The essays of Part V, "Purification and the Freedom of Death," return to the existentialist themes of death and freedom, but in order to dismiss the humanist conceits with which they were tinged in the early reception of Nietzsche. Both of the essays in Part V, in their very distinct ways, reject the claim that the human "experience" of death is such that it allows human beings to transcend the immanence of life, both organic and inorganic. Eduardo Nasser's essay, "Nietzsche and the Transformation of Death," traces the development of Nietzsche's conception of death from the perspective of his new conception of life based on the identity of matter with force, such that the inorganic world can no longer be thought of as an "inert" or "dead" world. The essay then proceeds to compare Nietzsche's conception of "freedom to death" with Heidegger's being-toward-death, leading to some new insights both in regard to Nietzsche's "Epicurean" take on death and also his general point of diminishing, rather than increasing, the awareness of death as the critical limit-experience for humanity. Also in Babette Babich's "Becoming and Purification: Empedocles, Zarathustra's *Übermensch*, and Lucian's Tyrant," death is the central object of inquiry, and as with Nasser, at issue here is contesting the idea that Nietzsche's "freedom to death" somehow allows the human being to overcome or transcend itself into an "overhuman" status. But Babich approaches this theme through a reading of Zarathustra's teaching of the overman as both an imitation of Empedocles, and also as a satirical exercise designed to show that, in the end, or through death, there is no elevation of humanity into over-humanity. To the contrary, basing her analysis on the subterranean links between Nietzsche's Zarathustra and Empedocles' life and thought, his activity as a lawgiver and his famous suicide by leaping into the volcano, as well as his teaching of eternal recurrence as eternal rebirth, Babich suggests that a proper understanding of the immanence of death to life and its eternal rebirth ought to rid us of any illusion as to our superiority to animals, as evidenced by Empedocles' rejection of carnivorism. Analogously, by recovering the links between Nietzsche's Zarathustra and Lucian's satire on tyranny, Babich suggests that Nietzsche wanted to rid us of the idea that the overman entails a superior form of tyranny.

Modern natural science obtains knowledge of objective laws of nature through its experimental method, but natural science is neither the sole nor the most significant space of experimentation. Nietzsche's call to see the source of normativity in life rather than knowledge also suggests that we may have much to learn from life's experimentalism and applying it to the becoming of the subject or "soul." This volume concludes with a section entitled "The Becoming of the Soul: Nomadism and Self-Experiment," in which Nietzsche's conception of life's becoming is discussed in relation to what is perhaps his fundamental teaching on subjectivity, namely, the doctrine of self-overcoming. Dieter Thomä's essay, "'Falling In Love with Becoming': Remarks on Nietzsche and Emerson," pursues the question of character and self-experimentation. Both Emerson and Nietzsche pointed out that who one is, is not a matter of having a fixed nature, because "the soul" is something that "becomes." The important question is how this becoming occurs, or how to avoid immobility in life. Emerson and Nietzsche advocate self-overcoming, by which Thomä understands the practice of taking distance from one's self, appreciating its "otherness," and simultaneously rejecting the myth that others are "furthest" from oneself. This attitude or ethics of taking distance from oneself and approaching what is "other" in order to overcome oneself is called by Emerson "intellectual nomadism," and Thomä shows the extent to which it influenced Nietzsche's thinking about life. But Thomä also takes distance from the Deleuzian interpretation of Nietzsche's nomadism, pointing out how Nietzsche, just like Emerson, ultimately rejected continuous self-overcoming because it did not allow for the building of character. Instead, both authors favor a more nuanced relation or oscillation between continuous movement and moments of rest and repose that are, according to Thomä, a more fitting description of human nomadic life on earth. Thomä concludes that the soul does indeed become, but that it needs to do so "slowly." The idea of self-overcoming is also at stake in Keith Ansell-Pearson's essay, "'We are Experiments': Nietzsche on Morality and Authenticity," where he focuses in particular on Nietzsche's middle period, namely, on the book *Dawn*, a period in which according to Ansell-Pearson, Nietzsche's views on self and self-experimentation are inseparable from his concern for the therapeutic treatment of human suffering or philosophical therapeutics, thus revitalizing for a modern age ancient philosophical concerns famously known through the figure of Epicurus. According to Ansell-Pearson, *Dawn* resurrects a Hellenistic conception of philosophy in which the love of wisdom is intimately bound up with the promotion of human flourishing and happiness, which, for Nietzsche, entails the experimental search for an authentic mode of existence. But whereas Thomä highlighted the need for distance from oneself in order to become oneself, Ansell-Pearson argues that Nietzsche understood authenticity in light of the kind of practices, which Foucault associates with "care of self," namely, with the care and cultivation of those things that are "closest" to oneself, from dietary habits to thinking habits. In a similar vein to Thomä's skepticism with regard to Deleuzian nomadism, Ansell-Pearson argues against the post-hermeneutic reading of Nietzsche proposed by Vattimo, according to which Nietzsche's overman is not a new subject but its end. For Ansell-Pearson, Nietzsche's soul or self is undoubtedly "plural," but it remains a self, in need of the right "care" if it is to become what it is.

The last essay of the volume, Gary Shapiro's "States and Nomads: Hegel's World and Nietzsche's Earth," offers yet a third way of thinking about nomadism and pluralism in Nietzsche's conception of the self. Shapiro approaches the question of life's becoming from the perspective of where this life becomes: do we live on earth or in the world? Shapiro argues that Nietzsche's conception of life and soul is from the start structured against the Hegelian, and later Heideggerian, privilege given to the world, and to history as the story of human freedom. Shapiro shows that whereas for Hegel the world is inseparable from the unity, eternity, and transcendence of spirit, for Nietzsche the earth signifies the radical immanence of life. Life's becoming on earth, therefore, is favored by assuming a nomadic form of life, which Shapiro opposes to Hegel's preferred form of human organization and inhabitation centered on the sovereign state. Like Thomä and Ansell-Pearson, Shapiro agrees that self-overcoming in Nietzsche entails the pluralization of the self. However, he also suggests that such a plurality does not only have an internal or soul-centered meaning, but that in Nietzsche one can also recover an affirmative idea of a multitude characterized by "migration, immigration, Diaspora, cosmopolitanism and hybridity," and which can be opposed, term by term, to the categories of the masses and the population, both of which are ultimately dependent on the state's dubious claim to exert sovereignty over an earth and over a life that are both common to all and yet belongs to no one.

In an age in which the biological sciences claim to have unlocked the deepest secrets and codes of life, the essays in this volume offer plenty of arguments to maintain a more skeptical view on the value of the results provided by the biological and evolutionary sciences, as well as their application to the human sciences. The essays in this volume give accounts of why life is in becoming precisely because life is both what is closest and what is furthest from us, because life experiments through us as much as we experiment with it, because life keeps our thinking and our habits always moving, in a state of recurring nomadism and, finally, because our best approach to life remains a mimetic one rather than a representational one: life is there to be lived and enjoyed rather than methodically studied and exploited. Nietzsche's philosophy is perhaps the clearest expression of the antinomy contained in the idea of "studying" life and in the Socratic ideal of an "examined" life, and precisely for this reason, his philosophy remains for our age the deepest source of wisdom about living.

PART I

Contesting Nietzsche's Naturalism

1

The Optics of Science, Art, and Life
How Tragedy Begins

TRACY B. STRONG

Where do we find ourselves?

—**R. W. Emerson, *Experience***

The greatest poverty is not to live
In a physical world, to feel that one's desire
Is too difficult to tell from despair.

—**Wallace Stevens, *Esthétique du Mal*, xv**

Emerson's five words raise four questions: of our place in the world; of who we are; of the difficulty of discovery; of becoming what one is. Stevens's poem reminds us that humans are self-impoverished, that they often and for manifold reasons resist living in and being of the world. It is also the case that it is au courant these days in Nietzsche-criticism to label him a "naturalist."[1] Yet on the face of it this seems a bit off. Whatever is meant by "naturalism"—be it *epistemological* in the sense that hypotheses must be explained and tested only by reference to natural causes and events, or *metaphysical*, in the sense of a worldview in which reality is such that there is nothing that counts but natural things, forces, and causes of the kind that the natural sciences study—neither of these understandings fit very well with Nietzsche. Yet Stevens enjoins us to live in the physical world, and Emerson queries as to how.

In the capsule history of Western thought entitled "How the 'True World' Finally Became a Fable: The History of an Error," Nietzsche famously closes with: "The true world we abolished: which world was left? The apparent one perhaps? . . . But no! *along with the true world we have also abolished the apparent one*" (*TI* "World" 6).[2] Generally speaking, the idea of a naturalism in either of these guises rests on a binary opposition between a "real" world and an "ideal" (or not-real) one and the rejection of the second in favor of the first. But just as Platonism—which we might read as that which naturalism attacks—remains Platonism when stood on its head, so "naturalism" depends on the preexisting opposition. When *both* are abolished, as Nietzsche tells us, what is left is not "naturalism," nor is it idealism. "I find myself more in agreement with artists than with any philosophers hitherto," writes Nietzsche. He continues: "For myself and all those who live—are allowed to live—without the anxieties of a Puritan's conscience, I wish an ever greater spiritualization and multiplication of the senses" (*KSA* 11:37[12]). Note: spiritualization *and* multiplication. Nietzsche's *umgedrehter Platonismus* is not to be understood as the valuation of the "natural" as opposed to that of the supersensuous. Nietzsche gets rid of *both* terms. Thus if he is to be a "naturalist," whatever he means by "nature" is far different from what is usually meant by that term, be it by Dennett, Dewey, Hook, Armstrong, Churchlands or Quine, . . . or Leiter or Clark.

What does Nietzsche mean by "nature"? I should start out by saying that over the period of my life that I have been engaged by Nietzsche, I have become increasingly convinced that his first book is not only among the most important, if not *the* most important, of his work, but it sets out the project or projects that are to occupy him for the rest of his life in sanity. This project is political in the most extended sense of the word—it is, one might say, to explore, critique, and to change the unconscious of the West, such that a new second nature replace and become a first nature, a project he lays out explicitly at the end of the third section of the "Use and Misuse of History for Life." In this sense, the problem is not ignorance—it is not that we lack information; it is rather how we know what we know. And for this we have no concepts: hence the critical task is much more radical, and much more complex even than Kant's. As Nietzsche remarks in criticism of Socrates: "That of which one cannot be conscious [*Unbewusste*] is greater than the ignoring [*Nichtwissen*] of Socrates" (*KSA* 7:1[43]).

But surely, you might say, there are at least three different *periods* to Nietzsche's work: an early romantic Wagner-intoxicated period, a second more positivistic (or "naturalistic") period that sees the volumes of *Human, All Too Human, Dawn*, and the first books of *The Gay Science*; a last "mature Nietzsche" reaching until sometime in 1888. Perhaps there is even a fourth period, that of the collapse. I find this unconvincing. *The Birth of Tragedy* was explicitly intended by Nietzsche as one prong of a triple attack. The other two were plans for a revision of the institutions of *Bildung* (his lectures *FEI*) and an exploration of what it would mean actually to be a philosopher in the contemporary world (*PTA*). When his first book fell, to borrow words from Hume, "still-born from the press,"[3] Nietzsche was dismayed. "How could this have happened?" he must have asked himself. I thus read the works of the late part of the 1870s as an attempt to discover for himself why he had been so wrong about the potential reception of *The Birth of Tragedy*, and the work of the 1880s as an analysis of what was it about various aspects of contemporary society that kept it from understanding (*Z* is to a great extent about social institutions; the *GM* is about morality; *TI* is about authority; *BGE* is about *Wissenschaft*, and so on).[4] While there are changes—he learns things—the project remains much the same from beginning to end.

A clue to that project comes in the preface he wrote in 1886 to a new edition of his first book. The phrase that serves as the first part of my title comes from the second section of the 1886 "An Essay at Self-Critique." It regards ("optic") three elements. And with few exceptions—one of them is Babette Babich's work, especially the last chapter of her *Nietzsche's Philosophy of Science* (to which I owe a special debt in this paper); another are some essays by Jacques Taminiaux and Gary Shapiro; a third (a prompt for all of them) is the section on "The New Interpretation of Sensuousness" at the end of the "Will to Power as Art" section of Heidegger's lectures on Nietzsche—with the exception of these and a few others, very little attention has been paid to *all* of the elements of this triple optic.[5]

When Nietzsche returns in 1886 to reclaim his early work with this series of new prefaces, he calls attention to what one might call the methodology of *The Birth of Tragedy*—how to understand (a) tragedy. It is to see "*science through the optic of the artist, but also to see art through optic of life*" (*BT* "Attempt" 2).[6] The emphasis is Nietzsche's. Note especially the "but also." This is not a matter of taking up now this lens, now that, now a third. Rather, as Nietzsche often tells us, it is to have many perspectives, to have all these at once. The term "*Optik*" is singular: lens, optic, point of view—and it warns us that this is to be a matter of perspectivalism. If we are moved to explore this, Nietzsche's phrasing invites us to take the terms sequentially.

What Is Science?

So, what is "science"? The first realization here is that we are to understand the subject matter of *The Birth of Tragedy* as science. Science is here understood in the sense of *Wissenschaft*, here with particular reference to the classical philological science in which Nietzsche was trained. By "*Wissenschaft*," Nietzsche means what any German would have meant (and to some degree still does): a learned and learnable body of knowledge, with a methodology appropriate to it that is transmissible.[7] The very beginning of *The Birth of Tragedy* makes this explicit:

> We shall have gained much for the science of aesthetics, when we have arrived *not only* at the logical insight but also at the unmediated certainty of experience [*Anschauung*] that the continuous production of art is tied up with the doubleness of the Apollonian and the Dionysian. (*BT* 1)

Anschauung can also mean contemplation and resonates with *anschaulich*—clear or vivid. In translations of Kant, it is given as "intuition." Nietzsche is speaking of attaining clarity of one's own experience, as if most of the time our experience was not clear or available to us. Again the "not only . . . but also" announce a *common* project for both science and experience. The project of the *Birth* is to recover the immediacy of experience *as part of our understanding*—a joining that Nietzsche thinks that the West has over time lost or rather denied itself. The joining of knowledge and clarity as to one's experience is necessary for a meaningful understanding.

One of the consequences of Socratism and Christianity is that humans no longer live—they merely exist. They lack what Thoreau had explored as and called a "natural life."[8] Thus Nietzsche's critique of Socrates will be that he cannot allow himself—or is perhaps unable—to *experience* the world, here the tragedy. Nietzsche says as a criticism: "Now, however, the tragic art never seemed to 'tell the truth' for Socrates" (*BT* 14). The accusation against Socrates is that he cannot be an authentic audience member: this is to say that he cannot be open to the world. When Wallace Stevens claims, as in my epigraph, that "The greatest poverty is not to live / In a physical world," he is talking about the impoverishment consequent to cutting oneself off from allowing oneself to experience the world.

Here, however, we can dispose immediately of the canard that Nietzsche was "opposed" to science—whatever that might mean. As Babich has written:

> There is a sense in which Nietzsche approves science. This approval is not for the sake of its truths or facts, but rather for the sake of its "honesty." The conception of honesty here reflects the character of the knower as an inquirer in the field of reality who still has integrity. For Nietzsche this integrity constitutes the most redeeming legacy of the scientific turn.[9]

This insistence on integrity as central to the practice and vocation of science will become the touchstone of Weber's 1917 lecture *Wissenschaft als*

Beruf.[10] As Emerson had remarked in *Experience*, an essay Nietzsche knew well: "I would gladly be moral . . . but I have my heart set on honesty."[11] For Emerson, as for Nietzsche, the questions of finding and self turn initially on honesty.

This is a science that is also passionate (again Weber will pick this up)—that is, the pursuit of scientific truth involves a particular kind of emotional experience.[12] Nietzsche has this to say in criticism of Aristotle: "According to Aristotle, science has nothing to do with enthusiasm, for one cannot rely on this unusual force: the work of art is the realization of the artistic insight of a proper artistic nature. A petit-bourgeois spirit!" (*KSA* 7:1[65]). However the science of which Nietzsche speaks (honest and passionate) is not science as it is practiced. Nietzsche entitles a section in the fourth book of *The Gay Science* "*Hoch die Physik*"—"Hooray for physics" (*GS* 335). We soon discover that "physics" here is not what one has been taught in courses. He goes on to say that practically *no one* knows how to observe anything and that when they do, they apply a straitjacket of rules that makes the elements observed seem the same. (Note the parallel to the accusation against Socrates.) Against this, he urges that we learn from physics to "limit ourselves to the purification of our own opinions and valuations" (*GS* 335). To become a being who "gives itself law," we must become:

> [T]he best learners and discoverers of everything that is lawful and necessary in the world: we must become physicists in order to be able to be creators in this sense—while hitherto all valuations and ideas have been based on ignorance of physics or were constructed so as to contradict it. Therefore: hooray for physics! And even more for that which compels us to turn to it—our honesty. (GS 335)

The praise of "physics" refers us to Φύσις[13] and is here linked explicitly by Nietzsche to what one might call a radicalized version of the Kantian project of autonomy. To give oneself a law was the very grounding of integrity for Kant. Nietzsche goes, one might say, beyond Kant, as this kind of self-critique involves five explicit steps, which Nietzsche details in the entry cited earlier. First, it entails the recognition that no actions are identical; second, that every action—past, present, and future—is unique and irretrievable; third, that any regularity that is posited deals only with the "coarse exterior" of actions; fourth, that all appearance of regularity is merely semblance; and finally, that no claim about the validity or worth of an action is conclusively resolvable.

Honesty is what science can give us. Honesty means to be critical and self-critical of all assumptions, in particular of claims on the order of "*X* is the same as *Y*" or "X is a subcategory of *Y*." This is why it is important to realize that no two actions are ever the same and that appearance of sameness is only sameness in what he calls appearance (*Schein*). Thus for science, "*Schein*, as I understand it, is the actual and unique reality of things—it is that only to which existing predicates apply and which in a certain sense could not be better defined but by all predicates, that is also by contradictory predicates" (*KSA* 11:40[53]). It is the subject matter of science (and science is not the less for that). Appearance is not opposed to "reality" (recall the passage from "How the 'True World' Became a Fable"), internally structured by and as the will to power. For if reality—the concern of science—*is* appearance, or rather the coming into appearance, it is, as Heidegger notes, a "perspectival letting-shine [*Scheinlassen*]."[14] The taking of appearance as reality is thus always and necessarily perspectival, thus an error, or sometimes, as in what becomes *Will to Power* (*WP* 853), a "lie" that we have in "order to live" (*KSA* 13:11[415]).

With the move to *Schein*, the analysis of science leads us to the question of art. Coming-into-appearance is the realm of art. It is as *artists* that we know that the world is brought into appearance, that it shines; hence, by art we are reminded of the need for criticality in science. Famously, he writes in 1888 that "we have art so that we do not perish from truth" (*KSA* 13:11[415]). Indeed, the philosopher who opts for truth "deserves a beating." Nietzsche goes on immediately to note that this was the subject of his first book; in his notes he reserves here a place for a previously composed section on "Art in the *Birth of Tragedy*" (*KSA* 13:225[17]). Note that the matter of his first book still concerns him in 1888.

What Is Art?

What then is art? In the notes of 1869, preparatory for *The Birth of Tragedy*, Nietzsche writes:

> What is art? Is it the ability to engender [*erzeugen*] a world of will without will? No. It is to engender as new the world of will, without that which is brought about by willing in its turn. It is thus an engendering of that which is without will by the will and instinctively. If there is consciousness one calls this a craft [*Handwerk*]. With this [the conscious craft] the relation to engendering appears plausible, however the fullness of the will reappears. (*KSA* 7:1[47])

An entry shortly before this one expands the idea of art (as opposed to "the arts").

> We are unfortunately accustomed to enjoy the arts in isolation: the insanity of art galleries and concert halls. The *absolute arts* are a sad

modern bad habit.[15] Everything comes apart. There are no organizations that collectively cultivate the arts as art, that is cultivate the spheres in which the arts go together. Rather each art goes a segment of the way alone and on another segment of the way accompanies the other arts. (*KSA* 7:1[45])

Thus when Nietzsche speaks of art he is speaking of something like *mousike*. Greek *mousike* refers to a vastly wider range of human activities than does our "music."[16] The "little" Liddell and Scott *Greek-English Lexicon* refers to μουσικός as a "man of letters, a scholar, an accomplished person." From this it follows that whatever is meant by music in Greek, it must refer to not only a much wider range of activities than "music," but also to an integration of those activities one with the other. We may take what Nietzsche means by "art" to have such a reference. It gives us some clue as to the spirit of music from which tragedy is born.

As Thrasybulos Georgiades notes, *mousike* denotes an ongoing activity and a "musical education" is only possible through "musical activity."[17] *Mousike* thus carries no implication of a tension between music and the (nonartistic) world. Not only was the world of *mousike* not apart from the world of life, but it served to create and maintain that world. Warren Anderson remarks, "the Greek term designates . . . oral training in poetry . . . that had for so long been the means of transmitting the values and precepts of Greek culture."[18] Plato says in the *Laches* that "A true musician has in his own life . . . a harmony of words and deeds arranged."[19]

Science gives us what we can call truth. Art tells us that truth is something we have made. We are thus pushed by our thought to the last term in Nietzsche's sequence. What is "Life"? One might start by noting that not all that is alive is life: Rousseau said that most of us die without having lived, and Thoreau will echo the same thought. Life is made of art and science, but they are in permanent tension with each other.

What Is Life?

The aforementioned has important implications for the understanding of life. As Nietzsche remarks: "Art and nothing but art. It is the great enabler of life, the great seductress to life, the great stimulation to life" (*KSA* 13:11[415]). The above arguments are in no way claims that everything is "subjective"—simply our point of view. Nietzsche explicitly says of such a conclusion that "even this is interpretation. The 'subjective' is not something given, it is something added, invented and projected behind what there is . . . Insofar as the word 'knowledge' has any meaning, the world is knowable . . . ; it does not have meaning behind it; it has countless meanings" (*KSA* 12:7[60]). All that we need to know and all that we can know is present in the world as we encounter it—this is the meaning of the "Midnight" poem in *Thus Spoke Zarathustra* (*Z* II "The Night Song") and what tragedy makes available.[20]

Thus nothing is closer to "reality" than anything else, for there is nothing to be close to. He writes:

> The "subject" is a fiction that many similar states in us are the effects of one substratum; but it is we who first created the "similarity" of these states; our adjusting them and making them similar is the fact, not their similarity—which had ought to be denied. (*KSA* 12:10[19])

He compares the "subject" to a regent at the head of a commonality, never so sure of its position that it can simply ignore the world around it.[21] The "ego" is an "apparent unity in which all is gathered as if bonded by a horizon" (*KSA* 12:2[91]).

With this we can arrive at a new understanding of Nietzsche's advocacy of "having many points of view"—many optics. In 1884, Nietzsche had written the following as an "insight":

> All estimations of value are a matter of a definite perspective: the maintenance of an individual, a commonality, a race, a state, a church, a belief, a culture. Due to the forgetfulness that there are only perspectival evaluations, all sorts of contradictory evaluations and thus contradictory drives swarm *inside one person*. This is the expression of the diseased condition in man, in opposition to the condition in animals, where all instincts play particular roles. This contradictory creature has however in his nature a great method of knowing: he feels many for's and against's—he raises himself up to justice—to a comprehension beyond the valuation of good and evil. The wisest man would be the richest in contradictions, who as it were, has feelers for all kinds of men: and right among them his great moments of grandiose harmony—the great accident in us also—a form of planetary emotion. (*KSA* 11:26[119])[22]

Justice is the ability to hold to contradictions. The holding of contradictions was what Nietzsche most admired in Aeschylus's Prometheus, already in *The Birth of Tragedy*.

> Raising himself to Titanic heights, man fights for and achieves his own culture, and he compels the gods to ally themselves with him because . . . he holds existence and its limits in his hands . . . . [T]he

most wonderful thing . . . [about Prometheus] . . . is its profound . . . tendency to *justice*: the limitless suffering of the bold 'individual' on the one hand, and the extreme distress of the gods . . . the power of both of these worlds to enforce reconciliation. (*BT* 9)

We are not to think of the subject as a unity but as a multiplicity, what he calls a "*Vielheit*" (*KSA* 11:40[42]). One might go to Whitman (whom Nietzsche had read),[23] but these thoughts call me back to Wallace Stevens:

And out of what one sees and hears and out
Of what one feels, who could have thought to make
So many selves, so many sensuous worlds,
As if the air, the mid-day air, was swarming
With the metaphysical changes that occur,
Merely in living as and where we live.[24]

"Who could have thought to make / So many selves"—who indeed? And how? But we do not hold to this: we put value into things, and this value has an effect on us after we have "forgotten that we were the donors" (*KSA* 12:5[19]). We do precisely that which the enthusiasm for physics in Nietzsche's sense should have warned us against. It is in those who rise up to "justice," however, that life remains multiple. In such life is an "experiment of the thinker . . . not a duty, not a fatality, not a deceit" (*GS* 324).

What does it mean to think of life as an experiment? It has some relation to what Jean Granier called "multiple ontologies,"[25] but it is also an "experiment, an endeavor, always subject to the temptation that one may call oneself finished, given and final" (*GS* 324). As above, one thinks of Whitman; one thinks also of J. S. Mill, who, in *On Liberty*, calls for "experiments in living."

It is worth noting in passing that this is *not* a theory of false consciousness. It is not that our place in the world keeps us from seeing what "really" is the case. The perspectival understanding places the emphasis not on "truth" and the lack thereof but on the consequences of perspectives for what counts as life. The point of the *Antigone* is that, as the audience, we see the world as both Kreon *and* Antigone. Our task is "to see things as they are. Means: we look at them from a hundred eyes, from many persons" and precisely *not* to see them "impersonally" (*GS* 345). As Nietzsche writes in *Beyond Good and Evil*: "It might be a basic characteristic of existence that those who would know it completely would perish, in which case the strength of a spirit should be measured according to how much of the 'truth' one could still barely endure" (*BGE* 39).

Thus the fact that we are alive—and that we die—means that we will always be unable to do full justice to the world, which would require that one have so transparent a contact with it (in all its becoming) that there would be no simplification of it. We must thus accept as a predicate of human existence that it is "unjust." In the 1886 preface to *Human, All Too Human* Nietzsche argues that one can never experience the world as other than unjust and that it is a sign of health that one forgoes any attempt to conceive of experience in the world as other than tragic. Already in the 1879 Basel lectures on *Oedipus Tyrannos*, Nietzsche had made the point that tragedy presents "the deepest conflict between life and thought" (*KGW* II, 3, 8). Greek tragedy shows us what it would mean (as an audience member) to accept the fact that all knowledge is perspectival, including that which we have of ourselves.

If there is nothing besides perspective, then it must not be the case that the world cannot be known, *but that it is in the nature of the world as we experience it to be known*. The danger is that we take our experience of the knowledge we have and conclude that this and this alone is *the* truth. If what we mean by nature is what is known, and known in multiple ways, then there is no naturalism, for there is no given nature. The world embodies all that we need to understand it, providing only that we do not insist on understanding it according to an arrogant and solipsistic notion of a unitary self. *Knowledge is never immaculate but it is not therefore necessarily flawed*—a radicalization of a lesson we first learned from Kant. We are *always* finding ourselves, unless we avoid doing so (as most of us do, most of the time).

The answer as to why humans insist on seeing the world as a unity is the subject of Nietzsche's genealogical investigations. The question as to what condemns us to experience the world as known and thus ensures that we will experience the world as a self, comes in the doctrine of the will to power. Here a few reminders. All life is/has will to power. Nietzsche calls the activity of the will to power "interpretation," "a means to become master of something" (*KSA* 12:161[47]). The will to power understands/interprets/makes in terms of the old; it extends the understanding and the categories of the life and action of a particular being over that which is not yet that being. A conclusion that follows from this is that Nietzsche is not "for" the will to power—he simply sees it as that which characterizes life, any form of life. The question will be what kind of life.

In the second section of *Beyond Good and Evil*, Nietzsche notes that "there would be no life at all if not on the basis of perspectival estimates and appearances" (*BGE* 34). Two sections later he introduces the notion of a "text without an author" and deepens his earlier statement by suggesting that to view the world as will to power is to view it from the "inside," that is on its own terms. The perspectival world is thus a text without an author, and is "determined and characterized according to its 'intelligible character'" (*BGE* 36). A text without an author has nothing behind it. It is exactly what it is, and there is no realm or arbiter—no author—to which or whom one can appeal for corroboration or final verification.[26] Hence when we speak of the world as will to power, we mean that the world as it presents itself to us in our claim to knowledge is *completely* intelligible. In 1887, Nietzsche notes the following as a "basic question":

> If the perspectival belongs to being [*Wesen*] as such? And is not only as a form of considering, a relation among different beings [*Wesen*]. Do the different powers stand in relation, such that this relation is tied to the observation-optic. This would be possible if all being (*Sein*) were essentially some kind of observation. (KSA 12:5[12])

I take this to mean that all *Sein* is in fact essentially some kind of observation. Perspectivalism is not therefore the perspective *of* something, for there can be nothing without perspective(s). It is not that we each have—with more or less tolerance—our picture of the world: there is no "world" of which to have a picture. The answer to the bright sophomore who asks "would there not be a world even if there were no people?" is that the question is meaningless: that there *is* a world means that there are perspectives. Indeed, "there would be nothing called knowledge, if thought did not reform the world into 'things'" (*KSA* 10:8[25]). I note parenthetically here that it follows that the unity (or unities) of Nietzsche's texts is to be found *in his readers* and that there is no authorial unity imposed by him on the texts, any more than a subject might impose a unity on the world. Thus any strictures that Nietzsche applies to his understanding of the subject apply also to his teaching on perspectivalism and life. Perspectivalism cannot be a doctrine or a point of view because, properly understood, it makes impossible the epistemological activism that such a doctrine would require. Nietzsche thus anticipates the position in relation to texts that one finds in Barthes or Foucault (not surprisingly since they get it from him). And more important, despite appearances to the contrary, Nietzsche never (well, hardly ever) speaks *ex cathedra*.

And this allows us to say something more about the optic of life. In *Twilight of the Idols*, Nietzsche has critiqued the Christian morality as a "revolt against life" (*TI* "Anti-Morality" 5). He immediately points out that a condemnation of life "by one who is alive is, in the end, just a symptom of a particular kind of life"; the question of the *value* of life is from the "optic of life" inaccessible (*TI* "Anti-Morality" 5). "Life itself values through us when we set out [*ansetzen*] values" (*TI* "Anti-Morality" 5). So the question becomes *what kind of life* has these values: his answer is that it is "declining, weakened, tired and condemned life" (*TI* "Anti-Morality" 5). Certain value judgments are consequent to certain kinds of life, but these can have no absolute standing (*TI* "Morality" 5). Indeed, in the last book of *Zarathustra*, Nietzsche will speak appreciatively of the tiger who has failed his leap and wants to go under: the tiger has accepted his "value judgments" for what they are (*Z* IV "On the Higher Men" 14).[27]

What Nietzsche (and tragedy) *cannot* accept is the moral judgment that moralizes itself, that takes its own value judgments to be absolute. Thus in the next section he says that

> The morality, insofar as it condemns on its own grounds [*an sich*] and not with regard to, in consideration of, from the purposes of life, is a specific error for which one can have no sympathy, . . . an error that has done an unspeakable amount of harm! (*TI* "Morality" 6)

This is what Stevens was to call "that evil in the self."[28] Life is an optic of which we are tempted to forget that it is one. And this is why Nietzsche's naturalism, if one were to speak that way, is other: the question is what *kind* of life. For those professional philosophers who profess naturalism, there is no question of what *kinds* of nature.

Three things follow: first the writer and thinker is forced to the necessity of an unrelenting honesty toward him or herself and the reader. All pretense must be shown to be pretense and all is, at some level, pretense. Second, it is impossible for a thinker honestly to claim to have found the solution to problems. Each must find the problems for him or herself—each group or country also—or they will not count—this is the democracy in Nietzsche because it is the democratic purpose of tragedy, and Nietzsche writes in such a manner to make this possible. Finally, there is no privileged position from which to discuss the world as if one were not part of it. All views are views from somewhere and it is the view that gives us something. This does not make rationality impossible—quite the contrary. All three are the stuff of tragedy. I started with Wallace Stevens and I end with him also, still on message:

> How cold the vacancy
> When the phantoms are gone and the shaken realist
> First sees reality. The mortal no
> Has its emptiness and tragic expirations.
> The tragedy, however, may have begun,
> Again, in the imagination's new beginning,

In the yes of the realist spoken because he must
Say yes, spoken because under every no
Lay a passion for yes that had never been broken.[29]

"The tragedy, however, may have begun, / Again, in the imagination's new beginning . . . ." One remembers that Zarathustra's return to the human world is announced in an entry entitled "*Incipit tragoedia*" (*GS* 342).

2

Nietzsche, Nature, and the Affirmation of Life

LAWRENCE J. HATAB

Nietzsche's critique of the Western tradition is gathered in the claim that "the fundamental faith of the metaphysicians is *the faith in opposite values*" (*BGE* 2). Our religious and philosophical belief systems have operated by dividing reality into a set of binary opposites, such as eternity and time, permanence and change, reason and passion—which can be organized under the headings of being and becoming. The motivation behind such divisional thinking is as follows: Becoming names the negative, unstable, dynamic conditions of existence that undermine our interest in grasping, controlling, and preserving life (because of the pervasive force of error, mystery, variability, destruction, and death). Being, as *opposite* to becoming, permits the governance or exclusion of negative conditions and the attainment of various forms of stability untainted by their fluid contraries.

Nietzsche wants to challenge such priorities in the tradition, so much so that he is often taken to be simply reversing priorities by extolling sheer becoming and all its correlates. This is not the case, even though Nietzsche will often celebrate negative terms rhetorically to unsettle convictions and open up space for new meanings. In fact, Nietzsche exchanges oppositional exclusion for a sense of *crossing*, where the differing conditions in question are not exclusive of each other, but rather reciprocally related.[1] Nietzsche suggests that "what constitutes the value of these good and revered things is precisely that they are insidiously related, tied to, and involved with these wicked, seemingly opposite things" (*BGE* 2). Rather than fixed contraries, Nietzsche prefers "differences of degree" and "transitions" (*WS* 67). As we will see shortly, Nietzsche rejects the strict delineation of opposite conditions, but not the oppositional *force* between these conditions.[2] He grants that circumstances of struggle breed in opponents a tendency to "imagine" the other side as an "antithesis," for the purpose of exaggerated self-esteem and the courage to fight the "good cause" against deviancy (*WP* 348). Yet this tendency breeds the danger of oppositional exclusion and its implicit denial of becoming's "medial" structure.

In restoring legitimacy to conditions of becoming, Nietzsche advances what I call an *existential naturalism*. The finite, unstable dynamic of earthly existence—and its meaningfulness—becomes the measure of thought, to counter various attempts in philosophy and religion to "reform" lived experience by way of a rational, spiritual, or moral "transcendence" that purports to rectify an originally flawed condition (*GS* 109; *TI* "Morality"). In turning to "the basic text of *homo natura*" (*BGE* 230), Nietzsche is not restricting his philosophy to what we would call scientific naturalism, which in many ways locates itself on the "being" side of the ledger. For Nietzsche, nature is more "wild and crazy" than science would allow; it includes forces, instincts, passions, and powers that are not reducible to objective, scientific categories. Retrieving the more primal sense of nature displayed in early Greek culture, Nietzsche insists that "the terrible (*schreckliche*) basic text of nature must again be recognized" (*BGE* 230). Nietzsche's naturalism is consonant with scientific naturalism in rejecting "supernatural" beliefs, yet these beliefs are not "errors" in the strict sense but perspectival contestants for "meaning." The source of supernatural beliefs, for Nietzsche, stems not from a lack or refusal of scientific thinking, but from an aversion to overwhelming and disintegrating forces in nature that science, too, suppresses and wants to overcome. Indeed, Nietzsche identifies nature with chaos, as indicated in his alteration of Spinoza's famous equation: "*chaos sive natura*" (*KSA* 9:11[197]).[3] At the same time, Nietzsche also rejects a romantic naturalism, which spurns science and calls for a return to an original condition of harmony with nature (*GS* 370). Naturalism, for Nietzsche, amounts to a kind of philosophical methodology, in that natural forces of becoming will be deployed to redescribe and account for all aspects of life, including cultural formations, even the emergence of seemingly antinatural constructions of "being." The focus for this deployment can be located in Nietzsche's concept of will to power, to be discussed shortly. First, I want to give some historical background for a discussion of naturalism, and then locate the historical focus for Nietzsche's naturalistic turn, namely the death of God.

The History of Nature

To understand Nietzsche's naturalism, it is helpful to begin with a brief excursion into the history of the words "nature" and "natural." For most philosophers today, including a number of Nietzsche interpreters, naturalism is shorthand for scientific naturalism, wherein philosophical topics are best explained by, or at least must be consistent with, findings in natural science. Although naturalism need not be equated with physicalism, nonetheless "nature" in naturalism refers to the full array of physical entities and forces that are properly ascertained by empirical investigation.

Analytic philosophers often complain that continental philosophy is bereft of precision and commitment to scientific reason. Continental philosophers often complain that analytic philosophy takes for granted terms or criteria that are not timeless but rather historically emergent and that thus at least are worthy of questioning. Nature is a good example (full disclosure: I am a continental philosopher). One might think that our sense of physical nature is nicely collected in the Greek word *phusis*, usually translated as nature; but this word had a much more complex meaning for the Greeks. *Phusis* is derived from the verb *phuō*, meaning to grow, to bring forth, to give birth. In Homer, *phuō* usually refers to plant life, with a specific meaning of bringing forth shoots, and earth is commonly called *phusizoos*, that which gives forth life.[4] With Aristotle we get a philosophical articulation of *phusis* as nature, but here also we have to be careful. Aristotle does not equate *phusis* with physical matter; *phusis* is manifest more in form than in matter.[5] And a prime instance of *phusis*, for Aristotle, is *psuchē*, life, including the human soul.[6] *Phusis* is not contrasted with the "supernatural." It is simply identified with movement and change[7] and is specified as self-manifesting movement, as contrasted with *technē*, artifice, or movement caused by an external agent in human production.[8] Aristotle also gives *phusis* a comprehensive ontological significance, going so far as to connect it with being itself.[9] The only sense in which Aristotle's conception of *phusis* could be distinguished from something "supernatural" is in the sense that sublunar natural movement does not admit of the permanence of the divine sphere; nature is the realm of temporal becoming as opposed to the eternal being of divinity. But to repeat, Aristotelian *phusis* is not strictly material because it includes a teleological principle of form; as distinct from the pure actuality of divine form, *phusis* exhibits a system of "dynamic" forms in the *process* of actualization.

In this way Aristotle blends two meanings in his understanding of *phusis*: self-manifesting movement and "essence," together indicating a kind of dynamic process of actualization indicated in his primary concepts of *dunamis* and *energeia*. Given that the manifestations of *phusis* display repeatable regularities, the "essentialist" meaning of *phusis* took shape in contradistinction to the manifest variety of cultural beliefs, gathered in the term *nomos*. It should be noted that Aristotle does not completely subscribe to the binary of nature and culture, especially since cultural capacities of the soul like *technē* and *phronēsis* are natural (*pephukos*) to the soul.[10] The same holds for the binary of *phusis* as an invariant order and *nomos* as the variance of convention: for Aristotle, sublunar nature, especially human nature, can admit of variance, even development that conflicts with erstwhile nature.[11]

In sum, an understanding of nature and the natural can unfold from a number of distinctions that do not reduce to a common form: natural-permanent, natural-artificial, natural-cultural, natural-accidental, and natural-supernatural. The last distinction in our sense was not operative in Greek thought; it emerged in modern thought, in part because of the complicated role of Christian theology in European philosophy. In general, the modern philosophical concept of nature developed out of two guiding criteria in modern science that, despite their apparent divergence into empirical and conceptual standards, were reciprocally related in scientific work: experimental verification and mathematical formalization. Both Descartes and Kant, among others, insisted that a science of nature was grounded in mathematics.[12] Modern science was a self-conscious repudiation of Aristotelian "physics," in part because central Aristotelian concepts of *telos* and *dunamis* eluded precise formalization and verification. As Newton put it, "the moderns, rejecting substantial forms and occult qualities, have endeavored to subject the phenomena of nature to the laws of mathematics."[13] And Descartes described his *Meditations* as the foundation of his physics, which deals a mortal blow to Aristotelian physics.[14] Consequently, in modern science, "nature" is no longer understood in an Aristotelian manner as the field of self-manifesting phenomena that guide inquiry according to their evident formations, but as re-formed phenomena according to a priori constructs and principles that are *not* evident in immediate experience. In the Sixth Meditation, Descartes claims that corporeal things in nature exist, but their true existence cannot be ascertained as a match with our sensory grasp (as in Aristotle), because sense experience can be confused. Things in nature exist only in the manner of clear and distinct ideas, which are ultimately grounded in pure mathematics, which is the ground of mechanical physics, and which, for Descartes, is ultimately guaranteed by God.[15]

Although many early modern philosophical and scientific developments were not divorced from theological principles, our contemporary understanding of naturalism can be called a deletion of any such principles and a reduction to a core of empirical and mathematical methods and constructions. My hope in this historical excursion is that it will help prepare and focus my later discussion of Nietzsche's distinct form of naturalism. Now I turn to the historical locus of Nietzsche's naturalistic turn, the death of God.

The Death of God

Nietzsche advances the death of God through the figure of a madman (*GS* 125), whose audience is not religious believers, but nonbelievers who are chastised for not facing the consequences of God's demise. Since God is the ultimate symbol of transcendence and foundations, his death is to be praised, but its impact reaches far beyond religion. In the modern world God is no longer the mandated centerpiece of intellectual and cultural life. But historically the notion of God had been the warrant for all sorts of cultural constructs in moral, political, philosophical, even scientific domains—so the death of God is different from atheism, since divinity had been "living" as a powerful productive force. From Plato through to the Enlightenment, a divine mind had been the ultimate reference point for origins and truth. With the eclipse of God, all corollary constructs must fall as well (*TI* "Skirmishes" 5). The death of God therefore announces the demise of truth, or at least that "the will to truth becomes conscious of itself as a *problem*" (*GM* III: 27). Even though God is no longer at the forefront of culture, we still have confidence in the "shadows" of God (*GS* 108), in supposedly secular truths that have nonetheless lost their pedigree and intellectual warrant. One of these "shadows" would be the modern confidence in scientific naturalism, which historically took shape by way of theological and metaphysical constructs purportedly dismissed by science.

The consequences of God's death are enormous because of the specter of nihilism, the loss of meaning and intelligibility. The secular sophistication of the modern world has unwittingly "unchained this earth from its sun," so that we are "straying as through an infinite nothing" (*GS* 125). The course of Western thought has lead it to turn away from its historical origins, but the unsuspected result has been that "the highest values devalue themselves" (*WP* 2) and we are faced with a stark choice: either we collapse into nihilism or we rethink the world in naturalistic terms freed from the reverence for being-constructs. "Either abolish your reverences or—*yourselves*! The latter would be nihilism; but would not the former also be—nihilism?—This is *our* question mark" (*GS* 346).

The complex question of nihilism in Nietzsche's thought cannot be addressed here. What can be said is that the threat of nihilism—the denial of any truth, meaning, or value in the world—is in fact parasitic on the Western tradition, which has judged conditions of becoming in life to be deficient and has "nullified" these conditions in favor of rational, spiritual, or moral corrections. If, in the wake of the death of God, the loss of these corrections is experienced as nihilistic, it is because the traditional models are still presumed to be the only measures of truth, meaning, and value—and thus the world seems empty without them (*WP* 12A). For Nietzsche, philosophers can embrace the death of God with gratitude and excitement, not despair, because of the opening of new horizons for thought (*GS* 343). Various motifs in Nietzsche's texts can be read as anti-nihilistic attempts to rethink truth, meaning, and value in naturalistic terms, in a manner consistent with conditions of becoming. A central motif in this regard is will to power.

Will to Power

"The world viewed from inside . . . would be 'will to power' and nothing else" (*BGE* 36). A world of becoming, for Nietzsche, cannot simply be understood as a world of change. Movements are always *related* to other movements and the relational structure is not simply expressive of differences, but rather resistances and tensional conflicts (*WP* 568). Will to power depicts in dynamic terms the idea that any affirmation is also a negation, that any condition or assertion of meaning must overcome some "Other," some obstacle or counterforce. Nietzsche proclaims something quite important for understanding his concept of power: "Will to power can manifest itself *only* against resistances; therefore it *seeks* that which resists it" (*WP* 656; [my emphasis]). What is crucial here is the following: Since power can *only* involve resistance, then one's power to overcome is essentially related to a counter-power; if resistance were eliminated, if one's counter-power were destroyed or even neutralized by sheer domination, one's power would evaporate; it would no longer *be* power. Power is *overcoming* something, not annihilating it: "there is no annihilation in the sphere of spirit" (*WP* 588). Will to power, therefore, cannot be understood in terms of individual states alone, even successful states, because it names a tensional force field, *within which* individual states shape themselves by seeking to overcome other sites of power. Power cannot be construed as "instrumental" for any resultant state, whether it be knowledge, pleasure, purpose, even survival, since such conditions are epiphenomena of power, of a drive to overcome something (*GM* II: 12, 18). For this reason, Nietzsche depicts life as "that which must always overcome itself" (*Z* II "On Self-Overcoming"). This accounts for Nietzsche's objections to measuring life by "happiness," because the structure of will to power shows that *dissatisfaction* and *displeasure* are intrinsic to movements of overcoming (*WP* 696, 704), and so conditions of sheer satisfaction would dry up the energies of life.

According to Nietzsche, any doctrine that would reject will to power in his sense would undermine the conditions of its own historical emergence as a contention with conflicting forces. All scientific, religious, moral, and intellectual developments began as elements of dissatisfaction and impulses to overcome something, whether it was ignorance, worldliness, brutality, confusion, or competing cultural models. Even pacifism—understood as an impulse to overcome human violence and an exalted way of life taken as an advance over our brutish nature—can be understood as an instance of will to power.

In historical terms, we can notice interesting links between will to power and Aristotle's conception of nature as *phusis*. We noted that modern physics departed from Aristotle in that the *being* of nature is reduced to precise, stable references of mathematical structure and the immediate findings of empirical verification—all this counterposed to Aristotelian physics and its dependence on developmental concepts of potentiality and purpose (*dunamis* and *telos*), both of which "exceed" immediate conditions of actuality. If Aristotelian *phusis* can be understood as a dynamic force of development, and *dunamis* is understood, as it was by Aristotle, as *capacious* potentiality—that is, not simply possibility, but potency, capacity, and power—then Nietzschean will to power can be seen as a radicalization of Aristotelian *phusis* and *dunamis*. For Nietzsche, "natural powers" would no longer follow Aristotle's proviso that they are developments toward actualities inscribed in reality by being fixed in divine form—which underwrites Aristotle's ultimate metaphysical principle that "actuality is prior to potentiality."[16] With will to power, Nietzsche turns this principle around: all actualization of form emerges within an irreducible force of power-relations. With the death of God, natural forms can no longer be traced to any "supra-dynamic" divine actuality. And Nietzsche's "physics" of will to power names the priority of dynamic force over *all* conceptions of actual being, whether ancient or modern (*BT* 2).[17]

Agonistics

A prefiguration of will to power can be found in an early text "Homer's Contest." Arguing against the idea that "culture" is something antithetical to brutal forces of "nature," Nietzsche spotlights the pervasiveness in ancient Greece of the *agōn*, or contest for excellence, which operated in all cultural pursuits (in athletics, the arts, oratory, politics, and philosophy). The *agōn* can be seen as a ritualized expression of a world-view expressed in so much of Greek myth, poetry, and philosophy: the world as an arena for the struggle of opposing (but related) forces. Agonistic relations are depicted in Hesiod's *Theogony*, Homer's *Iliad*, Greek tragedy, and philosophers such as Anaximander and Heraclitus.[18] In "Homer's Contest," Nietzsche argues that the *agōn* emerged as a *cultivation* of more brutal natural drives in not striving for the annihilation of the Other, but arranging contests that would test skill and performance in a competition. Accordingly, agonistic strife produced excellence, not obliteration, since talent unfolded in a struggle with competitors. In this way, the Greeks did not succumb to a false ideal of sheer harmony and order, and thus ensured a proliferation of excellence by preventing stagnation, dissimulation, and uniform control. The *agōn* expressed the general resistance of the Greeks to "unified domination" (*Alleinherrschaft*) and the danger of unchallenged or unchallengeable power—hence the practice of ostracizing someone too powerful, someone who would ruin the reciprocal structure of agonistic competition.

The Greek *agōn* is a historical source of what Nietzsche later generalized into the dynamic, reciprocal structure of will to power.[19] And it is important to recognize that such a structure undermines the idea that power could or should run unchecked, either in the sense of sheer domination or chaotic indeterminacy. Will to power implies a certain "measure" of oppositional limits, even though such a measure could not imply an overarching order or a stable principle of balance. Nevertheless, there *is* a capacity for measure in agonistic power relations. Nietzsche tells us that Greek institutions were healthy in not separating culture from nature in the manner of a good-evil scheme (*KSA* 8:5[146]). Yet they overcame sheer natural energies of destruction by selectively ordering them in their practices, cults, and festival days. The Greek "freedom of mind" (*Freisinnigkeit*) was a "measured release" of natural forces, not their negation. Accordingly, Nietzsche's concept of agonistic will to power should not be construed as a measureless threat to culture but a naturalistic redescription of cultural measures. The reciprocal structure of agonistic relations means that competing life forces productively delimit each other and thus generate dynamic formations rather than sheer dissipation or indeterminacy.[20]

Psychology and Perspectivism in Philosophy

A central feature of Nietzsche's naturalism, which distinguishes it from scientific naturalism, is that his diagnosis of the philosophical tradition goes beyond a conceptual critique of beliefs and theories: "the path to fundamental problems" is to be found in psychology (*BGE* 23). Nietzsche maintains that the origins of problematic constructs of "being" are not to be found in mistaken beliefs but in psychological weakness in the face of a finite world, an *aversion* to the negative conditions of life, which he describes as "decadence, a symptom of the *decline of life*" (*TI* "Reason" 6). Thus a certain kind of psychological strength is needed to affirm life and rethink it in ways that are more appropriate to its natural conditions of becoming. What follows is that Nietzschean psychology does not suggest a universal human nature, but a delineation of *types* along the lines of weakness and strength—hence Nietzsche's notorious objections to human equality[21] and his promotion of a hierarchical arrangement of types: "My philosophy aims at an ordering of rank" (*WP* 287).

Nietzsche rejects the notion that philosophy is an "impersonal" pursuit of knowledge; philosophy so conceived conceals a "personal confession," an "unconscious memoir," and so a philosopher's thought bears "decisive witness to *who he is*—that is, in what order of rank the innermost drives of his nature stand in relation to each other" (*BGE* 6). In considering a philosophical claim, one should ask: "What does such a claim tell us about the man who makes it?" (*BGE* 187). The turn to psychology means that knowledge cannot be based in an absolute, fixed, objective standard, but in a pluralized perspectivism: "There is *only* a perspective seeing, only a perspective 'knowing'" (*GM* III: 12). There are many possible takes on the world, and none could count as exclusively correct. And one's perspective can never be separated from one's existential interests, so "disinterested knowledge" is a fiction (*BGE* 207; *GM* III: 12, 26). Perspectives of value are more fundamental than objectivity or certainty. There is no being-in-itself, only "grades of appearance measured by the strength of *interest* we show in an appearance" (*WP* 588). Perspectivism entails that we exchange the connotations of strict knowledge and "facts" for the more open concept of "interpretation" (*GS* 374). Interpretation is the "introduction of meaning" (*Sinn-hineinlegen*) and not "explanation" (*Erklärung*) (*KSA* 12:2[82]).[22] Different, even conflicting positions can no longer be ruled out of play. Nietzsche expresses his outlook as follows: "Profound aversion to resting once and for all in any one total view of the world. Enchantment (*Zauber*) of the opposing point of view; refusal to be deprived of the stimulus of the enigmatic" (*WP* 470).

It can be noted how Nietzsche's turn to psychology reflects his naturalistic revision of philosophy, which focuses on thought as an embodied expression of psychological forces. Critical questions that follow such a focus would no longer turn on cognitive tests (How can you prove X?) but on psychological explorations and probes (Why is X *important* to you?). Accordingly, for Nietzsche, philosophy is always value-laden and cannot be reduced to descriptive, objective terms or to a project of logical demonstration; and he is consistent in recognizing this in the course of his own writing: "What have I to do with refutations!" (*GM* "Prologue" 4). He often enough indicates that philosophy, including his own textual work, is a circulation of writing and reading that stems from, and taps into, personal forces and dispositions toward life.[23]

I should mention one further methodological implication stemming from Nietzsche's naturalism. I call it a *presumption of immanence*. We can only think in terms of how we are *already* existing in the midst of manifest forces not of our choosing and not imaginable as stemming from, or implying, some "other" realm beyond the lived world. This mandates that we accept as *given* all forces that we can honestly recognize at work in our lives: reason and instinct, truth and lies, order and strife, love and hate, and so on. This includes the abiding *contest* between such forces, which undermines traditional projects of "eliminative" opposition (which can arise in any sphere, from religion to science). For Nietzsche, all evident forces play a role in cultural life, and a failure to embrace the whole package betrays weakness and the seeds of life-denial.

Again, "nature" in modern science is different from the notion of self-manifesting phenomena. In both conception and execution, modern science adopts a radical interrogation and re-formation of our initial confidence in lived experience. It is the radicality of such re-formation that can be called into question, and some of the rhetoric of early modern thought can open itself to critique. On the methodological path of Descartes's journey toward certainty and the warrant for physics, there is a wonderful moment in the First Meditation. Descartes confesses that his attempt to subject his normal beliefs to radical doubt meets stiff resistance:

> For long-standing opinions keep returning, and, almost against my will, they take advantage of my credulity, as if it were bound over to them by long use and the claims of intimacy. Nor will I ever get out of the habit of assenting to them and believing in them, so long as I take them to be exactly what they are, namely, in some sense doubtful, as has just now been shown, but nevertheless highly probable, so that it is much more consonant with reason to believe them than

> to deny them. Hence, it seems to me that I would do well to *deceive myself* [my emphasis] by turning my will in completely the opposite direction and *pretend* [my emphasis] for a while that these opinions are wholly false and imaginary, until finally . . . no bad habit should turn my judgment any further from the correct perception of things.[24]

In other words, the search for certainty must deploy self-deception and pretense to overcome the intimacies of "natural experience" that keeps asserting itself against the will of the investigator. Descartes mitigates his pretense of excessive doubt with the assurance that he will not fall into error because here he is "concentrating only on knowledge, not on action."[25] A Derridean could clearly relish the deconstructive exposure in Descartes's deployment of self-deception, and even a pragmatist can notice Descartes's vulnerability on the question of knowledge and action.

To continue with this deconstructive alert, the posture of experimental science with regard to nature may be far from a cooperative relationship (which marked Aristotle's account of scientific knowledge). Francis Bacon is disarmingly honest on this matter. The experimental method investigates "nature under constraint and vexed; that is to say, when by art and the hand of man she is forced out of her natural state, and squeezed and molded."[26] The point is that modern scientific naturalism emerged as a *struggle* with erstwhile conceptions of nature and lived experience. Such an agonistic relationship, in Nietzschean terms, does not prompt a rejection or dismissal of natural science; it simply opens up a redescription of its character and a check against its exclusive claims to truth.

If naturalism is associated with "objective" cognition and dispositions, Nietzsche would not sign on, because his naturalistic perspectivism mandates a constitutive *interest* in one's beliefs, as opposed to the "objective spirit" who stands for "disinterested" knowledge; such a spirit is weak in not being able to "affirm or negate" or to "take sides for good or evil" (*BGE* 207). Perspectivism is also not equivalent to skepticism (a frequent misreading of Nietzsche). The presumption of immanence will not permit a radical skepticism that goes all the way down to doubt the possibility of all beliefs at once in a given domain. To be precise, skepticism is permitted but diagnosed as an infirmity along the lines of objectivism. Perspectivism entails not only interest but a commitment to one's beliefs over others. A skeptical reserve is not only parasitic on the standard of certainty, it is also indicative of a "nervous exhaustion and sickliness" and a preference for "abstinence" that is fearful of the leap to any decisive "Yes and No" (*BGE* 208). In sum, Nietzsche's naturalism measures philosophy in terms of intellectual and existential capacities to affirm the finite conditions of natural life.

The Ascetic Ideal

Notable in this respect is Nietzsche's account of the ascetic ideal in the Third Essay of *Genealogy of Morals*. There the ascetic ideal names the life-denying impulse that renounces the conditions of natural existence—which is taken to be meaningless on its own terms—and aims for transcendent salvation. Surprisingly, Nietzsche declares that modern science is the latest and most potent form of the ascetic ideal, not because it shares a belief in religious transcendence, but because it maintains a belief in truth (*GM* III: 24). In *The Gay Science* (*GS* 344), Nietzsche had implicitly connected the modern commitment to truth with the ascetic ideal: A faith in scientific truth, for example, "*thus affirms another world* from the one of life, nature, and history." The belief in science "is still based on a *metaphysical faith*"—which we recall is manifested in binary-thinking, and which in this case would involve a secured scientific model of *truth* against the *errors* of nonscientific thinking.

In *Genealogy of Morals* (*GM* III: 25) Nietzsche concludes that science is not the genuine *natural* opponent of the ascetic ideal because in the matter of truth it is likewise alienated from the unstable forces of natural life. He then seeks to clarify how two seemingly different standpoints—asceticism and science—can yet share a common ideal. Religious asceticism is simply the most obvious and telling manifestation of the deeper issue animating Nietzsche's critical project: the diagnosis of life-alienating forces in human culture; *this* is the central meaning of the ascetic ideal, whatever form it takes. Obviously, modern science—in both its history and practice—has been antagonistic toward religion and transcendent doctrines in its drive for cultural authority. Yet Nietzsche insists that even with this contested relationship, science is still a manifestation of the *core* meaning of the ascetic ideal:

> Its opposition and battle are, on closer inspection, directed not at the ideal itself but at its outer-works, its apparel and disguise, at the way the ideal temporarily hardens, solidifies, becomes dogmatic. (*GM* III: 25)

Nietzsche then indicates how science is indeed more attuned to life than the transcendent versions of the ascetic ideal: "science liberates what life is in it by denying what is exoteric in this ideal" (*GM* III: 25). In other words, science opposes the "overt" manifestations of religion—its doctrines, theologies, and lifestyles—that do in fact stand in the way of something like science. Yet with respect to the core meaning of the ideal—which in this context could be called "esoteric" or "covert"—Nietzsche declares: "Both of them, science and the ascetic ideal, are still on the same foundation" (*GM* III: 25). And right away he identifies this common foundation with the matter of truth:

> that is to say, both overestimate truth (more correctly: they share the same faith that truth *cannot* be assessed or criticized), and this makes them both *necessarily* allies, so that, if they must be fought, they can only be fought and called into question together. An assessment of the value of the ascetic ideal inevitably brings about an assessment of the value of science. (*GM* III: 25)

After Nietzsche offers a provocative parenthetical remark about art being a better nominee for opposing the ascetic ideal, Nietzsche elaborates on how the alliance of science and asceticism can be understood in specific ways. The discussion focuses mainly on two elements: (1) How the practices and epistemological assumptions in science show a comparable antagonism toward more natural drives; and (2) How certain results of the modern scientific world-view have reinforced or reconstituted a central feature of the ascetic ideal: that natural life on its own terms exhibits no intrinsic meaning.

To the first point, Nietzsche briefly discusses the way in which scientific knowledge must fight off a host of natural dispositions, passions, and instincts in order to shape its aim toward an objective, disinterested understanding of nature, which is presumed to give truth that is independent of human interests and freed from the disorder and contingencies of lived experience. Despite the different spheres of *content* in science and religious asceticism ("natural" and "supernatural" spheres), when it comes to scientific criteria and the "discipline" required for training in science, Nietzsche asks us to notice a form of self-denial that is comparable to an ascetic denial of natural life impulses. This is why Nietzsche says that "science rests on the same base as the ascetic ideal: the precondition of both the one and the other is a certain *impoverishment of life*" (*GM* III: 25).

The second point requires some care in interpretation, and I think it is best viewed in light of the death of God, although here there emerges a different angle on its consequences. We have already noted that the eclipse of God in modern thought also threatens its "shadows," the supposedly secular beliefs that in fact have lost their historical anchor—thus the threat of full-blown nihilism. Nietzsche's analysis in *Genealogy of Morals* compresses this scenario into the problem of truth. According to Nietzsche, scientific truth is simply a modification of theological binaries, and so the modern displacement of God will have to deauthorize scientific confidences about knowledge. Yet in *Genealogy of Morals* (*GM* III: 25) Nietzsche pushes the science-asceticism equation even further, now in the light of asceticism's overt conviction about the meaninglessness of natural life, on its incapacity to find meaning on life's own terms.

Nietzsche continues to conflate the supposed differences between science and asceticism by taking up the "famous *victories*" of modern science over theology and religious world-views. There surely *are* such victories, he says, but they do not support the familiar binary-story of "natural science" overcoming and replacing "supernatural" beliefs. Nietzsche asks: Over *what* has science been victorious? Not the ascetic *ideal* but only certain of its trappings.

> The ascetic ideal was decidedly not conquered, it was, on the contrary, made stronger, I mean more elusive, more spiritual (*geistiger*), more insidious by the fact that science constantly and unsparingly detached and broke off a wall or outer-work that had attached itself to it and *coarsened* its appearance. (*GM* III: 25)

In what follows, Nietzsche elaborates on an *ideal* shared by asceticism and science—despite the "outward" battle between their world-views—and this ideal has to do with the meaninglessness of finite life, with the nihilistic erasure of meaning in the lived world. How can this be, when science deliberately separates itself from world-transcending beliefs and considers itself to be a highly meaningful endeavor? Nietzsche brings in the example of astronomy and asks if we can truly say that the Copernican defeat of theological astronomy was a defeat of the ascetic ideal. He thinks not, and it is here that the matter of a shared nihilism comes into play and the full complexity of the death of God is shown. If the modern alternative to God's eclipse is simply modern science, then Nietzsche seems to think that the nihilistic core of the ascetic ideal has not only been sustained but even strengthened, because it can now rest on much more evident and "natural" grounds (and therefore no longer requires a supernatural script).

We might comprehend Nietzsche's move by recalling the self-conception of modern science as a radical transformation of how nature is to be understood by way of mechanical physics. The new mechanical model of nature was thoroughly dependent on mathematical measures, which could provide the maximal degree of "objectivity," and which could not be compatible with less measurable or immeasurable matters such as purposes and values (goodness, beauty, goals, etc.). This is the source of the famous fact-value divide, where nature is viewed as a value-free set of measurable facts and values are no longer intrinsic to nature (as they were in ancient and medieval thought). Nature is now simply matter in motion measured by a quantified space-time grid; nature as such has no aim or purpose. The location of *values*, therefore, had to be redirected to the human subject—whether in the personal subjectivity of "taste" or in the transcendental subjectivity of universal principles intrinsic to any rational mind (as attempted by Kant). Yet in either case, values could no longer be attributed to natural "reality" because they were now "merely" subjective states projected "upon" objective nature (a sunset is not "really" beautiful; it only appears so to us). As a consequence, the status of certain meanings was not only sectioned off but also demoted to the point where it would be possible to say that human life is not "really" meaningful in the sphere of nature. Such, I think, is the context in which we can comprehend Nietzsche's subsequent remarks about astronomy in particular and science in general.

The reason why Nietzsche challenges the victory of Copernican over theological astronomy is that the ascetic departure from natural meaning no longer requires a supernatural story because, in effect, it has perfected an *immanent* departure from natural meaning *within* a natural setting.

> Has man perhaps become less *needful* of a transcendent solution to the riddle of his existence because his existence has since come to look still more arbitrary, more a loitering (*eckensteherischer*), and more dispensable in the *visible* order of things? Has not man's self-diminishment, his *will* to self-diminishment, been unstoppably progressing since Copernicus? (*GM* III: 25)

Nietzsche then alludes to the gradual reduction of human self-understanding to the "natural" condition of scientific findings, such as the "animal" characteristics given in biology (perhaps Nietzsche has Darwinism in mind here). He goes on:

> Since Copernicus, man seems to have been on a downward path,—now he seems to be rolling faster and faster away from the center—whereto? Into nothingness? Into the "*piercing* sensation of his nothingness"? (*GM* III: 25)

We should notice here a clear reference to the language of the madman passage in *The Gay Science* (*GS* 125) that announced the death of God—the loss of a divine center that has the earth unchained from its sun, "straying as through an infinite nothingness." Yet as I have suggested, the passage in question here pushes the matter further than just the loss of historical warrants in modern thought, which could be called a concealed nihilism; here Nietzsche seems to declare that modern science is a manifestation of ascetic nihilism made more *actual* in a worldly sense. This is why he can say of the growing diminishment of human meaning in modern science: "Well! That would be the straight path—to the *old* ideal" (*GM* III: 25).

Here is my take on Nietzsche's position: The original ascetic ideal found natural life meaningless and reached for transcendent relief. Modern science overcame religious transcendence, but with its *reductive* naturalism human meanings were robbed of their previous status and became superfluous in the natural order—despite (or because of) their being rendered "subjective" in modern thought. In this way science provides a *stronger* case for the meaninglessness of natural existence (compared with religious fantasy), and so within the sphere of natural life alone, *both* religion and science posit a lack of meaning. Moreover, since science restricts thought to the natural world, meaninglessness is now complete and exhaustive, because at least the old ideal provided the *solace* of an imagined deliverance. Nietzsche's argument seems to be that a reductive *scientific* naturalism is no less nihilistic than supernaturalism; it is even more dangerous because it can *consummate* nihilism if science is accepted as the only proper account of nature. What we are circling around here is the important matter of how Nietzsche's naturalism differs from scientific naturalism, and how Nietzsche's approach would be looking for a natural *affirmation* of life-meanings. That is why Nietzsche says that a strictly scientific picture of the world "would be an essentially *meaningless* world" (*GS* 373), and that the question of the *value* of existence lacks "any grain of significance when measured scientifically" (*GS* "Preface" 1).

Nietzsche proclaims that "*all* science" shares with asceticism a "humiliating and degrading effect" on human life by "seeking to talk man out of his former self-respect, as though this were nothing but a bizarre piece of self-conceit" (*GM* III: 25). By *all* science, Nietzsche means "natural as well as *unnatural*" science (*GM* III: 25). The unnatural form seems to reference Kant's critique of reason, in which knowledge is restricted to modern scientific knowledge, which renders knowledge of things like God, freedom, the soul, and immortality unattainable. Yet Kant recognized the crisis that this constraint represents, especially for human morality. Kant's solution was to limit scientific reason to "appearances," so that something like moral freedom could be posited as *possible* in a sphere of noumenal "reality." At least Kant recognized a crisis that had to be addressed, as opposed to those who take the deflation of human values as *not* disturbing—either by ignoring the issue or perhaps by way of a certain satisfaction taken in debunking cherished beliefs. Nietzsche agrees that the situation *is* a crisis that has to be met head on; but the crisis is *caused* by the presumption that scientific knowledge is the only way to properly understand nature, and the meaning-crisis is in fact the consequence of an ascetic inheritance in science and even the consummation of that ideal's nihilism. Without confronting that ideal as such, no solution to the crisis can be found.

In sum we can say that Nietzsche's critique of the ascetic ideal targets every dimension of European thought—theological, philosophical, and scientific—owing to a common failure or inability to find natural life meaningful on its own terms. In the final sections of the Third Essay, Nietzsche explores the possibility of overcoming the ascetic ideal and its nihilistic implications. If there is any way to do this (and Nietzsche seems tentative), it will have to follow from an *affirmative* posture toward worldly existence, one that can dwell with all the differentiated and conflicting elements of natural life.

PART II

Evolution, Teleology, and the Laws of Nature

3

Is Evolution Blind?
On Nietzsche's Reception of Darwin

VIRGINIA CANO

Nietzsche's criticism of Darwin's theory of evolution condenses in the figure of the English naturalist and the great spell that, to this day, it holds on biologists and philosophers when it comes to thinking about life. A final explanation, a "real world": this is the siren song that seduces with the idea of being able to capture life in the certainty of a *logos.* Here is the dream of conquest and also the goal of seduction.

As I illustrate in what follows, through his debate with Darwinian evolution Nietzsche finds a privileged route of attack against the two polemic fronts in nineteenth-century biology: teleology and mechanism. Both are modes of configuring a *logos*-logic that channels the dynamics of life into the same coordinates as the world of quantifiable entities. These two modalities of the same "dream" of a "real world" interweave in Nietzsche's reading of Darwin's theory. Nietzsche's reading, albeit flawed, reveals the importance nineteenth-century biological discourses recovered in Nietzsche's thinking about life, allowing me to reconsider the type of explanation undertaken by Nietzsche for the phenomenon of life. Darwin functions, in this way, as a kind of pretext to sketch out some of the basic lines of Nietzsche's argument regarding life.

Unlike Darwin's gradualist and predictive explanation, where a *logos* tries to reduce the phenomenon of the vital to a logic of calculus, Nietzsche presents a jovial discourse on life, a gay biology in which the "woman" that life is will never cease to exercise her *action at a distance.*

Nietzsche and Nineteenth-Century Biology

> Bisher sind beide Erklärungen des organischen Lebens nicht gelungen, weder die aus der Mechanik, noch die aus dem Geiste. Ich betone letzteres. Der Geist ist oberflächlicher als man glaubt.
>
> (*KSA* 11: 26[68])

How should we understand Nietzsche's thoughts about life? Is this discourse, this *logos* that reflects upon *bios*, a biological argument? After all, as Heidegger signals, "We are accustomed to call a kind of thinking that interprets all appearances as an expression of life a *biological one*."[1] And yet, it is Heidegger himself who offers us another way inside Nietzsche's philosophy, by rejecting the relegation of his argument regarding life to the confines of biological science. For "this current and, in a way, correct characterization of Nietzschean thinking as biologism presents the *main obstacle* to our penetrating his fundamental thought."[2] What is at stake here is not only Nietzsche's global vision of science, but also the manner in which these biological discourses interweave in a textual corpus that attempts to overcome the very limitations of nineteenth-century biology—the same limitations that are ubiquitous across the scientific disciplines of the age—posed by the distinction between teleology and mechanism. On this point, I follow Granier, who says that the "central problem is in knowing if these [biological] bases allow us to fully understand the ultimate meaning of the *Wille zur Macht* or if, on the contrary, they are no more than, as Jaspers says, 'the visible points of departure' of a reflection."[3] As I show in the following section, it is through the debate with certain positions in the biology of his age, mainly in his critique of Darwin, that Nietzsche will be able to establish the foundations of a conception of life.

It is important to point out the context in which Nietzsche develops his arguments on the will to power. The scientific paradigm of the biology of the age oscillates between the mechanistic tendencies belonging to Darwinism and the theses of the neo-Lamarckian physiologists who postulate a creative and inventive organism (that is, teleological tendencies).[4] Lenoir suggests reading the "research program" of German biology in the nineteenth century as an effort to "unify the teleological and mechanistic models of explanation."[5] Following this suggestion, Nietzsche's treatment of life will move at the limits of these two explanatory frameworks.[6] These two paradigms to explain life, sometimes united and sometimes apart, appear as the spells that have entranced scientists time and again. And as I will show, Darwin was, in Nietzsche's judgment, no exception.

"From the fact that something ensues regularly and ensues calculably, it does not follow that it ensues *necessarily*," Nietzsche would say, "*against determinism*" (*WP* 552; *KSA* 12:9[91]). He points out that "mechanical necessity" is not a fact, but rather one of the ways life becomes thinkable based upon an interpretation that converts the experienced world into something regular and stable. In this sense, Nietzsche's critique is directed against the strong influence of the will to truth that underlies every way of rendering existence intelligible. It represents a "making firm, a making true and durable, and abolition of the false character of things" (*WP* 522; *KSA* 12:9[91]) that allows us an extreme "logicizing, rationalizing, [and] systematizing" of experience. On this point, Nietzsche subjects the opposing, yet interlacing, explanatory paradigms in the development of the life sciences to the same critique. Nietzsche's objection to the deterministic positions applies equally to the teleological standpoints:[7] both paradigms exacerbate the logic of calculus and both express an underlying will to truth. At the bottom of both standpoints lies the strong fear of becoming, and a limitation of thinking reduced to the strategic construction of a "predictable world."

> As soon as we imagine someone who is responsible for our being thus and thus, etc. (God, nature), and therefore attribute to him the intention that we should exist and be happy or wretched, we corrupt for ourselves the *innocence of becoming* [*Unschuld des Werdens*]. We then have someone who wants to achieve something through us and with us. (*WP* 552; *KSA* 12:9[91])

In essence, the guilt-debt (*Schuld*) of "the apparent '*necessity*'" and the "apparent '*purposiveness*'" is the same: both deny the innocent character of becomings that escape and elude the will to make everything that exists stable, predictable, and durable. If mechanism and teleology have something in common, it, for Nietzsche, stems from this will to truth that wants "the thinkability of all beings" (*Z* II "Self-Overcoming"), and thus projects a "metaphysical world, as a thing-in-itself" (*WP* 552; *KSA* 12:9[91]) in order to achieve its aim. What Nietzsche claims for "'Reason' in Philosophy," also applies to reason in biological science. This hatred of becoming, this potent mummifying impulse constitutes one of the most persistent idiosyncrasies of philosophers.[8]

What does the constriction of the horizon of life to the sphere of calculability and predictability entail for becoming? The notion of becoming operates as a limit concept. It signals that which escapes the attempts to fix a world of being. If the will to truth attempts to make intelligible everything that exists, becoming is that margin that exceeds any formulation of the world. This is why Nietzsche maintains that "linguistic means of expression are useless for expressing 'becoming'; it accords with our inevitable need to preserve ourselves to posit a crude world of stability" (*WP* 715; *KSA* 13:11[73]). Against the stability of being, the inexpressible excess of intangible becoming impedes a definitive and mummifying systematization of the phenomenon of life. And in this way, life cannot remain imprisoned in any lethal logic of calculability and stability.

"Against the value of that which remains eternally the same (*vide* Spinoza's naiveté; Descartes's also), the values of the briefest and most transient, the seductive flash of gold on the belly of the serpent *vita*" (*WP* 577; *KSA* 12:9[26])—life is, for Nietzsche, a seductive serpent that eludes all attempts to reduce it to the logic of stability and predictability. His critique of Darwinian thinking may be summed up as a denunciation of the attempt to force the phenomenon of life into the corset-like logic of the plannable. In order to develop this critique, I will outline Nietzsche's interpretation of Darwin's theory of evolution. I will take a look at the sources and readings that led Nietzsche to see in the English naturalist that teleo-mechanism, which in Lenoir's opinion characterizes the core of the biology of the nineteenth century. To do this, Nietzsche needs to restore the capacity of vision to Darwin's blind watchmaker.[9]

The Spell of Darwinism

> I cannot persuade myself that a beneficent and omnipotent God would have designedly created the ichneumonidae (parasite wasps) with the express intention of their feeding within the living bodies of caterpillars.
>
> Charles Darwin to Asa Gray, May 22, 1860

One has to begin, then, with Nietzsche's reading of Darwin in order to evaluate its relevance and scope. "Anti-Darwin" and "Nietzsche contra Darwin": these are the proclamations with which Nietzsche characterizes his standpoint on Darwin's discoveries. In order to understand his opposition to Darwin, one must first be clear about who Nietzsche's "Darwin" is. Of whom (or what) is he thinking when referring to himself as anti-Darwinian? The fact is that Nietzsche's "Darwin" combines, as I have already indicated, the two greatest temptations of nineteenth-century science: determinism and teleology. Thus in order to make the case of "Nietzsche contra Darwin," I first have to sketch out what Nietzsche understands by Darwinian evolution and the various sources from which he drew in order to construct his reading of the theory of evolution. In this sense, Nietzsche's critiques are aimed at this complex reconstruction of "Darwin."

Nietzsche does not have first-hand access to Darwin's oeuvre. It is not known precisely which of Darwin's texts he did in fact read, with the exception of his "Biographical Sketch of an Infant."[10] His readings on evolutionary theory came mainly from Lange, who offered a teleological reading of Darwin, Ernst Haeckel (the German biologist who would be one of the most important defenders and promoters of Darwinism in Germany), and the biologists W. Roux and W. Rolph.[11]

Both Lange and Haeckel dwell on the central aspects of the Darwinian position that constitute the main target of Nietzsche's critique: the struggle for existence and natural selection.

> *Anti-Darwin.*—As regards the celebrated "struggle for *life*," it seems to me for the present to have been rather asserted than proved. It does occur, but as the exception; the general aspect of life is *not* hunger and distress, but rather wealth, luxury, even absurd prodigality—where there is a struggle it is a struggle for *power* . . . One should not mistake Malthus for nature.—Supposing, however, that this struggle exists—and it does indeed occur—its outcome is the reverse of that desired by the school of Darwin, of that which one *ought* perhaps to desire with them: namely, the defeat of the stronger, the more privileged, the fortunate exceptions. Species do *not* grow more perfect: the weaker dominate the strong again and again—the reason being they are the great majority. (*TI* "Skirmishes" 14)

Nietzsche not only rejects the idea of natural selection as a mechanism determining the preservation and growth of the fittest, but he also challenges another assumption of Darwin's theory of evolution, namely, the struggle for life, maintaining that this cannot constitute a law of life. Regarding the process of selection, what Nietzsche claims is the opposite of what would be postulated by Darwin. According to Nietzsche, if over the course of history one observes a process of selection of individuals, then it is the less fit, the weak and the mediocre, who get selected, and not the strongest individuals.

Thus, for Darwin, "when we reflect on this struggle, we may console ourselves with the full belief, that the war of nature is not incessant, . . . and the vigorous, the healthy, and the happy survive and multiply";[12] where Nietzsche, on the contrary, holds that "what surprises me most when I survey the broad destinies of man is that I always see before me the opposite of that which Darwin and his school see or *want* to see today: selection in favor of the stronger, better-constituted, and the progress of the species. Precisely the opposite is palpable" (*WP* 685; *KSA* 13:14[123]). On Nietzsche's view, the mediocre, the herd, have numerical superiority on their side. Contrary to what Darwin's subtitle to his masterpiece suggests ("the Preservation of Favored Races in the Struggle for Life"), it has not been the "favored races" that have triumphed in the struggle for life: it has been the weak, the sick, and the decadent that have won this war. In any case, Nietzsche says one ought to think of a "development in *decline*" (*TI* "Socrates" 3).

The struggle for life constitutes the crucial front of attack for Nietzsche. He addresses this question from two complementary perspectives. In the first, he discusses the relevance of the principle of self-preservation underlying the struggle for life by establishing a genealogy from the Spinozist *conatus* to the Darwinian struggle for life. The second perspective takes up the notion of struggle Darwin worked with. Let me begin with this second perspective.

According to Nietzsche, and in this he follows very closely in the footsteps of Roux, struggle cannot be understood on the basis of a combat between individuals. If for Darwin struggle is combat between organisms that compete over resources for survival, for Nietzsche struggle must refer first to an internal combat, to a struggle between the constitutive parts of individuals. In this sense, he displaces the coordinates along which struggle itself is conceived. For Darwin the relevant and decisive combat—in terms of his evolutionary explanation—is that which occurs between distinct individuals, and in this sense he assumes some stability in the identity of said individuals. For Nietzsche, instead, "struggle" is what produces and constitutes distinct individualities. In this way, these individualities never find a stable or closed identity. As Stiegler explains, "while Darwin believes that what is most decisive is what occurs between organisms, understood as finite individuals that are consistent and identical to themselves, Nietzsche will follow in Roux's footsteps and focus on the idea of the struggle of the parts that constitute organisms and make up an entity that is unstable and continually being formed."[13] The unity presupposed by Darwin as a point of departure is then, in fact, the result of a prior struggle. Rather than a stable beginning, it is a slippery place of arrival: "The amoeba-like unity of the individual comes at the end! And the philosophers started with it, as if it was already there!" (*KSA* 9:11[189]).

Rather than developing a critique that is internal to Darwin's theory of evolution,[14] Nietzsche displaces the site of struggle. But even so, the most ruthless aspect of his critique still latches onto the idea of a *struggle for life* considered as synonymous with the instinct for self-preservation. Against the idea of life understood under the formula of a struggle for survival,

Nietzsche advances the idea of life as will to power. As Granier says, "the Nietzschean notion of *Wille zur Macht* simply marks the substitution of Darwin's 'struggle for life' for the 'struggle for preeminence.'"[15]

> To wish to preserve oneself is a sign of distress, of a limitation of the truly basic life-instinct, which aims at *the expansion of power* and in so doing often enough risks and sacrifices self-preservation. It is symptomatic that certain philosophers, such as the consumptive Spinoza, took and indeed had to take just the so-called self-preservation instinct to be decisive: —they were simply people in distress [. . .] English Darwinism exudes something like the stuffy air of English overpopulation, like the small people's smell of indigence and overcrowding. As a natural scientist, however, one should get out of one's human corner; and in nature, it is not distress which *rules*, but rather abundance, squandering even to the point of absurdity. The struggle for survival is only an *exception*, a temporary restriction of the will to life; the great and small struggle revolves everywhere around preponderance, around growth and expansion, around power and in accordance with the will to power, which is simply the will to life. (*GS* 349)

To the struggle for life as self-preservation, Nietzsche opposes the struggle for the increase and expansion of power. But in Darwin self-preservation presupposes the domination and propagation of certain traits and individuals over others, and thus also the augmentation of power. So on what grounds does Nietzsche oppose self-preservation and increase of power? According to Nietzsche, preservation presupposes a logic of accumulation that in many cases is hostile to the possibility of any real augmentation of power. As he argues in the *On the Genealogy of Morals*, "even the partial *reduction in usefulness,* decay and degeneration, loss of meaning [*Sinn*] and functional purpose, in short, death, make up the conditions of true *progressus*: always appearing, as it does, in the form of the will and way to *greater power* and always emerging victorious at the cost of countless smaller forces" (*GM* II: 12). Increase of power cannot be equated with mere preservation, because it also presupposes and requires non-preservation, the risk of a confrontation with *thanatos.* The way of power does not detach the idea of life from the idea of death and dissolution. On the contrary, and I will return to this point shortly, life cannot be thought in the absence of death. "The amount of 'progress' can actually be *measured* according to how much has had to be sacrificed to it" (*GM* II: 12). Through the opposition between preservation and augmentation of power, Nietzsche introduces the notions of loss, sacrifice, and death into the sphere of life.[16]

For his part, Nietzsche also engages the Malthusian principle that posits the combat between individuals based upon the postulate of a scarcity of resources. Against this postulate, Nietzsche proposes a radically different initial condition: that of abundance and squandering. Thus Darwin's application of the Malthusian doctrine "with manifold force to the whole animal and vegetable kingdoms"[17] is replaced by a vision that considers situations of poverty and penury as exceptions to the rule, like the disproportionate growth of the (English) population in relation to its resources. Situations of overpopulation do not constitute the norm. In this sense, the struggle for life—which is a direct consequence of the alleged scarcity of resources—can only be seen as an equally exceptional situation. Thus Nietzsche lands his hammer blow at the center of Darwinian thinking: if resources are not (generally) scarce, then the war between individuals arising from their competition for resources would "dissipate," or at best be an exception, rather than a rule.

"The struggle for existence inevitably follows from the high geometrical ratio of increase which is common to all organic beings,"[18] affirms Darwin. But now, with Nietzsche, life appears in the guise of overflowing and overabundance. Thus the struggle for life cannot be seen as nature's starting point, nor as a necessary and inevitable outcome. It cannot, therefore, be the engine in the process of selection sustaining the evolution of living beings. Life can no longer be understood primarily through the principle of self-preservation that underlies Darwin's explanation of the development and selection of species. Thus, Nietzsche warns, "physiologists should think before putting down the instinct of self-preservation as the cardinal instinct of an organic being. A living thing seeks above all to *discharge* its strength—life itself is *will to power*; self-preservation is only one of the indirect and most frequent *results*. In short, here as everywhere else, let us beware of superfluous teleological principles—one of which is the instinct of self-preservation (we owe it to Spinoza's inconsistency). Thus method, which must be essentially economy of principles, demands it" (*BGE* 13). Self-preservation[19] cannot be anything other than an indirect consequence of the attempt by a living being to increase its power. And it is only as such that self-preservation is justified in the Nietzschean economy. As Frezzatti Junior says, "the attempt to dominate prevails over the attempt to preserve."[20] The intensification of power may require self-suppression, the nonconservation of self, since "that which is useful for the long life of the individual might be unfavorable to its strength and splendor; that which preserves the individual might at the same time arrest and halt its evolution" (*WP* 647; *KSA* 12:7[25]). In sum, what the will wants in its securing of greater power is nothing other than to overcome itself, its forms and its types; it does not seek fixation, but rather movement and plasticity.

> And life itself confided this secret to me: "Behold," it said, "I am *that which must always overcome itself.* Indeed, you call it a will to procreate or a drive to an end, to something higher, farther, more manifold: but all this is one, and one secret." Rather would I perish than forswear this; and verily, where this is perishing and a falling of leaves, behold, there life sacrifices itself—for power. (*Z* II "Self-Overcoming")

Life cannot want mere self-preservation because in order to increase its power, in order to be will to power, it is compelled to overcome itself. In this way, the will to power does not strive toward "one single thing," for otherwise it would remain tied to one single purpose and would cease to be what it is: overabundance, wealth, and overcoming. Life cannot be reduced to a mere economy of principles that strive toward one single mystery, whatever this may be. Is this not the case with Darwin's mechanism? Does one not have here the reduction of life to a single explanation, to a single purpose, as is the survival of the fittest? This is where Nietzsche sees a teleology in Darwin's thought. Through natural selection, the mechanism that "is daily and hourly scrutinizing, throughout the world, every variation, even the slightest; rejecting that which is bad, preserving and adding up all that is good; silently and insensibly working, whenever and wherever opportunity offers, at the improvement of each organic being in relation to its organic and inorganic conditions of life"[21] seems focused on one single purpose: the preserving accumulation of all that contributes to the survival of individuals and of species. For Nietzsche, this mechanism carries a teleological principle that strives toward a calculable economy of elements connected in terms of utilities and losses. Accumulation shows itself to be too intelligent to be blind. It is in this natural tendency toward progress, toward the organism's perfection[22] in terms of the selection of favored individuals, that Nietzsche discovers teleology in Darwin's mechanism. And in this misreading, which sees in utility, progress, and the struggle for life a form of teleology, one hears Lange's words:

> Meanwhile there's also a teleology which is not only compatible with Darwinism, but is almost identical with it . . . If Darwinism, as compared with the gross anthropomorphic teleology, appears as a theory of chance, this is only its thoroughly justified negative side. Adaptations proceed from the conservation of relatively fortuitous formations, but . . . [i]n the great whole everything, and therefore even the appearance of those formations which by adaptation and transmission

become the basis of new creations, is necessary and determined by eternal laws.[23]

The blind mechanism reveals itself, in its thrifty economy of principles, to be "*a continual growth in perfection*" (*WP* 684; *KSA* 13:14[133], [emphasis added]),[24] which Nietzsche like Lange, considers a teleology.[25] After all, "[t]he whole question of correct teleology may be reduced to this, that we inquire how far something may be found in this arrangement of nature, combined with the mechanically operating law of development, that can be compared to a 'cosmic plan.'"[26] This beauty and order betrays, behind the blind eyes of the unconscious maker, the existence of a single vision, explanation and purpose seeking to make of life a "stable" phenomenon. Here we have teleology united with mechanism. The two explanations of life united in this "vision" of the (not so) blind maker attempt to reduce the logic of the phenomenon of the vital to an economy of principles (natural selection and the *struggle for existence*). One single thing, one single explanation, one single vision, that makes life "firm." But life, per Nietzsche, withdraws from any ultimate explanation, warning: "I am merely changeable and wild and a woman in every way" (*Z* II "The Dancing Song"). Life remains an enigma. An enigma of a will to power that overcomes itself and escapes any teleo-mechanical reduction.

Nietzsche's Blindness, or: The "Miss" Reading of Darwinist Evolution

> But suppose I have found a watch upon the ground, and I should be enquired how the watch happened to be in that place, I should hardly think of the answer which I had before given, that, for any thing I knew, the watch might have always been there. [. . .] This mechanism being observed [. . .], the inference, we think, is inevitable; that the watch have had a maker; that there must have existed, at some time and at some place or other, an artificer or artificers who formed it for the purpose which we find it actually to answer; who comprehended its construction, and designed its use.
>
> [. . .] Every Indication of contrivance, every manifestation of design, which existed in the watch, exists in the work of nature: with the difference, on the side of nature, of being greater or more, and that in a degree which exceeds all computation."
>
> William Paley, *Natural Theology*

Darwin, as much as Nietzsche, fought against the idea of an intelligent watchmaker. Therein lies the blind spot of Nietzsche's critiques of Darwin.

One can sum up this misreading by returning once again to Paley's metaphor: Nietzsche's blindness stems, precisely, from his inability to see the blindness of Darwin's mechanism. Blind to Darwin's blindness, Nietzsche grants the mechanism of natural selection, and thus the *struggle for life*, an end, a goal, or a vision.

The metaphor of the watchmaker in Paley expresses the general outline of the creationist position, which postulates the existence of an intelligent craftsman who designs and creates the distinct forms of life. The argument from design has been one of the most productive justifications of a natural theology that maintains the existence of a transcendent maker of all creatures. The maker, just like the watchmaker, *intends* to create whatever it creates.[27] He possesses a vision that guides him in his work. Darwin, to the contrary, develops his theory of descent by constant modification through variation and natural selection as a revolutionary way of explaining the origin and the developments of life in direct opposition to any teleological vision. Thus his *Origin of the Species* develops an explanation of the emergence and modification of the natural species from a blind mechanism.

To return to the image of Dawkins: "Natural selection, the blind, unconscious, automatic process which Darwin discovered, . . . has no purpose in mind . . . It has no vision, no foresight, no sight at all. If it can be said to play the role of watchmaker in nature, it is the *blind* watchmaker."[28] Without a real craftsman, at most with a blind maker, evolution explains the emergence of species without resorting to any end or intention found in nature. That is why, in order to understand the critique that Nietzsche develops against Darwinian evolutionism, I had to make a detour through those interpretations by Lange and others that made it possible for Nietzsche to (re-)equip Darwin's blind maker with sight, converting the "*struggle for life*" into a form of teleology.

I now outline Darwin's automatic and unconscious mechanism in order to reevaluate Nietzsche's reading of it. The aim of the theory of evolution is the explanation of the process of the emergence and development of the species through a single *mechanism*. This mechanism is natural selection, according to which the "preservation of favorable variations and the rejection of injurious variations"[29] is achieved. In order for traits to be preserved, and consequently better-adapted individuals reproduced, natural selection requires some conditions without which its mechanism could not work. In the first place, the evolutionary process, by way of the selection of the most beneficial characters, presupposes the existence of variations in the organisms that may be found in the state of nature. Individuals experience modifications in their characters that distinguish them from one another. But natural selection does not only presuppose the existence of these changes or deviations (which configure the topology of these mechanics), but it also requires the inheritance of these variations. The transmission of the parents' characteristics to the next generation reveals itself as "a mysterious attribute connected with each character, but with no correlation between this capacity and the nature of the character *per se*."[30] Transmissibility is a fundamental presupposition for the explanation of evolution. If the variations of individuals were not transmissible, the evolutionary mechanism could not explain how the differences at the level of the individual function in the modifications undergone by the species. These modifications are due to the hereditary character of the variations that, with the passage of time, causes those favorable traits to be accumulated.

There exists a third presupposition of evolutionary explanation—namely, the "struggle for life." Inspired by Malthus,[31] Darwin will adopt the hypothesis of nature's scarcity of resources, especially of food. This scarcity determines the competition between the organisms over said resources such that the struggle for life signifies the struggle for nourishment—and also for reproduction—between distinct individuals. Given the limited character of resources, more individuals are born than can survive: those organisms that triumph in the struggle for life, those that accede to the scarce resources and survive, will have more descendants than those that are not successful in this competition.

The gradual and slow process of evolution is carried out by means of a natural selection, which presupposes the three principles: continuous variation, inheritance, and the struggle for life. The individuals that carry advantageous variations will triumph in the struggle for life and will have, as a consequence, more opportunities to reproduce themselves. Darwin's mechanism is "blind" because natural selection is necessary given the conjoint action of inheritance, variability, and the struggle for life. This triad operates in a conjoined manner, as necessary but not sufficient conditions of the process of natural selection. There is no agent, no intelligent "maker," that selects the favorable differences. These differences are preserved because the individual carriers triumph in the struggle for life and reproduce more than those individuals who fail to attain scarce resources. If resources were unlimited, the different organisms would not enter into a struggle for life. And if the traits and characters were not transmissible, those that proved beneficial in one generation could not subsequently be exhibited by the next generation. Thereby, the blindness of this watchmaker is explained by the combined—and indivisible—activity of these three pillars of evolution.

Nietzsche's critique of Darwin centers on natural selection and the struggle for existence. Here he takes a misstep by separating the elements of the struggle for existence, variability, and inheritance from each other. Nietzsche does not understand the struggle for existence is but one (alongside variation and inheritance) of the constitutive and indivisible elements of the unified mechanism of natural selection. His strategy consists in disaggregating natural selection and the struggle for life, lending to the latter a certain independence in the economy of this mechanism. In a certain sense, Nietzsche's reading produces a dislocation in the (unified) mechanism that Darwin deploys. And it is based on this mistaken reading that Nietzsche is able to characterize Darwin's thought as teleological.

Now, beyond signaling the injustice Nietzsche's reading commits against Darwin's theory, one can also ask whether his misreading still hits the mark. After all, Nietzsche's blind reading permits one to see a different logic of life based on overabundance, waste, sacrifice, and risk. So where does the blindness and limitation of a theory like Darwin's come from? What does Nietzsche have to say with regards to the unified mechanism of evolution, beyond its spurious re-teleologization?

At stake between Nietzsche and Darwin is the kind of theoretical model adequate for an explanation of the phenomenon of life. Darwin proposes a logic of life that makes it possible to project how much the species grows in relation to available resources, but this explanation makes scant or no space for the event, for the eruption of difference that is neither a function of a plan or a program for survival. Nietzsche develops a *logos* through which life cannot be subsumed under final explanations that distance it from the innocence of becoming. If life is a real enigma, it can never be deciphered by postulating a single goal or purpose. Nor can it be reduced to a mechanism (single or tripartite) that calculates its differing based on a triad of elements. Nietzsche's blindness brings to light what in Darwin's economy of life succumbs to the Circe-like spell of a "final" theory.

Jovial Biology: Monsters, Life, and Plasticity

> Knowledge, art, and philosophy are now growing into one another so much in me that I shall in any case give birth to a centaur one day.
>
> Nietzsche, Letter to Erwin Rohde, February 1870

> Do we really want to demote existence in this way to an exercise in arithmetic and an indoor diversion for mathematicians? Above all, one shouldn't want to strip it of its ambiguous character: that, gentlemen, is what good taste demands—above all, the taste of reverence

> for everything that lies beyond our horizon! That the only rightful interpretation of the world should be one to which you have a right; one by which one can do research and go on scientifically in your sense of the term (you really mean mechanistically?)—one that permits counting, calculating, weighing, seeing, grasping, and nothing else—that is a crudity and naiveté, assuming it is not a mental illness, an idiocy.
>
> Nietzsche, *GS* 373

"Christian morality has hitherto been the Circe of all thinkers—they stood in its service" (*EH* "Destiny" 6). The question is, then, whether Darwin has been yet another servant of that captivating woman who casts her spell on all thinkers. The western philosophical tradition has been entranced and entrapped by the spell of a single interpretation of reality. After all, if Christianity is "Platonism for 'the people,'" as Nietzsche claims in *Beyond Good and Evil,* it is so insofar as Christianity reiterates the same great mistake of Platonism. This is the mistake of believing in a "real world" that explains by virtue of its opposition to becoming, and that accounts for "everything" with a *single narrative.* Whether it is the Platonic world of ideas or the Christian Promised Land, the spell is always the same: *one* form, *one* type, and the illusion of capturing a *femina* that insistently attracts and escapes. They are figures of the monotonous and of the safe; variations of one and the same real, "stable," world in which calculations are possible and arrive at univocal explanations. What about Darwin's blind mechanism?

> So, too, it is with the faith with which so many materialistic natural scientists rest content: the faith in a world that is supposed to have its equivalent and measure in human thought, in human valuations—a "world of truth" that can be grasped entirely with the help of our four-cornered little human reason. (*GS* 373)

Nietzsche is on Darwin's side in their common struggle against theories that appeal to an omniscient creator and craftsman of nature. But Nietzsche also sees in Darwin yet another man seduced by a "real world," because his theory of evolution aims to explain the whole living world based on a calculus of variables[32] in order to fix life with a final explanation. If Christianity is Platonism for the people, the most subtle and feminized mode of the idea, then Darwinism is Christianity (Platonism) for the secular. After all, when Nietzsche asks himself: ". . . *what* is Christian morality?" and answers: "Chance robbed of its innocence . . ." (*A* 25), one finds in this formula the same charge that could be raised against Darwin's theory of evolution. To deprive chance of its innocence, Darwin reduces chance to an economy of principles that fit into a Triune mechanism (singular and triple at the same time). Chance is deprived of its innocence in this figure of the blind watchmaker because becoming finds the guidelines of its movement in the mechanical algorithm operating through the conjunction of a series of fundamental and determined variables. On this point, Nietzsche's critique of a final explanation is exempt from the imprecision that marred what I have called his "bad" reading of Darwin's theory.

Nietzsche transforms the theorist of evolution, of change, and of transformation into a convert to "monotono-theism," a dogmatic philosopher (who has little understood of women); a man enchanted by the illusion of being able to reduce life to a mechanism guided by the prejudice of survival. If there is any objection that can be made to Darwin from the perspective of Nietzsche's philosophy, as well as to Plato and to Christianity, it is that he proposes an explanation of the phenomenon of life that attempts to exhaust it. On this account, there is little difference whether the explanation is given by way of mathematical calculations or by way of an intelligent watchmaker with a purpose and plan (or even by way of their strange conjunction). Darwin's evolutionary thesis tries to reduce the phenomenon of life to a mechanics of inheritance and chance variation combined with a deficient vision of existence. Darwin speaks of a plastic organization of the living that takes into account its malleability and possibility of mutation. Nevertheless, the plasticity of Darwin's theory is minimal.

> Hence the canon of "Natura con facit saltum," which every fresh addition to our knowledge tends to confirm, is on this theory intelligible. We can see why throughout nature the same general end is gained by almost infinite diversity of means, for every peculiarity when once acquired is long inherited, and structures already modified in many different ways have to be adapted for the same general purpose. We can, in short, see why nature is prodigal in variety, though niggard in innovation.[33]

There are no monsters (discontinuous variations) to speak of. Centaurs do not reproduce according to Darwin's theory of evolution. Plasticity without monsters: here is a new formula for Darwinism. Only those minimal differences that strive to "progress toward perfection" are preserved.[34] It's one arduous path that climbs up "Mount improbable,"[35] attempting to capture life inside the corset of a monotonous explanation.

Nietzsche warns against the two great spells of mechanics and teleology. God has a myriad of shadows for Nietzsche. For this reason one must beware of the divine craftsman, against whom Darwin struggled with great passion, but one must also protect oneself "even of believing that the universe is a machine; it is certainly not constructed to one end, and the word 'machine' pays it far too high an honor" (*GS* 109)—and also too low. In Darwin's plasticity, and by "plasticity" I mean now that capacity for transformation and variation of life, there is no place for monsters or centaurs. Sudden and considerable anomalies (this is how Darwin defines monstrosities), if they ever become natural variations (small differences) and reproduce themselves, will "almost inevitably" lose "their abnormal character."[36] Nature does not take leaps. She does not give birth to centaurs. And if she does, her leaps and centaurs are rapidly reduced to the path of normalcy. Here, life is a sphere of normalization that conforms to the calculus of survival and natural selection.

Darwin's explanation supplies life with a plasticity that ends up being rigid. It falls once again into the hands of the enchantress Circe. It is Christianity for the learned, as I said earlier: the divine law secularized in the figure of a mechanism. "It also has no drive to self-preservation, or any other drives; nor does it observe any laws. Let us beware of saying that there are laws in nature" (*GS* 109). And the question is, "When will all these shadows of god no longer darken us? When will we have completely de-deified nature?" (*GS* 109). Perhaps the answer lies in not wanting to reduce nature to an economy of calculability—or of finality—in which the plasticity of evolutionary thought can do nothing but turn into a rigid and monotonous malleability. Perhaps one should think another economy of life, that changeable and obstinate woman, where there is room for monsters and monstrosities. The leap: a monstrous plasticity that gives birth to centaurs.

4

Nietzsche and the Nineteenth-Century Debate on Teleology

MARIANA A. CRUZ

General Outline of the Problem

In 1865 a wave of opposition to German idealism, already present since 1830,[1] becomes overt and widespread with Otto Liebman's proposal, in his *Kant und die Epigonen*, to "return to Kant."[2] This date marks the fall of German idealism, and with it the fall of "neo-classicist ideals . . . and . . . Romantic attitudes," leading to "the growth of popular materialism as the world-view corresponding to that new realism" in Germany[3]—that is, an interest in science, and above all, an interest in chemistry, embryology, physiology, and comparative anatomy. By shedding light on the characteristics of living organisms, this research not only provides philosophy with elements for critical reflection, but also offers general ideas concerning life from a descriptive and normative point of view.

One of the important figures in the fall of idealism and the rise of experimental critical reflection is Adolf Trendelenburg.[4] In one of his main works, the *Logische Untersuchungen* (*Logical Investigations*),[5] published for the first time in 1840, he revindicates Aristotelian preformism as the correct perspective to adopt with respect to the analysis of new scientific developments and, indeed, it does become established as a powerful current in embryology, comparative anatomy, and the physiology of the organs and the senses. In this particular work, Trendelenburg goes back to the writings of von Baer, Cuvier, and Johannes Peter Müller. The central idea he attempts to establish by doing so is that, as Aristotle maintained, in any natural entity "the end dominates the whole and controls the development of its parts."[6] Trendelenburg therefore returns to a teleological explanatory model, which under the name of *Zweckmässigkeit* became central to scientific debate in the early nineteenth century, in order to refute the idea that the same blind forces that rule over the inorganic world apply to the organic world. By restoring the Aristotelian program, Trendelenburg initiates a return to Kantian transcendentalism, attempting to integrate the transcendental aspects of Kantianism with the traditional Aristotelian perspective of final causation in the organic world.[7]

Trendelenburg begins by separating out the world of life, characterized by *Zweckmässigkeit* (functionality),[8] from nonliving, inorganic nature, characterized by *Gesetztmässigkeit* (legality, regularity, legitimacy). *Zweckmässigkeit* is a difficult term to translate, and therefore translation often fails to reflect the fuller sense of the debates on biology in Germany at this time. It is frequently rendered as "in accordance with ends" or "purposiveness," though depending on the context it can also mean "adequacy," or "functionality," and it refers to a unique directionality that is convenient, adequate, useful, and functional.[9]

While *Gesetztmässigkeit* refers to those natural laws that, following the Aristotelian distinction, belong to efficient causation, *Zweckmässigkeit*, is identified with final causation and with formal causation.[10] The mode of explanation that final causation establishes applies in a variety of ways to organic nature that cannot be considered applicable to inorganic nature. Although this type of causality is criticized for establishing a rift in the explanation of nature, in cell theory this feature is praised for preventing nature from being considered a continuum of differences merely of degree and not substantial. Teleology demands a rational and normative (*sollen*) directionality for the development of organisms, which presupposes the existence of ultimate unities. Teleology also presupposes a conception of organisms as atoms, as unitary wholes, whose unity and totality precede its parts and determine their "adequate" functioning.

Amidst this biological understanding of final causation, Nietzsche poses his questions: adequate for whom? functional to what? according to what criterion and value? This questioning is directed not only at Aristotelian conceptions, but also at the biology of his times. With the aim of developing these questions further, I briefly sketch out the central ideas of Aristotelian theory returning to prominence in the philosophical-scientific context of nineteenth-century German biology. I then present some of the central ideas of the philosopher Adolf Trendelenburg and the biologist Johannes Peter Müller[11] as representatives of Aristotelianism. In conclusion, I discuss Nietzsche's general critique of Aristotelianism, and in particular his critique of Trendelenburg. In order to explain the distinct components of his critique, I refer both to the core components of cell theory and to the figure of the *pre-Platonic* philosophers[12] with whom Nietzsche discusses, indirectly, his contemporaries' scientific and philosophical research. Throughout the chapter I use mostly fragments from Nietzsche's early writings between 1867 and 1873, and in particular, *Philosophy in the Tragic Age of the Greeks* and *Teleology since Kant.*

My intention is to show that although Nietzsche and Trendelenburg share a hostility toward the Hegelian equation of logic with metaphysics as well as toward the Platonic devaluation of the world of becoming, there are important differences between their ideas that limit their affinity. While Trendelenburg defends the teleological perspective, Nietzsche criticizes it; where the former seeks a scientific foundation of morality, the latter criticizes any attempt at moral foundationalism.

Aristotelian Explanation Reinstated

Trendelenburg's critique of idealism aims to reinstate the Aristotelian model of explanation, which contains a critique of Parmenides' theory as much as of Plato's theory in an attempt to "do justice to becoming and to our experience of it."[13] Aristotle explains organic development using notions of potentiality and act that presuppose acceptance of the existence of movement and of empirical reality. Aristotle critiques the reasoning by which Parmenides negates the reality of change. For Aristotle this ought to be accepted as a basic assumption of the natural sciences.[14] "The phrase 'that which is not' is not, for him, univocal."[15] Aristotle basically uses the distinction between act and potentiality in order to show that what is not may still be a form of being: being potentially (*dynamis*) what will come-to-be (*energeia*).[16] What the organism is, upon achieving its development, is given in its original potentiality; its form is foreseen in the potential.

Although it avoids the Eleatic-Platonic negation of the reality of movement, the determining factor in Aristotelian theory remains form,[17] and this causes it to remain trapped in a model of explanation targeted by Nietzsche's critique. In fact, Aristotelian theory does not call into question empirical reality by devaluating it as mere appearance, as is the case in the framework of the Platonic theory. Aristotle's affirmation of form is not made at the expense of the reality of matter; even his teleology is immanent to the development of species: it does not assume the devaluation of empirical reality and does not refer systematically to an external reason in order to explain natural occurrences. Nevertheless, this explanatory model typically starts from an organic whole and gives priority to organic structure over its parts as determining the function of the organs. Formal and final causes are combined in the structure as the plan for the development of the organism, and they predominate over material and efficient causes. Despite Aristotle's reliance on the concept of potentiality in his attempt to save empirical becoming, Nietzsche will criticize this type of explanation for remaining anchored to a reality that is given prior to it and that determines the way in which becoming develops. "Reality is ontologically prior to possibility . . . There is a preestablished reality that possibility has the potential to change, and change is always change of something . . . substance."[18] Things become, but only as an actualization of what was already given as reality in potentiality prior to its empirical realization. One can say that, on this view, becoming still *is not*, given that this understanding of becoming does not entirely relinquish the perspective of being it wishes to challenge.[19]

Johannes Müller and Adolf Trendelenburg

During the first decades of the nineteenth century, "the 'renaissance' of Aristotle seemed to be defined as the 'speculative' reflection of new scientific research in embryology and the physiology of the senses."[20] Starting in the 1820s, Trendelenburg's teacher the biologist Johannes Müller, as well as Virchow, and Helmholtz among others, urged a return to Aristotle. Müller defends a kind of teleological explanation that uses the concept of the rational [*Zweckmässig*] organization of organisms:

> As the foundation of any organism there is an idea, and it is in conformance with this idea that all organs organize themselves rationally [*zweckmässig*].[21]

This idea of biological explanation propounded by Müller is used by Trendelenburg in order to offer a philosophical explanation of organic life. His theory on natural organisms incorporates both the idea of tending toward an end and of a rational whole capable of being the source of the origin and development of organisms. Müller provides the framework within which Trendelenburg begins his own work. For Trendelenburg, too, "it is the task of philosophy to investigate and present the idea of the whole in its parts and the idea of the general in the particular."[22] Despite his struggle against Hegelian idealism, Trendelenburg does not question that logic and metaphysics are "interrelated and form a unity." What he questions is that they can become the same:

> The unity of logic and metaphysics results from the unification of the relations between reasoning and being. Therefore, logic and metaphysics are both the *theory of science*, but also the basic science, *philosophia fundamentalis.*[23]

In this way, the particular refers back to general being (metaphysics) and scientific methods are specializations of a perceptive thinking (logic). This interrelatedness establishes the necessity that Nietzsche rejects. Logical reasoning, based on the metaphysics of being, guarantees the emergence of the necessary.[24] In the kind of thinking proposed by Trendelenburg there remain echoes of a relationship between being and thinking, of the basis of the part in the whole, which contrast with the spirit of the Nietzschean philosophical project. Finally, it is important to emphasize the relationship between moral and logical philosophy and scientific research established by Trendelenburg. As Orsucci explains, Trendelenburg's conception assumes that social relations merely make more powerful what occurs in natural processes.[25] For Trendelenburg, as for many others in the nineteenth century, biology is an explanatory framework for society. Just as "what is specific to the character of the organic [is that] the whole, based upon an originary idea, be prior to its parts,"[26] so, too, the idea of an originary simplicity of the living, based on a final cause that is presupposed and that guides organic development, is asserted as much on the level of biology as it is on the level of moral philosophy.

Johannes Müller takes from von Baer the idea (which comes from early cell theory) that organic material is initially almost formless and that its development is governed and directed by the global essence of the animal that it is supposed to become.[27] Nevertheless, von Baer believes that the results call into question the possibility of asserting "the . . . dominant idea of a single progressive process of perfection leading from the monad to man."[28]

The new directions taken by biology in 1860 leave behind the Aristotelianism of Trendelenburg (the primacy of the end and of the totality, and the assertion of a preestablished harmony of the organic).[29]

> The growing aversion to final causation, and later also to the biological orientation of Müller and von Baer, is further reinforced by a particular coincidence, the contemporary assertion, in German science in the 1860s, of Darwinism and of the Helmholtzian perspective.[30]

In 1870 Trendelenburg reprints his *Logische Untersuchungen*, in a context that is no longer favorable to teleology; he insists upon the relationship between research on the organic world and moral philosophy. His defense of the primacy of final causation should be understood in light of his conviction that "if [this concept] were unknown in nature, it would also be unknown on the ethical plane."[31] Trendelenburg maintains that if one studies organic life only through the idea of efficient causality, one will not come to a satisfactory explanation for the development of the organs. And he revisits the classical example of the development of the eye. The eye that develops sight without seeing light is a clear example that it was generated not by or in response to light but was, rather, generated by its finality. Trendelenburg finds in the phenomenon of eyesight a good example of preestablished harmony.[32]

Nietzsche's Critique of Aristotelianism

Nietzsche's work also reflects this argument between the different explanatory models for organisms. In several of his early writings (published posthumously) one finds critiques of Aristotelianism and the reincorporation of finalism into the scientific explanation of natural organisms, as well as the critique of Kant's defense of teleological explanations. Among these are his writings on Democritus and Schopenhauer, as well as his text on teleology and the concept of the organic, *Die Teleologie seit Kant* or *Zur Teleologie* (*TSK*).

Nietzsche makes numerous references to Trendelenburg in his posthumously published work. The first references go back to fragments from fall 1867 to spring 1868 in which he systematically covers aspects of the explanation of Democritus, Empedocles, Anaxagoras, and Aristotle, placing particular emphasis on Democritus. In the fragment *Zur Teleologie* he puts forward a list of authors to bear in mind. The first name on this list is "Trendelenburg log. Untesuch. 2. Aufl. Leipzig 1862. II. S. 65 f." (*KGW* I/4, NF 58[46] Herbst-Frühjahr 1868, p. 491). In the same fragment he then refers to Gustav Schneider on Aristotle's final cause, Hume's dialogues on natural religion (in German translation), Kant's *Critique of Pure Reason* and the *Critique of Judgment*, and finally Rosenkranz's and Kuno Fischer's works on Kant. Nietzsche's writings on teleology inherently draw on his reflections on the explanations proposed by these philosophers, and the Greeks, in turn, become for Nietzsche a way of treating in an "untimely" manner the kinds of explanation put forward by his contemporaries in both science and philosophy.[33] One main focus of these first philosophical writings is the explanation of organic life, and whether and how such an explanation is at all possible. During the time Nietzsche wrote these fragments he was planning to abandon philology and take up the study of natural sciences—a plan that he ultimately abandoned.[34]

It is in this context that he develops the idea of dedicating his doctoral thesis to "the concept of the organic," an idea that would ultimately lay the foundations for his writings on teleology (*KGW* I/4, NF 62, pp. 548–578).[35] In 1868 he also restates, toward the end of the text, the project of reading Trendelenburg, along with "*Überweg, System der Logik*" (*KGW* I/4, NF 62[48], p. 572). Nietzsche seems to be struck by Trendelenburg's critique of the identification of logic with metaphysics in Hegel's system. Nietzsche's own critique of Hegel, and thus his interest in the argument over the relationship between these areas, is finally undertaken through a reading of Afrikan Spir.[36]

Nietzsche criticizes Trendelenburg's idea that philosophy ought to provide a foundation to science. Even though Nietzsche philosophizes by taking into consideration scientific developments, he does not believe that philosophy ought to be reduced to the grounding of the scientific enterprise, for this would be tantamount to eliminating philosophy itself: "To turn philosophy entirely into a science (as Trendelenburg) means to throw in the towel" (*KSA* 7:29[199]). The next fragment in which Nietzsche refers to Trendelenburg is from 1872, entitled *Bedrägniss der Philosophie*: if philosophy were to be reduced to the foundation of science, it could never serve as the foundation of a culture:

> . . . Philosophy—whether it can be the foundation of a culture? Yes—but not anymore: it is too refined and pointed, one cannot go by it anymore. Actually philosophy let itself be drawn into the current of contemporary education [*Bildung*]: it does not dominate contemporary education. At best it becomes a science (Trendelenburg). (*KSA* 7:30[15])

The reflection on culture, its tension with civilization and with the state, the need for philosophy to serve culture: these constitute some of the main points of Nietzschean philosophy. As the preceding fragment indicates, the proper relationship between philosophy and culture was once alive "even if [it] no longer" exists. That time was the age of the pre-Platonics, to which Nietzsche returns repeatedly, especially in this first period of his thought. But it was precisely this relationship that was eliminated by Platonic and Aristotelian philosophy, where priority is given to one or another kind of external reason (a *nous*) as the fundamental cause of existence, thereby turning philosophy into teleology. It is in this context that one comes across another reference to Trendelenburg:

University Philosophy [*Universitätsphilosophie*]
In the service of Theologist
of History (Trendelenburg) (*KSA* 7:32[75])

Trendelenburg and his philosophical proposal remain linked to the impossibility of philosophy to serve the ends of culture. The university, too, linked with idealist models of inquiry, is criticized by Nietzsche as a space in the service of theology more than of culture.

How is science related to religion? The science that Trendelenburg defends, in its Aristotelian variant, imposes a teleological model for scientific explanation, which for Nietzsche has its ultimate justification in the human need for certainties. Certainties that are provided by metaphysics (and the philosophy of Parmenides) depend on an external and rational foundation that makes organic nature knowable and understandable through logic, which assumes the task of consolation that religion possessed in antiquity. Without being formulated in the terms one finds later in his works, the idea that science assumes the place of religion once God is dead, is already present in these early texts.

The Pre-Platonics and Nineteenth-Century Science

In order to show where the model of philosophy proposed by his neo-Aristotelian contemporaries fails, Nietzsche returns to the pre-Platonics who were undervalued by Aristotle as being early physiologists who did not invoke final and formal causes in their explanations (*PPP* 14, p. 129). Nietzsche's return to the pre-Platonics must be read as a critique of Aristotle, but mainly as a rejection of the Aristotelian science of his own time: Aristotle, the model for Nietzsche's contemporaries, reviled the preeminence of matter over form in the pre-Platonics. In discussing Anaxagoras and Empedocles, Nietzsche emphasizes his opposition to Aristotelianism and, accordingly, to the teleology of his own contemporaries, taking sides with the materialism of the pre-Platonics, against his age.

One of the places where he expresses clearly his critique of the Aristotelian explanatory model is in *Philosophy in the Tragic Age of the Greeks,* where he sets up the problem of trying to transpose Parmenides' doctrine on being onto a world of becoming. The idea of transferring to the empirical world the existence of logical and abstract entities—beings that are not conditioned, but self-contained, containing the conditions for existence in themselves—while, at the same time, attempting to defend the reality of movement creates logical problems that Nietzsche works out in the section on Anaxagoras. There Nietzsche shows that the logic belonging to the idea of being (the assertion of essences that are "true and isolated," unconditioned), when transposed onto the material world, creates the problem of movement, of change. Nietzsche suggests that Parmenides could have objected to Anaxagoras's application of his theory of being to an empirical world in the following way:

> . . . two essences, each existent in itself with a totally different independently absolute being—and such are the Anaxagorian substances. With their nature as described, they can never collide, never move each other, never attract each other. There is no causality between them . . . . (*PPP* 14, p. 100)

Nietzsche describes Anaxagoras's effort to demonstrate the truth of movement, which he believed to be beyond question, without abandoning the idea of being. Anaxagoras transferred[37] to the empirical sphere what is valid in Parmenides' world of logical abstraction. But the eternal being—which is immutable, invariable, without any beginning—needs nothing, and is therefore consistent, in Nietzsche, with the image of death, and related to stillness, coldness, the "lack of blood," and not with the world of change (alive, changing) since it would have no reasons (given its completeness) to acquire movement on its own. But such eternal being would be consistent with the human need to ground normativity. The impossibility of movement in what is, from the point of view of the logic of Parmenides, imposes the necessity of an external "intellect" (the *nous*), a "force" that would set it in motion.[38]

> *Nous* was not dragged in by Anaxagoras to answer the specific questions, "how did motion come into being" or "how is it that there are regular motions." Yet Plato objects that he should have shown, but did not do so, that each thing in its own fashion and its own place is most beautifully, best, and usefully situated. (*PPP*, p. 122)

But what Nietzsche values in Anaxagoras's position is that he does not postulate a *nous* that is rational, but rather a *nous* that is artistic, creative, and that without purpose plays at setting the elements in motion, configuring different bodies out of the same material substances, determining, according to the form, a different being in each case. The creations of *nous* are not predetermined. *Nous* rather begins configuring beings like a game, and this is why Nietzsche claims that in Anaxagoras there is no teleology, since *nous* is not moved by an end in its configuration of the world. With the idea of a game comes the idea of an original arbitrariness (because of the lack of any determined character in the action of the *nous*), and after that first act, becoming finds itself already determined naturally by its own intrinsic movement. This idea of a beginning that is not a rational requirement, but rather a game, a creativity, is worked out by Nietzsche in his references to Heraclitus and to Empedocles. In *The Pre-Platonic Philosophers*, he announces another possible explanation, which does not need support from rational causes: "That which forms things is originally chance, necessity (ἀνάγκη), without any cleverness whatsoever. Love is clueless, too: she possesses only one single drive," (*PPP* 14, p. 117) namely, the drive "to allow the *ordered world* nonetheless to arise from these opposing forces without any purpose, without any mind" (*PPP* 14, p. 116). In these fragments, Nietzsche suggests two lines of interpretation: on the one hand, the intervention of an intelligence, but a creative intelligence, and, on the other hand, the intervention of strict natural necessity. In both cases, the ground of becoming is distinct from that provided by teleology and does not resort to an originary intelligence of the world of becoming.

The matter is different in the neo-Aristotelian science of Nietzsche's contemporaries. The idea that basic materials develop according to a form does not refer—except in cases where chance intervenes—to a purposeless creativity, but to a rationality that determines natural development. The idea of a metaphysical foundation of phenomena is emphatically maintained; this idea imposes an order as necessary, as good, as an end, and along with that introduces as a counterpoint the notion of what must be categorized as negative, as evil, as what ought not to have been and, accordingly, as what must be condemned. Thus Nietzsche appears to agree with the transference of values from the explanation of the biological world to the social, though he does not understand it as a logical transposition, and the values he proposes to transfer from the biological realm to society are also different than the ones of the neo-Aristotelian biologists. The coercion necessary to explain the world as organized unities whose parts respond functionally to a necessary (*zweckmässig*) organization is for Nietzsche inadmissible. Except in a case where "the purposiveness of those that continue to exist is reduced to the continued existence of those who act according to purposes," (*PPP* 14, p. 116) as occurs in the philosophy of Empedocles (a standpoint that is analogous, in nineteenth-century biology, to Darwin's theory, at least as far as the combination of chance and adaptation is concerned).

Contributions from Cell Theory

Nietzsche values the tendency in embryology to establish a continuity between the organic and inorganic world in the face of competing metaphysical and religious accounts. Nevertheless, he criticizes the idea that organisms share an amorphous plasticity and the same origin with inorganic natures. This can be seen in the theory of Theodor Schwann, and in the evolutionary theory of Haeckel, but not in Virchow's theory. Nietzsche appreciates Schwann's attempt to establish a continuity between the organic and the inorganic, but disagrees with the idea that organisms are simple in their origin and that they are characterized by an amorphous plasticity in this origin. For Nietzsche, organisms are characterized from the very beginning by the struggle between their elements, without any direction to guide them. In this he agrees with Virchow, whom Nietzsche knows from Friedrich Lange in *The History of Materialism.* Virchow proposes that organisms be observed as a sum of vital unities in which it is impossible to identify a center:

> . . . in all parts of the body a splitting up into a number of small centers takes place, and that nowhere, as far as our experience extends, does a single central point susceptible of anatomical demonstration exist, from which the operations of the body are carried on in a perceptible manner.[39]

The organism understands itself as a social network more than as a substantive unity. Anyone wishing to account for such a unity must enter into metaphysics:

> . . . one would need to go one step further for it, making an abstraction out of corporal things and taking refuge[40] with Stahl in animism. Only an immaterial soul permits a conception of true unity. But this is no more than a metaphysical conception. With it we abandon the domain of the natural sciences, of observation and of experiments. Not even the hypothesis of a single soul is enough to explain the life of the parts.[41]

In order to avoid the problem (the same problem Nietzsche sees) of explaining the life of parts by way of some vital center or exterior energy, Virchow characterizes the parts as active and as capable of shaping their environment. This idea is closer to the Nietzschean idea than to Darwinism and the passive subject. Physiology acquires an associationist explanatory paradigm, which is opposed to the earlier theory of unitary vital forces. The organism requires a continual counter-position of "local processes" that are unregulated beforehand by any central authority. This is essential to the claims made against teleology, for these do not refer to a center or a core that would constitute "the substantial vital force," and this absence of a unitary nucleus prevents the predetermination of the organism in a single project or direction.

Another important aspect of Virchow's conception has to do with Nietzsche's claim that teleology is anthropomorphic because it makes the idea of the physiological unity depend on our consciousness. For Virchow, it is human beings that establish something as being simple and unified, and human beings proceed always with the idea that every thing must be determined by this same unified character. The organism, even if it sees itself as an individual, remains a collection of parts, and Virchow refers to Goethe's theory of nature, which remains a leitmotif in his own inquiries.[42] What Virchow calls "territorial analysis" of organic disturbances must defend itself from the malice and lures of "consciousness," which is always ready to accentuate disproportionately the "unified character" of the vital processes.[43] There exists for this biologist no organic unity other than the one posited by consciousness. In Nietzsche's terms, one could say that organic unity is no more than our creation, starting with the forms belonging to the human intellect. Clearly referring to this possibility and the Goethean idea of organic plurality, Nietzsche writes in 1868 that, "[t]he organism is a form. Disregarding this form, the organism is a multiplicity" (*KGW*, I/4, NF 62[25], p. 558).

Orsucci emphasizes that Ehrenberg refers to the existence of a "philosophical" prejudice that, in the past, would have precluded from observation the complex and minute structures of even simple organisms. Such a prejudice rests on the tendency of scientists to abide by the Aristotelian idea that organization in the smaller bodies becomes progressively simpler.[44] In the same article, Orsucci maintains that, with the questioning of the Aristotelian ideas defended by Trendelenburg, their connection to moral doctrines is also called into question, which must have influenced Nietzsche.[45] In *The History of Materialism*, Lange asserts that Virchow's doctrine and the developments in cell theory have finally refuted Aristotelianism, revealing the "mystical" character of the principle that the whole governs over the parts. The organism is only a "relative unity."[46]

Nietzsche and Cell Theory

Consistent with Virchow's doctrine, Nietzsche supports the idea that organisms are not originally simple but contain within themselves varied elements in conflict that do not respond to one idea or form that predetermines the outcome of the conflict. The resulting configuration depends on the structuring power of the organism, which creates according to the needs of the organism and not as a function of given rational laws that may be understood as forces of self-organization. In any case, this organic necessity must be read as a negation of rational causes, in the sense of

Aristotle's final cause, but not as pure arbitrariness. This Nietzschean idea is best illustrated through the doctrine of Democritus. In discussing this doctrine, Nietzsche maintains that chance must be understood as,

> . . . "purposeless causality," "necessity (ἀνάγκη) without purposive intentions": precisely here there is no chance whatsoever but rather the most rigorous lawfulness, only not according to laws of reason. (*PPP* 15, p. 126)

The Nietzschean negation of *Zweckmässigkeit*, of purposiveness or functionality—according to the meanings of the term I specified earlier—does not entail its a posteriori negation. There can be purposiveness, but only in the sense of Empedocles—that is, the existence of what is functional, a posteriori, among things that are not functional themselves.

The existence of (ἀνάγκη), in Democritus's sense, is not questioned: it entails lawfulness, but not chance—understood as pure randomness—nor an original rationality. The logic of being, of the unconditional, is what makes us postulate the action of chance in the natural world. But in the Nietzschean explanatory context *chance* only means a lack of conscious, rational understanding, not necessarily a lack of natural, empirical necessity. This could be the place for the idea of necessity (ἀνάγκη). Here we might remember that the leitmotif of these reflections is the critique of Hegelianism. In the framework of Hegelian theory, the dialectical explanation of phenomena is rational: there is a rational connection from concept to concept, which is precisely what Nietzsche wants to contest.[47] In this sense, he asserts that "matter, moving itself according to general laws, produces a blind mechanical result, which appears to be the outline of a highest wisdom" (*PPP* 15, p. 126). For Nietzsche, then, the final cause, understood in an Aristotelian way as potentiality of the whole that promotes and sustains the harmony between its parts, becomes within the framework of contemporary theories an architecture of organic nature. It establishes that the natural is determined in its origin and development by an internal and rational force that prescribes to organic parts their characteristics based on the "entire vital economy."[48]

The Aristotelian potentiality of the whole makes the temporal order of organic development disappear, insofar as the end is transformed into the beginning, as the *raison dêtre*,

> in what ought to be developed, later, in its effect, the grounding of its characteristics and activity. Nature . . . proclaims as a simple piece of information that what results, in terms of efficient cause, the subsequent and the generated, becoming the antecedent . . . in the end.[49]

The whole is preformed in the seed. This is why Nietzsche could not agree with the preformist conception's imposition of an ought-to-be upon becoming, and its attendant negation of the temporal element in organic development, since what is developing already exists potentially in its origin.

Conclusion

In both the Platonic and the Aristotelian perspectives, the acceptance of an external *nous* that determines the course of becoming affords the possibility of interpreting the world as knowable. This knowledge tells us that the world is ordered and that it has a determinate mode of being. In this framework, the originary knowability of the world establishes the basis for its moral interpretation. Despite the fact that it does not devalue appearances, the architecture of the Aristotelian theory, its armature of concepts—potentiality and act, purpose and form, whole and part—establishes an explanatory model of becoming that, in Nietzsche's judgment, does not avoid the intervention of an ought-to-be in the world of becoming. Aristotelian theory has the virtue of rejecting an idealist—Hegelian—identification between logic and metaphysics, but it imposes being on becoming in another way. Natural development is determined in its origin by the idea of what the form of the organism is, and this idea acts as the interior force that allows the organism to develop, justifying its development.

It is Trendelenburg, as the representative of this Aristotelian standpoint, who Nietzsche sees as wanting to establish a knowledge that is secure and unifying, which grounds our existence, and does so not through religion but through science, the new idol replacing religion as the new foundation of praxis. The transposition of the logic of the world of being, of logic, to the empirical world creates the need to appeal to the *nous.* The *nous,* which is external, is what establishes order and intelligibility. The knowability of the world, starting with our capacity of comprehending the ideas of the *nous,* is what expresses itself in the idea of teleology. According to this paradigm, the world offers us, by way of the intellect, responses to what is good, what is evil, what ought to be and ought to be done. The originary intelligibility of the world, according to the teleological paradigm, involves a universal normativity without exception, where parts are merely functional and must comply with the universal norm.

In *Die Teleologie seit Kant*, Nietzsche critiques both the notion of a "grossly anthropological" (*grob anthropologische*) purposiveness as well as the idea of an immanent purpose (*Zweck*). I hope to have shown that the defining claim in this radical critique is that the preformist, Aristotelian assertion of *Zweckmässigkeit* necessarily imposes, as a presupposition, a rational structure on the empirical world, eliminating the importance of the temporal element in the explanation of organic development. Nietzsche makes multiple references to Trendelenburg as a theologian who wants to reduce philosophy to a foundation for an Aristotelian natural science characterized by introducing morality, rationality, and originary unity into the scientific account.

His rigorous critique of Trendelenburg can be understood in light of the fact that Nietzsche, in general, argues with greater vehemence against those who appear closer to himself, a paradigmatic example of this being his stance toward Darwin. Despite sharing with Nietzsche the struggle to eliminate the identification of logic with metaphysics in favor of the world of becoming, Trendelenburg remains a prisoner of a certain schema in which philosophy remains anchored to scientific-teleological knowing in view of the project of grounding morality.

5

Nietzsche's Concept of "Necessity" and Its Relation to "Laws of Nature"

HERMAN W. SIEMENS

Introduction

In a much-cited passage from *The Gay Science* 335, Nietzsche calls on us to become self-creators and self-legislators on the basis of what he calls "physics": knowledge of "all that is lawful and necessary in the world" (*GS* 335).[1] This passage is important because it illustrates the entanglement of Nietzsche's concept of *necessity* with his concept of *lawfulness* or "laws of nature," and the entanglement of both with *moral* concerns (self-legislation) and *artistic* concerns (self-creation). These entanglements are characteristic for Nietzsche, yet they are hard to understand. It is not just that necessity and lawfulness would seem to exclude creative and moral freedom. What Nietzsche means here is also hard to understand, given the weight of his sustained critique of moral legislation and even more: of lawfulness or laws of nature. Whatever he means by "lawfulness and necessity in the world," it cannot be the popular or physicists' concepts denounced by him as "naive-humanitarian" projections of moral categories onto nature (*KSA* 13:14[79]; *BGE* 22). Rather they need to be viewed as instances of the characteristic Nietzschean operation of "reinterpretation (*Umdeutung*, *Umbegreifung*)"; that is, as attempts to invest established or existing terms with new meanings. How, then, *are* we to understand "lawfulness and necessity in the world" or nature?

In this essay, my primary concern is with Nietzsche's concept of necessity. As so often with Nietzsche, his use of this term presents us with enormous difficulties, spanning as it does a bewildering range of positions from outright rejection ("let us get rid of the two popular concepts 'necessity' and 'law'" [*KSA* 13:14(79)]; "Against apparent '*necessity*'" [*KSA* 12:9(91)]) to unqualified affirmation ("Let us believe in absolute necessity in the universe [*im All*] [*KSA* 9:11(201)]; see also *BGE* 22). As my guiding thread, I will take the entanglement of "necessity" and "lawfulness," as illustrated by the opening passage from *GS*, with the thesis that *Nietzsche's concept of necessity needs to be understood in terms of his critical engagement with the scientific (mechanistic) concept of laws of nature (Naturgesetze).* In specific, I will try to describe a number of different meanings of the word "necessity" by examining some key moments in his engagement with laws of nature. In the process I will also take up the other entanglement exhibited in the passage from *GS* 335—that between Nietzsche's moral concerns and his engagement with laws of nature—by arguing that Nietzsche has primarily *moral* motivations for his engagement with the concepts of "lawfulness" and "necessity" in nature. For both theses, I draw on my work for the entry *Gesetz* in the *Nietzsche-Wörterbuch*[2] in what is intended as a test-case for the fruitfulness of this work. To start out, some preliminary orientation on Nietzsche's approach to laws of nature is needed.

Nietzsche's Attitude to Laws of Nature

Key Philosophical Impulses

It is hard to overestimate the formative influence of Nietzsche's early engagement with Heraclitus on his overall approach to the concept of law across his work.[3] Under his influence, Nietzsche's thought is shaped by the project to rethink law in *radically immanent* and *monistic* terms; that is, as an immanent feature of nature, conceived as one and the only reality. This leads him to reject transcendent, dualistic, and autonomous conceptions of law in favor of propinquities, analogies, and underlying similarities between different types or domains of law and legislation[4]. Nietzsche's immanentism is perhaps most clearly evinced in connection with the *moral* law. The autonomy of the normative sphere, essential to the self-understanding of both morality and jurisprudence (*Recht*), is consistently undermined by Nietzsche in contexts that denounce the transcendent and sovereign status of law as "anti-nature" (*Widernatur*) or a "'denaturing [*Entnatürlichung*] of morality'" (*KSA* 12:9[86]). Nietzsche's counter-proposal is a "naturalism of morality" or "moralistic naturalism," its task:

> to translate the seemingly emancipated and *de-natured* [naturlos *gewordenen*] moral values back into their nature—i.e., into their natural "immorality." (*KSA* 12:9[86])[5]

For Nietzsche this task is both theoretical and practical in nature. On the one hand, it requires a systematic "re-translation" (*Zurückübersetzung*), naturalistic redescription, or re-inscription of moral terms like "law" into the body, the drives, instincts, forces, individual and collective conditions for existence.[6] On the practical side, the first task is to overcome the "ignorance of physics or contradiction to it" upon which morality as antinature has been built (*GS* 335).[7] As we saw in the initial passage from *The Gay Science,* the question of "physics" or *knowledge of nature* therefore comes to occupy a central place in the practical project to construct a naturalized morality.[8]

This question is, however, profoundly complicated by a further tendency to which Nietzsche repeatedly draws critical attention: our projection of moral experience, and all its presuppositions, onto nature. Nietzsche's claim, in a nutshell, is that the progressive de-naturing (*Entnatürlichung der Moral*) of morality has gone hand in hand with a projection of our de-natured morality into nature (*Vermoralisierung der Natur*). In this light, his project to translate morality back into nature is pointless, unless it is combined with a translation of morality *out* of nature: Nietzsche's naturalization of morality (*Vernatürlichung der Moral*)[9] is inseparable from the project to demoralize nature (*Entmoralisierung der Natur*).[10]

On the Relation of Philosophy to Natural Science

Nietzsche's pronouncements on laws of nature need to be read from a perspective in his views on the relation between philosophy and science (in the broad sense: *Wissenschaft*). They exhibit a remarkable consistency across his work.

In two early *Nachlass* texts the *critical, evaluative,* and *supplementing* (*ergänzend*) functions of philosophy are set out in a programmatic manner. In one of them (*KSA* 7:23[45]) philosophy is played out "against the dogmatism of science" in that philosophy "shatters the belief in the inviolability [*Unverbrüchlichkeit*] of such laws." In *Philosophy in the Tragic Age of the Greeks* (*PTA* 3), philosophy is presented as a legislation of greatness (*Gesetzgebung der Grösse*) on the model of taste (*Geschmack*, sapientia); while making free use of the results of science (*Wissenschaft*), it leaps beyond them in the quest for "important knowledge," for "the things most worth knowing." For Nietzsche, as for Weber, science (*Wissenschaft*) is incapable of evaluation, and generates world-views that are bereft of value and meaning.[11] Philosophy-as-taste, by contrast, names a peculiar episteme that is normative or law-like (*Gesetzgebung*), without there being any actual laws of norms that could ground or demonstrate its judgments (*de gustibus non est disputandum*). Its task, according to Nietzsche, is to determine the *value of science*, and to prescribe its rights,[12] by elucidating the nature and limits of laws of nature, and by exposing their moral, metaphysical, and psychological presuppositions.

In Nietzsche's philosophical practice, this takes various forms, depending on the context and exact meaning of "law" therein. At one extreme is (1) *absolute negation*: "there are no laws" (*es giebt keine Gesetze*), the denial of the existence of laws of nature (*GS* 109).[13] Then there are (2) attempts at a radical reversal (*Umkehrung*) of the traditional properties and functions of the concept of law (eternity, universality, regularity, unification, ordering). Thus, for example, in a well-known note from the period of the eternal return, the *universality* and *eternity* of mechanistic laws are undermined by arguing that these laws "arose in a lawless play" (*gesetzloses Spiel*), as "exceptions" and "chance events" in a world that "is removed from mechanical laws" (*KSA* 9:11[313]).[14] In another note Nietzsche reverses the "regularity" encapsulated by laws of nature by relativizing it to its opposite, caprice: "regularity" (*Regelmässigkeit*) is interpreted as a "**whim become rule**" ("***zur Regel gewordenen Beliebens***"), a relatively long-term caprice (einer "*längeren* ***Laune***") that only arises in our corner of the world (*KSA* 9:11[311]). At the other extreme from Nietzsche's negation (1) of law is his affirmative usage in contexts where (3) he attempts to reinterpret or reconceptualize law (*Umdeutung*); that is, to retain the word "law" but invest it with new meanings. This can involve limited, pragmatic affirmations of laws of nature—as a "sign language" or "regulative fiction" (*Zeichensprache, regulative Fiktion*)—often coupled with the demand that they be *supplemented* with a philosophical world picture or "inner world" (Will to Power).[15] But it can also involve the unqualified use of "law" to describe reality or nature, as in *The Gay Science* (*GS* 335). This operational use of "law" occurs especially in connection with Will to Power, organic life, and physiology.[16]

It is these affirmative and/or operational uses of "law" (3), when placed next to texts at the other extreme that criticize and negate laws of nature (1), that bring us face-to-face with the problematic status of laws of nature in Nietzsche's thought. For how can he criticize and negate laws of nature, but also use "law" to describe nature or reality in other contexts? Is there a way to make sense of his affirmative and operational uses of law, in the light of his sustained critique and rejection of laws of nature?

In what follows, I will consider instances of the two extremes—absolute negation and the affirmative reinterpretation of law—asking in each case: What implications do these opposed positions on law have for the question of necessity, and what do they tell us about the meanings of this term for Nietzsche? But first we need to ask: What *is* Nietzsche's critique of laws of nature?

Nietzsche's Critique of Law

A number of constants stand out in Nietzsche's critical engagement with the concept of laws of nature. From an early date, laws of nature are understood by him as (1) *active anthropomorphic projections*, which (2) express *our* "laws" (laws of human perception) or at the most: the relation of the world to us; *not* the "things" themselves or the "in itself." As such they stand (3) in the service of *pragmatic ends* (signification, mutual understanding, calculation and mastery of nature), *not* of epistemic ends: explanation, understanding (*Erklärung / Begreifen*). They also stand (4) in the service of the *moral ends* of humanizing and ascribing meaning (*Sinngebung*) to nature.

1. With the conception of laws of nature as projections (*auferlegt, Interpretation, Erdichtung, Setzen*: "imposed," "poetization," "interpretation," "positing"), their "objective reality" and empirical origin are denied and effectively reversed: laws of nature are anthropological phenomena with sources in (human) activity. This conception can also be seen as a radicalization of Kant's Copernican turn, according to which it is the human intellect that prescribes its laws to nature. In Nietzsche's version, however, the categorial order of nature becomes the projection of physiologically conditioned errors (*Irrtümern*), fictions, simplifications (*Fiktionen, Vereinfachungen, Zurechtmachungen*) in the service of life-interests, not objectively valid judgments.

2. From early on, the realist conception of laws of nature is reinterpreted (*umgedeutet*) by Nietzsche in relational terms: as "*relations* of an x to y and z" (*KSA* 7:19[235]); or as "anthropomorphic relations" on the basis of the quasi-Protagorean principle: "*Man* as the measure of things" (Der Mensch *als Maaß der Dinge*) (*KSA* 7:19[237]; *KSA* 7:29[8]).[17] In later years Nietzsche writes of "lawfulness" (*das Gesetzmäßige*) as "the *relational character* of all occurrence" (Relations-charakter *alles Geschehens*: (*KSA* 11:26[36])), whereby "law" acquires an ontological meaning. This relational concept of laws of nature is developed further in two directions. On one side it is reduced to the laws of human perception ("the 'laws' of optics," "laws of perception"[18]), which in turn are referred back to our conditions of exis-

tence.[19] Where "laws of nature" carry this meaning, Nietzsche emphasizes the limits of their validity on the basis of the limits of human perception.

3. On the other side, the relational concept of laws of nature is also reinterpreted in pragmatic terms, as "formulae," "schemata," "images" or a "cipher" for an "unknown state of affairs" (*KSA* 9:6[429]).[20] In these contexts, Nietzsche's accent is often on the pragmatic functions or purposes of laws of nature, in sharp contrast to their epistemic value: laws of nature serve the ends of signification and mutual understanding (*Bezeichnung, Verständigung*), the mastery of nature, as well as "our everyday calculating needs" (*unserem Hausgebrauch der Berechnung*) (*KSA* 13:14[79]); *not*, however, explanation or understanding (*Erklärung, Begreifen*).[21] In this respect, Nietzsche comes close to Mach's phenomenalist opposition to panmechanism, which highlights the model-character of mechanistic concepts and abstains from explanation.[22] Characteristic of the late Nietzsche is the impulse to supplement (*ergänzen*) laws of nature in this sense with an interpretation of occurrences "from within (*von Innen her*)" (*KSA* 11:40[53]).[23] Just because of their instrumental value for life, however, this move allows for a limited affirmation of laws of nature in this relational-pragmatic sense.

4. Not so, when it comes to the *moral* goals served by laws of nature. Nowhere is Nietzsche's opposition to laws of nature more implacable or consistent than when he considers the moral meaning of "laws of nature." The chief polemical target across Nietzsche's writing is the subjective, essentially moral meaning of "laws of nature": the projection into nature (*Hineindichtung*) of the inner moral experience of obligation (*Sollen*), that is, of the *moral* law and the network of moral concepts that go with it ("mercy," "protection," "respect for 'laws'" (*KSA* 11:36[18])), and especially: voluntary obedience to the law with its metaphysical presupposition of free will.[24] This meaning of law is at work, says Nietzsche, not just in the "popular" conception of law (*KSA* 13:14[79]), but also in the physicists understanding, which he rejects as a "naive-humanitarian" distortion of nature (*BGE* 22).

There are contexts in which Nietzsche argues that the moral meaning of "ought" (*Sollen*) clings so firmly to the words "law," "lawfulness of nature" that we cannot utter them without a "moral aftertaste (*moralischen Beigeschmack*)" (*KSA* 11:36[18]). Thus, in a *Nachlass* note from 1879, where Nietzsche identifies our "law" talk with the moral meaning of ought (*Sollen*), he goes on to legislate—in a performative instantiation of this meaning—that the word "law" ought (*soll*) to be restricted to the moral domain of *Sollen*:

> Where something *must* be done, one ought not to talk of laws, but only there, where something *ought* to be done. Against the so-called natural laws and especially the economic [ones] etc. (*KSA* 8:44[6])[25]

A direct line can be drawn from this programmatic act of legislation to the numerous texts from *The Gay Science* (*GS* 109) on that they deny the existence of laws in nature (see note 13). Nietzsche's strategy (1) of absolute negation is, then, to be understood as the practical consequence he draws from the ineradicable moral connotations of the words "law," "lawfulness": If we cannot utter these words without a "moral aftertaste," then they are useless for the purposes of demoralizing nature. The only realistic chance of countering the moralization of nature involves a program to expunge the word "law" from our very language of nature in favor of a new, amoral, non-anthropomorphic vocabulary of power-relations.

If we now ask what the implications of this program are for the language of "necessity," Nietzsche's answer is equivocal, depending on the exact meaning he ascribes to it. In some contexts, "necessity" is perceived as part and parcel of the package of moral interpretation, as expressing the *moral* necessity of *Sollen*: the constraint, compulsion (*Zwang*) to follow the moral law (= N1).[26] In this case, the negation of law entails the negation of necessity, so that the task is to formulate a language of nature devoid of both "law" and "necessity," as false explanations of the calculability/regularity of natural processes (for example, *BGE* 21). In other contexts, the rejection of laws of nature does *not* entail a rejection of necessity. Here "necessity" names that which *remains* after thinking away anthropomorphic laws of nature, as an impersonal, amoral *Müssen* (*not Sollen*) aligned with the calculability or regularity of natural processes. Here necessity (= N2) is understood as *logically independent* of laws of nature, and the task is to rethink "necessity" in non-anthropomorphic, extramoral terms in a way that offers an alternative, non-legalistic explanation or interpretation of natural processes and the regularities they exhibit. These tasks are pursued by Nietzsche under the signs of *will to power* and *fate* or *fatum*.

However, it should not be thought that the will to power falls neatly within this program, nor that Nietzsche gives up entirely on the language of "law" in connection with nature or reality. As mentioned earlier, "law" is also affirmed and used by Nietzsche in connection with the will to power. This is partly because he does not always hold that the language of "law" is indelibly tainted with moral connotations. In some contexts, Nietzsche appears to believe that the problem of law lies less at the level of words than at the level of concepts, so that the task of demoralizing nature can be engaged by retaining the language of law and reinvesting it with new meanings, purged of moral connotations (strategy 3: *Umdeutung*). These suggestions call for a closer look at the will to power in relation to law, and the implications it has for the concept of necessity.

Will to Power, Law and Necessity

The status of law and necessity in the context of Will to Power is complicated by two factors. The first is that it is unclear whether the Will to Power is meant to supplement (*ergänzen*) mechanics or to displace (*ersetzen*) it as an alternative to pan-mechanism. Where the Will to Power is presented as a supplement (*Ergänzung*) of mechanics and mechanistic concepts like "force" and "law," Nietzsche intends what Mittasch calls a "deepening" ("*Vertiefung und Verinnerlichung*") of the concept of laws of nature by supplementing them with an "inner world" of nonmechanistic occurrence (*Geschehen*).[27] At issue, for one, is the explanation of motion in terms of a *principle of activity,*[28] what Nietzsche calls the problem of the "mobile" (*KSA* 12:1[30]).[29] In these contexts, mechanistic laws are sometimes assigned the pragmatic status of "formulae" or "means of expression" (*Formeln, Ausdrucksmittel*: *KSA* 12:1[30]), but also a quasi-ontological status as "symptoms," even "effects" (*Wirkungen*) (*KSA* 11:36[31]; *KSA* 11:43[2]) of a nonmechanistic, inner occurrence or process (*Geschehen*).

Where, on the other hand, Nietzsche looks to *replace* mechanics and mechanistic laws with the Will to Power, the question of laws and necessity is complicated by a second factor: Nietzsche seems to adopt at least three distinct positions on law in relation to necessity. In some contexts the absolute negation of laws includes a negation of necessity; in others, "necessity" names that which remains after subtracting laws of nature; and then there are the contexts where "law" is used affirmatively or as an operational term to describe reality or nature as Will to Power. Despite these differences, a survey of the relevant texts shows two things quite clearly: *first*, that Nietzsche's primary concern when discussing the question of law and necessity in connection with Will to Power is a critical interrogation of the concept of causality and the related issues of free will and determinism; and *second*, that the different positions he adopts on law and necessity are just so many different attempts to articulate a radically immanent knowledge of nature or reality. In this respect, the question of law and necessity is the "golden road" to Nietzsche's positive ontology, as I will try to indicate. Both points can be seen in the context of Nietzsche's affirmative use of law, with which I begin.

Will to Power and Law

One of the key meanings of "law" in connection with Will to Power and anticipations of the Will to Power concerns the *relational* character of reality. This can be seen in a note where Nietzsche writes:

> to all that is lawful, that is, the *relational character* of all occurrence [Relations-charakter *alles Geschehens*] there corresponds only a *thought-process* (memory und inference). (*KSA* 11:26[36])

Of importance for us is the emphasis on relations, which is already captured in an earlier *Nachlass* note from the time of *GS*, where Nietzsche looks to advance the cause of morality by overcoming the "I"/"Not-I" opposition in favor of a refined knowledge of nature: "a sharper grasp of the true in the other and in myself and in nature" (*KSA* 9:11[21]). He then calls on us

> [t]o **let** ourselves be **possessed** [*uns . . .* ***besitzen lassen***] by things (not by persons) and by the greatest possible range of *true things*! (*KSA* 9:11[21])

—an initiative that

> will perhaps end in such a way that, instead of the I we know the affinities and enmities of things [*Verwandtschaften und Feindschaften der Dinge*] thus *pluralities* [Vielheiten] and their laws. (*KSA* 9:11[21])

Later on, where the critique of substance, causality and the "doer-deed" schema makes talk of "things" more problematic, the emphasis in Nietzsche's use of "law" shifts to *dynamics*: activity, process, motion. Thus in one note he writes of the "inner laws of motion of the organic being" (*inneren Bewegungs-gesetzen des organischen Wesens*) of which we "still have no inkling" (*KSA* 11:26[81]). In another note he opposes "the absolute concept 'atom' and 'individual'" by referring the *relations* of "struggle" (*Kampf*) among atoms back to prior *processes* of aggregation (condensation) and disaggregation among power-centers (*Macht-Centra*) (*KSA* 11:43[2]). "Both processes," he insists, "that of dissolution and that of condensation [are] to be understood as effects of the will to power," and concludes

> world-bodies [*Weltkörper*] and atoms only different in scale, but the *same laws*. (*KSA* 11:43[2])

What, then, are we to make of this use of "laws" to describe the *relational* and *dynamic* character of reality as occurrence, given the weight of his critique of law as a distorting projection onto nature? And what are their implications for the concept of necessity?

One clue to this puzzle is given by *Heraclitus*, and the Heraclitean identity of *Dike* and *Polemos*, repeatedly described by the young Nietzsche as an "immanent lawfulness" (*immanente Gesetzmässigkeit*). Thus, for example:

> **Justice** (Δίκη) is not supposed to punish: it is the immanent lawfulness. (*PPP* 10)

> Conflict [*der Streit*] as the continuous effectivity [*Wirken*] of a unitary lawful rational **Justice** (Δίκη), an idea drawn from the deepest fundaments of Greek existence. It is Hesiod's good Eris made into the world-principle. The Greeks are distinguished by the contest [*Wettkampf*], above all by the immanent lawfulness in the deciding of the contest [*immanente Gesetzmäßigkeit im Entscheiden des Wettkampfes*]. (*PPP* 10)

> Heraclitus: the world an absolute lawfulness [*Gesetzlichkeit*]: how could it be a world of injustice!—so, a *moral* judgment "the fulfillment of the law" is absolute; the contrary [i.e., non-fulfillment of the law—HS] is a deception; even bad people do not alter this, the absolute *lawfulness* is fulfilled in them, just as they are. Here necessity is glorified and *felt* in a moral sense. (*KSA* 11:26[67] 11 (1884). Cf. *KSA* 7:19[116] 7: 'ethical anthropomorphism')

Or of the Heraclitean world-child:

> The child then throws the toy away: but soon it starts all over again in innocent caprice. But as soon as it builds, it connects, joins and forms in a lawful manner [*gesetzmäßig*] and according to inner orders [*nach inneren Ordnungen*]. (*PTA* 7; cf. *PTA* 19 "goalless"; *PPP* 10)[30]

But even stronger than Heraclitus are the affinities with Goethe, and his distinction between imposed (*auferlegte*) laws of nature and an *immanent* lawfulness of living nature.[31] At stake for Goethe here is not the kind of external, imposed laws that he identifies with natural science, but the *inner character of spontaneous effective beings*; not fixed, substantive models or primal images (*Ur-Bilder*), but *activity*; not eternally valid, constant laws, but laws that depend on *individual characteristics*. Above all, Goethe's concern with his concept of law or "type" is to assert "the *priority of relations or connections* among parts . . . over the analysis of parts."[32]

Clearly, two of these moments resonate strongly with what we have already seen and point to an *ontological dimension* of the lawfulness of Will to Power, one that is focused on the *relations between* diverse power-centers, conceived as *spontaneous, effective activity* without substance. In this light, Nietzsche's move is to extend Goethe's concept of law or "type" from living nature to all of reality-as-occurrence.

What, then, does this *immanent ontology of law* suggested by the affinity with Goethe imply for the concept of necessity in the context of Will to Power?[33] Among the later texts where "law" is used in connection with reality or Will to Power, only two make explicit reference to "necessity." Both provide important clues to Nietzsche's understanding of necessity that highlight key aspects of his immanent ontology of law. The first text involves the attempt, repeated throughout the late *Nachlass*, to deny mechanism's claim to knowledge:

> In mathematics [read: mechanism—HS] there is no *understanding* [*Begreifen*], but only *a registering of necessities* [*Feststellen von Nothwendigkeiten*]: of relations, which do not change, of laws *in* being [*Gesetzen* im *Sein*] (*KSA* 11:25[314]; cf. *KSA* 12:2[139])

In telegraphic form, this text performs a twofold reduction: of mechanism's claim to knowledge ("understanding") to a recording / registering (*Feststellen*) of necessities; and then—à la Hume—of necessity (Hume's "necessary connection") to constant relations (Hume's "constant conjunction"). But these constant relations are then—*contra* Hume—given an immanent-ontological status as "laws in being." Clearly, this claim places the burden on Nietzsche to do what mechanism cannot: to comprehend and explain necessity in the sense of constant relations, where these are understood as an immanent feature of reality or being (= N3). This is what we find Nietzsche doing in the second text that mentions "necessity" in connection with Will to Power, where he writes:

> "Laws of nature" as a registering of power-relations. [*Feststellung von Macht-verhältnissen*] / "Cause and effect" an expression for the necessity / and relentlessness of this assertion of power. [*Unerbittlichkeit dieser Macht-festsetzung*] (*KSA* 11:39[13])

Again in telegraphic form, we see Nietzsche looking to explain the constant relations in nature through the association of necessity with the "relentlessness" (*Unerbittlichkeit*) of power-relations. What Nietzsche means by "relentlessness" is somewhat filled out in another note where he refers the "law of nature" to "the unconditional establishment of power relations and degrees" (*die unbedingte Herstellung der Macht-Relationen und -Grade*: (*KSA* 12:1[30]). At stake here is clearly a sense of *constraint* (*Zwang*), but one that must be distinguished from the anthropomorphic-moral sense of constraint (*Sollen* as the necessity to obey the law) unequivocally rejected by Nietzsche. An important pointer for this impersonal-amoral sense of constraint is given in a note (mentioned earlier) where Nietzsche writes of the "laws" or "processes of dissolution and condensation" as "*effects* of the will to power" (*KSA* 11:43[2]). He goes on to write:

> All the way down to its smallest fragments, it [the will to power—HS] has the will to condense itself [*sich zu verdichten*]. But it is *constrained* to *condense* itself in a specific direction **around** itself [*gezwungen,* ***um*** *sich irgendwohin zu verdichten*], to thin itself out at another place [*sich zu verdünnen*] etc. (*KSA* 11:43[2])

Here Goethe's immanent ontology of law as *spontaneous, effective activity* without substance is specified as the *activity of increasing power* through processes of aggregation or condensation. This *general* principle is, however, situated in *concrete, particular* relations of struggle among diverse power-centers, each vying to increase its power. Thus, even if all power-centers are by definition activities of increasing power, the actual *direction* or *form* this takes for a given power-center is *limited* or *constrained* by the kind of resistance it encounters from the other power-centers in its vicinity. Here "constraint" refers not to the general "law" or activity of increasing power as such, which is spontaneous and "free," but to the *limits* imposed by the particular complex of counterpowers on the *direction* and *form* this activity can take (N4, meaning: the constraints (*Zwang*) imposed on the activity of increasing power by local resistances).

On this basis we can say: Where the term "necessity" is used in the sense of "constraint" (*Zwang*) in the context of Will to Power, it highlights another aspect of Nietzsche's radically immanent knowledge of nature or ontology: its attention to *concrete, situational* power-complexes for understanding the actual forms and directions taken by the spontaneous, effective activity that is reality. In this regard, Nietzsche's concept of necessity articulates the third moment or motivation behind Goethe's immanent ontology of law: its attention *not* to eternally and universally valid constants, but to the *diversity* of particular life-forms and their *individual characteristics*, or for Nietzsche: radically individual, situational complexes of powers and counterpowers.

Will to Power *contra* Law

So far, we have seen Nietzsche looking to explain constant relations as an intrinsic feature of reality (N3), with reference to the "necessity" or "constraints" that emerge in particular, concrete power-complexes on the general "law" or activity of power-aggregation (N4). If we now turn to those contexts where Nietzsche takes radically opposed positions on "law" and "necessity" in connection with the Will to Power, we find the same underlying concern to explain constant relations, or what he sometimes calls the "calculability" or "regularity" of nature. Nietzsche's commitment to immanent laws is, it seems, experimental rather than firm, and strictly secondary to his firmer commitment to explain constant relations in radically immanent terms. So, even in contexts where he negates one or both, his views on "law" and "necessity" throw further light on his positive ontology of immanence.

In aphorism 22 of *Beyond Good and Evil* (mentioned several times) Nietzsche denounces the physicists' "lawfulness of nature" as a "naive-humanitarian" distortion of nature in the service of modern, democratic instincts. In this text, Nietzsche's familiar critique of "law" as an anthropomorphic projection serving moral ends culminates in an absolute negation of laws. Laws of nature are opposed as a false explanation of constant relations by a (self-referential) interpreter who, with respect to "the same appearances"

> ends up claiming the same thing of this world as you [scientists], namely that it has a "necessary" and "calculable" ["*berechenbaren*"] course, *not*, however because laws rule in it, but because laws are absolutely *lacking* [fehlen], and every power draws its ultimate consequence in every moment. (*BGE* 22)

Here, the absolute negation of laws from nature leaves necessity, in the sense of (or a sense closely related to) the *calculability* (*Berechenbarkeit*) of natural events (N2). At stake here is the problem encountered earlier of understanding or explaining *constant relations*, understood as an intrinsic feature of reality. But at another level, it is the very possibility of science that needs to be explained; that is: the possibility of formulating mathematical laws that allow for predictive calculation of the course of nature on the basis of constant relations. And Nietzsche's laconic response at both levels runs: it is because "every power draws its ultimate consequence in every moment" (*BGE* 22).

What Nietzsche means by this is somewhat clarified in a *Nachlass* text with the heading: "*Critique of mechanism*." This is indeed a hyper-critical text that begins by negating not just the concept of law, but also "things" and a range of terms that in other, less critical contexts are used synonymously with the "calculability" of nature: "necessity," "constraint" and "regularity":

Will to power *Philosophy*
Power-quanta. *Critique of mechanism*

> let us here get rid of the two popular concepts "necessity" and "law": the first places a false constraint [*Zwang*], the second a false freedom in the world. "Things" do not behave with regularity [*regelmäßig*], not following a *rule* [*nach einer* Regel]: there are no things (—that is our fiction) they behave just as little under a constraint of necessity [*Zwang von Nothwendigkeit*]. Here there is no obeying: for that *something is as it is* [daß etwas so ist, wie es ist], as strong, as weak, that is not the consequence of an obeying [*Gehorchens*] or of a rule [*Regel*] or of a constraint [*eines Zwanges*] . . . (*KSA* 13:14[79])

Clearly it is the *moral* senses of "law," "necessity," "constraint," and "regularity" and their presuppositions (freedom, moral constraint, obedience) that are negated here ("necessity" as N1). None of this, however, touches on the meaning of necessity as *constant relations* or *calculability* (N2) that remains in *BGE* 22 after the negation of laws, as that which needs to be explained without recourse to laws. For this, we can look a little further in the same *Nachlass* text, where Nietzsche writes:

> There is no law: every power draws its ultimate consequence in every moment. That there is no mezzo termine, precisely that is the basis of calculability [*Berechenbarkeit*]. (*KSA* 13:14[79])

Here, what Nietzsche called "necessity" in *Beyond Good and Evil* (*BGE* 22): the *calculability* of natural events (N2) is explained with reference to the selfsame expression: "every power draws its ultimate consequence in every moment." But this time, he unpacks this with the claim: there is no "mezzo termine"; there is no middle or mediating term. According to Werner Stegmaier,[34] what Nietzsche is denying here is law (*not* in a moral sense, but) as a principle or term that would *stand outside* the actual course of events, understood as a play of forces or powers, in which each power only is what it is in any moment by virtue of its interactions with other counterpowers. At play here is Nietzsche's *dynamic, relational* concept of power, or rather *powers*; that is, (1) power as activity, the activity of increasing power, which can only be an *overpowering*, because (2) power-as-activity can only act *in relation to* the resistance offered by other counterpowers.[35]

Nietzsche, then, recurs to his dynamic, relational concept of power in order to negate the possibility of explaining the actual course of events by *abstracting* to any degree from this particular play of powers-and-counterpowers. Once again, the question of law directs us to the perspective *within* concrete, particular power-complexes required by Nietzsche's radically immanent ontology. But what does this imply for the concept of necessity? And what are we to make of Nietzsche's claim to explain the calculability of events from this internal perspective?

In contrast to the texts considered earlier, where "necessity" in the sense of constraint served Nietzsche to assert his concrete situational ontology (N4), there is at least one text where "necessity" and "constraint" are rejected on exactly the same grounds as those used here to reject law. In a *Nachlass* text that declares war on determinism (*Zur Bekämpfung des Determinismus*), Nietzsche writes:

> That something proceeds with regularity [*regelmäßig*] and proceeds in a calculable way [*berechenbar*] does not imply that it proceeds with *necessity*. (*KSA* 12:9[91])

But in what sense is necessity here denied? Nietzsche goes on:

> "Mechanistic necessity" is not a given fact [*Thatbestand*]: it is *we* who have interpreted it into occurrences. We have interpreted the *formulability* [*Formulirbarkeit*] of occurrences as the consequence of a necessity that holds sway over occurrences [*einer über dem Geschehen waltenden Necessität*]. But from the fact that I do something specific, it by no means follows that I do it under constraint [*gezwungen*]. *Constraint* [*Der* Zwang] as something in things cannot be demonstrated: the rule [*die Regel*, meaning here: regularity] demonstrates only that one and the same occurrence is not also another occurrence. (*KSA* 12:9[91])

It is, then, "mechanistic necessity" in a sense consonant with mechanistic law as *mezzo termine* that is here negated: necessity as an explanatory principle that stands outside or above (*über*), that "holds sway over" (*walten über*) a determinate occurrence (N5). "Necessity" in this (5th) sense is, by virtue of abstracting from the particularity of this determinate occurrence, a false interpretation of the formulability (*Formulierbarkeit*) of events, that is, their regularity or calculability (*Regelmäßigkeit, Berechenbarkeit*). Under "formulability" or "calculability," we have to understand the possibility of science, and Nietzsche goes on to interpret it, contra "necessity," in terms of *radical facticity*: that a given occurrence or force just is what it is:

> Against apparent "necessity"
> —this just a way of expressing that a force is not also something else. (*KSA* 12:9[91])

Thinking away "necessity" as the projection of moral constraint (N1) and as a *mezzo termine* that abstracts from determinate occurrences (N5) leaves a minimal concept of reality as facticity in the sense of: *so-sein* (being-thus); *so-und-nicht-anders-sein* (being-thus-and-not-otherwise); *so-beschaffen-sein*: that something is as it is, as strong or as weak, as a function of relations of power and the degrees of power-over and resistance.

With this notion of radical facticity, we have a settled position reiterated several times in the late *Nachlass*:

> The unchanging sequence of certain appearances does not demonstrate a "law," but rather a power-relation between 2 or more forces. To say: "but exactly this relation remains the same!" means nothing other than: "one and the same force cannot also be another force."—It is not about a *sequence* [lit. after-one-another: *Nacheinander*],—but rather an *interconnectedness* [lit. in-one-another: *Ineinander*], a process [*Prozeß*], in which the single moments that follow one another condition one another *not* as causes and effects. (*KSA* 12:2[139])

> But just this thus-and-not-otherwise [*jenes So-und-nicht-anders*, i.e. that something always occurs thus-and-thus—HS] could derive from the being itself [*aus dem Wesen selbst*], that behaves thus-and-thus not with regard to a law, but rather as being constituted thus-and-thus [*als so und so beschaffen*]. It means only: something cannot also be something else, cannot do this now, then that, is neither free nor unfree, but just thus-and-thus [*eben so und so*]. (*KSA* 12:2[142])

> [*T*]*hat something is the way it is* [*daß etwas so ist, wie es ist*], as strong, as weak, that is not the consequence of an obeying or a rule [*Regel*] or a constraint [*Zwang*] . . . The degree of resistance and the degree of power-over [*Übermacht*]—that is what is at play in all occurrence: if *we* know how to express it in formulae of "laws" for our everyday calculating needs, all the better for us! (*KSA* 13:14[79])

These notes are important because they bring the dimension of temporality into Nietzsche's concept of facticity. But they do so indirectly, by way of the concept of process (*Prozeß*), and in a manner that remains profoundly ambiguous. Ostensibly, they purport to show that facticity can explain the regularity of events in a way that law cannot. The key claim is that reality-as-process, understood as relations of antagonistic interdependence among force-centers, takes precedence over, and determines temporal sequences. In a sense we can say: temporal relations are derivative of spatial relations, insofar as the *Nacheinander* is mediated and conditioned by the *Ineinander* of antagonistic interdependence among an originary plurality of force-centers without substance (see *KSA* 12:2[139] cited earlier). On this processual understanding of reality, antagonistic relations of power-over and resistance (see *KSA* 13:14[79] above) constitute a dense multiplicity of constraints that determine the direction of each force-center and the form taken by the power-complexes they constitute: their being-thus-and-not-otherwise or *So-und-nicht-anders*. Being-thus (*so-sein*) is a function of being-thus-constituted (*so und so beschaffen sein*: *KSA* 12:2[142] cited earlier) by multiple relations of power-over and resistance. It is thus by appeal to necessity in the 4th sense: the constraints imposed by local force-centers on the direction taken by spontaneous effective activity (N4) that Nietzsche looks to explain regularity in nature. Insofar as relations of antagonism can only be understood to hold between force-centers that are qualitatively different or diverse, we can say that Nietzsche advances *pluralism*—an originary qualitative diversity of forces without substance—as the explanation of regularity.

In these texts, then, the concept of facticity as *being-thus-and-not-otherwise* is extended to include two interrelated meanings: 1. the constraints exerted by antagonistic relations with local force-centers that make a given force-center or power-complex what it is (*thus-and-not-otherwise* as a consequence of *being-thus-constituted*); and 2. the originary plurality of diverse force-centers presupposed by such antagonistic relations. It is, however, highly questionable whether this extended concept of facticity is adequate as an explanation of regularity. Even when situated in the context of Nietzsche's concept of reality-as-process, radical facticity is bound to the immanence of *this* situation or complex; as such, it seems eminently *incapable* of explaining regularity, which by definition involves some kind of repetition, extension, or generalization of the here-and-now. On the other hand, it's not clear that facticity is at all intended as an explanation of regularity in this sense. When Nietzsche writes: "To say: 'but exactly this relation remains the same!' means nothing other than: 'one and the same force cannot also be another force,'" he seems to be *collapsing* the meaning of regularity into facticity, rather than explaining it (*KSA* 12:2[139]).

Nor is it clear from these texts how Nietzschean facticity stands in relation to the concept of necessity. Certainly, facticity is consistently opposed to *laws of nature* in the senses criticized by Nietzsche. As such, it is advanced as part of an alternative, nonlegalistic, nonmechanistic, noncausal language of nature. But it's not clear whether it is meant as an *alternative to* the concept of necessity that would exclude the latter from this language, or as an *alternative interpretation of* necessity (*Umdeutung*): a *minimal concept of necessity* that remains and is affirmed by him after thinking away the moral and transcendent concepts (N1 and N5) he negates. In that case, we can speak of necessity in a 6th sense, advanced by Nietzsche as a minimalist reinterpretation (*Umdeutung*) of necessity in the 2nd sense (N6: radical facticity or *so-sein* as a reinterpretation of N2: a non-anthropomorphic, extra-moral necessity that remains after subtracting laws of nature).

Conclusion

In my concluding remarks, I will sketch an interpretation that does not settle these ambiguities, but does enable us to understand them better, and throws light on the essentially *moral* motivations or functions of Nietzsche's concept of facticity. As my frame of reference, I take three modalities of judgment or being: (I) necessity (must-be-thus: *so-sein-müssen*); (II) actuality (being-thus: *so-sein*, being-thus-and-not-otherwise: *so-und-nicht-anders-sein*); and (III) possibility (can-be-thus-or-otherwise: *so-oder-anders-sein-können*). My claim is that Nietzsche's concept of facticity collapses all three modalities into one.

I. With the concept of facticity, Nietzsche collapses necessity (*so-sein-müssen*) into actuality (*so-sein*) with two consequences: (1) Nietzsche hereby excludes determinism or the "unfree will," and in doing so (2) frees up actuality toward *radical contingency*. Or one could say: Nietzsche thereby transforms the meaning of actuality from *presence* to the *radical contingency* of just being-thus:

> Toward the fight against *determinism*.
>
> That something proceeds with regularity [*regelmäßig*] and proceeds in a calculable [*berechenbar*] way does not imply that it proceeds with *necessity*. That a quantum of force is determined and behaves in one and the same manner in every particular case does not make it into the "unfree will." (*KSA* 12:9[91])

III. With the concept of facticity, Nietzsche also collapses possibility (*so-oder-anders-sein-können*) into actuality (*so-sein*) with two consequences:

1. This move enables us to understand better Nietzsche's puzzling claim to "explain" regularity and with it, the possibility of science. As was noted earlier, radical facticity is bound to the immanence of *this* situation or complex, and so seems eminently *inadequate* to explain regularity, involving as it does some kind of repetition, extension, or generalization of the here-and-now. Yet how can this extension be performed other than by appealing to counterfactuals (it could have been otherwise, but was not; it could be otherwise, but is not; it could turn out otherwise in the future, but it will not)? And how can the explanatory deficit of facticity be specified other than by appealing to counterfactuals? (What if the regularity of

this event were to cease tomorrow?) By collapsing possibility into actuality, Nietzschean facticity excludes counterfactuals, so that the explanandum (regularity) cannot even be formulated. Or perhaps one should say: Nietzsche's explanans (facticity) has the effect of collapsing the explanandum (regularity) into the *impossibility* of explaining regularity. In that case, Nietzschean facticity should be understood, not as an explanation of regularity that somehow does better than laws of nature, but as an *interpretation* of reality that asserts the *impossibility* of comprehending or explaining regularity in the way that laws of nature are supposed to.

2. By collapsing possibility (*so-oder-anders-sein-können*) into actuality (*so-sein*), Nietzschean facticity also has the crucial consequence of excluding possibility from the past, and specifically: the past subjunctive of "it could-have-been-otherwise" (*hätte-anders-sein-können*). Nietzsche hereby excludes the presupposition of the "it could-have-been-otherwise," the nondeterminism of the free will[36] that is the condition for the moral imperative: the *so-sein-sollen* or ought-to-be-thus. For Nietzsche, the concept of facticity has the strategic value of undermining the moral imperative by attacking the opposition that is its presupposition: both free will *and* "unfree will" (consequence I.1 above), determinism and nondeterminism:

> something cannot also be something else, cannot do this now, then that, / is neither free nor unfree, but just thus-and-thus [*eben so und so*]. (*KSA* 12:2[42])

> Removal of the will, the free and unfree. / of the "must" ["*Muß*"] and of "necessity" . . . (*KSA* 11:26[296])

If this, or something like this is right, then Nietzschean facticity leaves us with a concept of reality as radical contingency beyond the opposition of free will and determinism, an *extra-moral* contingency that, in excluding free will also excludes the ascription of responsibility, and the negation of the past, the "it was," on the grounds that it *could have been otherwise.* Nietzschean facticity thereby frees up reality toward *innocence* and towards *unconditional affirmation*. In these respects, Nietzsche's concept of facticity, this incredibly simple but unthinkable thought that is the result of his life-long engagement with laws of nature, forms the core of his project to demoralize nature.

In the published works, Nietzsche's efforts to rethink or think away "necessity" beyond mechanistic laws and beyond the free will–determinism opposition are pursued through the concept of *fate* or *fatum*. In Nietzsche's critique of mechanistic laws, as we have seen, it remains unclear whether facticity is meant to *displace* the concept of necessity as an *alternative to* the language of necessity, or to *reinterpret* it as a *minimal concept of necessity*. It is in connection with *fate* or *fatum*, rather than laws of nature, and in the domain of human life and culture, that Nietzsche takes up and develops the minimal concept of necessity won from his critique of mechanistic laws. That is the subject for another essay, but an important link between the two domains of thought can, I think, be seen in a speculative moment recorded in the *Nachlass*, when Nietzsche extends facticity by way of the eternal return into the thought of the "recurrence of identical cases":

> The *calculability* [Berechenbarkeit] *of an occurrence* lies
> not in the following of a rule [*eine Regel befolgt wurde*]
> nor in the obeying [*gehorcht*] of a necessity
> nor in our projecting of a law of causality into every occurrence:
> it lies in the *recurrence of identical cases* [Wiederkehr identischer Fälle].
> (*KSA* 13:14[98])

Appendix

The main meanings of "necessity" identified in this essay are:

N1: "necessity" as the *moral* necessity or constraint (*Zwang*) to follow the law: ought-to-be-thus (*so-sein-sollen*) that is often "read into" mechanistic laws of nature.

N1 is criticized and rejected by Nietzsche as part of the anthropomorphic, moral meaning ascribed to (mechanistic) "laws of nature" (as if things or forces followed laws of nature out of voluntary obedience).

N2: "necessity" as a non-anthropomorphic, extra-moral necessity: must-be thus (*so-sein-müssen, not sollen*) often connected with the calculability or regularity of natural processes.

N2 is retained and affirmed by Nietzsche as that which *remains* after thinking away anthropomorphic laws of nature. It is *logically independent* of laws of nature, form, even order (for example, *GS* 109).

N3–N6 occur in the context of the will to power:

N3: "necessity" in the sense of constant relations (*Verhältnisse, welche nicht wechseln*), where these are understood ontologically: as an immanent feature of reality or being (*Gesetzen* im *Sein*) (see *KSA* 11:25[314]). Affirmative usage.

N4: "necessity" as the multiple constraints (*Zwang*) imposed on a given power-center or -complex by local resistances or counterpowers that *limit* its activity of increasing power and determine the specific *direction* and *form* this activity can take.

N4 is used by Nietzsche to express his concrete situational ontology.

N5: "necessity" as *mezzo termine* (closely tied to the concept of law as *mezzo termine*), a principle that governs or "holds sway over" (*walten über*) a determinate occurrence and can therefore explain the regularity or calculability (*Regelmäßigkeit*, *Berechenbarkeit*) of events.

N5 is criticized and rejected by Nietzsche as a false explanation of regularity, precisely because it is as a principle that stands outside or above (*über*) and so abstracts from the reality of this determinate occurrence.

N6 (?): a minimal concept of necessity as radical facticity: being-thus, being-thus-and-not-otherwise (*so-sein, so-und-nicht-anders-sein*).

N6 is affirmed by Nietzsche as that which remains after thinking away the moral and transcendent concepts of necessity (N1 and N5) and law that he negates. N6 serves, above all, to oppose the moralization of nature, since being-thus (*so-sein*) excludes the moral concept of necessity (N1): *so-sein-sollen* and its presupposition in free will (*hätte-anders-sein können*). N6 can perhaps be understood as a minimalist reinterpretation of N2: a non-anthropomorphic, extra-moral necessity that remains after subtracting laws of nature.

PART III

Justice and the Law of Life

6

Life and Justice in Nietzsche's Conception of History

VANESSA LEMM

Introduction

In this famous essay dedicated to a consideration of the value of history,[1] Nietzsche claims to have detected in the superfluity of historical knowledge (*Erkenntnis-Überfluss*), a sickness and consuming fever that has befallen his contemporaries (*HL* "Preface"). What his contemporaries and, in general, modern man are lacking is an awareness of the genuine necessities (*Notwendige*), needs (*Bedürfnisse*), and requirements (*Nöthe*) of life (*HL* "Preface"). Nietzsche's thesis is that history is needed solely for the sake of life and action and insofar as it serves and is employed in view of the building of future life. As long as modern man fails to acknowledge this need for and value of history, historical knowledge inevitably leads to a degeneration of life.

Whereas historicism understands history as the objective knowledge of the past and sees in the necessity of the past the standard of the truth of historical knowledge, Nietzsche wants to shift historical knowledge away from science toward life and action. For him, life entails a constructive orientation toward the future, which commits an injustice toward the past. The historical knowledge of historicism claims to be true to the past and to do justice to the past. But, seen from the perspective of life, historical knowledge will have to become unjust toward the past in view of being true to life and its future becoming. This essay explores the problem of how a historical knowledge that is inherently unjust can nonetheless provide the material for the constitution of a just order of life. I argue that as long as modern man fails to appreciate the injustice of historical knowledge, he also remains closed to the justice of life.

But Nietzsche not only detects the symptoms of his age; he also sets out to cure modern man of the sickness of historicism. Against an overdose of historical knowledge, he prescribes the antidotes of the unhistorical, understood as the art and power of forgetfulness, and of the suprahistorical, understood as that which gives to reality the characteristic of the eternal exemplified in art and religion (*HL* 10). Most needful is to follow the old maxim: "Know yourself," which here is meant to recall one's genuine necessities (*Nothwendige*) and needs (*Bedürfnisse*) (*HL* 10).[2] In other words, a cure from the sickness of historical fever requires that modern man submit himself to the government (*Regierung*) of life. Not surprisingly, the three forms of history that are in the service of life—the monumental, antiquarian, and critical forms of history—all respond to real-life needs: the need to act and thrive, the need to preserve and revere, and the need to judge and condemn. Each of the three forms of history belongs to a certain soil and to a certain climate, and it is only in their own soil and climate that they can come into their own right (*Recht*) (*HL* 2). For Nietzsche, becoming aware of the needs of life will lead to a valuable use of history. Moreover, this use of the past for the sake of life and action is a form of justice. But how can history in the service of life be just or justified if, as Nietzsche says, every form of history in the service of life is inherently unjust? The past suffers as long as history stands under the rule of the needs of life and is dominated by its drives (*HL* 3). This essay wishes to shed light on the relationship between life and justice in Nietzsche's new conception of history in the service of life.

History and Justice under the Government of Life

In the opening passage of "On the Use and Disadvantage of History for Life," one learns that human life (*Dasein*) is a form of life that is inherently historical because it "lives off [*lebt davon*] negating, consuming, and contradicting itself" (*HL* 1). The process of negation, consumption, and self-contradiction is directed toward the future, where the future is understood as that dimension of human life which constitutes a continuous transfiguration of what was into what shall be. To account for this transfiguration, which the past cannot bring about by itself, Nietzsche brings into play the power of forgetfulness, an inherently unhistorical force of life. For Nietzsche, human life needs both the historical and the unhistorical, memory and forgetfulness, and it is thanks to their fruitful interrelation that human life becomes like a plastic force: "I mean by plastic force [*plastische Kraft*] the power [*Kraft*] to grow out of oneself in one's own way [*eigenartig*], to transform and incorporate [*einzuverleiben*] into oneself what is past and foreign, to heal wounds, to replace what has been lost, to re-create broken molds" (*HL* 1). One finds this plastic force at the core of each of the three forms of history in the service of life: whereas the monumental expresses the power to develop out of oneself in one's own way, the antiquarian expresses the power to transform and incorporate what is past and foreign, and the critical form of history is defined by its power to heal wounds, replace what has been lost, and re-create broken forms. History in the service of life therefore means history as a form of life, not cut off from life but as an expression of life. History here reveals itself to be a representative of life[3] as that force which lives off the past (historical), but is also directed toward the future (unhistorical). It responds to a need of life and also fulfills the aspiration of life to negate the past in view of future life to come. As such, history constitutes a form of knowledge that, in its injustice, is fully justified (*steht im Recht*) by standing in the service of life.

For Nietzsche, "an age, a culture, a nation" stands in a living relation to its past when it recovers a "natural relationship" to the past "evoked by hunger, regulated by the extent of its needs, held in bounds by its inherent plastic powers" (*HL* 4). In such a natural relationship, knowledge of the past is desired "only in the service of the future and the present and not for the weakening of the present, for depriving a vigorous future of its roots" (*HL* 4). Life is a plastic force that uses the past as nourishment for the sake of constituting an order of justice. When life governs (*regiert*), excessive desires (such as that for knowledge) are constrained and limits (*Grenzpfähle*) are erected and respected (*HL* 4).[4] What characterizes the order of justice produced by life is that it establishes a "natural relationship" between knowledge (memory/historical) and action (forgetfulness/unhistorical). Knowledge and action are now productively and creatively involved with each other and give rise to forms of life that are not only inherently future-promising and life-enhancing, but also just or justified (*stehen im Recht*).

From the beginning of the essay, Nietzsche makes clear that life and history, action and knowledge, art and science are diametrically opposed to each other. The historicist conception of justice is on the side of history, knowledge, and science. Nietzsche rejects this "historical" or "pure" justice because "it always undermines the living thing and brings it down: its judgment (*Richten*) is always annihilating" (*HL* 7). The problem of historicist justice is that its "historical drive does not also contain a drive to construct" (*HL* 7). "If the purpose of destroying and clearing is not to allow a future already alive in anticipation to raise its house on the ground thus liberated, . . . then the instinct for creation will be enfeebled and discouraged" (*HL* 7). Against the man of historical consciousness, Nietzsche praises the human being who feels unhistorically, whose horizon is as narrow as that of a dweller of the Andes, whose judgments may involve injustice and who falsely supposes that all his experiences are original to him, for despite these injustices and errors, such a person's unhistorical sensibility leads to superlative health and vigor (*HL* 1). By contrast, the human being who feels overly historical and hence who is far more just (*Gerechtere*) and instructed (*Belehrtere*) sickens and collapses "because he can no longer extricate himself from the delicate net of his judiciousness [*Gerechtigkeiten*] and truth for a simple act of will [*Wollen*] and desire [*Begehren*]" (*HL* 1).[5] The overabundance of historical knowledge clouds this person's insight into its real-life needs and desires and, moreover, inhibits it to act upon them. The example of the "just and instructed" man proves that an overdose of historical knowledge debilitates a person's creative instincts of life.

Historical knowledge destroys "the mood of pious illusion in which alone anything that wants to live can live" (*HL* 7). According to Nietzsche, this "illusion is produced by love, that is to say, in the unconditional faith in right and perfection" as the only mood in which man can be creative (*HL* 7).[6] The true historical actor is like a "man seized by a vehement passion, for a woman or for a great idea" (*HL* 1) who betrays all the features of a person who is typically seen as lacking any sense of justice, but who instead possesses an unconditional faith in right and perfection:

> It is the condition in which one is the least capable of being just [*der ungerechteste Zustand von der Welt*]; narrow-minded, ungrateful to the past, blind to dangers deaf to warnings, one is a little vortex of life in a dead sea of darkness and oblivion: and yet this condition—unhistorical, anti-historical through and through—is the womb of not only the unjust but of every just deed too: and no painter will paint his picture, no general achieve his victory, no people attain its freedom without having first desired and striven for it in an unhistorical condition such as that described. (*HL* 1)[7]

The blindness and injustice in the soul of him who acts, is the essential condition of all happenings (*HL* 1)[8] and, for Nietzsche, this is why the finest deeds always take place in such a superabundance of love.[9] The superabundance of love is creative and productive of future life, in contrast to the superabundance of historical knowledge, which destroys and inhibits the becoming of life.

Nietzsche concludes, first, that the power to feel unhistorically is more fundamental to life than to feel historically and, second, that the unhistorical constitutes the "foundation upon which alone anything just [*etwas Rechtes*)], healthy and great, anything truly human can grow" (*HL* 1). In other words, he argues that injustice and error are not only more important to life, to its preservation and enhancement, than truth and knowledge, but also that injustice and error provide the conditions of justice. This means that the origin of justice is no longer found in the purity of knowledge, but must be constructed from out of injustice and error. Nietzsche is seeking for a new idea of justice that is not imposed onto life but that arises from and is inherent to life. This new idea of justice is subject to the rule of life and finds in life its true growing ground.

When it comes under the rule of life, history is redirected away from the past and toward the future. This redirection is the work of a historical knowledge that must do violence or injustice to the past so that justice may become a "subverting" and "renewing" power (*SE* 3; see also *SE* 4), which longs for that which shall be rather than for that which has been:

> As he who acts is, in Goethe's words, always without a conscience, so is he also always without knowledge, he forgets most things so as to do one thing, he is unjust toward what lies behind him, and he recognizes the rights only of that which is now to come into being and no other rights whatever. (*HL* 1; see also *HL* 8)

This desire and passion for what shall be turns justice from being merely a passive instrument of measuring or evaluating in the service of science into an active force of life invested in the becoming of future life. Then "the study of history is something salutary and fruitful for the future" for as "the attendant of a mighty new current of life," it is now dominated and directed by the higher force of life and does not itself dominate and direct (*HL* 1).

In order to learn more about what Nietzsche means by justice or what justifies a form of history, one needs to turn to the sixth subsection of "On the Use and Disadvantage of History for Life." This section is dedicated to the question of whether modern man has a right (*ein Recht*) to call himself just (*gerecht*) because of his historical objectivity, that is, because he is true to the way things really were. Nietzsche claims that the idea of justice arising from historical objectivity is a delusion because it does not originate in a genuine need (*Bedürfnis*) and demand (*Verlangen*) for justice (*HL* 6). The historians of his age claim to be in a position of superiority where they can bring judgment upon the entire history of humanity whereas, in fact, they are in a position of weakness. Modern historicism writes history in the "naive belief that all the popular views of precisely their own age are the right and just views and that to write in accord with the views of their age is the same thing as being just" (*HL* 6). Nietzsche rejects the modern historicist way of relating to the past, but nevertheless does not want to give up on objectivity and hence calls for the truly just historian as the only one able to restore true objectivity (*wirkliche Objectivität*).

For Nietzsche, the idea of justice arising from the subordination of history to the higher forces of life is infinitely more valuable than the idea of "historical" or "pure" justice professed by his historicist contemporaries. Nietzsche regrets that the age of historicism suffers from a lack of "a stern and great sense of justice" (*HL* 6):

> Only insofar as the truthful man possesses the unconditional will to justice is there anything great in that striving for truth which is everywhere so thoughtlessly glorified: whereas in the eyes of the less clear-sighted men a whole host of the most varied drives such as curiosity, flight from boredom, envy, vanity, the desire for amusement, for example, can be involved in the striving for truth, which has its roots in justice. (*HL* 6)[10]

The servants of science not only lack any sense of justice, but their excessive production of historical knowledge leads them to imagine that their age "possesses the rarest of virtues, justice, to a greater degree than any other age" (*HL* 5).[11] They live in the illusion that what they call "historical objectivity" is the highest expression of justice. But their idea of objectivity has nothing to do with justice (*HL* 6). Following the words of Socrates, Nietzsche warns that such an imagined virtue of justice makes this age only more unjust for "justice as an illusion [*Gerechtigkeit als Einbildung*] makes more unjust" (*HL* 6). Against the idea of "historical objectivity," Nietzsche calls for a new "true objectivity" (*wirkliche Objectivität*) where the latter is the expression of an artistic and creative force (*HL* 6).[12] He imagines a form of historiography in which the human being's creative and artistic instincts would come to be fully realized: "Thus man spins his web over the past and subdues it, thus he gives expression to his artistic drives—but not to his drive toward truth or [historical or pure] justice" (*HL* 6). Such a form of historiography conceives of history as a form of art (*Kunstwerk*), and one could imagine that it would have in it "not a drop of common empirical truth and yet could lay claim to the highest degree of objectivity" (*HL* 6; *KSA* 7:29[156]).[13] This form of historiography is not ruled by a drive for truth as pure knowledge, but instead by a drive for truth as justice. However, the question remains how to reconcile the injustice done by historical knowledge to the past with the truth and justice arising from the government of life.[14] I suggest that the three forms of history, the monumental, the antiquarian, and the critical offer an answer to this question.

Antiquarian History: Self-Preservation as a Measure of Justice

According to the historicist perspective, the past stretches its power over all of historical knowledge, such that historical knowledge is only conceivable as being about the past. In so doing, according to Nietzsche, historicism becomes the accomplice of the injustice done by the past toward the present and the future. From the perspective of life, instead, the past receives its due only from one kind of historical knowledge, that is, from the antiquarian mode of history. This keeps the past from overflowing into the present and the future: through antiquarian history, life preserves the past as something past. Thus, life's injustice to the past at the hands of the antiquarian mode of history is not letting the past be hegemonic over the becoming of history, reveals itself to be the most appropriate, the most measured; in sum, the most just way of approaching the past. From the perspective of life's ordering of becoming, the antiquarian form of injustice is a way of doing justice.

Justice is typically associated with the ability of applying the right measures and proportions. Antiquarian history is unjust insofar as it lacks this sense for the right measure and proportion:

> The antiquarian sense of a man [*eines Menschen*], a community, a whole people, always possesses an extremely restricted field of vision; most of what exists it does not perceive at all, and the little it does see it sees much too close up and isolated; it cannot relate what [*kann es nicht messen*] it sees to anything else and it therefore accords everything it sees equal importance and therefore to each individual thing too great importance. There is a lack of that discrimination of value and that sense of proportion which would distinguish between the things of the past in a way that would do true justice to them; their measure and proportion is always that accorded them by the backward glance of the antiquarian individual [*Einzelnen*] or nation [*Volk*]. (*HL* 3)[15]

By taking everything as equal and equally important, the antiquarian historian fails to appreciate the higher distinction of the singular, unique, and irreducible. In this sense the antiquarian historian resembles the modern historicist who measures the past "according to the everyday standards of the present moment [*Allerwelts-Meinungen des Augenblicks*]," thus lowering "the past to contemporary [*zeitgemässen*] triviality" (*HL* 6).

Antiquarian history is inherently unjust for it privileges the preservation of the past, of tradition, and of an established way of life at the cost of obstructing the becoming of new forms of life. The problem is that antiquarian mode of history simply does not know how to value the becoming of life:

> For it knows only how to preserve life, not how to engender it; it always under-evaluates that which is becoming because it has no instinct for divining it—as monumental history, for example, has. (*HL* 3)

The kind of injustice exemplified by the antiquarian reflects in many ways what Nietzsche will later refer to as the "necessary injustice [*nothwendige Ungerechtigkeit*] of the perspectival." What predominates here is the project of the preservation and consolidation of a weak form of life:

> You shall learn to grasp the sense of the perspectival [*Perspektivische*] in every value judgment—the displacement, distortion and merely apparent teleology of horizons and whatever else pertains to perspectivism [*Perspektivischen*]; also the quantum of stupidity that resides in antithesis [*entgegengesetzte*] of values and the whole intellectual loss which every For, every Against costs us. You shall learn to grasp the *necessary* [*nothwendige*] injustice in every For and Against, the injustice as inseparable from life, life itself as *conditioned* by the sense of perspective and its injustice. You shall above all see with your own eyes where injustice is always at its greatest: where life has developed all its smallest, narrowest, neediest [*dürftigsten*], most incipient and yet cannot avoid taking *itself* as the goal and measure of things and for the sake of its own preservation secretly and meanly and ceaselessly crumbling away and calling into question the higher, greater, richer—you shall see with your own eyes the problem of the *order of rank* and how power [*Macht*] and right [*Recht*] and spaciousness of perspective grow into the heights together. You shall—enough: from now on the free spirits *know* what "you shall" he has obeyed, and he also knows what he now *can*, what only now he—*may* do . . . . (*HH* "Preface" 6)[16]

This form of injustice is necessary because it pertains to the government of life. Insofar as the injustice of antiquarian history satisfies a need (necessity) of life, it is justified in its injustice. Antiquarian history manifests the features of the necessary injustice of life in the following way: the antiquarian historian's plastic force to transform and incorporate what is past and foreign is, on the one hand, guided by its need (of life) to preserve and revere. In other words, its way of relating to the past is inherently perspectival and subject to "the displacement, distortion and merely apparent teleology of horizons and whatever else pertains to perspectivism" (*HH* "Preface" 6). On the other hand, its ways of measuring and evaluating are entirely dependent upon its relative strength (of life): since the antiquarian form of history reflects a weak form of life, self-preservation stands in the foreground when it comes to establishing the value of the past for the sake of life. Taking itself—that is, its self-preservation—as "the goal and measure of things" it calls into question "the higher, greater, richer" (*HH* "Preface" 6). The antiquarian mode of history is just or justified because it obeys the limits imposed on it by the government of life and its *Du solltest* and hence, just like Nietzsche's posterior vision of the free spirit, knows what it can and may do (*HH* "Preface" 6). Nevertheless, the form of justice associated with the antiquarian mode of history constitutes only an "incipient stage of justice" (*Anfänge der Gerechtigkeit*) that rests on self-preservation and, more generally speaking, is "animal like" (*tierhaft*) (*D* 26). In this sense, this form of justice is ranked lower than that which is associated with the power and right arising from "spaciousness of perspective" (*HH* "Preface" 6).

Monumental History: Action as a Measure of Justice

Whereas, from the perspective of life, the past receives its due only from the antiquarian mode of history, what justifies monumental history is that its historical knowledge has the power to protect the present against the past and the future. The injustice peculiar to the monumental form of historical knowledge consists in taking from the past only what is useful for the present. The monumental historian seeks in the past exemplary instances of action that he can imitate or repeat in the present. The interest of life in a monumental history is the interest of life in the power to act in the present. But, just like in antiquarian history, the injustice of monumental history with respect to the past is a form of justice with respect to life because one can only act justly in the present; the temporal horizon of just action is neither the past nor the future. Monumental history is therefore that form of history which allows for the existence of justice as action. Insofar as action stands higher than self-preservation, monumental history is assigned a higher place in the order of rank of justice than the antiquarian mode of history.

What characterizes the monumental historian is his faith in the everlasting greatness of humanity:

> For the commandment which rules over him is: that which in the past was able to expand the concept "man" and make it more beautiful must exist everlastingly, so as to be able to accomplish this everlastingly. That the great moments in the struggle of the human individual constitute a chain, that this chain unites mankind across the millennia like a range of human mountain-peaks. (*HL* 3)[17]

As such, the monumental historian responds to the need of life to strive and act in the present and turns to the past in view of finding models worthy of imitation. But there is here no reverence toward the past. On the contrary, the monumental historian commits an injustice to the past because what it is looking for in past models is not what makes them past, or historical, but rather what makes them inimitable: the monumental historian seeks to imitate of the past only what is most inimitable about it, that is, what is most everlasting about it.[18] The monumental historian will therefore always privilege the great and heroic over the regular, average, and normal:

> As long as the soul of historiography lies in the great *stimuli* that a man of power derives from it, as long as the past has to be described as worthy of imitation, as imitable and possible for a second time, it of course incurs the danger of becoming somewhat distorted, beautified and coming closer to free poetic invention; there have been ages, indeed, which were quite incapable of distinguishing between a monumentalized past and mythical fiction, because precisely the same stimuli can be derived from the one world as from the other. (*HL* 2)

Under the predominance of the monumental mode of history, "the past itself suffers *harm*: whole segments of it are forgotten, despised, and flow away in an uninterrupted colorless flood" because, from the perspective of the monumental, there exists only the eternal present of a series of inimitable, singular, and unique actions: "only individual embellished facts rise out of it like islands" (*HL* 2).

Furthermore, the injustice pertaining to the monumental historian in many ways resembles that which Nietzsche typically refers to as the injustice of the genius:

> *Injustice on the part of the genius* [*Ungerechtigkeit des Genies*].—Genius is most unjust toward genius, when they happen to be its

> contemporaries: in the first place it believes it has no need for them and thus regards them as superfluous for it is what it is without them; then their influence clashes with the effect of *its* electric current: on which account it even calls them *harmful.* (*HH* 192)[19]

Since the plastic force of the monumental historian designates the power to grow out of oneself by oneself, such a being typically depreciates the value of his contemporaries, be they other geniuses or simply average men. He is like the artist who overestimates himself and the quality of his work and is not in a position to do justice to the work of others. However, the depreciation of the other is vital for the one who is entirely motivated by the imperative to extend the everlasting greatness of humanity through his actions. The monumental historian cannot but distinguish himself from his contemporaries, even if this means incurring an injustice against them.

Although monumental history shields the present from falling back into the past, it does not do so in view of eternalizing the present. In fact, for the monumental historian "to feel historically" means to have surpassed both past and present (*KSA* 8:5[157]). Monumental history inscribes into the present a task, a duty to fulfill—namely, that of accomplishing an action that is as inimitable and unique as its exemplars. In this sense, the injustice that establishes the priority of the present and of action, considered from the perspective of the becoming of life, is a form of justice. However, this duty can be fulfilled only by an action that occurs in the present, but whose truth and meaning lie beyond it. This is why the monumental historian adopts an untimely perspective when he evaluates the past or the present.

According to Nietzsche, monumental history is needed especially in an age where greatness is lacking. The monumental historian must then adopt the perspective of the philosopher "who deliberately under-assess[es] it [the present age] and, by overcoming the present in himself, also overcomes it in the picture he gives of life" (*HL* 2). In other words, the monumental historian must stand above his age and become untimely, thus incurring the risk of meeting everywhere the hatred and resistance of the average men: "For everything else that lives cries no" (*HL* 3). The untimeliness of the monumental historian is reflected in his way of evaluating the past—namely, by measuring it against his own singular standard.[20] The idea of singularity as a measure of justice should not, however, be confused with an individual, subjective, and arbitrary way of measuring, because Nietzsche holds that with the increase of individual standards of measurement (*individuelle Massstäbe*), injustice also increases (*KSA* 9:4[101]). Rather, singularity provides us with a just measure because it exemplifies an incomparable fullness of life.[21] In contrast to modern historicists who measure what is great in the past against the mediocrity of the present age, thereby assimilating the fullness of life of the former to the poorness of life of the latter, the monumental historian is just when he interprets the past out of the fullness of life of the present:

> *If you are to venture to interpret the past you can do so only out of the fullest exertion of the vigor of the present*: only when you put forth your noblest qualities in all their strength will you divine what is worth knowing and preserving in the past. Like to like [*Gleiches durch Gleiches!*]. (*HL* 6)

The untimeliness of monumental history is due to the fact that the action it seeks must be such as to stand out in the present as what is inimitable by the present. This it can never ultimately achieve by itself: the actor himself does not decide on the greatness of his deed. From the perspective of life, the truth of the action lies always beyond the present, and is the object of the third form of history, critical history.

Critical History: Truth as a Measure of Justice

Whereas from the perspective of life, the past receives its due only from the antiquarian mode of history, the present from the monumental mode, what justifies critical history is that its historical knowledge has the power to safeguard the future against the past and the present. The interest of life in a critical history is the interest of life in re-beginnings, which require the destruction of the past: "man must possess and from time to time employ the strength to break up and dissolve a part of the past" (*HL* 3). The injustice peculiar to the critical form of historical knowledge consists in judging and condemning the past and the present for the sake of the becoming of future life. In other words, the injustice of the critical historian consists in giving the future a past from which it would like to originate, a past that fits its needs of renewal, and which is not the past from which it derived.

Critical history is a response to the need of life to judge and condemn the past and the present, but this destructive drive of the critical mode of history is directed toward the liberation of a new and incipient form of life. From the perspective of life, only those who construct the future have the right to judge the past (*HL* 6). The critical historian has the right to judge the past because its objective is to implant "a new habit, a new instinct, a new second nature" (*HL* 3). This is how it gives expression to the plastic force of life which "heals wounds," "replaces what has been lost," and "re-creates broken molds" (*HL* 1).

Whereas antiquarian history measures the value of the past from the needs of self-preservation, and monumental history does so from the needs of action, critical history measures the value of the past from what Nietzsche calls the will to truth as justice. Critical history therefore takes the highest place in the order of rank of justice, for the standpoint of truth as justice reflects the most spacious perspective. In contrast to both the antiquarian and the monumental, the critical form of history is the only properly historical form of history that strives for knowledge of the past. It arises from a genuine need for memory (historical) in contrast to the need for forgetfulness (unhistorical) found in the other two modes of history:

> Sometimes, however, this same life that requires forgetfulness demands a temporary suspension of this forgetfulness; it wants to be clear as to how unjust the existence of anything—a privilege, a caste, a dynasty, for example—is, and how greatly this thing deserves to perish." (*HL* 3)

The critical historian takes on the role of the judge who desires and demands truth as final judgment, truth as the "*ordnende und strafende Richterin*":

> [F]or he [the just man] desires truth, not as cold, ineffectual knowledge [*folgenlose Erkenntniss*], but as a regulating and punishing judge [*ordnende und strafende Richterin*], truth, not as the egoistic possession of the individual, but as the sacred right [*heilige Berechtigung*] to overturn all the boundary-stones [*Grenzsteine*]; in a word, truth as final judgment [*Weltgericht*] and not, for instance, as the prey joyfully seized by the individual huntsman. (*HL* 6)

The measure of truth upheld by the critical historian does not correspond to the ideal of scientific truth found in modern historicism. The critical historian who stands under the government of life condemns as untruth "what to him, as a living being and one productive of life, is destructive and degrading" (*HL* 4), and declares as truth what to him as a living being is life-enhancing and future-promising.

According to Nietzsche, justice requires the ability to judge, measure, and evaluate correctly. For instance, to do justice to the Greeks requires that we evaluate them correctly (*KSA* 8:6[51]).[22] Here greater knowledge appears as a condition of justice insofar as it makes our judgments more measured (*mässiger*) and more just (*gerechter*) (*KSA* 8:3[76]).[23] However, this condition of justice is not met by the critical mode of history, for it is life and not knowledge that here judges, measures, and evaluates the past:

> It is not justice which sits here in judgment [*zu Gericht sitzt*]; it is even less mercy which pronounces the verdict [*Urtheil*]: it is life alone, the dark, driving power that insatiably thirsts for itself [*sich selbst begehrende Macht*]. Its sentence is always unmerciful, always unjust, because it has never proceeded out of a pure well of knowledge [*reinen Borne der Erkenntniss*]; but in most cases the sentence would be the same even if it were pronounced by justice itself. "For all that exists is *worthy* of perishing. So it would be better if nothing existed [*entstünde*]." (*HL* 3)

The injustice of the critical historian is due to the fact that he does not rely on pure knowledge as the measure of justice, but on his own vitality as a living being: a "dark, driving power that insatiably thirsts for itself" (*HL* 3). However, from the perspective of life, one needs to be a living being (*ein lebendiger Mensch*) before one can be a fair judge (*gerechter Richter*) (*HL* 3), and the verdict of the critical historian is just when the increasing or decreasing vitality of life provides the measure of justice.

In other texts, Nietzsche offers a series of conditions that need to be observed in order to avoid injustice in one's judgment of the past. Nietzsche claims, for example, that in relation to the past, one should evaluate the past from within, according to its own standard of measure. Rather than imposing upon the past a standard of measure that does not do it justice, one should better refrain from judging at all: "*Judge not*" (*HH* 101). Furthermore, with respect to the tragedies of Aeschylus and Sophocles, for example, one should acknowledge that it is impossible to do them justice because it is impossible to fully understand them on the basis of what we know about them (*GMD*).[24] In both cases Nietzsche recommends, in the name of justice, to remain silent and refrain from judging when one lacks the right measures or is simply not in a position to know or understand the object in question. The historian who seeks to reach a just verdict of the past must therefore have the strength to acknowledge his own limitations and in certain cases be able to withhold judgment. This requires cultivating the right temperament to attain justice, showing that being able to apply the right measures also means that one has become oneself more measured.[25] Justice does not simply arise from the instrumental application of correct measures and proportions, but requires that one knows how to incorporate and impose on oneself order and measure.[26]

In the case of the critical historian, the difficulty is not to avoid injustice, but how to build a new and just order on the basis of error and injustice. The critical historian is fully aware of the extent to which "to live and to be unjust is one and the same thing" (*HL* 3), or, as Nietzsche later writes, that "the whole of human life is sunk deeply in untruth" (*HH* 34). The kind of injustice the critical historian sees himself confronted with reflects what Nietzsche in *Human, All Too Human* calls "necessary injustice [*nothwendige Ungerechtigkeit*]":

> All judgments as to the value of life have evolved illogically and are therefore unjust. The falsity [*Unreinheit*] of human judgment derives firstly from the condition of the material to be judged, namely, very incomplete, secondly from the way in which the sum is arrived at on the basis of this material, and thirdly from the fact that every individual piece of this material is in turn the outcome of false knowledge [*unreinen Erkennens*], and is so with absolute necessity [*voller Nothwendigkeit*]. Our experience of another person, for example, no matter how close he stands to us, can never be complete, so that we would have a logical right to a total evaluation of him; all evaluations are premature and are bound to be. Finally, the standard [*Maass*] by which we measure, our own being, is not an unalterable magnitude, we are subject to moods and fluctuations, and yet we would have to know ourselves as a fixed standard to be able justly to assess [*gerecht abzuschätzen*] the relation between our self and anything else whatever. (*HH* 32)[27]

The dilemma of the critical historian is that of the heroic human being who, "however much he may strive after justice," is "bound, according to the human limitations of his insight, to be unjust" (*SE* 4).

The false or impure basis of judgment is particularly problematic for critical history because, in relation to the other two forms of history, critical history judges the past as a function of its drive to truth: critical history wants knowledge, more so than antiquarian and monumental history. Seen from the perspective of life, critical history is life's knowledge, where antiquarian history aims for the preservation of life, and monumental history for the action of life. Critical history expresses life at its highest level of self-awareness. But since life lives of untruth and illusion and injustice, the judgment that is brought about by life's knowledge can never be based on a pure, whole knowledge of the whole. What form does such knowledge take so as to remain true to its ground in falsity and illusion, in the impossibility of having a pure knowledge? How can life be just (and justified) when its essence is injustice? Nietzsche's answer is that critical history is a form of tragic wisdom.

The justice of critical history is a tragic form of justice. It is so in two senses. First, tragic knowledge is the awareness that the essence of the world is expressed by life and not by knowledge. Tragic knowledge is an awareness of the intrinsic limitations of knowledge in all spheres of life: the solutions for the problems of life never come in the form of knowledge but of illusion, dreams, art. That is why, as Nietzsche says in *The Birth of Tragedy*, it is ultimately only art that justifies life, this life which teaches that "it would be better if nothing existed" (*HL* 3). In a second sense, the justice of critical history is a tragic justice because the critical historian knows from the very beginning that justice will never be attained: he has to believe that his judgment is the last judgment (*Weltgericht*) in order for new life to emerge, and yet it can never be sure that this coming life will prove it to have been in the right (*HL* 8; see also *KSA* 9:15[3]). The final paradox in Nietzsche is that the justice that critical history metes to the past and the present for the sake of bringing about a new life, a re-beginning of life, itself enjoys only a posthumous existence.

7

Life, Injustice, and Recurrence

SCOTT JENKINS

Thus Spoke Zarathustra reaches its climax at the end of the third part, where Zarathustra finally confronts what he terms his "abysmal thought" and whispers his wisdom to the figure of Life (*Z* III "The Convalescent"; *Z* III "The Other Dancing Song"). Readers of Nietzsche are in almost universal agreement that the thought Zarathustra slowly confronts and then whispers to Life is the doctrine of the eternal recurrence. Here I argue that this position is mistaken. It is not the eternal recurrence that torments Zarathustra, but instead a pessimism that arises from confronting what I will call the injustice of life.

My argument for this conclusion draws on Nietzsche's earlier remarks on life and injustice in "On the Use and Disadvantage of History for Life" and *Human, All Too Human*. In section one I consider Nietzsche's claim that life is essentially unjust and argue that this is a claim about the indefensibility of all evaluative judgments. Section two examines Nietzsche's account of the pessimism he takes to follow from apprehending human events from what he terms the suprahistorical standpoint. In section three I show that these positions on injustice and pessimism reappear in *Human, All Too Human*. Section four connects these earlier views with central elements of *Thus Spoke Zarathustra*. Section five then argues that in light of these points of contact, we must conclude that Zarathustra's abysmal thought is the thought of the injustice of life—not the thought of the eternal recurrence. I conclude in section six by providing an explanation of why Nietzsche nevertheless chooses not to draw attention to the importance of this thought of injustice in his account of Zarathustra's development.

Life and Injustice in *Uses and Disadvantages*

Nietzsche's claim that life is injustice receives its clearest expression in "On the Use and Disadvantage of History for Life." There he asserts that injustice is inseparable from life, and that as parts of life we are unavoidably guilty of injustice—". . . to live and to be unjust is one and the same thing" (*HL* 3). We can approach this claim by appealing to Nietzsche's understanding of life in terms of wills or drives. These drives underlie a set of distinctive ends and activities, in relation to which objects have a particular status. The drives that underlie these ends and activities thus present the living thing with a world that is "colored" with value (*HL* 1; *GS* 7, *GS* 301). As living beings, then, we are *valuing* beings existing in a world full of things that appear agreeable or disagreeable, tasty, repulsive, inspiring, worthy of love, and so on. And this kind of value—a matter of standing in relation to an act of valuing rooted in a drive—is the only sort of value that Nietzsche takes to exist (*Z* I "On the Thousand and One Goals").[1]

Of course, we are not the only valuing beings. The drives that constitute us are just one way in which life presently exists and has existed in the past. And as Nietzsche repeatedly emphasizes in his notes, he takes even simple organisms such as amoebas to possess drives that color their world with value. Nietzsche does recognize that there are significant differences between an amoeba's drives and the drives that distinguish modern human beings, such as a drive to truth, or to equality. He aims to account for these differences by providing diverse explanations of drives, sometimes appealing to biological selection, sometimes to historical contingency, sometimes to social forces, and so on.[2] I am not concerned here with the details of Nietzsche's categorization and explanation of drives, or with the question of whether Nietzsche's theory of drives is plausible. For my purposes, it is sufficient to note that Nietzsche understands our values to be essentially connected with drives that have particular, contingent histories.

This is where the charge of injustice first becomes comprehensible. Our evaluative judgments are unjust because we cannot demonstrate their authority by showing that they are privileged in relation to any other estimations of value.[3] Nietzsche sometimes expresses this point by claiming that we are unjust because our value judgments are illogical (*HH* 32; *GS* 111). The claim here is not that in making evaluative judgments we necessarily make a logical or factual error of some sort, perhaps by taking the objects of those judgments to possess value in themselves.[4] It is rather that an accurate understanding of why we take something to possess a particular sort of value does not provide us with any way of defending our judgment in the face of a radically different judgment. While there always exists some explanation of why an individual, group, or species possesses a particular drive and associated estimation of value, that explanation does not demonstrate that another individual, group, or species with a different drive and associated estimation of value is in the wrong. The same sort of explanation could be given in the other case, and Nietzsche maintains that these processes lack an inner logic that might enable us to rank their products as more or less rational.[5] In short, there is nothing logical about being the outcome of a contingent historical, social, or biological process. Our drives are just one way in which life does exist, or could exist. Thus we have no *right* to privilege our present estimations of value, or the value-properties that constitute the world as we currently see it, in relation to the estimations and value-properties connected with some other configuration of life.

We can now explain Nietzsche's claim that living things are necessarily unjust. To live is to value, and all valuation is illogical and thus unjust.[6] As living beings, then, we possess unprincipled preferences for some objects and states of affairs, as well as unprincipled aversions to others. Nevertheless, we cannot help but retain our value judgments and respond to the value-properties that we see in the world. It is a consequence of this injustice in valuation that all of our actions, which express our drives and are responses to what we take to be valuable, are likewise unjust. In "On the Use and Disadvantage of History for Life" Nietzsche remarks that a person who acts, "recognizes the rights only of that which is now to come into being and no other rights whatever" and is for this reason (borrowing Goethe's phrase) "always without a conscience" (*HL* 1).

While Nietzsche holds that all life is unjust in this sense, he also maintains that most people have very little awareness of this injustice in their valuations. He describes such people as living within a "horizon as narrow as that of a dweller in the Alps" (*HL* 1) insofar as they are not aware of what exists outside the "valley" of their own conative and affective perspective. He also notes that a parochial outlook of this sort has its advantages. Nietzsche says of the Alps-dweller that "in spite of this injustice and error he will nonetheless stand there in superlative health and vigor, a joy to all who see him" (*HL* 1). We might think of this vitality as resulting from the fact that the value-properties that stimulate action "shine" at their brightest when a living being has no reason to doubt the authority of its own evaluative judgments. In a later context Nietzsche speaks of life as "*conditioned* by the sense of perspective and its injustice" (*HH* "Preface"), and in

"On the Use and Disadvantage of History for Life" he describes injustice as creating the "atmosphere" in which we can live, "germinate," and be "fruitful" (*HL* 1, *HL* 7). These remarks yield a second sense in which injustice is essential to life. A living being not only cannot help but be unjust, but also flourishes in its injustice.

These remarks first appear in an essay on history because Nietzsche regards some ways of practicing history as capable of damaging this atmosphere and thus retarding life. There are many strands in Nietzsche's critique of the practice of history, and I will consider just a couple. On the one hand, Nietzsche claims that history "confuses the feelings and sensibility when these are not strong enough to assess the past by themselves" (*HL* 5). While some persons see in the past a range of persons, events, ways of life, and values that they might emulate in creative ways, others are overcome by this diversity. These weaker types have less confidence in their own perspective of value once they encounter other perspectives that cannot be understood as parts of their own. The result of this encounter, for the weaker person, is an increased sense of justice that damages the atmosphere in which such a person lives (*HL* 7). In these cases a "retreat to the Alps"—perhaps through a denial of unnerving historical diversity—is necessary for life. Nietzsche sees a second form of historical justice in the recognition of what is "crude, inhuman, absurd, or violent" in the past (*HL* 7). Awareness of these features of history is said to undermine the "pious illusions" that shape our lives. This talk of piety, weakness, and confusion suggests that Nietzsche holds in high regard the justice involved in facing up to these historical phenomena. In fact, he terms justice the "rarest of virtues" (*HL* 5). I will set aside the question of why Nietzsche regards this justice as a virtue and will instead consider a relation to past and present that has an even more severe effect on the subject.

The Suprahistorical Standpoint

The two instances of justice I have described involve engaging with the past while at the same time seeing oneself within history. Nietzsche maintains that the practice of history can also lead one to what he terms the "suprahistorical" (*überhistorisch*) standpoint *outside of* history. From this standpoint, he claims, surveying the series of human events reveals a single timeless structure underlying the diversity of ways of life that overwhelm the weaker person (*HL* 7). But apprehending this structure leads to disgust or nausea (*Ekel*) in the suprahistorical person, accompanied by a reluctance to go on living, and it's this response to history that will tie Nietzsche's remarks in "On the Use and Disadvantage of History for Life" to *Thus Spoke Zarathustra*.[7]

> . . . in opposition to all historical modes of regarding the past, [suprahistorical persons] are unanimous in the proposition: the past and the present are one, that is to say, with all their diversity identical in all that is typical [*typisch gleich*] and, as the omnipresence of imperishable types, a motionless structure of value that cannot alter and a significance that is always the same [*ewig gleicher Bedeutung*]. Just as the hundreds of different languages correspond to the same typically unchanging needs of humanity, so that anyone who understood these needs would be unable to learn anything new from any of these languages, so the suprahistorical thinker beholds the history of nations and of individuals from within, clairvoyantly divining the original meaning [*Ursinn*] of the various hieroglyphics and signs: for how should the unending superfluity of events not reduce him to satiety, over-satiety, and finally to disgust [*Ekel*]? (*HL* 1)

I will consider three questions in connection with this passage. First, what exactly is this imperishable structure that underlies the past and future and renders them (in this respect) identical? Nietzsche describes it as a *value* possessing a meaning or significance that is always the same. Just as all languages are identical in the sense that they express those basic needs that are distinctively human, all nations and individuals are said to be identical in that they express the same unchanging value. Nietzsche does not name this value, but the value essential to all nations and individuals could only be one connected with life itself. As I have already stated, I take Nietzsche to understand life as a matter of being driven one way or another. But there is one further essential quality of life, which Nietzsche states in "On the Use and Disadvantage of History for Life" by describing life as that "dark, driving power that insatiably thirsts for itself" (*HL* 3). In addition to aiming at particular ends, a living thing *also* aims at itself, that is, at the maximal expression and expansion of its particular drives. This second-order drive is the other essential feature of life in *HL*. We can see in this feature of life the influence of Schopenhauer's talk of a will to live—a "greedy" relation of life to itself that Schopenhauer regards as the "most real thing we know" and the "kernel of reality itself."[8] Nietzsche's talk of life thirsting for itself also anticipates his own theory of life as will to power. To be sure, Nietzsche opposes his theory to Schopenhauer's, claiming through his mouthpiece Zarathustra that where there is life there is "not will to life but—thus I teach you—will to power" (*Z* II "On Self-Overcoming"). What matters for my purposes here is not the differences between these two views (which concern the question of whether life aims at self-preservation or at self-overcoming), but rather the general form of these theories. Both Nietzsche and Schopenhauer understand life as having an immutable structure, take that structure to involve a relation of life to itself, and aim to explain phenomena such as animal life, the human will, and world history through appeal to that structure. In "On the Use and Disadvantage of History for Life," the suprahistorical person is described as one who grasps that all of history is a matter of life aiming at, and thus *valuing*, the maximal expression and expansion of particular drives. That life aims at itself is an essential part of what Nietzsche describes as the "wisdom" characteristic of the suprahistorical person (*HL* 1).

My second question concerns the claim at the end of this passage that all events in history are superfluous. Why should apprehending the essential features of life that underlie human history lead one to regard all individual events and actions as superfluous? If anything, it would seem that apprehending life's thirst for itself would lead one to grant even greater importance to the particular drives that shape world history. The answer to this question lies in the fact that as a "power that insatiably thirsts for itself," life is indifferent to what its constitutive drives are. In thirsting for itself, it wants its drives—whatever those may be—to be exercised and to grow. But this means that any *particular* drive, and any action based upon it, is superfluous in the sense that it could, in principle, be replaced by another. Suprahistorical wisdom is the apprehension of this superfluity. It sees in all human history only the essential structure of life and takes any particular drive and associated action (that is, a drive with a particular content, or an action with a particular effect or end) to be unnecessary. In "On the Use and Disadvantage of History for Life" this wisdom is connected with the virtue of historical justice—both because this wisdom is a matter of regarding individual actions as they are, and because the suprahistorical standpoint is opposed to the partiality toward one's own drives and evaluations characteristic of the injustice of life.

At this point we can turn to a third question—namely, why is the suprahistorical person's reaction to this superfluity one of disgust? I will begin by noting that disgust is a state of a *living* being, a bodily response composed of an aversion and an unpleasant affect. Disgust is also triggered by a particular object, such as a piece of feces or rotting food. In this case, the state of unpleasant aversion on the part of the suprahistorical person arises from apprehending the "unending superfluity of events" (*HL* 1). The claim, then, is that as living beings, we find ourselves with an unpleasant aversion to the human actions and events that constitute world history once we apprehend that they are all superfluous. This is the case, I suggest, because living beings regard their own actions as good only if they are in pursuit of an end that is itself valuable. This assurance that one's ends are valuable is precisely the state of the Alps-dweller described in "On the Use and Disadvantage of History for Life." But from the suprahistorical point of view, it becomes clear that this condition is never satisfied, and cannot be satisfied. Actions and drives have value not by way of their orientation toward a particular end or activity, but only as instances of life itself. Our ends have value only in relation to a particular drive, and this drive is contingent and unnecessary in relation to the whole of life. Thus the living being finds itself driven to pursue certain ends and to engage in particular activities, while its suprahistorical wisdom at the same time ensures that it regards those particular ends and activities as arbitrary and completely lacking in worth. It recognizes "the delusion, the injustice, the blind passion" present in its own actions (*HL* 1). The result of this clash of standpoints is a state analogous to a particular case of disgust, such as the disgust that arises from a drive to eat in the presence of rotting food. In the more general case, suprahistorical wisdom ensures that not just the drive to eat, but all of one's first-order drives are in the presence of a world that is contrary to the conditions of their satisfaction. Thus the atmosphere of value in which the living being acts and strives has been destroyed, and the living being finds itself "sated" (as Nietzsche puts it), and ultimately in a state of total disgust. And because no feature of a particular human life underlies this disgust, the suprahistorical person ultimately finds all of human existence to be superfluous. From the suprahistorical standpoint outside the perspective of a particular living being, individuals and their actions simply don't matter.

Suprahistorical wisdom thus yields an extreme form of pessimism. Nietzsche and Schopenhauer both turn to literature in expressing their pessimistic assessments of human existence. In "On the Use and Disadvantage of History for Life" Nietzsche describes the historical justice opposed to the injustice of a particular living perspective as the Mephistophelean view that "all that exists is worthy of perishing . . . So it would be better if nothing existed" (*HL* 3). Earlier in the work he states that the suprahistorical person might be able to "say to his heart" these words by Giacomo Leopardi:

> Nothing lives that is worthy
> Thy agitation, and the earth deserves not a sigh.
> Our being is pain and boredom and the world is dirt—nothing
> more.
> Be calm.
>
> (*HL* 1)

Lurking behind Nietzsche's interest in talk of pain, boredom, and calm is Schopenhauer. It is Schopenhauer, of course, who understands human existence as a pendulum swinging between pain and boredom.[9] And Schopenhauer believes that apprehending this fact leads one to an ascetic life of minimal willing. This process of living beings coming to understand their predicament as parts of life gets summed up through the epigraph of *The World as Will and Representation*, "*Ob nicht Natur zuletzt sich doch ergründe? (Goethe)*"—roughly, the question of whether nature will finally fathom itself. For Schopenhauer, this self-fathoming does occur in living individuals, and it leads them to a pessimistic asceticism.

This sort of pessimism has its origins in Greek poetry and tragedy. Schopenhauer lists Theognis and Euripides among his predecessors, noting that we can find in their writings the claim that it would be best for all of us never to have been born—with the next best thing to pass quickly out of existence.[10] Nietzsche of course orients *The Birth of Tragedy* around the wisdom of Silenus, which he formulates using a remark from Aristotle's *Eudemos*—"The very best thing is utterly beyond your reach not to have been born, not to *be*, to be *nothing* . . . the second best thing for you is: to die soon" (*BT* 2). The theory of life as injustice that we find in Nietzsche's work functions as a demonstration of this tragic wisdom. It aims to make clear those features of our existence that, when apprehended by the individual, generate a pessimistic response to life and an inability to go on living.

Pessimism in *Human, All Too Human*

So far I have focused on the awareness of injustice characteristic of the suprahistorical standpoint and the pessimistic assessment of life that Nietzsche takes to follow from it in "On the Use and Disadvantage of History for Life" and *The Birth of Tragedy*. But this pessimism is not limited to Nietzsche's earliest writings. It appears clearly in *Human, All Too Human*, and as I will argue in the next section, it serves as the central problem of *Thus Spoke Zarathustra*.[11] In *Human, All Too Human* Nietzsche asserts that we are "unjust beings *and can recognize this*: this is one of the greatest and most irresolvable discords of existence" (*HH* 32). As in "On the Use and Disadvantage of History for Life," Nietzsche here asserts that the discord of existence arises when our awareness of injustice clashes with the point of view of an individual living being, which is characterized by an inability "to live without evaluating, without having aversions and partialities" (*HH* 32).

More important for my purposes, this opposition between two points of view a living being can occupy also yields a pessimistic assessment of existence. This "discord of existence" is the topic of the section of *Human, All Too Human*, which is entitled "Error regarding life necessary for life" (*HH* 33). There Nietzsche states that it is only through our inability to "feel our way" into others and partake in their fortunes and sufferings that we can take existence to have value (*HH* 33). This lack of imagination enables us to privilege our own perspective, and to see the world and our actions as "lit up" with value (*HH* 33). On the other hand, Nietzsche here imagines a process through which a single person might experience what he terms the "total consciousness of humanity," thus leaving behind his own particular point of view and treating all as equal (*HH* 33). The result is similar to the disgust described in "On the Use and Disadvantage of History for Life."

> . . . if he succeeded in encompassing and feeling within himself the total consciousness of humanity he would collapse with a curse on existence—for mankind has as a whole *no* goals, and the individual man when he regards its total course cannot derive from it any support or comfort, but must be reduced to despair [*Verzweiflung*]. If in all he does he has before him the ultimate goallessness of man, his actions acquire in his own eyes the character of useless squandering [*Vergeudung*]. But to feel thus *squandered* [*vergeudet*], not merely as an individual but as humanity as a whole, in the way we behold the individual fruits of nature squandered, is a feeling beyond all other feelings. (*HH* 33)

The affinity between these remarks and the pessimism of "On the Use and Disadvantage of History for Life" should be obvious. Because apprehending the total consciousness of humanity reveals that no perspective is privileged, that each contains a set of contingent drives and values and nothing more, the person who takes this point of view is no longer able to find any course of action worth pursuing. As in "On the Use and Disadvantage of History for Life," the individual's assessment of his own existence is quickly generalized, yielding the result that the efforts of humanity are squandered, superfluous, and in vain. And this thought leaves the individual in an affective state beyond all others.

Thus in both "On the Use and Disadvantage of History for Life" and *Human, All Too Human*, Nietzsche identifies essential features of life and argues that our recognition of those features leaves us, as living beings, in a state of disgust and despair, incapable of going on living. We simply cannot continue to live and will if we fully apprehend the essential features of our own existence. The route to this apprehension varies. In "On the Use and Disadvantage of History for Life" Nietzsche appeals to a standpoint outside history, while in *Human, All Too Human* the multitude of individual perspectives plays this role. Earlier, of course, it was Greek tragedy and Wagnerian opera. But Nietzsche's understanding of the effect of apprehending our predicament does not change. As he puts it in *The Birth of Tragedy*, "knowledge kills action" (*BT* 7).

Pessimism in *Thus Spoke Zarathustra*

I will now turn to some points of contact between my reading of these passages and central elements of *Thus Spoke Zarathustra*. First there is Zarathustra's distress in hearing the soothsayer's doctrine "All is empty, all is the same, all has been" (*Z* II "The Soothsayer"; *Z* III "The Convalescent"). This doctrine closely resembles the claim in "On the Use and Disadvantage of History for Life" that past and present are identical insofar as they contain a single structure of value determined by essential features of life (or, as a "soothsayer" like Schopenhauer might put it in this context, by the nature of the will).[12] Nietzsche also describes the doctrine as claiming that all of our fruits have turned rotten, and that all of our work is in vain (*Z* II "The Soothsayer"), which echoes his earlier talk of human action as a useless squandering similar to the squandering of the fruits of nature.

Second, consider Zarathustra's distress in considering the persons he encounters—"Naked I had once seen both, the greatest man and the smallest man: all-too-similar to each other, even the greatest all-too-human" (*Z* III "The Convalescent" 2). If we understand seeing something naked as seeing only its essential qualities, then it would be clear why Zarathustra finds this vision distressing. The great person would be, in this respect, no different from anyone else, and would offer no ideal for action. We might see here the wisdom of the suprahistorical standpoint, which takes all human drives and actions to be equal—and equally superfluous. Zarathustra's suggestion that the greatest and the smallest are both instances of the "small man" (*der kleine Mensch*) encourages this reading. He states, for instance, that he has been troubled by the thought that ". . . man recurs eternally! The small man recurs eternally!"—a remark that presents his notion of the small man as a matter of regarding all humanity as insignificant (*Z* III "The Convalescent" 2).

Third, consider Zarathustra's reaction of disgust (*Ekel*) upon confronting an unnamed "abysmal thought" (*abgründlicher Gedanke*) sometimes characterized simply as his abyss (*Abgrund*) (*Z* III "The Convalescent" 2).

Whatever this thought is, Zarathustra first reacts to it by collapsing as a dead man would and remaining on the ground as if he were dead. Upon regaining consciousness, he continues to lie on the ground, pale and shaking, and has no desire for food or drink. We can see here a reaction similar to the disgust of "On the Use and Disadvantage of History for Life," which leaves a person disinclined to go on living. Zarathustra's reaction to his abysmal thought is first one of an apparent lack of life, followed by mere consciousness without the most basic drives of life, those for food and drink.

Eternal Recurrence and Zarathustra's Abysmal Thought

These three points suggest a remarkable conclusion. The abysmal thought that plays such an important role in *Thus Spoke Zarathustra* is not the thought of the eternal recurrence, as many have assumed, but instead the thought of the essential injustice of life—or something quite close to this.[13] Zarathustra's response of disgust and a lack of interest in food, drink, and life more generally is the same as that of the suprahistorical person, and at one point this response is tied directly to the soothsayer's doctrine (*Z* II "The Soothsayer"). In addition, his realization that all persons are small and insignificant (no matter how great they appear within history) furnishes him with the object of the suprahistorical person's disgust, namely the superfluity of all events in relation to an unchanging structure of life. The abyss (*Abgrund*) that Zarathustra gradually confronts as *Thus Spoke Zarathustra* progresses must be the fact that all that human action involves injustice—is *groundless* in the way described in "On the Use and Disadvantage of History for Life"—and is thus a useless squandering.

The claim that Zarathustra's abysmal thought is not the eternal recurrence also gains support from other parts of Nietzsche's writings. In *Ecce Homo*, for example, Nietzsche characterizes Zarathustra as one who has the hardest, most terrible insight into reality that has thought the "most abysmal idea," nevertheless does not consider it an objection to existence, not even to its eternal recurrence (*EH* "Zarathustra" 6). Understanding the abysmal thought as that of the eternal recurrence seems to make nonsense of the passage.[14] Consider as well Zarathustra's characterization of himself as "the advocate of the circle" moments before he summons up his "most abysmal thought" (*Z* III "The Convalescent" 1). This suggests that the abysmal thought cannot simply be the thought of the circular course of all things. Thus my approach is at least consistent with other important passages.

But what, then, is the relation between the abysmal thought and the doctrine of eternal recurrence? This passage from *Ecce Homo* suggests that accepting the doctrine of recurrence makes the abysmal thought even more difficult to accept, which would explain why Nietzsche would refer to the eternal recurrence as the "highest formula of affirmation" (*EH* "Zarathustra" 1). The interpretation I have articulated fits this point neatly. In *Thus Spoke Zarathustra* Nietzsche connects the thought that "all is empty, all is the same" (*Z* II "The Soothsayer") with the conclusion that "everything deserves to pass away" (*Z* II "On Redemption"), and in "On the Use and Disadvantage of History for Life" awareness of injustice is said to produce the judgment that everything is worthy of perishing (*HL* 3). For a person in possession of this wisdom, the thought that all individual events—including all human actions—actually recur infinitely many times would be exceedingly difficult to accept.[15] Thus following my interpretive approach, affirming recurrence requires more of a person than does affirming a world in which all is injustice and emptiness. Zarathustra's own words also suggest this approach. In "The Convalescent" he distinguishes between a satiety (*Überdruss*) with humanity, which follows from the thought of the small man, and a satiety (*Überdruss*) with "all existence," which follows from "the eternal recurrence even of the smallest" and leads to the almost unbearable disgust (*Ekel*) that Zarathustra endures at the beginning of this section (*Z* III "The Convalescent" 1). Thus Zarathustra's most extended discussion of recurrence presents that doctrine as combining with the doctrine of the small man to generate a thought that is even more difficult for Zarathustra to confront.[16]

Understanding the doctrine of recurrence as serving only to intensify a person's reaction to the injustice of life has two more significant virtues. First, it does not require that the doctrine of recurrence be true. Following this approach, Nietzsche would be concerned with the question of whether a person thinking the abysmal thought of injustice could endure taking recurrence to be true, or could even want it to be true. Neither question requires that we read Nietzsche as maintaining that individual events do recur eternally. This is a benefit of my approach because nowhere in the published writings does Nietzsche himself state that the recurrence doctrine is true. Figures such as "the spirit of gravity" (*Z* III "On the Vision and the Riddle" 2), Zarathustra's animals (*Z* III "The Convalescent" 2), and the demon of *The Gay Science* (*GS* 341) state that all events recur eternally—but Nietzsche does not. In fact, in "On the Use and Disadvantage of History for Life" he states clearly that individual entities do not recur. He ridicules the Pythagorean doctrine of recurrence and states that the chain of causes in the future will *not* produce any individual persons or events "exactly similar to what it produced in the past" (*HL* 2). He also describes the question of whether one would want to relive the past simply as a test of one's attitude toward life (*HL* 1).

Second, my approach also explains why other figures in *Thus Spoke Zarathustra* have no trouble confronting the eternal recurrence (*Z* III "The Convalescent"). They have not thought Zarathustra's abysmal thought of the injustice of life. To use the image from "On the Use and Disadvantage of History for Life," they remain safely enclosed within the atmosphere of their injustice. From this point of view—what Nietzsche previously termed the "unhistorical" (*HL* 1)—affirming recurrence is exceedingly easy and also somewhat ridiculous. Zarathustra suggests as much in "The Convalescent" when he mocks his animals as "buffoons" for repeatedly formulating the recurrence doctrine.[17] Consider as well Zarathustra's earlier response to the dwarf's claim, in "The Vision and the Riddle," that "time itself is a circle" (*Z* III "On the Vision and the Riddle" 2). Zarathustra responds angrily, "do not make things too easy for yourself!" and he later speaks of "my thoughts and the thoughts behind my thoughts" (*Z* III "On the Vision and the Riddle" 2). Here again Zarathustra presents the thought of recurrence by itself as rather easy to confront, and he suggests that another thought lies behind his engagement with eternal recurrence.[18]

It might seem, however, that if we understand the doctrine of recurrence as serving only to intensify a person's reaction to the injustice of life, we cannot then make sense of the importance that Nietzsche himself accords to the eternal recurrence. After all, Nietzsche later describes himself as "the teacher of the eternal recurrence" (*TI* "Ancients" 5) and flags the eternal recurrence as "the fundamental conception" of *Thus Spoke Zarathustra* (*EH* "Zarathustra" 1). Is this really compatible with taking the injustice of life to be the content of the abysmal thought that Zarathustra slowly confronts? I will respond by noting, first, that my approach is compatible with recurrence being the fundamental conception of *Thus Spoke Zarathustra*. Nietzsche makes this remark as he labels the idea of eternal recurrence "the highest formula of affirmation that is at all attainable," and my interpretation is compatible with this being the case. Because the thought of recurrence intensifies a person's reaction to the injustice of life by postulating the infinite recurrence of what is "empty" and thus "ought to perish," it is difficult to imagine a higher form of the affirmation of life. Thus, as the highest formula of affirmation, the eternal recurrence can serve as the fundamental conception of *Thus Spoke Zarathustra*, even though eternal recurrence is rather easy to affirm if one has not recognized the injustice of life and drawn a pessimistic conclusion from it.

The more pressing worry concerns the relative prominence of the eternal recurrence in Nietzsche's thought. If the thought of the injustice of life is this important for Zarathustra's development—and for Nietzsche's thought more generally—then why do we hear relatively little about it, and so much about the eternal recurrence? Why does Nietzsche describe himself as the teacher of recurrence—not the teacher of injustice? I will make two points in response to this worry. First, Nietzsche actually refers to the doctrine of injustice on a number of occasions. Within *Thus Spoke Zarathustra*, for example, Zarathustra is chastised with the remark—"You will, you want [*begehrst*], you love—that is the only reason why you *praise* life" (*Z* II "The Dancing Song"). That life appears praiseworthy only from within a perspective of willing and desiring is one of the central doctrines of "On the Use and Disadvantage of History for Life." And in *Ecce Homo*, Nietzsche concludes his discussion of *Thus Spoke Zarathustra* by drawing attention to Zarathustra's "great disgust [*Ekel*] over man" (*EH* "Zarathustra" 8). The injustice of life does remain a central theme in these contexts.

The second point to consider in accounting for the relative prominence of eternal recurrence in *Thus Spoke Zarathustra* and in *Ecce Homo* concerns Nietzsche's aims in his writing. Nietzsche's many allusions to the eternal recurrence count against my identification of injustice as Zarathustra's abysmal thought only if we assume that Nietzsche aims to draw the most attention to the doctrine that he takes to be most fundamental, most troubling, and most problematic in connection with life affirmation. While this assumption might sound reasonable, there is good reason to question it. Here again it is useful to return to "On the Use and Disadvantage of History for Life."

The Antithesis of Life and Wisdom

Nietzsche begins "On the Use and Disadvantage of History for Life" with a remark from Goethe: "In any case, I hate everything that merely instructs me without augmenting or directly invigorating my activity" (*HL* Preface). This remark serves as the starting point for Nietzsche's critique of the practice of history because he will argue that to each form of history there belongs a distinctive sort of harm that serves to retard human activity—"historical justice . . . is therefore a dreadful virtue because it always undermines the living thing and brings it down: its judgment is always annihilating" (*HL* 7). The purpose of the essay is to uncover these "disadvantages" of history for the sake of understanding how the practice of history can become most useful for life. In the particular case of suprahistorical wisdom concerning the injustice of life, Nietzsche maintains that in almost every case this wisdom is disadvantageous for life. Thus, immediately after describing the disgust that arises within the suprahistorical standpoint, Nietzsche proposes to leave the topic behind.

> But let us leave the suprahistorical men to their disgust [*Ekel*] and their wisdom . . . Let us at least learn better how to employ history for the purpose of *life*! Then we will gladly acknowledge that the suprahistorical outlook possesses more wisdom than we do, provided we can only be sure that we possess more life: for then our unwisdom will at any rate have more future than their wisdom will. (*HL* 1)

Suprahistorical wisdom receives relatively little attention in "On the Use and Disadvantage of History for Life," but not because Nietzsche takes the injustice of life to be unimportant. He clearly states that it is the content of a fundamental sort of wisdom, and he notes that its effects on an individual are overwhelming. But he turns his attention to other topics because he sees an "antithesis of life and wisdom" (*HL* 1) and thinks it unlikely that this wisdom will enhance the lives of his readers.

Zarathustra also sees an antithesis between life and wisdom. In "The Dancing Song" he states that he is entranced by Life precisely when he finds her unfathomable (*unergründlich*) (*Z* II "The Dancing Song"). This remark recalls Schopenhauer's epigraph to *The World as Will and Representation*—the question of whether nature will finally fathom (*ergründen*) itself. Thus Zarathustra is telling us that he appreciates the vitality that is possible when one lacks wisdom concerning the essential injustice of life. Later in this section Zarathustra notes that he is well disposed toward wisdom as well. On the reading I have offered, this attitude toward wisdom eventually results in Zarathustra fathoming life and its injustice. Thus by the end of the third part of *Thus Spoke Zarathustra*, Zarathustra is acquainted with both the life-enhancing effects of lacking wisdom and the disgust that fathoming the abysmal character of life inevitably produces in a living thing.

We should not be surprised, then, if Zarathustra chooses his remarks largely through consideration of their likely effect on the lives of his listeners—not simply with the aim of expressing the greatest wisdom. And Zarathustra's remarks do exhibit a concern for his listeners. For example, after describing his animals as "buffoons and barrel organs" due to their formulation of the doctrine of recurrence, Zarathustra reacts to their repeated statements of recurrence with silence (*Z* III "The Convalescent" 2). This desire to spare others the effects of his wisdom reappears in "The Other Dancing Song" (*Z* III). In this final confrontation with the character

Life, Zarathustra chooses to whisper his wisdom into her ear, leaving others (including the reader) in the dark concerning the content of that wisdom. This choice is surely motivated by the unsettling, disadvantageous nature of Zarathustra's wisdom. Both Life and Zarathustra weep after confronting it. All of this shows that my account of Zarathustra's abysmal thought is not only consistent with the relative prominence of the recurrence doctrine, but also capable of explaining exactly why Zarathustra becomes secretive and silent as the third part of *Thus Spoke Zarathustra* concludes.

In arguing that the injustice of life is actually the content of Zarathustra's abysmal thought, I have not even begun to engage with some of the most intriguing questions that arise in this context. Zarathustra's reasons for aiming to confront the injustice of life remain unclear. It is also a mystery why Zarathustra says, following his confrontation with Life, that "life was dearer to me than all my wisdom ever was" (*Z* III "The Other Dancing Song"). Obviously Zarathustra does find a way to affirm the series of events that evokes disgust in the suprahistorical person. He succeeds in saying "yes" to all things—a task that Nietzsche describes as his own task as well (*EH* "Zarathustra" 8). Understanding how Zarathustra accomplishes this, and why Nietzsche chooses to present the solution to his own task in allegorical form, would require that we return to the antithesis between life and wisdom first announced in "On the Use and Disadvantage of History for Life." While nothing I have said suggests a way of overcoming this antithesis, recognizing its importance within *Thus Spoke Zarathustra* does point to a way forward in interpreting this enigmatic work.

8

Heeding the Law of Life

Receptivity, Submission, Hospitality

DANIEL CONWAY

> As the will to truth thus gains self-consciousness—there can be no doubt of that—morality will gradually perish now: this is the great spectacle [*Schauspiel*] in a hundred acts reserved for the next two centuries in Europe—the most terrible, the most questionable, and perhaps also the most hopeful of all spectacles.
>
> **—Nietzsche, *GM* III: 27**

In this essay, I attempt to make sense of the conclusion of Nietzsche's *On the Genealogy of Morals*,[1] which was written and published in 1887. In doing so, I direct my focus not to the final section of the book, whose contributions are by no means trivial, but to the penultimate section of the book, which is Section 27 of Essay III. I further restrict my focus to the concluding sentences of this unusually dense section.

My reason for restricting so severely the focus of my investigation is that I am interested in charting the various endings that Nietzsche is obliged to provide as he approaches the conclusion of the book. He is most obviously obliged to bring to an end the Third Essay, thereby completing his promised account of the *meaning* of ascetic ideals. Equally obvious, he must bring to an end the free-swinging "polemic" (*Streitschrift*) that is *On the Genealogy of Morals* itself. Less obviously, he must bring to an end the program of education and training that informs the book with its peculiar rhetorical-dramatic structure. It is not often noticed that *On the Genealogy of Morals* is presented as a didactic training exercise, wherein Nietzsche conducts a largely one-sided conversation with his intended readers, instructing and guiding them as he advances the book's wandering narrative toward its oft-deferred conclusion. As he concludes *On the Genealogy of*

Morals, will he now expose this program of education and training as a rhetorical prop, perhaps even as a writerly indulgence? Or has this program induced genuine, discernible change in those readers whom it has escorted, supposedly, from innocence to experience?

Even less obviously, Nietzsche somehow must bring to a close the complex rhetorical exercise that comprises Sections 23–27 of Essay III, wherein he communicates only indirectly with his best readers as they wrestle with the startling implications of his exposé of the ascetic ideal. Unwilling to identify them directly and unambiguously as the last knights of the Christian-ascetic ideal—and not, as they wishfully suppose, as the long-awaited conquerors of the ascetic ideal—he deploys an array of rhetorical devices that are designed to help them to arrive on their own at this painful realization. Were they to do so, he believes, they would finally be in a position to oppose the will to truth that motivates their scholarly pursuits. In that event, he allows, the will to truth would "become conscious of itself as a problem" (*GM* III: 27). It would do so, moreover, in and through *them*, on the strength of their Nietzschean regimen of self-directed experimentation.

According to Nietzsche, the stakes associated with these endings are exceedingly high. Nothing less than the future of humankind (or overhumankind) hangs in the balance. The "great spectacle [*Schauspiel*]" that will unfold in the centuries to come, featuring the collapse of Christian morality, will be "the most terrible, the most questionable, and perhaps also the most hopeful of all spectacles" (*GM* III: 27).[2] Presumably, Nietzsche means in *On the Genealogy of Morals* and related writings to influence the eventual modality of this "perhaps," such that his readers (or, more likely, their progeny) will partake of the hopefulness that he associates, counterintuitively, with the demise of Christian morality. That this "spectacle" will qualify as the "most terrible" and "most questionable" known to human history is probably beyond dispute. That it also might qualify as the "most hopeful of all spectacles" is plausible, or so we might speculate, only if humankind were somehow to emerge strengthened, rather than devastated, by its long, costly apprenticeship to morality.

As if to suggest that some such result might be in the offing, Nietzsche cheerfully predicts that the survivors of morality, for whom he presumes to speak in the first person plural, will realize (and say) that "our old morality too is part of the comedy" (*GM* "Prologue" 7). He presents this realization as having a potentially libratory effect on them, inasmuch as it affords them the luxury of looking back (and down[3]) on morality. Having done so, he suggests, they are likely to laugh at, and make light of, the leaden seriousness of their moral investments. He goes so far as to predict that these survivors will come to see morality as a dramatic innovation scripted and staged by a trickster deity—"the grand old eternal comic poet of our existence" (*GM* "Prologue" 7)—who delights in the struggles of human beings cast in absurd and increasingly complex roles. If *On the Genealogy of Morals* is to have the effect Nietzsche immodestly claims for his writings, such that he is entitled to speak here on behalf of a genuine "we," the book must play some role in placing his best readers in a lineage that also includes these envisioned survivors of morality.

In short, one of his central aims in *On the Genealogy of Morals* must be to connect his best readers with a possible future in which humankind not only survives the death of God, but also thrives in its new, extra-moral, post-theistic, overhuman incarnation. He endeavors to forge this connection, as we have seen, by resorting to a tried-and-true dramatic artifice that he attributes, approvingly, to the nobles of Greek antiquity: We (or "we") are to understand ourselves as players on stage, performing comic roles designed for us by spectator deities (*GM* II: 23). The mortal spell of morality will be broken, and the burden of guilt lifted from our shoulders, when we come to share in the realization he ascribes to the survivors of morality: *This, too, is part of the comedy*. If we follow the recipe perfected by the noble Greeks, we will come to understand our most heinous transgressions not as the inevitable expressions of a flawed and sinful soul, but as transient fits of lunacy produced in us by gods who delight in recalling the extroverted cruelty that is native to our core animality (*GM* II: 23).

It is at least mildly ironic that Nietzsche would nominate himself for the post of managing the endgame of late modernity. Adept at opening new vistas, fresh channels of inquiry, unexplored lines of interrogation, and novel angles of vision, he was notoriously inept at bringing his various experiments and investigations to a satisfying conclusion. He regularly revisited his finished works, improving and expanding them while advancing new interpretations of their aims and accomplishments. To his *Zarathustra*, pronounced complete in its original, tripartite form, he famously added a parodic fourth part modeled on a satyr play. To the writings from the pre-Zarathustran period of his career, he added new titles, prefaces, sections, poems, and other materials. To the writings from his post-Zarathustran period, he appended all manner of postscripts, epilogues, songs, and so on. Perhaps the most extreme instance of this dilatory tendency is *The Case of Wagner*, which he finally relinquished only after adding a conclusion that expressed three summary "demands" (*Forderungen*) (*CW* 12), a postscript, a second postscript, and an epilogue. When Nietzsche sought to brand European modernity as unable to be done with anything—and, so, as in need of an emetic—he may have had himself in mind.

Nor does this concern pertain exclusively to his oft-remarked fussiness about style, drama, rhetoric, and presentation. His prodigious gifts as a thinker and critic naturally lent themselves to labors of diagnosis, disclosure, retrieval, and interpretation. He was chronically unsure about what course of action, if any, his interpretations might warrant, what prescriptions and prognoses his diagnoses might support, and so on. Toward the end of his sanity, moreover, he became increasingly enamored of a cheerful fatalism that Robert Pippin has recently linked to the "equanimity" that was prized by the French moralists.[4] The decadence of late modern European culture has advanced to the point, he came to believe, that we can do little more than to suffer the decay to run its full course. Arresting the spread of decay, much less reversing it, is simply beyond the capacities (and aspirations) of most late modern Europeans.

In this light, in fact, it becomes increasingly apparent how curious it was (and is) that Nietzsche offered to steer the late modern epoch toward an appropriate and timely close. If the aforementioned "spectacle" is slated to unfold in any event, then how might he (or we or "we") possibly ensure that it is "hopeful" as well as "terrible" and "questionable"? More fundamentally, how can it possibly matter if his readers do or do not grasp the full implications of the insights embedded in his genealogy of morality? What is it that we (or "we") are supposed to have learned, or perhaps become, as a result of faithfully following the tangled thread of his genealogical narrative?

Still, it must be said of Nietzsche that he was unusually sensitive to the need for European philosophers, and European culture in general, to attend more honestly to the practice of preparing for death. Long distracted by the false promise of a rewarding afterlife, Europeans had largely failed to consider what it would actually mean for an individual, an institution, a people, an epoch, or a civilization to die well.[5] In their anticipations of a terminal stage, or so he observed, late modern Europeans tended to misplace their most powerful resource—namely, *science*—reverting instead to the heavily moralized fables and superstitions disseminated by the priests. Nietzsche is thus distinguished from most philosophers by the scientific intensity of his morbid preoccupations. He knew that God was dead, that Christian morality would soon perish, and that late modern European culture was drawing to a close. Yet he refused to conclude on the basis of the available evidence that all was lost. He maintained until the end the buoyant cheerfulness that marks his post-Zarathustran writings.

We might say of Nietzsche that he was neither an optimist nor a pessimist with respect to the future of humankind, but a realist. As such, he encouraged in his readers a degree of hopefulness that was consistent with his grim diagnosis of late modernity. Although we are powerless to alter the decay of late modern European culture, he believed, we are not yet authorized to surrender ourselves to cynicism, resignation, pessimism, or defeatism. We still may position ourselves to affirm the demise of Christian morality and contribute thereby to the dawning of a post-theistic, extra-moral successor epoch.[6]

Section I

Toward the end of *On the Genealogy of Morals*, in an apparent attempt to tease something resembling a conclusion from his rambling indictment of the ascetic ideal, Nietzsche suddenly (and ominously) invokes the law of life:

> All great things bring about their own destruction through an act of self-cancellation [*Selbstaufhebung*][7]: thus the law of life [*das Gesetz das Lebens*] will have it, the law of the *necessity* of "self-overcoming" ["*Selbstüberwindung*"] in the nature of life—the lawgiver [*Gesetzgeber*] himself eventually receives the call: "*patere legem, quam ipse tulisti*" [Submit to the law you yourself proposed.] (*GM* III: 27)

Hoping to impress upon his best readers that he and they occupy a node of world-historical transformation, Nietzsche dangles before them the tantalizing possibility that their seemingly unremarkable labors of *self-overcoming*—most notably, as we shall see, their experimental, self-directed challenge to the will to truth—may converge with, and in fact expedite, the historical *self-cancellation* of Christian morality. Owing to the unprecedented opportunities afforded them by their unique historical situation, that is, he and they are poised to host the final stage in the demise of Christian morality.

This is Nietzsche's first reference in *On the Genealogy of Morals* to the "law of life,"[8] and it appears at a crucial (and conspicuously *late*) juncture in the elaboration of his main narrative. We very well may wonder if this "law of life" is anything more than a *lex ex machina*, clumsily devised to allow a beleaguered author to tame an unruly tale. Or is this reference perhaps meant to test how closely we have followed the lessons of *On the Genealogy of Morals*? Is this not precisely the kind of self-serving, *ad hoc* appeal that Nietzsche's genealogical approach is generally supposed to expose and banish? If it is not, then we certainly are entitled to wonder why he did not mention this law earlier in *On the Genealogy of Morals*, especially if he intended all along to spring it on us in the eleventh hour. Surely he might have revealed earlier in the book that Christian morality and the ascetic ideal—the ostensible targets of his polemic—are already and irreversibly deathbound, owing to their implication in a suspiciously Hegelian dynamic of self-cancellation. Indeed, the collapse of Christian morality is presented here as a fait accompli. There is nothing that Nietzsche's readers can or must do to seal the demise of Christian morality. It would appear, in fact, that the "law of life" actually absolves his readers of any responsibility for causing or facilitating the collapse of Christian morality. In that event, however, we would be led back to the questions raised earlier about the intended aims of the book: What is the point of acquainting us with the irresistible enforcement of the "law of life"? How are we meant to respond to this revelation?

More charitably, we may understand Nietzsche's reference to the "law of life" as a natural extension of his observations thus far. Throughout *On the Genealogy of Morals*, he has commented instructively, if sporadically, on the nature and essence of life, often refining his position in antagonistic response to positions staked out by rival theorists. In one such instance, he explicitly opposes himself to Herbert Spencer, who, he claims, defined "life itself . . . as a more and more efficient inner adaptation to external conditions" (*GM* II: 12). In doing so, he elaborates, Spencer managed to misplace the very "essence of life, its *will to power*," a blunder that obliged him to disregard "the essential priority of the spontaneous, aggressive, expansive, form-giving forces that give new interpretations and directions" (*GM* II: 12). In general, we find that Nietzsche was keen to insist, as he puts it elsewhere, that the will to power—and *not* the will to self-preservation—is the "cardinal impulse [*Trieb*]" of all living beings (*BGE* 13).

Nietzsche's allegiance to life becomes progressively more visible in Essay III of *On the Genealogy of Morals*, where he explains that the ascetic priest, "this apparent enemy of life," in fact deserves to be counted "among the greatest *conserving* and yes-creating forces of life" (*GM* III: 13). Like Nietzsche himself, that is, the ascetic priest is in fact an agent in the service of life itself. (So much for the simplistic "us versus them" opposition that Essay III originally and "misleadingly" appeared to promote![9]) This insight, in turn, licenses Nietzsche to claim that his own struggle (*Kampf*) with the ascetic priest, a struggle that he endeavors to disclose to his readers as ultimately self-referential and self-consuming, also serves the deepest interests of life. Just as life appointed the ascetic priest to gather, tend, protect—and, ultimately, *exploit*—his herd of sickly sufferers (*GM* III: 15), so life now authorizes Nietzsche to engage the ascetic priest in a struggle destined to result in their mutual assured destruction. Up to this point, that is, life has allowed the ascetic priest to degrade the diversity of human types as he schemed to prolong the decay (and misery) of the sufferers entrusted to his care. But no more. Now, at this specific moment in European history, life deputizes Nietzsche to end the reign of the ascetic priest and to halt the degradation of the highest human types. Life does so, Nietzsche observes, just in the nick of time, as the priest's campaign to eradicate predatory expressions of human excellence nears its species-threatening conclusion.

What life wants, we are now in a position to understand, is for morality to come to an end. (Although this is also what Nietzsche wants, his wishes are relevant, or so he claims, only insofar as they reflect the interests of life [*TI* "Morality" 6].) Having served the interests of life, morality now must expend its residual authority in a final, self-directed act of negation. It must do so, moreover, in and through the efforts of Nietzsche and his best readers, who, he claims, are ultimately responsible for staging this final act. Toward this higher end, Nietzsche urges his best readers—albeit via an extremely indirect mode of communication—to attune themselves to the interests of life itself. What life wants, as we shall see, is for its authorized lawgivers—including Nietzsche and the "*unknown* friends" whom he is keen to recruit—to submit to the legislations they have prescribed to others. In particular, they are enjoined to submit voluntarily to the demands for probity and truth that they have leveled against others.

Section II

At the behest of life, Nietzsche exhorts his best readers to join him in commencing the terminal stage in the demise of Christian morality. Having already grown wise, they now must cultivate and display the virtues of *receptivity*, *submission*, and *hospitality*. In particular, as we shall see, they must *receive* the call to *submit* to the laws they have imposed on others, and *host* the final act in the self-overcoming of Christian morality. They must do so, moreover, as a sincere expression of their own volition, which they will have aligned, voluntarily, with the "law of life." As active, engaged participants in the "spectacle" that is about to unfold, they may say of the ensuing crisis, "Thus *we* willed it!"

If they are successful in doing so, he hopes, they will experience the demise of Christian morality not as an adventitious calamity, but as an expression of their undivided, collective will. To be sure, they will not have caused the collapse of Christian morality, but they nevertheless will regard the necessity of its collapse as compelling their allegiance and commanding their volition. Their communal expression of affirmation will enable them in turn to exert a formative influence on the eventual disposition of the successor epoch. Simply put, Nietzsche believes that the way in which Christian morality comes to an end will play a role in shaping the future of humankind (or over-humankind). Indeed, his recommendation of the virtues of receptivity, submission, and hospitality is meant to ensure that the end of Christian morality will be maximally conducive to the dawning of an extra-moral, post-theistic, overhuman epoch.

Receptivity

The most intriguing aspect of Nietzsche's reference to the "law of life" is his claim that the lawgiver receives the *call* (*Ruf*) to submit to the legislations he has prescribed to others. The reception of this call is thus presented as potentially separable from the lawgiver's inevitable submission to the "law of life." Although the lawgiver must submit in any event, his receptivity to this call positions him to do so of his own volition, on the strength of his voluntary submission to the laws he has prescribed to others. The possibility of receiving this call in advance of one's eventual submission thus introduces an unexpected element of freedom, or self-determination, into Nietzsche's otherwise grim exposition of the "law of life."

Although the source of this mysterious call is not identified, Nietzsche's background historical narrative indicates that he has in mind the call of *conscience*. As we shall see, in fact, the ultimate (and highest) expression of the conscience is the demand of Christian morality, on behalf of Christian truthfulness, that it deliver an honest account of itself. Upon doing so, Nietzsche believes, Christian morality will wither and die, as it acknowledges (and subsequently disowns) its untenable reliance on an unsecured faith in truth. More important, those who press this demand—ultimately, as we shall see, against themselves—will be able to say of the ensuing calamity, "Thus we willed it!"

The conscience has played an important role in the development of the main narrative of *On the Genealogy of Morals*.[10] In a crucial section of Essay II, Nietzsche explained the emergence of human interiority, of which the conscience is emblematic, as resulting from the mandatory inward discharge of instinctual energy (*GM* II: 16). Prohibited from visiting their natural instinct for cruelty upon others, or so he hypothesized, the earliest civilized human beings were obliged to vent their pent-up aggression against themselves. Under the civilizing influence of this enforced regimen of self-directed aggression, human beings involuntarily acquired with respect to themselves an internal point of reference and a corresponding set of self-regarding relationships.[11] The suffering that resulted, which the earliest civilized humans experienced as unbearably meaningless (*GM* III: 28), was instructively linked by the priest to the failure of these sufferers to keep their promises and pay their debts. Eventually, the conscience became popularly associated with the hectoring voice of God, whose authority was believed to underwrite the obligations to keep one's promises and pay one's debts.

The typical human experience of interiority thus manifests itself as what Nietzsche calls the *bad conscience*, inasmuch as this experience pertains exclusively to a reckoning of one's failings, shortcomings, debts, disabilities, errors, vices, and sins. The suffering one endures as a consequence of this inward discharge of animal aggression is thus interpreted as a nagging reminder of one's unfulfilled promise and unrealized aspirations. From here it is but a short step to the *guilty* conscience. According to Nietzsche, the experience of *guilt* is nothing more than a particular, moralized interpretation of the suffering associated with the "bad conscience." Guilty parties suffer, or so they come to believe, because they *deserve* to suffer—owing, supposedly, to an irreparable flaw in the very nature of their being (*GM* III: 15). This interpretation of the pain of the "bad conscience" is ingenious, Nietzsche concedes, for it renders our suffering meaningful and charges us with the impossible task of atoning for our guilt.

The conscience reappears toward the conclusion of Nietzsche's main narrative. Borrowing a passage from Section 357 of *The Gay Science*, Nietzsche explains that the most recent evolution of Christian morality has merged it, improbably, with its former nemesis—namely, modern science:

> The confessional subtlety of the Christian conscience [has been] translated and sublimated into the scientific conscience, into intellectual cleanliness at any price. (*GM* III: 27; *GS* 357)

What Nietzsche would like for his best readers to understand at this point is that *their* conscience, which he identifies as the "scientific conscience," is actually a trustworthy and reliable guide. If they follow their conscience, in fact, they eventually will have no choice but to demand of Christian morality that it face the truth about itself—namely, that its enabling will to truth rests on an unacknowledged faith in truth.[12] (As we shall see, this would be an unmistakably *moral* demand, for it would derive its force from the authority of "Christian truthfulness," which is all that now remains of Christian morality).[13]

This is a potentially momentous revelation on Nietzsche's part, especially in light of his earlier remarks on the origin and development of human interiority. Unlike all previous manifestations of the conscience, which threatened to poison the enjoyment and self-fulfillment associated with spontaneous expressions of instinctual energy, the "scientific conscience" emboldens its possessors to indulge the full measure of their righteous cruelty. Like all civilized expressions of animal instinct, to be sure, their extroversions of cruelty are and must be self-directed. (As we have seen, the target of their purity campaign, the will to truth, now resides only in them.) At the same time, however, Nietzsche apparently means to suggest that the self-directed violence sponsored by the "scientific conscience" admits of a degree of enjoyment, freedom, and self-fulfillment that is virtually unknown to civilized human beings. As they purge themselves of their residual faith in truth, Nietzsche's best readers will understand and experience themselves to be possessed of an undivided will, a functioning system of complementary instincts, a viable network of passions and affects, and a fully integrated "second" nature. In fact, here we might be tempted to identify the "scientific conscience" as an index of the "sovereign individual," in whom, supposedly, the conscience has become the "dominating instinct" (*GM* II: 2).[14]

Channeling their priestly obsession with purity—this, too, is ingredient to the legacy they inherit—they will undertake to purge themselves (*qua* representatives of Christian morality) of their unwashed faith in truth. If they demand of themselves "intellectual cleanliness *at any price* [emphasis added]," moreover, they will risk everything—including their own lives *and* the future of humankind—to banish the untruth that pollutes their otherwise pristine scholarly investigations.[15] This means, as we shall see, that the call of their conscience will conform with, and enable them to comply with, the "law of life." While they must submit to this law in any event, they are historically positioned to express the alignment of their will with its demands.

This call is delivered in Latin, which is the noble language of empire, most notably of the currently vanquished forces of *Rome* (*GM* I: 16). Of course, Latin is also a priestly language, as Nietzsche makes clear when he cites at length from—though refusing to translate into his native German—the hateful teachings of St. Thomas Aquinas and Tertullian (*GM* I: 15). Presumably, those who receive and heed this call will restore Latin to its former position of imperial privilege, even if they do so from within the priestly lineage to which they belong. In them, in fact, we may expect to discover a historically unique and potentially productive mixture of the *noble* and the *servile*, of the *legislative* and the *submissive*, and of the *imperial* (Rome) and the *priestly* (Judea).[16] Fluent in both Latin dialects, Nietzsche's best readers stand a good chance of issuing *and* heeding the call to submit.

Submission[17]

Nietzsche does not identify the lawgivers who are called to submit to their own legislations, but he does provide some instructive clues. From *Beyond Good and Evil*, we know that he regards "*Genuine philosophers . . .* [as] *commanders and lawgivers* [*Befehlende und Gesetzgeber*]," in large part because they decree, "*thus it shall be*!" (*BGE* 211). Presumably, then, the lawgivers referenced in Section 27 will include philosophers. From *The Gay Science*, moreover, we know that Nietzsche places himself and his fellow "*good Europeans*" in the lineage of those German *philosophers*—he names Leibniz, Kant, Hegel, and Schopenhauer—whose legislations have propagated "Europe's longest and bravest self-overcoming" (*GS* 357). Thus we may assume with some confidence that the lawgivers in question are meant to include Nietzsche and his best readers, but only if their contributions to this ongoing process of "self-overcoming" earn them a place within this noble lineage. That they are poised to join this lineage is reinforced by Nietzsche's (indirect) identification of his best readers with those "unconditional honest atheists" whom the passage imported from *The Gay Science* (*GS* 357) reveals as "*good Europeans*" (*GM* III: 27).[18]

If they are to join this lineage, Nietzsche's best readers must acknowledge the unique responsibility that now accrues to its bearers: The time has come for them to submit to the laws they have prescribed to others. It would seem, moreover, that Nietzsche has in mind one particular piece of legislation. Just as their predecessors in this lineage ruled against the lie that had sustained belief in the Christian God (*GM* III: 27), so are they now called to legislate against the kindred lie that sustains *their own* belief in the divinity of truth. In doing so, he further implies, they will submit voluntarily to the law they have prescribed to others, just as they have been called to do. As the imported passage confirms, moreover, they are uniquely qualified to accomplish precisely this, by virtue of the "rigor" (*Streng*) with which their "scientific conscience" asserts itself. Having called to order the entirety of European civilization, they now must call themselves to order.

He continues: Christian truthfulness, which is all that now remains of Christian morality, will draw its "*most striking inference*,"—that is, "its inference against itself"—"when it poses the question '*what is the meaning of all will to truth?*'" (*GM* III: 27). Let us note the similarity of the question that now demands to be asked—"What is the meaning of all will to truth?" (*Was bedeutet aller Wille zur Wahrheit?*)—to the question that serves as the title of Essay III: "What is the meaning of ascetic ideals?" (*Was bedeuten asketische Ideale?*) This similarity, I propose, is no coincidence. Nietzsche's question here advances a more specific formulation of the general question embedded in the title of Essay III. Presumably, those who will pose this question will understand, as his best readers as yet do not, that the will to truth simply *is* the ascetic ideal in its most current incarnation. As he explains,

> [T]his will [to truth], this *remnant* of an ideal, is, if you will believe me, this ideal itself in its strictest, most spiritual formulation, esoteric through and through, with all external additions abolished, and thus not so much its remnant as its *kernel*. (*GM* III: 27)

In other words, asking after the meaning of the will to truth turns out to be the most effective and historically precise way of asking after the meaning of ascetic ideals.

Although Nietzsche does not name the agent(s) who will pose this question on behalf of Christian truthfulness, the question itself recalls the *task* he earlier defined for himself and his best readers. There, as we recall, he explained that:

> From the moment faith in the God of the ascetic ideal is denied, a *new problem arises*: that of the *value* of truth. The will to truth requires a critique—let us thus define our own task [*Aufgabe*]—the value of truth must for once be experimentally [*versuchsweise*][19] *called into question*. (*GM* III: 24)

Owing to the unique historical conditions associated with the "death of God," the task defined here by Nietzsche has become, *for the first time*, both possible and desirable to pursue. In short, the time has come for him and his best readers to assay, truthfully and experimentally, the *genuine* value of truth.[20]

If we now interpret this "task" as authorizing the question that will compel Christian truthfulness to draw "its inference against itself," we may assume that this question will be posed by Nietzsche and those who will join him.[21] Within the context of their experimental assessment of the value of truth, moreover, they will be obliged to pose this question to themselves. No one else is in a position to comply credibly with this inquiry, for the will to truth now resides only in them. Once they pose this question to themselves, or so he apparently means to suggest, they will have no choice but to conclude that "the meaning of all will to truth" lies in its untruthful reliance on an unacknowledged *faith* in the inestimable value of truth. This would mean, of course, that Christian morality, which derives its authority from its animating will to truth, is fundamentally immoral, for it has not been truthful about its faith in truth. Duly obliged to draw its "*most striking inference*," Christian truthfulness will turn the full force of its authority against itself, thereby sealing the demise of Christian morality.[22]

From this point forward, Nietzsche means for his best readers to interrogate the meaning of the will to truth precisely as he has interrogated the meaning of the ascetic ideal. If he has trained them well, moreover, they will arrive at a similar conclusion: Just as the preponderance of ascetic ideals *means* that a will to nothingness has covertly guided the progress of Western civilization (*GM* III: 28), so the preponderance of the will to truth *means* that Western science has advanced only under the aegis of a veiled expression of the will to nothingness. Rather than provide a welcome exit from the ruined labyrinth of late modernity, that is, modern science only exacerbates the ruin it illuminates. Instead of recoiling from this will to nothingness, however, Nietzsche's readers are urged to harness its destructive power in the service of *their* task, which, as we have seen, involves them in an experimental appraisal of the value of truth. By asking after the truth about truth, they may succeed in turning the will to truth—which, as we have seen, shelters a potent will to nothingness—*against itself.*

Hospitality[23]

Although Nietzsche is reluctant to say so explicitly, he thus envisions for himself and his best readers the role of representing Christian truthfulness in its final (and finest) hour, as it issues a mortal challenge to Christian morality.[24] This means, however, that his well-publicized "struggle" with Christian morality is far more complicated and nuanced than we might have thought. In particular, as we shall see, this "struggle" must incorporate and express a counterbalancing measure of respect for, and positive identification with, Christian truthfulness. In short, Nietzsche must recruit readers who are willing, along with him, to *host* the final act in the self-overcoming of morality, to serve collectively as the world-historical agents in and through whom Christian morality asserts and exhausts its residual authority.

This they can accomplish, however, only if they are able to own and affirm their historical identity as representatives of Christian truthfulness. In addition to the enmity that inflames their desire to destroy Christian morality, that is, they must cultivate and display *hospitality* toward the current incarnation of Christian morality. They must do so, moreover, not (simply) in the service of a stratagem or ruse, but as indicative of a sincere, full-throated affirmation of their status as the final representatives (and arbiters) of Christian morality. (This may explain why Nietzsche believes that "the most serious Christians have always been well disposed toward [him]" [*EH* "Wise" 7]). Christian morality may be the target of this strange "polemic," but it is also the source of its authority and must be honored as such.

Here we see most clearly the significance (and complexity) of Nietzsche's allegiance in *On the Genealogy of Morals* to the interests of life. If he and his best readers are to host the final act in the self-overcoming of Christian morality, they must align their interests with those of life. Although they are historically positioned to host the terminal stage in the self-overcoming of Christian morality, they cannot limit or resign themselves to a strictly instrumental role in this process. Indeed, they must own and embody the residual authority of Christian morality. Notwithstanding their enmity for Christian morality and the joy with which they anticipate contributing to its self-destruction, they must affirm Christian morality—including themselves as its final representatives—as a historical development authorized by life itself.

Hence Nietzsche's justification for calling his best readers to cultivate the virtue of hospitality: A relationship to Christian morality predicated exclusively on antagonism will not suffice to further the complex interests of life. As paradoxical as it may sound, Nietzsche and his best readers must identify fully, positively, and unambiguously with the current incarnation of Christian morality, even as they work from within to engineer its (and, so, *their*) demise. The rhetorical indirection and dramatic complexity that inform the concluding sections of Essay III are thus intended to help Nietzsche's best readers to become what they are—namely, double agents in the service of life.

Their performance of this divided office is possible, he explains, because the "law of life" has delivered Christian morality, through a series of self-overcomings, to its final and minimal incarnation. That which remains viable in Christian morality is now concentrated in its animating will to truth, which manifests itself in its final generation of adherents as an unconditional, unflinching demand for truthfulness. As this demand is pressed against the source of its authority, against the will to truth itself, Christian morality will expend its remaining authority and cease to exist as a vital, generative source of meaning and justification. Although Europeans are likely to continue to rehearse the familiar rituals and routines of

Christian morality for centuries to come, they will cease to do so in resolute pursuit of a truth that might set them free.

If Nietzsche and his best readers are to complete the "task" he has defined for them, he will need to convince them that he and they are in fact the last knights of the ascetic ideal. This is precisely the aspect, however, under which they are least inclined to regard themselves. As scientists and scholars in their own right, they pride themselves on their principled opposition to, and liberation from, the ascetic ideal. They are, or so they believe, the truly free spirits whom Nietzsche ostensibly seeks as his rightful companions.[25] Hence the final irony of the program of education and training that Nietzsche undertakes in *On the Genealogy of Morals*: Somehow, he must liberate his best readers from the illusion that they are already liberated from the ascetic ideal. The will to truth will finally become "conscious of itself as a *problem*," he explains, in and through the experiments that he and his "*unknown* friends" will perform on themselves (*GM* III: 27).

This particular claim merits further attention, for it sheds welcome light on the kind of readership, or "we," that Nietzsche has endeavored to build in *On the Genealogy of Morals*. Here he explicitly links their newly determined task to their desire (and corresponding quest) for *meaning* (*Sinn*).[26] That he appeals here to the *meaning* to be found in a collective challenge to the will to truth is indicative of his refusal thus far of "modern science" and its nihilistic campaign to deprive existence—and especially human existence—of the meaning formerly accorded it (*GM* III: 25; *GS* 373).[27] Despite the "death of God" and the impending collapse of Christian morality, that is, a meaningful, future-oriented existence remains possible for them, but only if they pursue and complete the "task" they have defined for themselves.

By implicating himself in a communal quest for collective meaning, moreover, Nietzsche finally acknowledges the full extent of his dependence on his best readers. Earlier, we recall, he alluded to his reliance on them to define and execute the "task" that is uniquely theirs (*GM* III: 24).[28] Here, however, he adverts to a far more basic human need, which only his "*unknown* friends" can meet: He needs their companionship and support if he (and they) are to make adequate sense of—and thereby generate sufficient meaning for—the "task" they are about to undertake. While addressing his "*unknown* friends," in fact, he explicitly identifies *his* problem—viz., the problem of securing adequate meaning (*Sinn*)—as "*our* problem" (*GM* III: 27). Inasmuch as the meaning he seeks is available only if it is shared with them, he effectively acknowledges[29] that he must immerse himself fully—with none of his usual caveats, loopholes, conditions, or reservations—in "*our* whole being" (*Sein*) (*GM* III: 27).[30] In typical fashion, of course, he pointedly withholds himself from his contemporary readers, claiming that "as yet I *know* of no friend" (*GM* III: 27).

Here, I suspect, he is not simply being playful or gnomic. Despite his preference for an increasingly nomadic form of existence, Nietzsche knew several individuals whom he readily acknowledged as current or former friends. What none of these flesh-and-blood friends provided, however, was the genuine sense of meaningful belongingness and collective destiny that his new "task" compels him to cultivate.[31] In short, he needed to assemble a brotherhood of like-minded scholars and "free spirits" who would undertake in his name a coordinated, yet hospitable, assault on Christian morality. And although he says very little here about the "friends" he hoped to attract for this final quest, the perils native to their task suggest a level of intimacy and eroticism that was known to him only in his fantasies. Presumably, the "friends" he seeks will be sufficiently committed to their cause that they will agree voluntarily, even joyfully, to his risky agenda of self-experimentation.

That these "*unknown* friends" will belong to a distant future is treated by Nietzsche as both regrettable and nonnegotiable. As he regularly observes, his contemporary and late modern readers could not possibly sustain the intensity of commitment that the task at hand demands.[32] Aware that he would not take part personally in the final battle against Christian morality, he endeavored to ensure that the "we" in question would consecrate itself in his name. While this may be wishful thinking on his part, he envisioned his contribution to their eventual success as anything but trivial. It was he, after all, who identified for the first time the historical opportunity and historical task that would unite and galvanize this "we." It was he, moreover, who devised the program of education and training that would deliver his readers (*qua* warriors) first to wisdom, and then to the self-referential insight into their own allegiance to the ascetic ideal. Finally, it was he who identified the signature virtues—receptivity, submission, and hospitality—that would prepare this "we" to host the final stage in the auto-destruction of Christian morality. Should such a "we" emerge from the gloaming of late modernity, and should this "we" acknowledge Nietzsche as its progenitor, then he may be "born posthumously" after all, just as he predicted would be his fate (*A* "Preface").

He thus concludes his program of education and training by designing a contest that is meant to remain open-ended.[33] His provocative challenge to his best readers—namely, that *they* are the "last idealists" described in Sections 24–25 of Essay III—effectively invites them to prove their avowed opposition to the ascetic ideal. They will fail in their efforts to do so, of course, for they are in fact the last knights of the ascetic ideal. Indeed, they will arrive at the desired realization only as a result of failing, perhaps repeatedly, to establish their independence from the ascetic ideal. The contest in which Nietzsche has enrolled his best readers is thus intended to continue indefinitely the program of education and training begun in *On the Genealogy of Morals.* As his best readers struggle to assert their avowed independence from the ascetic ideal, failing in the process to establish themselves as free spirits, they will fortify themselves—albeit unwittingly—to undergo the final transformation reserved for them. This means that they will complete their education and training, if at all, on their own time and terms. Of course, Nietzsche's hope is that his best readers eventually will realize that they are *not* liberated from the ascetic ideal, that their scholarly pursuit of science rests on an unscientific will to truth, and that they are morally obliged to tell the truth about truth. They will do so, he further hopes, while acknowledging his formative role in their education and training.

Section III

Obviously, a great deal more needs to be said about these virtues, especially since they stand in such stark contrast to the strong, "manly" virtues that Nietzsche more regularly associates with the highest human types. Our consideration, thus far, of the concluding sections of *On the Genealogy of Morals* supports the following observations.

First of all, these virtues are meant to be cultivated and displayed as *social* virtues, predicated not of any particular individual, but of the collective itself. As such, these virtues contribute to the shared identity of the "we" that will host the final act in the self-destruction of Christian morality. Apparently, a lawgiver will receive and heed the call to submit *only* if he or she is already immersed in the collective identity of a properly constituted "we."

Second, these virtues are presented not as universally expressive of the flourishing of the highest human types, but as specific to the twilight epoch of late modernity. As such, these virtues are not to be confused with the virtues of tragic heroes, world-transfiguring artists, architects of empire, or rampaging beasts of prey. Rather, these virtues pick out the *relatively* higher human types—for example, the "last idealists," the "so-called 'free spirits'"—of late modern European culture. As we have seen, in fact, Nietzsche recommends these virtues only to a circumscribed audience, and only under the exigency of the historical conditions uniquely associated with the death of God. In promoting these virtues to the target audience of *On the Genealogy of Morals*, that is, Nietzsche neither contradicts nor undermines his more familiar expressions of esteem for the noble virtues of the predatory peoples of bygone epochs. Although these are not the virtues that we typically associate with the "higher" human beings whom Nietzsche esteems, they *are* the virtues that he praises and promotes for the transitional historical setting in which his best readers are likely to find themselves.

Third, these virtues are unmistakably *moral* in nature, even if they are cultivated and displayed in the service of Nietzsche's ongoing campaign *against* Christian morality. Much has been made of Nietzsche's avowed opposition to morality, whose precise force and focus scholars continue to dispute.[34] For such an outspoken critic of Christian morality, his readers often note, Nietzsche operates very much within the gravitational pull of Christian morality. He regularly delivers what appear to be moral objections and evaluations, which he directs most vehemently against morality itself. He refers with surprising frequency to the "obligations," "virtues," and "responsibilities" that he acknowledges as pertaining to him and those who are like him, especially in the context of their prescribed assault on Christian morality. In Essay III of *On the Genealogy of Morals*, as we have seen, he reveals that he and his "*unknown* friends" will represent Christian morality in its final hour. As they demand of themselves a truthful account of their faith in truth, they will speak with the full authority of Christian morality.

In short, Nietzsche's opposition to morality is a good bit more complicated than it initially appears. As *On the Genealogy of Morals* confirms, Nietzsche knew himself to be a kind of moralist and endeavored in this capacity to turn morality against itself. Although he opposed himself to Christian morality, he framed and conducted this opposition in distinctly moral terms, appealing both directly and indirectly to the moral authority vested in him. He was, as he explains elsewhere, an *immoralist,* which means, in brief, that he understood himself to be a moral critic (and opponent) of morality (*EH* "Destiny" 2–4).[35] As such, his case against morality remains irreducibly moral in nature. In the end, of course, we may judge Christian morality to have failed on any number of counts, many of which Nietzsche himself has cataloged. According to Nietzsche, however, Christian morality will fail most decisively with respect to its own (moral) standard of truthfulness.

Fourth, these virtues are emblematic of morality only in its death throes, as it pivots and turns against itself. Sponsored by wisdom, who favors those warriors who are not afraid to die, these virtues become prominent and valuable only as a people or culture prepares for death and self-overcoming.[36] Nietzsche thus promotes these virtues in the context of his efforts to manage the endgame of late modernity. These are the virtues that will enable him and his "*unknown* friends" to vanquish Christian morality in the name of Christian truthfulness. Accordingly, these are the virtues that will embolden the last knights of the ascetic ideal—again, Nietzsche and his unsuspecting "we"—to compel the will to truth to acknowledge its reliance on an unscientific faith in the inestimable value of truth.

Fifth, Nietzsche's promotion of these virtues is both continuous with and expressive of the estimable legacy of the "good Europeans." As we have seen, he immodestly endeavored to place himself and his best readers in a philosophical lineage that has contributed decisively to "Europe's longest and bravest self-overcoming" (*GM* III: 27; *GS* 357). This means, I take it, that Nietzsche and his "we" are positioned to submit to the "law of life" only inasmuch as they are evolved creatures of conscience. If this is what Nietzsche means to suggest—and his intent in this dense passage is by no means clear—then he is offering his best readers the truly wondrous opportunity to satisfy simultaneously the demands of morality *and* the "law of life." Apparently, that is, the unique confluence of historical conditions that defines their historical situation has steered Christian morality into momentary convergence with the "law of life." This in turn means that life, which is usually and ultimately indifferent to morality and all other anthropogenic artifacts, temporarily favors those whose aim it is to tell the truth about truth itself.[37]

Here it is interesting to note that Nietzsche regards his confrontation with Christian morality as integral to, rather than independent from, this grand process of self-overcoming. In cultivating the virtues of receptivity, submission, and hospitality, his readers will propagate, rather than suspend, the lineage of the "good Europeans." What is not clear is whether the post-Christian, extra-moral epoch to come also will bear the legacy of the "good Europeans," or whether it will be something entirely new. In light of Nietzsche's abiding Eurocentric chauvinism, we might suspect that he retains some hope that the legacy of the "good Europeans" will survive the disruptions and discontinuities introduced by this particular generation of "good Europeans."

Finally, it bears noting that these virtues are presented as potentially descendant from the virtues that distinguish the readers whom Nietzsche trains in *On the Genealogy of Morals*. His express wish for ruminant readers, those who can afford the time and effort needed to digest his pithy teachings (*GM* "Preface"), adumbrates one of the signal insights delivered in *On the Genealogy of Morals*. As much as he may wish to speak directly and efficaciously to the readers of the future, those who will join him in his assault on Christian morality, *On the Genealogy of Morals* explains precisely why he may and must not do so. The "*unknown* friends" whom he seeks are neither contemporaneous with him nor categorically unrelated to his current audience. So although it would have been (and in fact was) tempting for Nietzsche simply to ignore his contemporary and late modern readers, he endeavors instead to provide these readers with the education and training that will prepare them to vouchsafe the possible emergence of the readers he seeks. Disciplined in the ways of the herd, Nietzsche's ruminant readers will take the time to chew on his untimely teachings. In so doing, they may yet position themselves to beget those future generations of readers that will cultivate and display the virtues of receptivity, submission, and hospitality.

Conclusion

As we have seen, the penultimate section of *On the Genealogy of Morals* announces Nietzsche's intention to inaugurate a distinctly *communal* moment in his campaign against Christian morality.[38] Suspending the nomadic individualism for which he is best known, he not only identifies himself with an unmistakably collectivist "task," but also apportions to a "we" the meaning this "task" is likely to engender. Although he does not say so explicitly, we may assume with some confidence that the virtues sponsored by wisdom—receptivity, submission, hospitality—are meant to be understood as virtues of reciprocal dependency, that is, as belonging or pertaining exclusively to the emerging collectivity.

Nietzsche's devoted readers may bristle at the suggestion of a final, communal moment of collective action. According to him, after all, only the weak are "naturally inclined" to "congregate" in the manner indicated by my interpretation of Section 27 (*GM* III: 18). Here it may be helpful to point out that the collective in question is formed not on the basis of Nietzsche's independent judgment of the political options available to him, but at the behest of life itself. If left to his own devices, or so we might speculate, he may have preferred to engage the ascetic priest *mano a mano* in a winner-takes-all millennial death match. Life, however, has other plans for him, which involve his voluntary immersion in precisely the sort of collective that he has regarded thus far with contempt and suspicion. In other words, it may be psychologically comforting for Nietzsche to claim, and for his readers to hear, that this was not his idea. No less an authority than life itself has decreed that he and his best readers must congregate like weaklings, while habituating themselves in the process to a suite of virtues that they have ridiculed as unacceptably base and servile. Such, however, is the unyielding force of the "law of life," which bends everyone and everything, strong and weak alike, to the necessity of its iron will. What we may hope for with respect to this law is not an exemption from its indiscriminate application, but an opportunity to align our will with its inviolable decrees.

Although this communal moment receives precious little elaboration in the penultimate section of *On the Genealogy of Morals*, it is clearly important to Nietzsche's larger aims. This is the moment, after all, in which he and his "*unknown* friends" will host the final act in the self-overcoming of Christian morality. The arrival of this moment thus presupposes the final transformation that his program of education and training is supposed to induce. If the envisioned collective never materializes, if he and his fellow critics of Christian morality cleave stubbornly to their independent plans of attack, they will squander the unique historical opportunity available to them. As we have seen, moreover, this is the moment in which Nietzsche and his "we" may align their collective will with the "law of life," thereby affirming the necessity of their own self-overcoming.[39]

Finally, it is in this moment that Nietzsche will deliver the various endings that he owes to the readers of *On the Genealogy of Morals*. The book itself, Essay III, the program of education and training, and the indirect communication that occupies Sections 23–27—all point to, and are meant to facilitate, this final transformation of Nietzsche's best readers. As they take up the "task" they have defined for themselves, these warriors beloved by wisdom will become the "we" that will host the final act in the demise of Christian morality. By impressing a distinctly Nietzschean stamp on the conclusion of the late modern epoch, or so he hopes, they may influence the eventual disposition of the successor epoch.

The evolution of Nietzsche's envisioned relationship to his best readers thus reproduces in broad outline what he takes to be the general developmental trajectory of Western history. In particular, we see that a sustaining (noble) hostility to the need and wish for collectivity eventually yields a communal moment in which the whole is consumed and the new epoch inaugurated. Notwithstanding the nomadic, anarchic, and autarkic impulses that have guided Nietzsche's critical engagement with modernity, the late modern epoch must and will end in an explosive expression of a uniquely collective will.

Here we may detect, in fact, a certain resonance with a particular strain of Marxist thought: The internal contradictions native to Christian morality have the cumulative effect of raising to consciousness a previously unacknowledged truth,[40] which catalyzes the production of a primitive communal moment, wherein the prevailing structure is subverted and the stage (and tone) set for what is to follow. Whereas Marx foresaw the revolution and subsequent dictatorship of the proletariat, Nietzsche here anticipates the experimental self-interrogation, and eventual self-cancellation, of an omega caste of warrior-scholars. In both cases, a collective expression of will, undaunted by the likely prospect of imminent self-destruction, is expected to exert a formative influence on the emergence of the successor epoch.

PART IV

The Becoming of a New Body and Sensibility

9

Toward the Body of the Overman

DEBRA BERGOFFEN

The Hypothesis

This paper is (pre) occupied with two bodies: the body of the last man and the body of the overman. Finding, with Nietzsche, that the overman will appear only when the last man has disappeared, it examines the body of the last man to discern what this disappearance might entail. It finds that the body of the last man, as the embodiment of the ascetic ideals of Christianity and Platonism also embodies the misogyny of these Western traditions. The body of the last man is the paradigmatic masculine body. It is a self-possessed autonomous body; a body unsullied by messy materialities (these are deposited onto paradigmatic women's bodies). It creates itself in the image of an invulnerable body, a self-enclosed coherent entity that looks out onto the world but refuses to engage it on anything other than the laws of its making. As a controlled and controlling body, it knows nothing of the risks and joys of becoming. By Nietzsche's criteria of life affirmation, it is a sick, if not dead body. How to find a way from this body to the body of the overman is the question.

Posing the question in this way, I propose the following thesis: the route to the body of the overman lies in a woman's body divested of its stigma. Taking this route, I discover that the body of the overman will live the myth of the eternal return as a riddle whose answer to the question of how to affirm the once more of life lies in an affirmation of the risks of pregnancy and its threat to the stabilities of a coherent and autonomous subjectivity, rather than in the nauseating demand that we affirm the last man's return.

This reading of Nietzsche finds that however blind he usually was to the ways that his announcement of the Death of God and his critique of modernity were also and necessarily a critique of patriarchy, there are places where he seems to be aware of this link—places where the figure of woman challenges hallowed patriarchal truths and speaks both as critic of modern Western culture and as an opening for the coming of the overman. There is the "Supposing truth were a woman" of the Preface to *Beyond Good and Evil*. There are the women life and truth of *Thus Spoke Zarathustra*. There is the woman on her wedding night of *The Gay Science* (*GS* 71), to name a few. Nietzsche's women live the truth of their bodies in shock, shame, and silence. Some of them whisper this truth stripped of its shame to Zarathustra in their dancing songs. We do not hear what they say. It is not clear that Nietzsche understands what he hears. This paper is a gamble. It wagers that we can decipher the whispered truths of Nietzsche's women if we put Nietzsche in conversation with two women who did not dance to his tunes, Luce Irigaray and Julia Kristeva. It bets that staging and listening in on this conversation can show us how to cut a path from the diseased body of the last man to the life affirming body of the overman.

A Word on Translation/Translation of a Word

Nietzsche used the term *Übermensch* to refer to the being that would walk the earth after humanity overcame the ascetic ideal. This term has had an interesting English life. Thomas Common translated *Übermensch* as "superman." James Birx in his amended translation of Common's *Zarathustra* translated *Übermensch* as "overman." In explaining the changes he made to the Common's translation, Birx does not point to his rejection of the English superman for the German *Übermensch*. He simply says that he "replaced archaic words with modern usage and [strived] to achieve a text that is easier to read."[1] Why "overman" is less archaic or easier to read than "superman" is a mystery to me. Walter Kaufmann in his introduction to *The Portable Nietzsche,* which includes *Thus Spoke Zarathustra* says that his new translation was necessary because the older ones of Alexander Tille and Commons were unacceptable. Discussing the particulars of *Zarathustra,* he accuses older translations of missing the cadence and play on words of Nietzsche's German. In his editor's note to *Zarathustra*, he addresses the issue of translating the term *Übermensch*. He explains that he opted for the term "overman" rather than "superman" for philosophical, literary, and historical reasons. Philosophically, he says, the term "overman" brings out the relationship between self-overcoming and the overman. Further, he finds that in terms of literary style it captures Nietzsche's play on the words "over" and "under" in *Zarathustra*'s Prologue. Finally, he notes that since Shaw popularized it as an ironic term, superman has become associated with the comics without losing its ironic twinge.[2] Kaufmann never mentions the ways that the English term "overman" neutralizes the militant, racist chords of the English "superman." This is especially odd given his campaign to absolve Nietzsche of all accusations of anti-Semitism and of his efforts to demonstrate Nietzsche's abhorrence of Fascist, militarist, and racist ideologies. Thus, though Kaufmann, unlike Birx, gives us some explanation of the decision to replace "superman" with "overman," I find his silence on the racist affect of the term "superman" puzzling.

Most recently, Graham Parkes has stepped into the translation fray. He adopts the term "Overhuman" for the German *Übermensch*.[3] He opts for a literal translation—one that is strictly speaking more accurate than either "superman" or "overman." The Parkes translation of *Übermensch* as "Overhuman" has much to recommend it. Like the term "overman," there is no militarist cadence, no comic book character image, no ironic smirk, and no racist resonance lurking in its sedimentations. It has the further advantage of capturing the nonsexist dynamic of the German *Mensch*. Indeed, when Brix amends Common's translation of "*Ich lehre den Übermenschen. Der Mensch ist was,* Überwunden werden Soll" as "I teach you the overman. Humankind is something to be overcome," one wonders why he would render the *Mensch* of *Übermensch* "man," and then translate the *Mensch* that follows immediately as "humankind."[4] It seems that Parkes's Overhuman rendering of *Übermensch* is long overdue.

So why do I not use the Parkes translation in the title of this paper? Surely as a feminist I should welcome this more literal androgynous rendering of *Übermensch*. Translations, as Kaufmann makes clear, are more than a matter of substituting the words of one language for another. They involve literary and philosophical decisions. Given that in titling this paper "Toward the Body of the Overman" I, too, am taking a philosophical position, a word (or two) about this decision would seem to be in order. Two aspects of the decision are broadly feminist and philosophical. One is particular to this paper. Though adopting the term "Overhuman" surely makes the point that the English term "man" cannot legitimately be used to signify humanity, and though it opens the way for Nietzsche's women readers to see themselves included in the charge to take up the rigors of overcoming, adopting this term runs the risk of ignoring the ongoing feminist interpellations of the ways that the materiality of our bodies is lived through the complex ways that our bodies are raced, classed, sexed, gendered, nationalized, and more. It would forget that there is no human being, only diversely embodied human beings. This feminist problem is complicated by a philosophical one. Translating *Übermensch* as "Overhuman" reinforces the meaning of *Mensch* that opposes the human being to the animal. It inscribes the human within a binary operation that I think undermines Nietzsche's project of affirming the animal materiality of the body. Though it would take me too far afield to adequately pursue this issue here, a few words are in order; for Nietzsche's rejection of the binary opposition between the human and the animal is not entirely unrelated to the issue that preoccupies this paper—undoing the stigma that adheres to the body that openly lives its animal materiality—the woman's body.

In her paper "The Overhuman Animal," Vanessa Lemm steps into the translation fray. She adopts the term "overhuman" for Nietzsche's *Übermensch* but follows it with the term animal to make the point that far from opposing the human to the animal, Nietzsche refuses to endorse a hierarchy of being where the human supersedes the animal. In Lemm's reading, Nietzsche's overman "announces the future of human animal becoming."[5] Helping us understand why at the end of his unfruitful search for human companions, Zarathustra surrounds himself with his animals, Lemm argues that:

> The overhuman animal becoming points to a movement of overcoming and self-overcoming that is engendered through a return of animality as that force that irrupts the human, exceeds and tears it apart, to open up the space for its future becomings. The future, instead of being reduced to one and only one "all too human" form of life, opens up to an infinity of possible human animal becomings.[6]

Jennifer Ham shows us what this has to do with women. She writes:

> Both women and animals challenge the philosopher on his way to "becoming what he already is": a fully assumed animal unafraid of the feminine, indifferent to masters, "forgetful" of gender distinctions—open to a limitless, unknown future.[7]

Like Lemm and Ham, I see the issue of animal materiality and women's bodies as central to the question of Nietzsche's project of overcoming and the overman, and like them I tackle this question through the question: What is it about human beings in their current condition that requires overcoming? Without disputing their readings I take a somewhat different, but I think complimentary direction. This different direction puts me in a different place on the translation issue.

The heart of the matter in terms of this paper is that the term "Overhuman" masks the ways that it is not the human being that must be overcome, but the human being as man that must be overcome. The term "Overhuman" suggests that human beings already exist and that they must become something other than human. As I read Nietzsche's descriptions of the sick animal, however, it is not human beings, but the fantasy of masculinity (a fantasy that degrades the animal and woman as animal) that passes itself off as the human that is at issue. What must be overcome is the idea that this fantasy is the reality of the human; for only in overcoming this fantasy can we get to the human. We must, in short, get over man, not the human, if we hope to cure ourselves of the disease of modernity. Or, in getting over man we will also and necessarily get over the denigration of the animal that informs our humanity. Thus, like all translation preferences, my translation of *Übermensch* as "overman" is philosophically packed. One way of reading this paper, is to see it as both an unpacking and as a defense of this preference.

The Fantasy of the Disembodied Man

Nietzsche directed us to pay attention to modernity's denigration of the body, and to the ways that the last man, as the embodiment of this deprecation fashioned himself in the image of a Cartesian disembodied man. Feminists, too, critique modernity's degradation of the body. Being more specific than Nietzsche, however, they consider the ways that this degradation is sexed and gendered. They note for example that women are denigrated because they are identified with the materiality of the body. As bodies, they are compared with nature and animals and are found to be dangerous and uncontrollable. Reduced to being bodies, women are taught to be ashamed of themselves for being bodies. Men, identified with the rational powers of culture and civilization, are said to be in control of their bodies. They are authorized to use their higher powers to regulate unruly bodies, women, animals, and the forces of nature. Their disciplined anti-body Cartesian bodies are idealized as the truth of the human (as distinct from the animal) body. Within the codes of current sex gender systems, the deprecation of the body is synonymous with the denigration of women. From a feminist point of view, or at least from my feminist point of view, Nietzsche's project of validating the body, of re- embodying the human in the figure of the overman, will fall short unless it takes account of the ways our bodies are sexed and gendered and unless it exposes the relationship between the asceticism of the last man's denigration of life and the sex gender systems, which validate this denigration.

Sex/gendered myths of masculine and feminine bodies allow the last man to believe that he is immune from the threat of a world that cannot be managed. They give him license to create an idea of happiness grounded in the utilitarian ideal of a world ruled by the calculations of cause, effect, and usefulness. Within this world women's bodies are good for, that is, useful for, two things: sexual pleasure and reproduction. And here is where things get interesting; for however much the last man wants to keep the disorder of women at a distance, he wants to appropriate her (re)productive powers. On the way to the overman, we need to ask how the last man affects this appropriation. We need to understand what the desire to evade the material realities of creation means. To do this, we need to attend to and become suspicious of the tired metaphors of birth and creation used by male philosophers from Plato to Nietzsche. The Platonic tradition of equating men's mental gymnastics with women's embodied labor, so that men's abstract ideas, which according to Socrates are not of this world, may still be said to have life, is perpetuated by Nietzsche, who, despite his upset with Socrates, will follow him in equating writing and thinking with birthing. Going one better than Socrates, he will be the mother, not the midwife. His innocent child, the creator of new values, will be born the old philosophical way, cleanly and antiseptically from a lion. For the one who is on the way to the overman, the issue is not the legitimacy of the desire to create new ways of being, but the misogynous form this desire has taken. It is a question of detecting this misogyny and of developing the necessary skepticism to confront it. It is a question of finding the right teachers. Nietzsche directs us to three possibilities: the sage, the old woman, the bride.

Learning to Listen to Women

The sage teaches Nietzsche how to listen to women; for though the sage does not claim to know who women are, he does know that in their current form they are nothing more than Platonic reflections of impossible masculine ideals. In his words in the *The Gay Science*: "it is man who creates for himself the image of woman and woman who forms herself according to this image" (*GS* 68). Or at least young women fashion themselves in this way; old women are a different story.

In the *The Gay Science,* Section 64, Nietzsche calls old women skeptics. He writes, "I am afraid that old women are more skeptical in their most secret heart of hearts than any man; they consider the superficiality of existence its essence; and all virtue and profundity is to them merely a 'veil' over this truth." I take these old women to be products of the wedding night where upper-class women,

> brought up as ignorant as possible of erotic matters . . . with a profound sense of shame in such matters . . . [are] hurled as by a gruesome lightning bolt into reality and knowledge by marriage—precisely by the man they love most! To catch love and shame in a contradiction . . . Thus a psychic knot has been tied that may have no equal . . . the ultimate philosophy and skepsis of woman casts anchor at this point. (*GS* 71)

Staying with the sage, the old women, and the young bride for a moment, we may say that women brought up to believe the myth of femininity are schooled in the aesthetics of the ascetic ideal. Following the instructions of sex/gender codes, they learn to be ashamed of their bodies and its passions. They are taught to believe in the romance of marriage only to discover that it is not romance that their husbands want but sex; that the flowers decorating the wedding tables are a prelude to the deflowering of the bridal chamber that is sometimes painful and always bloody. Nietzsche could have stayed with the diagnosis of shame, but good doctor that he is, he went further. What begins as women's shame ends with the truth of the body and its passions unmasking the myths of sex/gender systems and bearings its burdens. Women's bodies as Nietzsche's camel spirit.

Many years later Simone de Beauvoir speaking not of the wedding night (wedding nights having changed considerably since Nietzsche's time) but of abortion, reports a similar awakening of skepticism among women. Women who choose abortion, Beauvoir tells us, are vilified for violating the feminine values of patriarchal motherhood. If they choose to give birth to their illegitimate children, however, the fathers of these unwanted children disavow both mother and child. Women discover that where men "contradict themselves with dizzying cynicism . . . [a] woman feels the contradictions in her wounded flesh."[8] Like Nietzsche, Beauvoir grounds women's skepticism in the truth of their bodies. She writes, ". . . the one sure thing is the manipulated and bleeding womb, these shreds of red life, that absence of a child. With her first abortion, the woman begins to "understand."[9]

Nietzsche's and Beauvoir's women understood. They kept their knowledge to themselves. They rebelled in silence. Nietzsche does not challenge their silence. Beauvoir does. So do the "Madres de la Plaza de Mayo." They took the bodied truth of children torn from their lives to the streets. They exposed the lie of the cold monster who claimed to honor motherhood but violated the mothers of children who were seen as a threat to the power of a state that pursued a policy of invulnerability. (Ironically this myth of motherhood also protected the Madres from the full wrath of the authorities.) The Madres de la Plaza de Mayo refused to play their assigned roles. They refused to suffer in silence. They spoke the truth of the body in pain. They did not, however, equate this truth of the body in pain with the truth of the body. Instead they saw this truth as a violation of the body's truth and turned to the discourses of the law to demand that the state accept responsibility for enforcing their rights as mothers/birthing bodies.

The Materiality of the Maternal Body

Irigaray and Kristeva do not turn to the law. They believe that a politics of motherhood that appeals to the state and its laws carries the risk of supporting the reactive forces of the status quo. They fear that the protest of mothers also can be written off as an episodic event. They fear that once their children are accounted for, their protest will end and the mothers will return to their traditional homebound nurturing roles. In the case of the Madres, this did not happen. The group remains a force for accountability. Nevertheless, these fears are not unfounded; for in appealing to the gendered role of the mother, the Madres are not undermining the patriarchal structure of the law that lies at the heart of the problem of the injustice of their disappeared children. Something more fundamental and radical than a protest in the name of motherhood is necessary—a radical revision of the law's concepts of subjectivity and autonomy; or in Nietzsche's language, a radical challenge to the last man's notions of subjectivity. Kristeva and Irigaray find resources for this revision in the materiality of the maternal body; for they find this body speaking in ways that throw the autonomous body and the subject it validates into turmoil (or as Kristeva might say, psychosis).

The last man is not aware of this danger. He expresses his anxieties in his (mis)reading of the Oedipus tragedy. First he establishes it as the defining account of generational and sexual difference. Then he reads its lesson of the danger of violating the incest taboo through an image of a devouring maternal body that threatens his destruction. Hélène Rouch calls the last man to account. The last man's image of the maternal body is an Oedipal imaginary construct. Invoking the authority of biology, Rouch finds that the last's man's vision of the maternal body bears no resemblance to the material birthing body. Whether one is a cemented last man or capable of his overcoming may be measured by whether or not he can bear to hear Hélène Rouch, as she describes the maternal body as structured through the placenta, a tissue that allows for the embryo's individuation from the mother while remaining related to her. Rouch writes, ". . . the placenta is the mediating space between mother and fetus . . . there's never a fusion of maternal and embryonic tissues . . . it . . . establishes a relationship between mother and fetus."[10] Describing the placenta as relatively autonomous, she finds descriptions of the fetus-maternal body relationship that appeal to images of fusion and aggression "quite poor and . . . extremely culturally determined."[11]

Autonomy in this placental schema denotes a singularity that embraces its ground in the other. This placental economy thinks autonomy in terms of an individuation inscribed in a logic of mediating difference and an ethics of generosity. One comes into being as a singular being through an inscription in the other. Rouch tells us that in order for the placenta, a tissue formed by the embryo, to be produced, "[t]here has to be a recognition of the other, of the non-self by the mother and therefore an initial reaction from her . . . It's as if the mother always knew that the embryo (and thus the placenta) was other and that she lets the placenta know this, which then produces the factors enabling the maternal organism to accept it as other."[12] Though the maternal body's generosity provides the ground for the placental tissue's production, the fetus must respond in kind. It must produce unique placental factors that allow the maternal organism to accept it as other. It must signal that as an alien body, it is not an enemy body—that it does not threaten the mother's body.

The idea of relative autonomy is critical here; for it is not a matter of rejecting the value of autonomy but rather a matter of transvaluing its meaning. Placental mechanisms support the autonomy of the fetus and the mother by regulating an exchange between them where the otherness of the fetus is distinguished from the otherness of a foreign body that threatens the mother's body. These mechanisms do not pit the autonomy of the fetus against the autonomy of the mother. The fetus does not establish its difference by attacking the mother's body. Neither does it deactivate the mother's defense mechanisms against infections. Within the dynamic of the maternal body, there is no contest of Hegelian wills where only one or the other survives, or where the survival of both requires that one submit its identity to the other. The maternal body teaches a different lesson: autonomy figured as absolute is a pawn of the death drive. A fetus that identified itself as absolutely autonomously other would be attacked by a defense system designed to experience the other as a foreign agent and a threat. If the fetus escaped this fate by demanding that the mother's body deactivate its defense mechanisms, the maternal body's survival would be threatened. The pregnant body would be indistinguishable from the AIDS body. Happily for both mother and fetus, the placental economy does not work this way. Ignorant of the dialectic, it deploys what Irigaray calls the labor of love.[13]

In following Irigaray's directive to create an ethics guided by the placental economy, I am not claiming that this is the only economy of the body. The body gives us two models of autonomy and otherness: one maternal, the other medical. The medical model provides us with a paradigm for autonomy. In this economy of disease, infection, and antibodies, the other is identified as a threat to the body's integrity. Acting to maintain its health, the body treats the foreign body as an enemy that must be either destroyed or expelled. If I follow Irigaray's assessment of the relationship between nature and culture, that is, if I find that there is no break between the two, but a process by which one is taken up by the other, then I might suggest that the sexed culture of Oedipus, the culture of the independent autonomous subject and the binary logic of either/or is a cultural appropriation of the medical mechanisms of the body. In directing us to the cultural possibilities of the placental economy, I take Irigaray's point, like Nietzsche's, to be genealogical, ethical, and political. Western culture, having adopted the medical economy of the body, is treading a dead end path. The maternal economy of relational autonomy and generosity offers modernity a life line—an antidote to the anti-life modes of sociality of the last man.

Irigaray's discussions of wonder alert us to the ways that a cultural translation of the maternal body's script of relational autonomy and bodily generosity challenges the last man's world. Nietzsche called us the sick animal. Irigaray agrees. Nietzsche's diagnosis unmasks the ascetic ideal. Irigaray's diagnosis unmasks the blind spot of Oedipal culture.

We can get to the ways that Nietzsche's critique of modernity and Irigaray's critique of phallocentric culture speak to each other by attending to Irigaray's reading of Descartes's *Meditations* in *Speculum* and Descartes's essay on the *Passions* in *An Ethics of Sexual Difference*. Her reading of the *Meditations* establishes the father of modern philosophy as a last man of the first order; for, as Irigaray reads Descartes, his pursuit of a first truth of philosophy is a pursuit of autonomy and the pursuit of autonomy signals a flight from the relational truth of the maternal body.

Reading Descartes through Irigaray comes to this: the desire for certainty, specifically the desire for the certainty of self-identity, must be understood as the desire for an imaginary wholeness/autonomy. The doubt that makes self-affirmation possible must also be understood as a refusal to acknowledge our relationship to the (m)other. The method of doubt, Irigaray tells us, is "a refusal of anything not his same self [and therefore] . . . a refusal of all beginnings."[14] To doubt is to refuse the "precariousness of existence . . . *the chain of relationships, the cord* . . . the mysteries of conception."[15] To escape the precariousness of existence, Descartes will stage his own birth. In solitary confinement, his disembodied thinking will produce the "I" that will assure him of his existence, his God, his truth, and finally of the fact that the body he believed he could discard is intimately his. How different the history of modern Western philosophy might have been if Descartes had heeded Zarathustra's advice and after saying farewell to his body became silent (*Z* I "On the Despisers of the Body").

Reading Irigaray's account of Descartes's *Meditations* from the perspective of her essay on Descartes's *Passions*, I am struck by the ways that Descartes's attempt to escape the precariousness of existence is also and necessarily a repudiation of wonder. In his essay on the *Passions,* Descartes describes wonder as synonymous with surprise with regard to both the new of the unknown and the unexpected of what we already know. The uniqueness of wonder lies in the fact that insofar as we are taken by surprise, we are unable to calculate and must therefore simply attend to the givenness of the phenomena.

Wonder is accompanied by a mood. Whether that mood is anxiety or joy determines the way that wonder situates us in the world and with each other. If accompanied by anxiety it is experienced as a passion to be evaded or overcome. Accompanied by joy, it delights in its encounter with the chance of the world. Directed by Irigaray to return to Descartes's wonder and making this return in the shadow of Nietzsche's last man, I read Descartes's account of the first passion of wonder for its lessons in what must be done for God's ghost to be laid to rest. The lessons are: (1) we must disengage wonder from anxiety; (2) we must learn to prefer the joyful yes of uncertainty that welcomes the unknown, the surprise, the other, to the anxious yes of certainty.

The test of our ability to live these lessons will be found in our tolerance for the proximity of women's bodies—the bodies that speak of the wonder and of the love for the surprises of the other/otherness. The test may be phrased in terms of Nietzsche's description of the relationship between the artist and women. In *The Gay Science*, aphorism 59, Nietzsche tells us that artists love women so long as they maintain their distance, that they resent the woman who gets too close—the woman who confronts them with her bodily being and natural functions. I take these artists to be products of the ascetic ideal. I take them to be the creators of the myth of woman as the eternal feminine—the one whose body in its veiled beauty can lean on the body of the autonomous man for balance and protection so long as she does not get close enough to disturb him with her blood. A lesson in distinguishing the last man from the overman—measure the distance they keep between themselves and women.

Reading Irigaray, we are alerted to the ways that the structure of the placental economy undermines the authority of the autonomous subject. We are not, however, apprized of the full force of the maternal body's threat to the last man. For this, we need to turn to Kristeva; for it is her account of the questionable subject in process, the birthing body as the material instantiation of the poetic subject, and the dangers of psychosis, that leads us to confront the stakes of following the directives of embodied maternal creativity.

Almost echoing Irigaray's descriptions of the almost ethical of the placental economy, Kristeva describes the woman as mother as

> . . . a strange fold that changes culture into nature, the speaking into biology. Although it concerns every woman's body, the heterogeneity that cannot be subsumed in the signifier nevertheless explodes violently with pregnancy and the child's arrival.[16]

This account of the maternal body leads Kristeva where it led Irigaray—to a recognition of the depths of the sexual difference, and to a call for a "herethical ethics" that gives the law "flesh, language and *jouissance*."[17] Confronting what she calls the impossible syllogism of motherhood, Kristeva gives Irigaray's almost ethical of the placental economy another reading. Under Kristeva's eye, the maternal body becomes the site of the event she calls the It. She writes:

> Cells fuse split and proliferate; volumes grow, tissues stretch and body fluids change rhythm, speeding up or slowing down. Within the body growing as a graft indomitable there is an other. And no one is present, within that simultaneously dual and alien space, to signify what is going on, It happens but I'm not there . . . I cannot realize it but it goes on.[18]

The relational subject of Irigaray's placental economy is not yet here. The dual and alien space of becoming a mother lives at the vanishing point where the subject and its speech split apart; the point that Kristeva calls the semiotic, which, lest we be tempted to romanticize, she also identifies as the space that comes close to negating the social symbolic bond—the space of psychosis.[19]

If I align Kristeva's idea of the maternal body as existing in the mode of the luminal subject, with her ideas of the psychotic threat of this liminality and the poesis of maternal-cosmic creativity, I find her asking Nietzsche's artist, who I hear as speaking for the last man, the following questions:

Could you, by coming closer to women, create an art and ethics of the liminal subject of psychosis? Could you embody a cosmic creativity that happens within you but without you? Could you become the voice of a symbolic, social, cultural, and political life that remembered the birthing body? Could you become a semiotic poet?

What occurs invisibly and unconsciously within the maternal body is culturally reproduced in semiotic poetic practices. Mimicking the negative space of the maternal body, poetic language undermines the ideological and metaphysical tendencies of the symbolic by pluralizing the denotations of the word. From the perspective of the subject committed to the project of happiness and its symbolic calculus, the transgressions of poetic language are intolerable. From the perspective of the one who in the process of becoming the overman, the one who has forgone the project of happiness for the risks of wonder and joy, and who in pursuit of these risks and joys is learning to speak the poetic language of music (Zarathustra's language), what Nietzsche calls the illness of pregnancy promises to teach him/her how to revive the symbolic's Greek tragic powers (*GM* II: 19).

In asking us to embrace the creative and ethical space of the maternal body, Irigaray and Kristeva ask us to renegotiate our sense of ourselves as subjects and to reconsider our understanding of the ethical; for Irigaray's almost ethical placental economy, like Kristeva's splitting pregnant body, guides us to an ethical transvaluation where attentiveness rather than willing births new ways of being and becoming.

Wonder and the Riddle

In catching the last man out, the maternal body catches Nietzsche's error of turning to the will to overcome the ascetic ideal. Creativity is not a matter of willing. Nietzsche got it right in *Z* I "The Three Metamorphoses." It is a matter of innocence and wonder. He cannot, however, escape the lure of the will. And so rather than a clear affirmation of the active passivity of the wonder of the child, there is throughout Zarathustra an undecidability and a tension—will willing or innocence become the path of overcoming? We may, following Robert Gooding-Williams, attribute this tension to the fact that Zarathustra is the lion spirit and not yet the child, and then read Nietzsche's talk of the will to power as the will to master in terms of the lion's nay-saying—the no that masters modernity's decadence. Going further, we may find this will to mastery present in all human bodies and read it in terms of a power that in revaluing the passions as a source of enjoyment and delight creates a being beyond man.[20] Finally we can read Nietzsche's will to power as the signature of his

Dionysian body ". . . a body that can go under to passional chaos and subsequently overcome itself."[21] Read in this way, the will to power bears no resemblance to the will of the despisers of the body who, in positing an autonomous fixed stable substance as the subject, dams the flows of the flesh. This going under and overcoming version of the will to power seems to be an affirmation of Kristeva's account of the maternal body. Alan D. Schrift's description of the will to power as the play of becoming that emphasizes the fluidity of relations also seems to direct us to the maternal body's placental economy as described by Irigaray.[22] Looking more closely, however, I find that though these accounts of the will to power may provide us with a way to overcome the last man as a despiser of the body, they do not give us a way to overcome the idealization of power embedded in the last man's idealization of the imaginary masculine body. They are not affirmations of the maternal body's will-less creativity, that active passivity that gives the other its place to become. They are not, as I see it, a bridge to the overman. The undergoing driven by the will to power is endured for the sake of overcoming oneself, not for the sake of the birth of an-other. The fluidity of relations of Nietzsche's will to power becoming is not the placental relationship that refuses the adversarial notion of otherness, but the relationship of friendship where the friend is described as either the welcomed adversary or as the one who helps me cultivate my solitude so that I can walk the path of overcoming (*Z* I "On the Friend"). Though Zarathustra is constantly seeking companions, given his descriptions of overcoming, if he found suitable companions, it is not clear that he would/could overcome the current structures of social and political life in his relationships with them.

My suspicions are fed by the variant version of the *Ecce Homo* section "Why I Am So Wise," discovered in 1969 and discussed by Jean Graybeal, where Nietzsche describes his relationship to his mother and the mother's body in distinctly Oedipal terms. Here it is not the nausea of the last man that argues against the eternal recurrence. Here, "The most profound objection to the eternal recurrence, my truly abysmal thought is always mother and sister."[23] Whatever the sage, the women skeptics and the old women may have taught Nietzsche is now forgotten. In this version of *Ecce Homo,* Nietzsche speaks in the culturally over determined language of the devouring maternal body. He describes his mother as "a perfect hell machine" who can "with unfailing certainty . . . bloodily wound me."[24] Standing before this hell machine and bloodily wounded, Nietzsche is emasculated, ". . . all strength is lacking to defend oneself against poisonous vermin."[25] The body of the living mother is the kiss of death. It is the dead father who carries the gift of life.

It may go too far to rely on this text, written just before Nietzsche's descent into madness and silence to argue that Nietzsche's truth of the body is a return to the all too familiar truth of the masculine body. It may be unfair to read Nietzsche reinstating the male female hierarchy when he claims the mantle of the dead father to escape the hell machine of the living mother. If these were the only texts where Nietzsche's Oedipal blind spots appeared, charges of over-interpretation might be justified, but Irigaray, never mentioning this text, finds this murder of the mother in the name of the father throughout Nietzsche's thought.

Specifically she finds it contaminating his desire for overcoming and particularly pernicious in his desire for the eternal recurrence. This is not to say that she rejects the project of overcoming. Calling herself Nietzsche's Marine Lover, Irigaray expresses her love for the overcoming of man as she critiques Nietzsche's way of overcoming. Asking Nietzsche why he leaves the sea, why he never chooses sea creatures as companions, why his teaching of the meaning of the earth forgets the fluid depths that engendered him, she answers her questions by accusing Nietzsche of harboring the spirit of ressentiment in his presumption that the seas wish to become mountain tops and light. She describes Nietzsche as someone who says, "[a]s long as the sea remains sea, some movement resists my will. Some path of light is hidden from me in the sea."[26] Fleshing out the implications of this ressentiment in terms of the will to autonomy and domination, Irigaray continues,

> Wanting to find the sun again at mid- night, doesn't that amount to wanting to steal the other man's midday from him? . . . Isn't your sun-worship also a kind of ressentiment? Don't you measure your ecstasy against the yardstick of envy? And isn't your circle made of the will to live this irradiation—there will be no other but me?[27]

In her love letter, Irigaray accuses Nietzsche of fleeing the birthing body and of only seeing women in terms of their availability for impregnation. Wanting to forget the source of his life, he wants to become the source of the child to come. In short, Nietzsche only wants women who can be bent to his will. This, Irigaray writes, is the meaning of Nietzsche's desire for the eternal return. Going further and recalling Nietzsche's *Ecce Homo* preference for the dead father over the living mother in the authorized published text, Irigaray writes:

> And your whole will, your eternal recurrence, are these anything more than the dream of one who neither wants to have been born, not to continue being born at every instant, of a female other? Does

your joy in becoming not result from annihilating her from whom you are tearing yourself away?[28]

Warning Nietzsche that he "will hear nothing of women so long as you are bending them thus to your will,"[29] Irigaray entreats him to abandon his affirmation of willing that ties him to a desire for an eternity of the same and to come to women "without wanting to fill her to the brim, overwhelm her with your gifts. Let her return to the rhythm of her blood. To that happiness in living that remains a mystery to you. And that you do not want to receive from her."[30]

In their advocacy of an ethics of the maternal body, in their affirmation of the ways that this body affirms the becoming, wonder and risk of life, neither Irigaray nor Kristeva intend to return us to the ideology of woman as mother; for this ideology, as Irigaray makes clear in her admonitions to Nietzsche, is not an affirmation of the pulsations of life, but an affirmation of the will that would rather control, contain, and master life than abandon the project of willing for the chance of the dice throw. An ethics of the maternal body as an ethics of relational autonomy and risk is an ethics that welcomes the mystery of the other's singularity and otherness. It prefers the surprises of the wonders of becoming to the comforts of an assured identity and a calculable world.

Listening to Nietzsche's women life and truth under the tutelage of Irigaray and Kristeva, I discover that the tragedy of Oedipus (and of our Oedipal civilization) is not the tragedy of the murderous son who breaks the incest taboo, but the tragedy of figuring the desire to learn the secrets of the life giving body according to the terms of the will; for it is not through the murder of the father that the son gains access to the mother, but through the will to master the riddle of the woman-animal Sphinx that the son becomes the law of the city and the lord of its queen. Listening to Irigaray and Kristeva, the one on the way to the overman might discover that the tragedy of Oedipus lay in his conviction that riddles were meant to be solved; for if the city seemed to be threatened by the plague of the Sphinx's unsolved riddle, this threat was nothing compared to the cycle of death and destruction that followed the closure created by Oedipus' answer. Learning this, the one on the way to the overman, having taken on a woman's body divested of its stigma, would know that riddles are not meant to be solved; that the desire to create is kept alive by following the logic of the placental fluids and is kept awake by the wonder that asks the question in order to invigorate the polymorphous semiotics of "answers" that return us to the play of the once more of life.

10

Nietzsche's Synaesthetic Epistemology and the Restitution of the Holistic Human

RAINER J. HANSHE

> [The heart] nourished in seas of blood which leaps back and forth, and there especially it is called understanding by men; for men's understanding is blood around the heart.
>
> —**Empedocles**[1]

> If a *revolt* is to come, it will have to come from the five *senses*!
>
> —**Michel Serres**[2]

In opposition to the orthodox philosophic, religious, and aesthetic conception of the senses, in Nietzsche's epistemic order, every sense is not only positively valued but also often "crossed" with other senses. If three of the just four scholars who actually address Nietzsche's conception of synaesthesia assert that his depiction and use of it is strictly metaphoric,[3] in fact, it is often if not as a rule precisely the opposite—Nietzsche conveys the phenomenon as something real, actual. Nietzsche was knowledgeable of synaesthesia through medical, aesthetic, and philosophic sources and a persistent engagement with it can be traced throughout his corpus. Further, his interest in synaesthesia may signal that he himself was synaesthetically inclined. If that cannot be definitively ascertained, aside from the testimony of his philosophy, several intriguing allusions in letters indicate that he may have had experiential knowledge of the phenomenon. Whatever the case, as an experimental mode of epistemology, Nietzsche was sensitive to it and, as will be illustrated, considered it a phenomenon demanding serious attention.

In counseling us to develop our synaesthetic potentiality, I propose that Nietzsche is recuperating an ancient praxis and advancing *a sense-oriented epistemology* in order to refine and intensify our attunement to the world. It is the cultivation of a new mode of "common sense" (in Greek, *koinê aesthêsis*, in Latin, *sensus communis*) completely different from Kant's and that of orthodox philosophy—data received via the sensory domain is not condemned or abnegated. In Nietzsche's *Umwertung aller Werte*, the mode for obtaining knowledge is no longer reason alone—it will also be obtained through a meditative praxis that engages the entire body, which Nietzsche refers to as "a great reason" and "a manifold with one sense" (*Z* I "On the Despisers of the Body"), presaging the view in contemporary synaesthetic literature that we do not have five sense organs, but one sense organ with five sub-organs.[4] A particularly rich concentration of the synaesthetic figures in his magnum opus, *Thus Spoke Zarathustra*, with Zarathustra and the *Übermensch* representing holistic types who not only embrace the senses as well as reason as means for acquiring knowledge, but more important, *unite* both as the ultimate epistemological tool. Synaesthetic epistemology is therefore concordant with Nietzsche's perspectivalism and functions as one of the most optimal methods for acquiring more objective and truthful analyses of reality, a method that enables us to see with "more eyes," which Nietzsche asserts enables us to develop more complete "concepts" of things.[5] In what follows, I will examine the philosophical precedents of synaesthesia on which Nietzsche's conception may in part be founded, trace the synaesthetic in Nietzsche's corpus, focusing most on *Thus Spoke Zarathustra*, briefly address the question of Nietzsche being synaesthetic, then conclude with an outline of Nietzsche's constellation of the sensory order and explain how comprehending the *Übermensch* demands activating our synaesthetic capacity.

Ancient Philosophical Precedents

> Wretched mind, from us [the senses] you take your certainty, and yet you would overthrow us?—Our defeat will be your downfall.
>
> Democritus[6]

> What can we find more certain than the senses themselves, to mark for us truth and false-hood?
>
> Lucretius, *De rerum natura*[7]

Aside from its largely aesthetic orientation, synaesthesia also has ancient philosophical precedents and as a philologist, historian, and philosopher, Nietzsche was cognizant of that heritage. Of crucial concern here is the positive valuation that thinkers such as Heraclitus and Empedocles gave to the senses, and their recognition of them as valid epistemological tools.

In numerous fragments, Heraclitus presents a varied view of the senses and though critical of them, demanding that they be considered with discernment, he never condemns them *in toto* but recognizes the instrumental role they serve in acquiring knowledge of the world. For the Ionians, the senses are "instruments of discovery and signposts to truth."[8] Phenomena "can only be granted a decent scientific status if our senses, by which the phenomena are apprehended, have some claim to be regarded as dispensers of truth."[9] The most positive valuation of the senses Heraclitus advances is where he notes that "whatsoever things [are] objects of sight, hearing, [and] experience—these things I hold in higher esteem."[10] If he believes that the "eyes are more accurate witnesses than are [the] ears,"[11] both senses are inadequate witnesses if people have what he calls "uncomprehending (literally, 'barbarian') souls."[12] When stating that most people do not understand what they encounter via the sensory dimension, he outlines the necessity for sensing and thinking *together* as opposed to rejecting the senses in favor of reason. Yet sensing must always be coupled with thinking, otherwise one will sense as if one is not sensing. "The 'know nothings,' on the other hand, are 'unjudging hordes,' whose senses are senseless, their 'eye sightless, their hearing full of noise.' Heraclitus pictures such people as sleepwalkers."[13]

In his *Poem*, Empedocles presents us with another forceful alternative to the orthodox devaluation of the sensory order. In at least two fragments, and these are fundamental to his thinking, Empedocles articulates a "refusal to choose either the senses or reason, *nous*, to the exclusion of the other. This is most explicit," Trépanier notes, in the fragment "where he instructs the disciple to place *no more trust* in one sense than the other" and is further reinforced in another fragment "where he includes 'grasping with the mind' alongside the senses, as one of the means whereby the disciple could follow his teachings."[14] As with Heraclitus, there is an important union of sensing and thinking:

> But come, consider, by every device, how each thing is clear—not holding any sight as more reliable than what you hear, nor the resounding hearing [as more reliable] than the clarities of the tongue and do not in any way curb the reliability of the other limbs by which there is a passage for understanding, but understand each thing in the way that it is clear.[15]

If Sextus Empiricus believes there is a contradiction in Empedocles' views, critics such as Trépanier demonstrate that the contradiction is but ostensible and predicated on a misreading of the fragment "where Empedocles does not reject either the senses or reason completely, but merely the status of either as final and authoritative, to the exclusion of the other."[16] It is this Heraclitean and Empedoclean epistemology, where both reason and the senses function together, that I believe Nietzsche is recuperating. Indeed, it is what underlies his own epistemology and in thinking this, we can trace an expansive arc (the *pre-Platonic* lineage) stretching from Heraclitus and Empedocles directly to Nietzsche's thought. As Barnes says, Empedocles "establishes that what is grasped through each of the senses is trustworthy provided that reason is in charge of them."[17] Despite his criticism of Empedocles' views, Sextus Empiricus clearly recognizes this balance and affirms that "perception through each of the senses is reliable, provided reason is in control of them, even though previously disparaging their reliability."[18] Vlastos makes a similar assessment when he states that,

> If used aright, the senses are "openings for understanding"; there is no necessary conflict between their reports and the highest truth that the mind can discover. When we see "earth with earth," what we see is not "deceitful" appearance, but Being. Perception and judgment can thus be in perfect harmony. There, the same physical condition is appropriate to both, and the formulae for "most accurate sense-perceptions" and "wisest thoughts" coincide.[19]

Nietzsche makes precisely the same point in *Thus Spoke Zarathustra* and *Twilight of the Idols*, and it is exactly this coupling of sense perception *and* reason that informs his synaesthetic epistemology.

During Empedocles' time *koinê aesthêsis* (common sense) had a completely different meaning from what it does in modern times. As Peter Kingsley proposes,

> For Empedocles the discovery of common sense—of that consciousness which is able to hear and see and touch and feel and taste at the same time—was a matter of direct experience. And to experience it was to start waking up from the chaotic dream of human existence into another state of awareness.[20]

This conception of synaesthesia is incredibly more complex and is not the mere crossing of two senses, but the simultaneous unification of *every* sense. For Empedocles, *koinê aesthêsis* functions as a means for the purest experience of the world or, in Nietzsche's terms, for a perspectivalist one, the knower's "discipline and preparation of the intellect for its future 'objectivity' . . ." (*GM* III: 12). It is a heightened if not possibly the most accurate mode of perception.[21] The Austrian doctor Jean Nüssbaumer avowed that his synaesthetic experiences were objective and asserted that those who aren't synaesthetic are the ones who are actually imagining things.[22] Indeed, like Empedocles, Nietzsche is after as direct, full, and accurate an experience of the world as possible and his sounding out of all idols is a method for freeing us from what Kingsley calls "the chaotic dream of human existence," or, in Nietzsche's own terms, "the lie of the ideal." As Barnes notes, what Empedocles promises his disciples, and Zarathustra promises something similar, is "knowledge (and with it some magical powers). He insisted, against the Eleatics, that the senses, if properly used, are routes to knowledge."[23] And it is precisely the "proper" use of the senses as routes to knowledge that Nietzsche advocates throughout his philosophy, and this we can propose is the uniting of the human with its animal nature.

Synaesthesia in Nietzsche's Corpus

> All that philosophers have been handling for thousands of years is conceptual mummies; nothing real has ever left their hands alive.
>
> Nietzsche, *TI* "Reason" 1

One of the earliest instances of Nietzsche's positive valuation of the senses and of his awareness that they were all once united is in his 1870 essay "*Das griechische Musikdrama*." There, Nietzsche critiques the common aesthetic axiom that the union of two or more arts is indicative of "a barbaric error of taste." What this axiom actually betrays is the modern bad habit of lacking the ability to enjoy things with all of our faculties: "we are, as it were, torn into little pieces by absolute art forms, and hence enjoy as little pieces, in one moment as ear-men, in another as eye-men, and so on. Let us contrast this view with . . . the drama of antiquity as total work of art . . ." (*GMD*). Instead of cultivating the ability to unite all of the senses, we sever our bodies into pieces and augment and expand the separate parts and convince ourselves that we have become geniuses through inflating those individual fragments. From the very beginning of his philosophical life, Nietzsche's thought is grounded in a conviction in the centrality of the total body, of the body as holistic anchor of human experience.

In *Philosophy in the Tragic Age of the Greeks*, Nietzsche criticizes Parmenides for precisely the kind of abnegation and fragmentation of the body Zarathustra derides. Since Parmenides observed with his senses a world of becoming, he condemned his eyes and ears for what they recognized, refusing to accept his observations as epistemologically valid. Because of this, Parmenides warns us against being guided by the senses of sight, hearing, and taste. Instead, we should trust in the power of thinking alone. For Nietzsche, this is the first and most dire critique of our apparatus of knowledge, by which he implies the body and the mind operating in unison. "By wrenching apart the senses and the capacity for abstraction, in other words, by splitting up mind as though it were composed of two quite separate capacities, he demolished intellect itself, encouraging man to indulge in that wholly erroneous distinction between 'spirit' and 'body' which, especially since Plato, lies upon philosophy like a curse" (*PTA* 10). Nietzsche declares further that "the absolute separation of senses and concepts" is a falsehood (*PTA* 13), precisely the kind of Platonic-Christian moral division of the body and mind that leads to barbarism. As with Socrates, the figure of Parmenides haunts Western thought and is one of the opponents in Nietzsche's agonistic ring. Whether his assessment of Parmenides is wholly accurate or not is here inconsequential.[24] What we already begin to see through these passages is a continuity of thought that Nietzsche will sustain until the end of his writing life regarding the senses and the body.

In the 1886 preface to *Human, All Too Human*, Nietzsche constitutes the book not merely as a text, but as *a musical artifact* when declaring that it "must be capable of some kind of music and flute-player's art by which even coy foreign ears are seduced to listen" (*HH* "Preface" 8).[25] Thus, "understanding" the book demands more than reading it with one's eyes alone—it must also be *heard* with the eyes or ears; yet the book has not only "been read most carelessly" but, more crucial Nietzsche emphasizes, it has been "*heard* the worst." To truly comprehend it then requires becoming *Übermenschlich*, that is, it requires "refined and experienced senses" (*HH* "Preface" 8). As Nietzsche diagnoses later in the book though, our senses have become blunted and our ears are no longer capable of hearing fine distinctions, such as between C-sharp and D-flat, a result of "the complete dominance of the well-tempered tonal system . . ." and our inquiring after reasons instead of after "what things are." "In this matter," Nietzsche believes, assessing the cultural climate of his time, "our ears have become coarser" (*HH* 217).[26] Now, over a hundred years later, our senses may be even more blunted. As Wordsworth diagnosed, presaging Nietzsche's critique of decadence by half a century, urbanization, which includes a loss of the rich sensory contact with the natural world, is in part what blunts "the discriminating powers of the mind [. . .] unfitting it for all voluntary exertion to reduce it to a state of almost savage torpor."[27] Because of coarseness or barbarity, we intellectualize the senses, too, and this intellectualization of the senses is one of the consequences of the Parmenidean-Platonic-Christian derision of the body. It results in an enervating of the perceptual faculties, the rationalization of joy, and the supplanting of the real.

> The more the eye and ear are capable of thought the more they reach that boundary line where they become unsensual. Joy is transferred to the brain; the sense organs themselves become dull and weak. More and more, the symbolic replaces that which exists—and so, as surely as on any other path, we arrive along this one at barbarism. (*HH* 217)

The necessity of coupling the perceptual and the rational faculties is exemplified in another aphorism where Nietzsche imbues the thinking organ with the attributes of the feeling one when conceiving of a double-brain with two *brain-ventricles* for the perceptions of science and nonscience (*HH* 251).[28] This provocative image, of a brain with throbbing chambers that pulsate, of an organ of cognition that requires blood to function, is emblematic of Nietzsche's radical epistemological concept, and it will receive a significant transformation in *Zarathustra*. It can function as a powerful guiding image for contemplating Nietzsche's synaesthetic epistemology. Let us sustain it in our imagination during this meditation.

In *Daybreak*, there is a similar demand for special readers, for readers with keen ears and delicate eyes and fingers, for readers capable of becoming still and slow, or of deeply ruminating like the cud-chewing cow Nietzsche admires. In his positing that our senses may even have had different functions, too, and in exploring that possibility, it is clear that synaesthesia is not merely metaphoric. When discussing the history of the eye, Nietzsche claims that after demonstrating its evolution, one "must arrive at the great conclusion that vision was *not* the intention behind the creation of the eye" (*GS* 122).[29] Similarly, in the *The Gay Science*, he explicitly declares that our eyes had a completely different function; "our eyes," he pronounces, "are also intended for hearing" (*GS* 223). Whereas in general Nietzsche positively values the senses, in *Daybreak*, as throughout his corpus, there is a persistent emphasis on feeling and its importance, of the primacy feeling has over thought in life. This further reinforces the centrality of the body, of the nerves in Nietzsche's philosophical vision, a vision that one could say is in part neurologically based, though this never descends into mere positivism or biologism—body for Nietzsche is a fluid, amorphous entity. Thoughts are but "the shadows of our feelings—always darker, emptier, and simpler" (*GS* 179).[30] And when discussing two different kinds of deniers of morality and avoiding and resisting what would be considered "immoral" acts versus doing and encouraging "moral" acts, Nietzsche stresses that "the one should be encouraged and the other avoided *for other reasons than hitherto.* We have to *learn to think differently*—in order at last, perhaps very late on, to attain even more: *to feel differently*" (*D* 103). Here, in this hierarchy, feeling is valuated higher than thinking. If in his later work he may have a different view of morality, the centrality of feeling remains consistent throughout. Consciousness itself, or our "so-called consciousness," as Nietzsche says, is also "a more or less fantastic commentary on an unknown, perhaps unknowable, but felt text" (*D* 119). Conceiving of the world as a text is a prevailing if not now even mundane aspect of postmodern thought, but, tellingly, what the postmodern appropriation of Nietzsche's view neglects is its sensory nuance—it is, as he differentiates, a *felt* text, perhaps akin to Braille texts which the blind "see" with their fingers.[31] The world is not something that we read as the text-centric insist, but *sense,* and to sense it requires possessing "subtle eyes, ears and noses" as well as a degree of inventiveness and an imagination "*unchained* by acuteness and knowledge" (*D* 428).

In the preface to the second edition of the *The Gay Science,* Nietzsche begins with a warning to the reader: to understand the book requires having *lived* through similar experiences.[32] Reading alone—that is, rational comprehension—will not yield its secrets or enable the reader to fathom its knowledge. In *Ecce Homo,* Nietzsche repeats this warning when stating that if one has no access to something from experience, one will have no "ear" for it (*EH* "Books" 1). As Bertram notes, subsequent to beholding the Eleusinian mysteries, Aristotle "says the same thing when he reports that this act of beholding is a *παθεῖν*, an 'experiencing,' not a *μαθεῖν*, a 'learning.'"[33] And, Bertram continues, it is as an Eleusinian mystagogue, "as a great educator of secrecy through secrets, that Nietzsche embraces this Aristotelian *παθεῖν* as the highest form of all fruitful learning and 'knowledge.'"[34] Beyond that, the hermit of Sils Maria asserts that the book "seems to be written in the language of the wind that thaws ice and snow: high spirits, unrest, contradiction, and April weather are present in it" (*GS* "Preface" 1). Thus, Nietzsche endows this work with a sensorial and meteorological dimension and, as is well known, posits that philosophy has been nothing but "an interpretation of the body and a *misunderstanding of the body*" (*GS* "Preface" 2). Thinking itself is *bodily* and the philosopher

> simply *cannot* keep from transposing his states every time into the most spiritual form and distance: this art of transfiguration *is* philosophy. We philosophers are not free to divide body from soul as the people do; we are even less free to divide soul from spirit. We are not thinking frogs, nor objectifying and registering mechanisms with their innards removed. (*GS* "Preface" 3)

Earlier, in "On Truth and Lies in an Extra-Moral Sense," Nietzsche makes an analogous assertion when claiming that nature mystifies and confines us "in a proud, deceptive consciousness, aloof from the coils of the bowels, the rapid flow of the blood stream, and the intricate quivering of the fibers!" (*TL* 1). Later, he will pronounce in "On Immaculate Perception" that our entrails are what is strongest in us, and in the opening of *Thus Spoke Zarathustra* he makes the even more intriguing assertion that the head is simply the entrails of the heart (*Z* "Preface" 5), a clear inversion of the orthodox hierarchy of the body. Further, if we do not "hold on to our hearts," according to Zarathustra, we can also lose our heads (*Z* II "On the Pitying"). In this, it is the heart, classically the feeling or emotive organ, that is the guiding or predominant force of the body. Parkes does not observe this in the footnotes to his translation, but Nietzsche may very well be evoking Empedocles' thought that the blood around the heart is the thought of the human.[35]

There is a bodily or sensorial dimension to the death of God (*GS* 125), too, and it is emblematic of Nietzsche's sensory orientation. While the sacrifice of God causes us to *feel* the breath of empty space and the temperature of the world grows more frigid, the madman asks if we can *hear* the noise of the gravediggers burying God and if we *smell* the divine decomposition. The act of murdering God also results in our being saturated with blood so that we need to be cleansed. In the closing passage, the madman explains that the tremendous event has not yet reached the *ears* of men and that it is a deed that requires time to be *seen* and *heard*. Thus, Nietzsche imbues his dramatization of the sacrificial murder of God with a striking and powerful sensory dimension as opposed to demonstrating that "God" is a conceptual construct and not an actual or metaphysical entity. When speaking of the event of the death of God later in the book, Nietzsche construes it *visually* and speaks of it as a spectacle that only those "whose eyes, the *suspicion* in whose eyes is strong and subtle enough for this spectacle, some suns seem to have set and some ancient and profound trust has been turned into doubt: to them our old world must appear daily more like evening, more mistrustful, stranger, 'older'" (*GS* 343). Also, when Zarathustra speaks of God dying, he notes that God offended "the taste of [his] ears and eyes . . ." (*Z* IV "Retired"). As a philosopher of the present and the future who has unlearned the fear of the senses, the sensorial dimension of events is an instrumental aspect of earthly life for today; all such philosophers "are believers in the senses," and "*not* in theory but in *praxis*" (*GS* 372).[36]

If some of Nietzsche's positions regarding the development of the sensory organs are understood as merely straightforward utilizations of nineteenth-century evolutionary arguments, as recent neuroscience research has proven, synaesthetic perceptions "are actual perceptions and, as such, clearly distinguishable from metaphorical associations or hallucinations."[37] Further, and more appositely, basing the classification of the senses strictly on the visual organs is essentially crude, for those largely external structures are not the sole mediums of sense experience. The process of vision, for instance, includes numerous body structures that include the eye itself, nerves, and different areas of the brain. Thus, as Cretien van Campen explains, the

> division of sensory experience on the basis of physical external characteristics (eyes, nose, etc.) into five sensory domains is somewhat misleading [. . .]. [Various] sense researchers stress that the senses cannot be isolated but should be considered and understood in their relationships to one another.[38]

According to Greta Berman, "we all possess 'relative synaesthesia,' which, like relative pitch (and unlike perfect pitch), can be developed,"[39] and Nietzsche seems to have understood this as he compels us to cultivate the ability, which is part of his project of reinstituting the holistic human, the human who embraces its animal nature. "When technically discussing the phenomenon of synaesthesia," Berman asserts, "we should be dealing with the senses not as metaphors, but as separate and distinct realities."[40]

Synaesthesia in *Zarathustra*

In *Zarathustra*, Nietzsche frequently implies that Zarathustra's teaching can only be comprehended via the senses. When after first presenting his teaching and it is not understood, Zarathustra observes that he is still distant from human beings, suggesting that he is possibly not human, but *Übermensch*. That is to say, he possesses qualities or abilities that the average human does not or has not yet cultivated. More pertinently, and this is an illuminating passage, perhaps one of the most instructive regarding Nietzsche's synaesthetic epistemology, Zarathustra realizes that his "sense does not speak to [the] senses" ("*Aber noch bin ich ihnen ferne, und mein Sinn redet nicht zu ihren Sinnen*") of those he addressed (*Z* "Preface" 7), clearly indicating that it is *through the senses themselves* that one will come to "understand" his teaching in its fullest dimension. Once again, multiple perspectives must be employed to gain any accurate knowledge of an idea, concept, or the world. In another passage, Zarathustra asks his disciples if they are the *commanders* of their senses (*Z* I "On Child and Marriage"), accentuating the necessity of controlling the senses as opposed to passively receiving perceptions.[41] Since the *Übermensch* is not spoken of in conceptual terms, but in strictly material or sensorial ones—it is the sense of the earth, it is the sea, it is lightning, and earth and animal and plant are to be prepared for its sake (*Z* "Preface" 4) just as there is a rainbow that leads to the *Übermensch* (*Z* "Preface" 9); it is definitively not something that can be comprehended via cognition alone, but requires the attention of the entire body. And if it "comes to" Zarathustra as a specter (*Z* I "On Love of the Neighbor") and a shadow that is "still" and "light" (*Z* II "Upon the Blessed Isles"), to continue to grapple with the *Übermensch* from a strictly cognitive position is to refuse to encounter the figure as Nietzsche intimates it needs to be encountered, to refuse to cultivate the precisely singular epistemological mode necessary to *sense* the *Übermensch*.

As is often remarked, it is not that Zarathustra is a failure as a teacher or that his teaching is inadequate, for clearly, it is effective, but that those who have struggled to receive his teaching lack the abilities necessary to receive and animate it. If Zarathustra is synaesthetic, as all synaesthetes, not only would he consider his own perceptions to be normal, he might not even be aware that others lack his innate abilities. It might not be too bold to speculate that Nietzsche designed the text to illustrate that Zarathustra's teaching can be fully grasped *only* synaesthetically. As he says in the preface to *The Gay Science*, if one hasn't had similar experiences to those elucidated in the book, it is doubtful if prefaces alone, that is, instructive intellectual guidance, will bring one closer to such experiences. What is necessary is *experience, sensing with the entire body* what the book expresses, for the book is a metaphor of bodily experiences, a series of nerve stimuli that have been transformed into images, and the reader must activate them bodily to regenerate their sensuous power.[42]

Immediately subsequent to the very first presentation of his teaching, Zarathustra realizes that he is not understood and then wonders, "Must one first smash their ears before they learn to hear with their eyes?" (*Muss man ihnen erst die Ohren zerschlagen, dass sie lernen, mit den Augen hören?*) (*Z* "Preface" 5). This is another deeply illuminating passage that demands a different stress and focus. The task of hearing with one's eyes is not metaphoric and recurs throughout the narrative, most dramatically when Zarathustra commands his abyss-deep thought to rise up and to *hear* with its *eyes*, which it achieves, as do other synaesthetic tasks, events, episodes, and entities. Zarathustra proclaims that he is able to listen to trees (*Z* "Preface" 5), that he can shut and open his ears as if they were eyes (*Z* II "On the Rabble" and *passim*),[43] that he can hear the eye of Life speaking (*Z* II "On Self-Overcoming"),[44] that he can hear the Stillest Hour speaking without voice (*Z* II "The Stillest Hour"), that he can see and smell spirit (*Z* III "The

Homecoming"),[45] that his soul sneezes (*Z* III "The Homecoming"), that a tree can act as a seeing witness (*Z* III "On the Spirit of Gravity"),[46] that his eyes and entrails laugh (*Z* IV "The Shadow"), that eternity has a fragrance and odor (*Z* IV "The Sleepwalker Song"),[47] and so on. All of these factors designate that the text operates according to an altogether different epistemological order. Now, let's briefly consider the possibility of Nietzsche being synaesthetic.

On 10 February 1883 Nietzsche makes an intriguing allusion to having experiential knowledge of synaesthesia in a letter to Overbeck. "How can I help having," Nietzsche states, almost with excitement, "*an extra sense organ* and a new, terrible source of suffering!" (Letter Nr. 373, *KSB* 6:325f [emphasis added]). This admission corresponds precisely with accounts given by synaesthetes of their experiences, some of which include painful sensations in the fingertips due to certain consonants, of letters being bitter, scalding hot, and capable of producing terror, while color hearing can cause fatigue and headaches. These experiences offer insight into what Nietzsche articulates in the passages now under discussion. In another letter to his sister written in Venice on 20 May 1885, he claims that his words "have *other colors* than the same words from other people" and that with him "there is much *multicolored* foreground" (Letter Nr. 602, *KSB* 7:51f).[48] Similarly, in the final aphorism of *The Gay Science* (383), he refers to *painting* gloomy question marks, and in the final aphorism of *Beyond Good and Evil* he speaks of his *painted* thoughts as being once "so colorful" and "full of thorns and secret spices" (296) that they caused him to sneeze and laugh. When such thoughts are transformed into words, they lose their "fragrance" or sensorial dimension, but, Nietzsche protests, he alone has "colors, many colors perhaps, many motley caresses and fifty yellows and browns and greens and reds" for his wicked thoughts. While these may unquestionably be figurative statements, the parallel with the experience synaesthetes have of words is truly arresting.

Synaesthesia and the *Übermensch*

If the genuine philosopher once feared the senses because they "thought that the senses lured them out of their world, the cold realm of 'ideas,'" Nietzsche insists that the philosophers of the future should "regard ideas, with their cold, anemic appearance, and not even in spite of this appearance, as worse seducers than the senses" (*GS* 372). Freeing the senses from the domain of morality, Nietzsche positively endows each of them in order to develop a new attunement to the world. In his aesthetico-philosophic project, all of the senses become valid means for acquiring knowledge—

the senses, Nietzsche declared, "do not lie at all. What we *make* of their evidence is what gives rise to the lie; for example, the lie of unity, the lie of materiality, of substance, of duration [. . .]. 'Reason' is what causes us to falsify the evidence of the senses. If the senses show becoming, passing away, change, they do not lie" (*TI* "Reason" 2).[49] Synaesthetes, as has been verified by neuroscientific research, do not all experience the same perceptions. Thus, their mode of perception reveals more accurately the degree to which we are not passive perceivers of a fixed reality, but that perception is to some degree a creative act; that when perceiving the world we are active participants. Through considering the possibility of perceiving the world from three completely different nonhuman perspectives, we will, Nietzsche asserts, be led to realize that there is no regularity to nature. What is doubly intriguing about this passage from "On Truth and Lies in an Extra-Moral Sense" is that a sight stimulus is considered capable of producing sound:[50]

> If each us had a different kind of sense perception—if we could only perceive things now as a bird, now as a worm, now as a plant, or if one of us saw a stimulus as red, another as blue, *while a third even heard the same stimulus as a sound*—then no one would speak of such a regularity of nature, rather, nature would be grasped only as a creation which is subjective in the highest degree. (*TL* 1 [emphasis added])

Synaesthesia here reveals, as normative perception does not, the radical state of becoming of the world, its perpetual and dynamic flux.[51] Yet, despite Nietzsche's substantial transvaluation, despite the little and larger conceptual earthquakes that have occurred since his time, even today, we still remain at large in the grip of the Parmenidean-Platonic-Christian sense hierarchy.

Like Empedocles, Nietzsche clearly knew that "to open the way to a world of stillness quite unknown to our restless minds—is to become aware of the common factor linking each sense together, motionless, featureless, placeless and timeless, which is the consciousness we are."[52] It is not the abnegation of the senses that is at work in Nietzsche's philosophy, for that would be to perpetuate a misunderstanding of the body, but precisely the celebration and engagement of the senses. What is necessary is *spiritualizing* and *multiplying* them (*WP* 820; *KSA* 9:37[12]), and this most probably refers to the new mode of *sensus communis* that I believe Nietzsche outlines.[53] If she never discusses synaesthesia but tantalizingly circles within its vicinity, Jill Marsden recognizes that the *Übermensch* is to be approached via radically other means. "To develop the conditions for sensing the overhuman, one has to suspend the intellectual values that guide one's thought and be guided in turn by one's senses."[54] With this approach, a new praxis for encountering the *Übermensch* is initiated.

When stressing the importance of the senses, it must be emphasized that Nietzsche is not expunging reason altogether, but restoring a balance that for centuries had been disrupted, predominantly because of moral valuations, to a refusal *per se* of a perspectivalist epistemology. Nietzsche creates a new or rather, *revives* an ancient pagan constellation wherein reason and the senses operate together. Without reason, one cannot of course think one's senses through to their end. Here the parallel with Empedocles noted previously is so exact, Nietzsche may even be paraphrasing him. For Nietzsche, perception and judgment can function in perfect harmony, just as Vlastos remarks that they do for Empedocles. Reason always remains within Nietzsche's epistemology, but it is a different kind of reason; as he notes, there are diverse kinds of "reason" just as there are diverse kinds of the "sublime." In *The Gay Science*, he distinguishes between those who "thirst after things that *go against reason*" and others, Nietzsche's infamous "we," "we others who thirst after reason" (*GS* 319). In *Zarathustra* he speaks of the body itself as being "a great reason" and observes that what we have called "spirit" is but a tool of the body and "small reason," the "toy" of our great reason (*Z* I "On the Despisers of the Body").[55] As noted earlier, the body is spoken of in the same chapter as being "a manifold with one sense" (*Z* I "On the Despisers of the Body"). Nietzsche also construes reason positively when speaking in *Twilight of the Idols* of his "*restored* reason" (*TI* "Errors" 2). Thus, there is the body itself as a great reason, small reason, and Nietzsche's "renovated" reason, all functioning as faculties along with what he explicitly refers to as the single sense of the body.

With this conception of *sensus communis*, Nietzsche develops a unique epistemology born of his restitution of the body. In this recuperation of the Heraclitean and Empedoclean epistemological heritage, the senses are unified and function together with reason, which serves as a guide and enables us to think our senses through to their ends, to develop a perspectivalism *par excellence*. Here, I must return again to Marsden, for she comes closest to distinguishing what is necessary for this holistic approach to philosophy. "To be affected by the *Übermenschlich*—to experience it—is not to take up an intellectual position. Somehow," Marsden surmises, "we are required to develop sensitivity to different cues, to push the exercise of thinking beyond its usual range."[56] However, it is not only that we are to impel thinking into a different range, but that it is necessary to cultivate a more dynamic use of our senses, that we think and sense *together*. What, Marsden argues, must be abandoned is "the assumption that the overhuman is to be approached conceptually."[57] Instead, Marsden suggests, "we might say that the overhuman is to be sensed in Nietzsche's thinking at the very point where cognition fails."[58] One might conceive this somewhat differently though—the *Übermensch* is to be sensed not where cognition fails completely, but where it *acquiesces* to the body, where a new harmonic constellation of the senses and reason is developed. And when illustrating in *Ecce Homo* how his *felt text* is to be received, Nietzsche stresses that the book is constituted of *alpine air* and that its *halcyon tone* must be *heard aright* if we are not to be unjust to "the meaning of its wisdom" (*EH* "Preface" 4), a "meaning" which is clearly also sense-oriented. To exercise this justice is then an equally, if not predominantly, sensorial task. Following this counsel, Nietzsche quotes a profoundly suggestive passage from his magnum opus that offers further illumination into Zarathustra's teaching. It also directs us toward explicitly *how* it is to be embodied or incorporated. In the passage, Zarathustra compares his teachings to good, sweet figs that are so ripe they are about to burst and invites us to "drink their juice and their sweet flesh!" Once again, we are given a sense-oriented task, this time a gustatory or digestive one, and this must be thought beyond the realm of mere metaphor, for it is precisely here that Nietzsche evokes his most honored and ancient synaesthetic forbear, Empedocles.

In his *Poem*, Empedocles offers similar counsel to his disciples when commanding them to press his words down underneath their dense-packed diaphragms and to let them grow. As to Zarathustra, words to Empedocles are food, or *seeds*, and in order to cultivate such nutrients, his disciples have to *breathe* them in and "bury them deep inside [their] own entrails like seeds,"[59] not just comprehend them rationally.[60] "Perceive," he instructs, "just as the pledges from our Muse command after splitting what I am saying in your entrails."[61] Throughout *Thus Spoke Zarathustra*, Nietzsche uses the exact same agricultural metaphors as Empedocles but, oddly, Lampert does not make this observation, nor to my knowledge have any other commentators.[62] Aside from Nietzsche's referring to Zarathustra as a sower who casts forth his seed (*Z* II "On the Three Metamorphoses"), Zarathustra instructs humanity that it must plant the seed of its highest hope in order to give birth to a dancing star (Z "Preface" 5). Zarathustra also believes that truths are engendered from seeds (*Z* III "The Convalescent") and that "a genuine son and consummate heir" will grow from the seed of the superior humans (*Z* IV "The Welcome"). Like Empedocles, Zarathustra discusses the necessity of *chewing* on words and of grinding and crushing them until *they flow like milk into his soul* (*Z* IV "The Ugliest Human Being"). This art of rumination, of chewing thoughts like cud, is exactly akin to Empedocles' instruction to his disciples to force his teachings deep inside themselves like seeds, to *split* them, to give birth to them in their entrails. Beyond thinking alone, there is *a bodily process* that must occur in order to truly fathom these teachings or, more dynamically, to *activate* them. "Thinking" though is not just a rational process, or it is not one that can easily be differentiated from the body. "The skin," as Deane Juhan recognizes, "is no more separated from the brain than the surface of a lake is separate from its depths . . . . The brain is a single functional unit, from cortex to fingertips to toes. To touch the surface is to stir the depths."[63] Thus, our entrails, which Nietzsche believes is the strongest part of us, like other parts of our bodies, may very well be involved in the process of "thinking." And this precise parallel with Empedocles is further solidified through Nietzsche's referring to Zarathustra's teaching as a living plantation, garden, and fine soil. As the advocate of the earth who ritually counsels us to remain faithful *to* the earth and to be courageous enough to believe even in our entrails, Zarathustra is clearly evoking this aspect of Empedocles' praxis. When Kingsley illustrates that what makes the use of *metis* crucial for Empedocles "was its capacity to carry [him] beyond human existence altogether,"[64] there is an analogous desire in him to overcome the human and to become *Übermenschlich*. Or, the concept of the *Übermensch* is infused with an Empedoclean ethos. When Empedocles instructs his disciples "to become aware of the common factor linking each sense together, motionless, featureless, placeless and timeless, which is the consciousness we are,"[65] we discover a further corollary with Zarathustra and the figure of the *Übermensch*, the holistic human type *par excellence*.

Conclusion

If Zarathustra's voice is "thunder enough that even graves will learn to listen!" and, more pertinent, it is "a healing potion even for those born blind" (*Z* III "The Convalescent"), something distinctive is operating in the text that demands careful consideration.[66] To construe such rhetoric negatively as simple hyperbole, as does Gooding-Williams for instance, is to be insensate to the philosophical task Nietzsche struggles to achieve. Alerting the reader to the "synaesthetic epistemology" and new mode of *sensus communis* that he advances, as opposed to stating it, Nietzsche *attunes* us to what is quite clearly an instrumental aspect of his philosophy, seducing us to *sense* it. As careful readers, we must not neglect these signals—the synaesthetic dimensions of his texts are far from strictly metaphoric.[67] Nietzsche explicitly avows in the *Nachlaß* that "our eyes hear much more keenly than our ears" (*KSA* 10:3[1]415). Since he limits "truth" to what is humanly thinkable, visible, and sensible, in projecting before humanity its former holistic totality, he calls us to *animate* a modality we are capable of animating. If, as some neuroscientists assert, (relative) synaesthesia *can* be developed, Nietzsche presents humanity with a spectacular challenge that demands consideration.[68] When he asks repeatedly in *Ecce Homo* whether or not he has been "understood," we might wonder if one of the main reasons why we have failed to "understand" him is because we have not approached him synaesthetically. Nietzsche does state that "the more abstract the truth which one wishes to teach, the more one must first entice the *senses*" (*BGE* 128). At the very least, Zarathustra's teaching clearly seems to demand this, which Marsden also recognizes, and if "understanding" also requires "understanding" another's blood as Zarathustra asserts, the task of knowing Zarathustra sets for us is clearly a body-oriented one.[69] Nietzsche's conception of the body, however, includes not only the senses and the nerves, but mind, too. When informing us that "there is more reason in our bodies than in our finest wisdom" (*Z* I "On the Despisers of the Body"), it is to a more complete constellation that Nietzsche directs us, where mind is not separated from the body or the nerves or the sensuous dimension, but is inextricably connected to it. "Formerly, the proof of man's higher origin, of his divinity, was found in his consciousness, in his 'spirit.' To become *perfect*, he was advised to draw in his senses, turtle fashion, to cease all intercourse with earthly things, to shed his mortal shroud: then his essence would remain, the 'pure spirit'" (*A* 14). Having learned differently, having at last overcome the lie of the ideal, "We no longer derive man from 'the spirit' or 'the deity,' we have placed him back among the animals." As Nietzsche affirms in the same passage, "The 'pure spirit' is a pure stupidity: if we subtract the nervous system and the senses—the 'mortal shroud'—*then we miscalculate*—that is all!—" (*A* 14). But in tearing ourselves to pieces, in reducing ourselves to nothing but "ear-men and eye-men," we reduce ourselves to the emaciated stalks Zarathustra castigates, inverse cripples incapable of activating our synaesthetic capacity and *uniting* reason and the senses, which would create the most powerful, if not truthful, epistemological mode, or the most ultimate and many-sensed form of perspectivalism. We have been severed from the ancient heritage of the synaesthetic body predominantly due to morality, to limited, single perspectives born of Platonism and the Platonism of the people, monotheism. In order not only to sense Nietzsche anew, but to achieve our highest potentiality, we must recover that ancient pagan heritage.

11

Nietzsche's Naturalist Morality of Breeding

A Critique of Eugenics as Taming

DONOVAN MIYASAKI

Introduction

Nietzsche's endorsement of a "morality of breeding" (*Züchtung*), which he opposes to the morality of "taming" or "domestication" (*Zähmung*), invites worry that his philosophy may be compatible with ethically dangerous forms of eugenics and, consequently, with the historically associated practices of discrimination, racism, and genocide.[1] While there is a general consensus that Nietzsche does not actively or directly endorse racial discrimination or political violence, the failure to clearly exclude such egregious views would be sufficient reason to seriously question any major positive contribution Nietzsche might make to ethical philosophy.[2]

In this paper, I directly oppose Nietzsche's morality of breeding to all forms of comparative eugenics. By comparative eugenics, I have in mind any eugenic program that identifies benefit or harm to individuals or the species on the basis of comparatively evaluated traits. For example, to genetically engineer intelligence or talent for the purpose of making an individual competitive in the economic, cultural, or social spheres would count as comparative eugenics, since in this context ability must be greater than the norm to count as improved.

I will argue, further, that Nietzschean breeding is directly opposed to both positive and negative forms of comparative eugenics, that is, to both the genetic promotion of beneficial traits and the genetic elimination of harmful ones. While this allows for the possibility that Nietzschean breeding might be compatible with non-comparative eugenics, the category is sufficiently broad to include the most ethically dangerous historical forms, as well as contemporary forms that, while ethically controversial, are generally perceived to be more innocuous. It includes the forms of Social Darwinism that were common in the United States, the United Kingdom, and Scandinavia throughout the twentieth century, with their comparative conceptions of health and hygiene, the racial eugenic theories of National Socialism, with its comparative evaluations of racial superiority, and the contemporary liberal or voluntary forms, with their comparatively grounded conceptions of ability and disability.

I will begin by explaining Nietzsche's contrast between moralities of breeding and taming. I will argue that the ethical danger of comparative eugenics is grounded in its status as a form of taming, which promotes positively evaluated character types through the active elimination of negatively evaluated ones. The morality of taming—and, consequently, comparative eugenics—is not an authentic form of selection, but in fact a disguised de-selection: the production of anti-types through the elimination of de-selected traits. Consequently, taming tends necessarily toward violence as the elimination of de-selected forms of human life.

In contrast, Nietzsche's notion of breeding indicates a morality that selects traits and types by protecting them from de-selection—specifically, by destroying moral ideas, values, and practices designed to weaken or eliminate natural traits. Such a morality tends not toward the destruction but preservation of types; its negativity targets not life, but ideas and practices that disable and disempower forms of life.

I will argue, further, that the fundamental ethical difference between breeding and taming, and so between Nietzschean morality and eugenics, is found in their attitudes toward the natural world. The violence of eugenics as taming is grounded in its status as anti-natural, while Nietzsche's morality of breeding resists violence through its foundational affirmation of the conditions and limitations of the natural world—that is, through a form of moral naturalism.

Finally, I will apply my interpretation of breeding and taming to two cases of comparative eugenics: the historical case of discriminatory racial eugenics and the debate surrounding so-called designer baby cases in contemporary theories of liberal eugenics. I will argue that Nietzsche must resolutely condemn both as forms of the anti-natural morality of taming, to which the morality of breeding is diametrically opposed.

Breeding as the Cultural and Biological Selection of Psychological Types

As many commentators have noted, Nietzsche uses the language of breeding (*züchten*) both literally and figuratively, to refer to both biological and cultural methods of selecting, promoting, and enhancing human traits and abilities.[3] However, he principally uses this language to describe moral and social values, practices, and institutions as means of human transformation.[4] For example, in the *On the Genealogy of Morality*'s description of the "breeding" of an "animal with the right to make promises,"[5] Nietzsche describes a process not of reproductive selection, but of sociocultural character production.[6] Individuals are made "necessary, uniform . . . calculable" through the "morality of mores and the social straightjacket" (*GM* I: 2).

Likewise, in *Beyond Good and Evil*, Nietzsche's discussion of breeding focuses on the influence of education, religious instruction, and moral discipline: "Asceticism and puritanism are almost indispensable means for educating and ennobling a race" (*BGE* 61). And, when discussing the ancient Greek city-state as an example of "an arrangement for breeding," Nietzsche again emphasizes social practices: moral severity in "the education of youth, in their arrangements for women, in their marital customs, in the relation of old and young, in their penal laws" (*BGE* 262).

Even where these practices include biological means of selection, such as marital customs, Nietzsche's constant emphasis upon moral practices and psychological traits indicates that the aim of breeding is to produce a psychological and social kind, not a biological type. Moreover, even as a means, breeding is only secondarily biological, since the psychological type that is to be reproduced through breeding is itself cultivated through social training, rather than through biological inheritance. In other words, biological means are attractive to Nietzsche only given his Lamarckian belief in the inheritance of culturally acquired traits. For example, when he explicitly contrasts discipline (*Zucht*) of body and soul (or "thoughts and feelings") in *Twilight of the Idols*, he identifies the former with disciplined activity. To "convince the body" requires the "internalization" of behavior through habit: "one's society, residence, dress, sexual gratification . . . a significant and select demeanor, an obligation to live only among men who do not 'let themselves go'" (*TI* "Expeditions" 47). Consequently, the intended contrast is of volition and habit, rather than culture and biology, as opposing means of selecting human types.

With this in mind, in my discussion I will assume that breeding refers to the selection of psychologically, not biologically, identified types. And I will focus on breeding and taming as general categories, not specific instances, so I will not attempt to identify which specific traits or character types a Nietzschean morality of breeding would promote. This question, while important, is not central to my topic: I would like to determine, not what kind of human being Nietzsche wishes to promote, but in what way he wishes to accomplish that promotion, as well as how his methods of achieving his own ideal forms of human personality and life might affect those forms to which he is opposed.

In addition, I will not address the ethical and political question of authority—that is, whether or not it is a process to be effected coercively through the state, non-coercively through social institutions, or individually on the level of values and practices.[7] This question does not bear on the ethical status of Nietzsche's notion of breeding in relation to eugenics, since any coercive form of human improvement, not just breeding, is ethically problematic on grounds unrelated to means or aim.

Finally, it should also be noted that Nietzsche occasionally uses *züchten* in a broad sense that refers to any attempt to promote specific human types. In this sense, breeding is not opposed to taming. Instead, it includes taming as one particularly harmful form of the broader, normatively neutral category.[8] We could, then, contrast breeding and taming as positive and negative forms of breeding in this more general sense.[9] However, to avoid confusion, I will use "breeding" only in the narrower sense in which it is distinct from and opposed to taming.

Breeding as Selective Empowerment, Taming as De-Selective Disempowerment

I will begin by showing that Nietzsche's distinction of moralities of breeding and taming is continuous with his critical contrast, in *Twilight of the Idols*, of natural and anti-natural forms of morality. We can identify breeding as natural, and taming as anti-natural, in three key ways: first, in their effects upon natural affects and abilities (their relation to human nature); second, in their consequences for the natural diversity of types in the human species (their relation to natural contingency); and third, in the destructiveness of their methods of morally transforming humanity (their relation to natural forms of change). I will first consider their effects upon human nature.

Nietzsche's notion of moral breeding does not imply a strong conflict between natural and artificial forms of development. Breeding is not a radical departure from, or against, natural selection.[10] Although usually translated as "breeding," "discipline," or "cultivation," *Züchtung* can also suggest "selection," as in the title of H.G. Bronn's influential 1860 German edition of Darwin's *On the Origin of Species*, which translates "natural selection" as *naturliche Züchtung*. This accidental interpretive twist in the German reception of Darwin is fortuitous, since for Nietzsche there is no essential divide between natural and non-natural selection. Breeding and selection both refer to the development of the species through the preservation, reproduction, or extinction of traits and types—a process that remains natural, whether the product of accident or human intervention, because both processes operate through the contingent preservation of naturally originated traits.[11]

Nevertheless, Nietzsche does believe there are "natural" and "anti-natural" moralities and, consequently, anti-natural ways of intervening in the process of natural selection. Anti-natural moralities are distinctive in their negative foundation, method, and purpose: they express a "condemnation" of "the instincts of life," while natural moralities are "dominated by an instinct of life" (*TI* "Morality" 4). Nietzsche does not, of course, consider every negation, limitation, or restriction of natural instinct to be a "condemnation." Rather, an instinct is condemned by a morality when that morality seeks to completely eradicate its influence and to prevent every form and instance of its satisfaction.

Anti-natural moralities are, consequently, against nature in the sense that they do not simply alter or enhance the natural process of selection, but actively oppose or work against it: they do not select, but rather de-select; they do not breed traits into individuals and the species, but rather breed them out.[12] They produce supposed improvement by removing undesirable natural traits rather than by authentically selecting, choosing from, and preserving desirable natural traits.

In contrast, natural moralities are authentically selective, because they directly affirm and preserve traits, and only indirectly and accidentally negate non-selected traits. Natural moral negations are indirect, because they serve more primary affirmations. When a natural morality condemns, it does so in order to promote another affect, instinct, or trait: "Some commandment of life is fulfilled through a certain canon of 'shall' and 'shall not'" (*TI* "Morality" 4). The condemnations of natural moralities are merely apparent rather than true negations because they are aimed at negative values or actions; they negate only negations: "Some hindrance and hostile element on life's road is thereby removed" (*TI* "Morality" 4).

Consequently, Nietzsche's distinction of selective and de-selective moralities helpfully clarifies how a morality can condemn while remaining consistent with the affirmation of the natural world. A natural morality can condemn only what directly negates an aspect of life—what itself condemns in the strong sense of seeking to exterminate. For this reason, Nietzsche characterizes the negative aspect of natural morality not as true negation, not as annihilation, but as transformation: a natural morality tries to "spiritualize, beautify, deify" a passion, in contrast to anti-natural moralities, which seek to "exterminate" (*vernichten*), "excise" (*ausschneiden*), or "castrate" the passions and, in so doing, to eliminate the variation they bring to human types (*TI* "Morality" 1).

This distinction of negative and positive *objects* of condemnation clarifies Nietzsche's seemingly contradictory call for a "pruning" (*beschneiden*) of the contemporary individual's contradictory instincts. Nietzsche argues that because these instincts "destroy one another," it is necessary that "at least one of these instinct-systems should be paralyzed beneath an iron pressure, so as to permit another to come into force, become strong, become master" (*TI* "Expeditions" 41). How does this technique of "pruning" differ from the "excision" practiced by anti-natural morality?

Our first clue to their difference is in Nietzsche's contrast of *beschneiden* (to cut back, pare) and *ausschneiden* (to cut out or away). Anti-natural morality tries to completely eradicate the instinct, to remove it entirely from one's personality. Nietzsche's call to "prune" a contradictory instinct, on the contrary, requires that we cut *back* or moderate the instinct. The instinct is only temporarily "paralyzed" beneath an "iron pressure" until another instinct has developed sufficient strength to master it. The result, then, is not the complete paralysis or extinction of the instinct, but instead its incorporation into an order and hierarchy of instincts—in other words, its moderation.

So, the first difference between natural and anti-natural ways of controlling an instinct is simply that a natural morality reduces a troublesome instinct's power, while an anti-natural morality tries to destroy it. The second, and perhaps more crucial, difference bears on what *form* of instinct is the object of "cutting back" or "cutting away." I have said that natural morality never truly "condemns" because it negates only values, instincts, and practices that are directly hostile to life—it only condemns what condemns. It is in this sense that we should understand Nietzsche's claim that the contemporary individual's instincts *contradict* (*widersprechen*), rather than merely conflict with, one another. They do not hinder, but destroy (*zerstören*) each other.

This conflict is not based merely in accidental differences in instinctual aims. It is possible only given the presence of *anti-natural* instincts—of incorporated values and behaviors that are specifically aimed *against* other instincts, which directly negate rather than merely obstruct other instincts.[13] Consequently, while natural morality only limits or restrains natural instincts, it can consistently eliminate anti-natural ones. For the excision of an anti-natural instinct does not harm a positive ability, only the negative ability to weaken other abilities. To "prune" a self-contradictory soul is to empower and enable it, not "paralyze" or weaken it.

This is also the decisive difference between moralities of breeding and taming: "Both the taming [*Zähmung*] of the beast man and the breeding [*Züchtung*] of a certain species has been called 'improvement' [*Besserung*]" (*TI* "Improvers" 2). However, taming does not truly improve individuals: "Whoever knows what goes on in menageries is doubtful whether the beasts in them are 'improved' [*verbessert*]. They are weakened, they are made less harmful, they become sickly beasts through the depressive emotion of fear, through pain, through injuries, through hunger" (*TI* "Improvers" 2). Consistent with anti-natural morality, taming is a condemnation, a negation, a removal of characteristics: sickness, fear, and pain as the direct negation of health, confidence, and happiness. Although Nietzsche does not directly describe the contrasting form of breeding, its character is clear in contrast: if taming weakens and sickens, then breeding strengthens and enhances health. While it might be objected that this claim depends on Nietzsche's questionable evaluative assumptions about strength and health, it is, on the contrary, a simple, non-evaluative, and substantive distinction: regardless of the value we attribute to an ability, taming disempowers and disables, while breeding empowers and enables.[14]

Consider a literal example: while I might, in the process of breeding a horse for its swiftness, breed out other traits such as the horse's unique color, the negative effect on other traits is contingent, extrinsic to my purpose. Breeding is, consequently, aptly described as a form of "cultivation" in two senses. First, it cultivates in the sense of promoting positive characteristics rather than destroying negative ones. Second, it cultivates in the sense of tending to and working with a natural process, rather than directly imposing or creating new forms. Breeding cultivates natural traits by preserving and protecting their natural reproduction, not by introducing or engineering new traits.[15]

Of course, it might be argued that Nietzsche's frequent characterization of the higher type as a product of self-overcoming, discipline, and self-mastery suggests a more positive and individualistic form of breeding, the active self-introduction of new traits rather than their protection and preservation. Nietzsche's "highest type of free man" is characterized by "the maximum of authority and discipline toward oneself" (*TI* "Expeditions" 38). Goethe, for example, "disciplined himself to a whole, he created himself" (*TI* "Expeditions" 49). Even where human enhancement is not the product of personal discipline, Nietzsche describes it as the product of a creative, productive social or cultural form of discipline: "What is essential 'in heaven and on earth' seems to be, to say it once more, that there should be obedience over a long period of time and in a single direction: given that, something always develops, and has developed, for the sake of which it is worth to live on earth" (*BGE* 188).

Such passages misleadingly suggest a voluntaristic morality in which higher individuals are not products of breeding but self-produced. Yet Nietzsche consistently counters and qualifies such suggestions. Although higher types possess greater authority over themselves, this is only the outcome of a conflict of drives: "Freedom means that the manly instincts that delight in war and victory have gained mastery over the other instincts" (*TI* "Expeditions" 38). Freedom is not the result of individual agency, but of conditioned necessity, of a danger which "compels us to be strong . . . . One must need strength, otherwise one will never have it." Goethe's self-creation, for example, was not a development against or independent of nature but "a return to nature" (*TI* "Expeditions" 49). He did not produce or reinvent his character but instead "affirmed everything which was related to him" and dared "to allow himself the whole compass and wealth of naturalness." His development was an affirmation of nature rather than its redesign, achieved not autonomously but through "a joyful and trusting fatalism . . . the faith that only what is separate and individual may be rejected, that in the totality everything is redeemed and affirmed."

Consequently, although the higher type is characterized by self-discipline, it does not independently produce that capacity for self-discipline. Freedom is an outcome, a produced character type, not the cause of its own production. Ultimately, human enhancement is not the product of individual but social discipline, not voluntary self-control but "the morality of mores and the social straightjacket" (*GM* II: 2).

Nevertheless, Nietzsche's description of social forms of discipline may still support the objection that breeding actively produces new traits and types, rather than merely promoting naturally occurring traits and types. To produce the "sovereign individual" through the morality of mores is, after all, to "breed [*heranzüchten*] an animal with the right to make promises [*das versprechen darf*]" (*GM* II: 1), to introduce a new type characterized by the unique trait of conscience.

However, in the *Genealogy* Nietzsche has not yet introduced the *Twilight of the Idols*' critical contrast between breeding and taming. The social and moral production of conscience is clearly a morality of taming in the later, pejorative sense, rather than a true morality of breeding. For it does not aim at the production of the sovereign individual or a distinct human type, but rather at the very opposite: it "makes men to a certain degree necessary, uniform, like among like, regular, and consequently calculable" (*GM* I: 1). It seeks, in other words, to make individuals type-less, to breed out the natural qualities that differentiate them, to weaken or eliminate rather than enhance their capacities.

The sovereign individual is, then, an accident of the morality of taming, rather than the intended product of a morality of breeding. More important, the sovereign individual as a higher type is defined in opposition to the taming process that produced it. While the morality of mores (*Sittlichkeit der Sitte*) makes individuals "necessary, uniform, like among like [*gleich unter Gleichen*]," the sovereign individual is "like unto himself [*nur sich selbst gleiche*] . . . autonomous and supramoral [*übersittliche*]." In other words, Nietzsche's morality of breeding is a counter-breeding that turns the disciplinary practices of the morality of taming against its own ends, not in order to introduce new character traits, but in order to breed *out* the traits that taming has introduced.

And since, as we have seen, those traits are negatively defined, anti-natural traits, produced through the repression, weakening, or elimination of natural ones, Nietzschean breeding does not redesign nature but seeks "to translate man back into nature" (*BGE* 230). This "return to nature" is "not really a going-back but a going-up—up into a high, free, even frightful nature and naturalness" (*TI* "Expeditions" 48 and 49), because it does not undo the work of the morality of taming entirely. The morality of breeding preserves its "ripest fruit": it naturalizes the higher faculty of conscience by freeing it from bad conscience, the domination of conscience by the values of the morality of taming.

Taming, in contrast, is an anti-natural moral method: it does not intend to preserve and enhance desirable powers, but to de-select and exterminate undesirable ones. Taking, again, a literal example: to domesticate a wild animal is to intentionally breed out the traits of size, strength, aggressiveness, and independence. Even if we argue that such traits can be harmful or undesirable, we are not rejecting Nietzsche's claim that taming disempowers. We are, instead, arguing that disempowerment is sometimes beneficial or justified—a removal of harmful abilities, but abilities nonetheless.

It might also be argued that taming can sometimes empower or produce positive traits—for example, when we breed domesticated dogs for sociability. However, this depends on which trait we are identifying as "sociability." As a product of taming, sociability is a negative trait, a disempowerment: the absence of aggression. However, as a positive trait—say, friendliness or social intelligence—sociability is the product of breeding rather than taming. For the breeder does not eliminate the traits of undomesticated dogs: they are already a domesticated species. Instead, the breeder selects and preserves the naturally given trait of sociability that some domesticated dogs possess. To breed a more sociable domesticated dog is, then, not truly an example of taming at all.

The crucial distinction is whether the aim is negative or positive in relation to the trait: whether the goal is to reduce or enhance a characteristic or ability, to preserve or eliminate it. This is why Nietzsche's claim that the morality of taming makes humanity weak or ill is meant quite seriously: "In the struggle with the beast, making it sick can be the only means of making it weak" (*TI* "Improvers" 2).[16] If a morality reduces the power to act, it weakens; and if it weakens to the point of disabling, it can plausibly be likened to an illness. The morality of taming makes sick precisely because it has no other means: as an anti-natural morality it attacks the passions and desires as such, "at their roots," rather than in their excessive manifestation (*TI* "Morality" 1). This means it cannot entirely or truly excise a passion without destroying the patient. Such a morality can practically succeed only by failing to eliminate de-selected abilities entirely, instead reducing the patient's power to act upon its abilities—through disempowering rather than fully disabling.

This brings us to a second, crucial point about the naturalness of breeding. Taming is anti-natural because it de-selects and disempowers rather than selects and empowers. This is, in turn, related to a broader issue in Nietzsche's ethical philosophy—his rejection of strong conceptions of metaphysical free will and, consequently, of forms of morality that rely on the free, voluntary agency of the moral subject to effect change in individual character and action:

> When the moralist merely turns to the individual and says to him: "You ought to be thus and thus" he does not cease to make himself ridiculous. The individual is, in his future and in his past, a piece of fate [*ein Stück fatum*], one law more, one necessity more for everything that is and everything that will be. To say to him, "change yourself!" means to demand that everything should change, even in the past. (*TI* "Morality" 6)

It is precisely because Nietzsche does not believe slave morality can be effected on a voluntary level—through a free choice to constrain a condemned passion or instinct—that it is necessary for a natural form of morality to be achieved through breeding: through the cultural production of human types, rather than through rational or moral persuasion.[17]

If the individual cannot be substantially changed through moral persuasion, then humanity can only be changed in its future character. But because the present character of the individual cannot be directly changed, future humanity can only be changed through the preservation or extinction of presently existing individuals as types. Breeding "improves" through the selection, preservation, and reproduction of higher individual types. It is a modest, indirect means, because it does not directly change forms of humanity, but selects and preserves natural changes. It does not create types or impose new forms, but chooses the "highest" naturally occurring exemplars and protects them from extinction.

Consequently, breeding is natural, not only as the selection and preservation of natural powers and abilities, but also as an improvement of human types rather than individuals, through the medium of natural necessity rather than volition. Breeding is not vulnerable to Nietzsche's critique of the "so-called improvers of mankind," because it affirms the "fatality" of the individual, the impossibility of changing humanity qua individual (*TI* "Improvers" 2, *TI* "Errors" 8).[18]

We may conclude, then, that Nietzsche's critical distinction of moralities of breeding and taming is continuous with that of natural and antinatural morality. Moreover, these moralities' positive or negative relation to nature determines their consequences for life as empowering or disempowering, enabling or disabling—generally, as beneficial or harmful to life.

Breeding as Proliferation and Variation, Taming as Reduction and Normalization

Breeding and taming also reflect Nietzsche's contrast of natural and antinatural moralities in their relation to natural processes as a whole. As a natural morality that selects and preserves abilities rather than de-selects and disempowers, breeding affirms nature as a whole in its basic characteristic of contingency: as an accidental, purposeless, and endless process of selection, lacking progress in any absolute sense. Breeding tends necessarily toward proliferation, the preservation of new types, as well as toward variation through the preservation of the diversity of types. Taming, in contrast, tends toward reduction, the elimination of negatively evaluated types, and normalization—the universal reproduction of a single moral type in all members of the species, the "last man."

For Nietzsche, variation and proliferation are processes intrinsic to natural selection and development. Natural processes have no governing aim; their contingency thwarts every attempt to bring human development to a single, lasting end. The human individual, he says, "is not the subject of an attempt to attain to an 'ideal of man' or an 'ideal of happiness' or an 'ideal of morality'—it is absurd to want to hand over his nature to some purpose or other. We invented the concept 'purpose': in reality purpose is lacking" (*TI* "Errors" 8). Given this absence of teleological end, nature tends inevitably toward a rich diversity of contradictory, blossoming and perishing, forms and types; it is characterized by a "wealth, luxury, even absurd prodigality" that is indifferent to human evaluations of progress and even tends, on the contrary, toward the "defeat of the stronger, the more privileged, the fortunate exceptions" (*TI* "Expeditions" 14).

This natural condition of contingency, purposelessness, and impermanence does not support moral attempts to transform humanity as a species into a single improved or perfected type: "The entire morality of improvement [*Besserungs-Moral*] . . . has been a misunderstanding" (*TI* "Problem" 11). Indeed, Nietzsche's self-proclaimed "tragic" form of philosophy is grounded in the affirmation of life's "sacrifice of its highest types" (*EH* "Books" 3). Any morality that actively seeks to reduce humanity to a single type acts, then, directly against a fundamental limitation of nature: "Reality shows us an enchanting wealth of types, the luxuriance of a prodigal play and change of forms: and does some pitiful journeyman moralist say at the sight of it: 'No! Man ought to be different'?" (*TI* "Morality" 6).

As with Nietzsche's fatalism about the individual, this fatalism about the species ("the fatality of all that which has been and will be," [*TI* "Errors" 8]) is both natural and moral: a recognition of the necessity of lower types and the extinction of higher types, as well as a normative demand to *affirm* this necessity. Consequently, humans cannot be absolutely "improved" (*bessern*, *verbessern*); they cannot be changed universally or permanently, nor can they be fundamentally "bettered": made qualitatively better or worse. Instead, we must understand human enhancement both relatively and quantitatively.

First, the relative enhancement of humanity as a whole is determined according to the production of higher types within that whole, rather than the universalization of a single type. "Enhancement" in the sense of "raising" or "heightening" (*Erhöhung*) (*BGE* 44, 239, 257) improves one individual or type relative to the norm of the species, so there cannot be absolute enhancement of the species as a whole.

Instead, breeding seeks to produce and preserve higher types among other types, to add to or preserve nature's "enchanting wealth of types" rather than transform all human beings into one higher type.[19] Consequently, enhancement is primarily a matter of quantitative, not qualitative, change: "enhancement" as "expansion," "increase," or "greatness" (*Vergrößerung*,

Grösse) (*BGE* 212)—as "making more" (more diverse and stronger drives and abilities) rather than "making good" (morally or aesthetically better drives and abilities).

Second, the improvement of types within the whole is relative to contingent historical conditions. If there are no purposes in nature, there are no absolute criteria according to which we can measure the well-being or excellence of higher types. Consider, as an analogy, the process of natural selection. The "fitness" or well-adaptedness of a species is determinable only relative to the conditions of its environment, since attributes beneficial under one set of environmental conditions might be harmful under others. Consequently, a species is "better" or "worse" adapted only relative to its current environmental state. Individual traits do not have adaptive value for every species or individual in a species, and even within the same species a trait's value varies with its changing environmental conditions.[20]

Likewise, because human well-being depends upon a changeable human type's relation to contingent historical circumstances, whether or not a human type is "well turned out" (*wohlgerathen*) cannot be evaluated absolutely, but only in relation to the actual historical conditions in which it exists.[21] Therefore, there cannot be a single vision of moral improvement for all human beings that would serve as the criterion of moral breeding: what is an enhancement of life for a given individual or group in contemporary historical circumstances may tomorrow be harmful. Consequently, human well-being, like evolutionary fitness, is best served not by direct improvement but by diversity. The greater the diversity of types, the greater the likelihood that any one will be well suited to its conditions of existence.[22]

Breeding, then, does not conceive and create a specific higher type. It is designed to take advantage of fortunate exceptions rather than engineer them. It is an experiment rather than an art, one that (1) produces the conditions for the proliferation of all types, not just the higher, and (2) selects from and preserves accidentally produced higher types. So, we may conclude that, on Nietzsche's view, human improvement is best served through the proliferation of human types, rather than through the defining and engineering of an "overman" as ideal type—a method which would repeat the same error of selective narrowing that Nietzsche condemns in the "last man" ideal of moral taming (*Z* "Prologue" 5).[23]

Nietzsche repeatedly suggests this connection between variation and human improvement. On the level of the individual, he tells us that "the greatness of man" lies in "being capable of being as manifold as whole, as ample as full" (*BGE* 212). The same is true of the conditions for human development: humanity is made great precisely by maintaining its unity while diversifying the types within it, increasing its manifoldness. Historical epochs in which a diversity of human values, types, and ways of life flourish promote overall "variation, whether as deviation (to something higher, subtler, rarer) or as degeneration and monstrosity" (*BGE* 262). In such epochs, "the individual dares to be individual and different," in turn creating "a splendid, manifold, junglelike growth and upward striving, a kind of tropical tempo in the competition to grow" (*BGE* 262). To be sure, this manifoldness is the condition of harmful variations as well as beneficial ones, but Nietzsche's point is precisely that it is the condition for both.

From Nietzsche's naturalistic fatalism, it follows that the morality of taming, in contrast, is anti-natural in two ways. First, because the well-being of humanity is relative to contingent historical circumstances, the morality of taming is opposed to the natural conditions that maximize effective breeding. Second, by prescribing a single moral ideal for all humanity, it pits itself against a natural world that tends, intrinsically, toward the proliferation rather than perfection of types.[24] Its ideal is anti-natural in the dangerous sense that it can succeed only through the active destruction of naturally proliferating variations from that ideal. If everyone cannot be tamed, if every individual cannot be transformed into the "last man," then the last man can be realized only through the elimination of every other type.

Breeding as Preservation of Types, Taming as Destruction through Anti-Types

The final way that breeding and taming reflect Nietzsche's distinction of natural and anti-natural moralities is in their relation to natural change—specifically, in the destructiveness of their methods of preserving selected types against non-selected types. Unlike taming, breeding does not actively eliminate non-selected types. It is "selective" in the truest sense: it refuses to de-select. In keeping with Nietzsche's commitment to the affirmation of the whole of existence, the love of fate (*amor fati*), breeding does not engage in authentic destruction. It only selects against anti-types—false types defined by the absence of traits. It destroys only ideals and practices that produce such anti-types through actively disabling; it affirms, in contrast, all variations of authentic types within the diversity of the species.

We have already seen that the selective character of breeding tends toward an increased diversity of types. But *amor fati* is not merely a refusal to actively condemn non-selected types, but an active affirmation (*Jasagen*) of their existence as part of the whole sphere of life: "We immoralists have . . . opened wide our hearts to every kind of understanding, comprehension, approval. We do not readily deny, we seek our honor in affirming" (*TI* "Morality" 6). Unconditional affirmation is a part of Nietzsche's strategy of spiritualizing rather than exterminating passions: enmity is transformed through recognition of "the value of having enemies" (*TI* "Morality" 3).

This is not abstract generosity on Nietzsche's part; he expressly affirms the continued existence of the church and Judeo-Christian morality as enduring philosophical enemies. "We immoralists and anti-Christians see that it is to our advantage that the Church exists." In a later section he adds:

> We have come more and more to appreciate that economy which needs and knows how to use all that which the holy lunacy of the priest, the diseased reason of the priest rejects; that economy in the law of life which derives advantage even from the repellent species of the bigot, the priest, the virtuous man. (*TI* "Morality" 6)

Nietzsche repeatedly insists he can simultaneously affirm and condemn, that he can select or promote without de-selecting or eliminating: "I do not want to wage war against what is ugly . . . . Looking away shall be my only negation!" (*GS* 276). We can conclude, then, that he does not intend the same "destruction of enemies" that he criticizes Christianity for, that a morality of breeding produces higher human types alongside others rather than through their exclusion. In some way, his morality preserves the very ideals and types it condemns.[25]

Can Nietzsche's morality promote higher types without making war against the lower? Of course, no morality, breeding included, can *fully* affirm what it morally condemns. It is not in a merely exaggerated way that Nietzsche repeatedly and explicitly appeals, despite his love of fate, to "destruction" (*Vernichtung*) as a necessary moral means. However, can we interpret Nietzsche's endorsement of destruction in a way consistent with affirmation?[26]

Nietzsche often uses the language of warfare and violence figuratively, but there are instances in which he appears to condone actual harm. For example, in one deeply troubling passage, he says that the "higher breeding [*Höherzüchtung*] of humanity" calls for "the remorseless destruction [*schonungslose Vernichtung*] of all degeneracies and parasites [*Entartenden und Parasitischen*]" (*EH* "The Birth of Tragedy" 4). In another, he complains that Christianity preserves "what ought to perish" (*BGE* 62).

We should first note that Nietzsche uses *Vernichtung* for "destruction," which he has already identified with anti-natural morality's extermination of the passions. So we should be wary of attributing a meaning to this positive use of *Vernichtung* in *Ecce Homo* that would directly contradict his critical use of the term in *Twilight of the Idols* (*TI* "Morality" 1), a work completed the same year.

More important, such comments, although literally intended, are misleading in their reference in two ways. First, they do not refer to the destruction of types as collections of human individuals, but types as such. It is not the perishing of beings but forms of character, not persons but forms of life.[27] Second, they refer not to the destruction of authentic, positively determined types, but rather to the destruction of "anti-types" which, I will argue, does not involve authentic destruction at all.[28]

Although Nietzsche's morality of cultivation allows unselected types to perish, it is essential to remember that this is a *morality* of breeding: a sociocultural selection and preservation of psychological types. Likewise, the de-selection of types is also a sociocultural process: an undoing of the values and habits that produce and reproduce the deselected type. Consequently, the destruction of character types does not entail the destruction of persons possessing those characters.[29]

For example, in *On the Genealogy of Morality*, Nietzsche suggests we can reverse the development of bad conscience (the principal harmful effect of moral taming) through a transvaluation of values, an evaluative fusing of the feeling of guilt to unnatural rather than natural instincts (*GM* II: 24). This is the paradigmatic case of Nietzschean "destruction," the refusal to preserve what "ought to perish": he is calling for the destruction of the guilt-ridden personality, the elimination of bad conscience as a form of human life.

The priest, in contrast, responds to the suffering of the guilty by preserving their type. By offering temporary relief in the form of forgiveness and penance, by continuing to interpret suffering as moral punishment for sin, the priest preserves not individual lives, but guilty conscience as a form of personality. Nietzsche's reinterpretation of suffering as the innocence of becoming is an attempt to destroy this form of life: to end the continued production of guilty character by destroying the interpretation of suffering that regenerates it.

This is an exemplary case of "philosophizing with a hammer": a philosophical interpretation that destroys a form of character production, thus ultimately destroying an entire human type: guilty conscience. This interpretation of the metaphor of the hammer best captures both of its intended connotations, the martial imagery of destruction and the gentler image in the forward to *Twilight of the Idols*: the tuning fork used to "sound out" hollow idols, destroying not realities but falsehoods, not beings but values, practices, and personality types that negate reality. In the latter respect, *vernichten* suggests not annihilation, but rather a revealing or releasing of the nothingness of which such "ideals" are constituted: "The characteristics which have been given to the 'true being' of things are the characteristics of non-being, of nothingness; the 'true world' has been constructed from the contradiction of the actual world" (*TI* "'Reason'" 6).

This is not merely one possible, minor example of innocuous "destruction"; it is the principal kind with which Nietzsche is concerned. For moral guilt is the fundamental harm that the taming has inflicted upon humanity, the fundamental obstacle to the survival of higher types and, therefore, the principle cause of humanity's decline. Christian morality has "waged a war to the death" against higher types (*A* 5). It has attempted to "break the strong, sickly over great hopes, cast suspicion on the joy in beauty, bend everything haughty, manly, conquering, domineering, all the instincts characteristic of the highest and best-turned-out type of 'man,' into unsureness, agony of conscience, self-destruction" (*BGE* 62).

Consequently, to destroy guilt as a form of character is to attack decline at the very root. Nietzsche's provocative endorsement of destruction means, not that we should harm or let perish those who suffer, but that we should cease harming those who do *not* suffer. What ought to perish is the systematic reproduction of a destructive form of personality—*not* the victim of this form of personality. We should, then, understand Nietzsche's call for the destruction of types as a call to cease their intentional production and reproduction.[30]

This is not, however, a claim that his language of destruction is metaphorical. It is literally destruction in two senses. First, it is a destruction of types and, second, to cease reproducing these types requires the destruction of the ideals, values, and practices that condition them.

It should be added that the destruction of types and values rather than persons is not accidentally beneficial, a fortunate side effect of Nietzsche's preoccupation with types over individuals. The effects of breeding are intentionally beneficial to the deselected, since breeding is designed to negate only negative qualities. It follows from breeding's selective character that it can only select against false types: negatively defined forms of character based in values and practices that actively disempower, disable, and exterminate true types.

As we have seen, moral taming is a form of de-selection: it produces types characterized by the absence of negatively evaluated traits. They are not authentic character types, but non-types defined by negative attributes, by a lack or weakness of traits—for example, charity as unselfishness, humility as lack of pride, or purity as lack of sensuality. Consequently, Nietzsche's irresponsible language of "degeneracies and parasites" is consistent with his commitment to *amor fati*, because it refers to these negative forms of personality. They are literally degenerate (*Entartet*) because they eliminate formal traits: they are anti-forms, anti-kinds (*Entarten*) rather than kinds (*Arten*), existing parasitically upon the traits and types they weaken or destroy.

Thus, taming does not produce competing types at all: it systematically destroys all competitors. It is intrinsically destructive, a "common war on all that is strange, privileged, the higher man" (*BGE* 212). And, consequently, breeding does not authentically destroy at all, but instead conducts, as the saying goes, "a war on war." The destruction of anti-types does not remove form but preserves it, destroying what are in the strongest sense "ideals" (anti-traits and anti-types) rather than realities, a destruction that is accomplished simply through the *preservation* of positively determined forms of character.[31]

In this way, breeding indirectly preserves all true types, including non-selected ones, by destroying the values and practices that undermine them, and by protecting the existence of character as such from the truly destructive morality of taming, which seeks the eradication of all character through the universal realization of a negatively-defined moral ideal.

Comparative Eugenics as a Morality of Taming: A Nietzschean Critique

We are now in a position to conclude that all comparative forms of eugenics are instances of the morality of taming, that they share in its dangerous tendency toward destructiveness, and that they are diametrically opposed to Nietzsche's morality of breeding. By comparative eugenics, I mean the promotion or elimination of traits based in comparative values, such as evaluations of superiority and inferiority or type, trait, or ability.[32] I will begin with the most extreme case: historical forms of racial eugenics that have led to racism, discrimination, oppression, and genocide. I will then close with a discussion of contemporary liberal eugenics and so-called designer baby cases.

The principal characteristic of racial eugenics is its foundation in what Nietzsche calls the slavish mode of evaluation: its concept of the good, the health of the race, is comparatively defined in relation to a more primary negative evaluation, the identification of one or more out-groups as inferior. This negative foundation grounds the primary, supposedly positive, concept of "purity." The good is equivalent to the elimination of evil: racial superiority is defined by what it excludes rather than what it includes, by the absence of traits rather than their presence.

As in the morality of taming, racial eugenics produces a moral ideal that rejects competing types. Because the ideal is both universal (claiming superiority as species) and negative (defined as exclusion of an out-group), it cannot exist alongside competing types. Like the negative anti-types of taming, a racial eugenic ideal is realized precisely through the direct negation of competing types, and so it tends necessarily toward domination and violence. Consequently, racial eugenics is clearly an instance of the morality of taming. Indeed, any eugenic theory whose conception of superiority is universal and grounded in direct negation must be a morality of taming. The distance between Nietzsche's morality of breeding from ethically dangerous historical forms of eugenics is, then, not simply substantial, but absolute: they are related only in their direct opposition.

Finally, we can conclude that contemporary liberal or non-coercive varieties of comparative eugenics also fall into the category of taming for the same reason: their positivity is an illusion; they do not select for true traits, but against them. This is also their ethical failure: they do not truly benefit the selected, but rather harm the de-selected.

I will focus on what I will call perfectionist eugenics, in which parents use direct genetic intervention to enhance their child's abilities (sometimes referred to as "designer baby" cases). The principal ethical worry is that these parents' children will have an unjust advantage over others. Now, I have emphasized that Nietzsche's morality of breeding affirms ability, power, and difference. Surely, we might argue, this includes the affirmation of *superior* ability. Must we conclude that Nietzsche would endorse perfectionist eugenics as a morality of breeding?

On the contrary, it is a morality of taming, for it does not involve the selection of positive abilities, but rather the de-selection of comparative disadvantages, falsely perceived as disabilities. Since we are concerned only about cases where fairness or justice is endangered, I will limit the argument to cases involving the introduction of abilities significantly superior to the norm; for example, superior intelligence, talent, or beauty.

Perfectionist eugenics selects abilities for their relative value: *comparative* abilities.[33] For example, suppose it one day becomes technologically possible to eugenically enhance intelligence. Parents choosing such a procedure would not wish merely to make their children intellectually able, but to give them an educational advantage—to make them more able than other children. But a comparative ability like greater intelligence is not an ability different in kind from that of intelligence; it is one and the same ability, evaluated relationally. So, parents who genetically select for intelligence are not really selecting *for* intelligence, but *against* average or inferior intelligence, perceived as disability.

Moreover, this de-selection is of a disadvantage rather than an authentic disability: inferior intelligence is only comparatively negative. In itself, it is a positive ability. The parents are not really de-selecting average or inferior intelligence in their own child, but instead indirectly de-selecting intellectual equality or superiority in other children. The target of their genetic intervention is not their child's intelligence, but the social norm against which their child will be measured. While they claim to select for a positive ability in their own child, they are instead manipulating the norm in order to produce a negative, relative disability in other children.

The illusion that perfectionist eugenics positively promotes authentic abilities has its basis in the very same inversion of good and bad, being and non-being, ideal and reality, that Nietzsche attributes to slave morality in *On the Genealogy of Morality*. While the nobles affirm their own positively existing traits as good, the slaves negate the positive traits of the nobles, affirming their destruction as good.

Likewise, while the ability of intelligence is a positive trait, perfectionist eugenicists identify its possession by others as a harmful disadvantage to their own child, thus identifying the relative reduction of other children's intelligence as a good. While claiming to positively improve the populace by improving intelligence, perfectionist eugenicists instead manipulate comparative intelligence in a way that weakens the relative intelligence of others. They disguise a negative evaluation of the child's intelligence as a positive one, and a reduction of other children's relative abilities as an absolute promotion of ability.

Consequently, perfectionist eugenics is a morality of taming, characterized by de-selection rather than selection, disempowerment rather than empowerment, the reduction and normalization of types rather than their variation and proliferation, and active harm to the de-selected, rather than the protection of differentiated types. We may conclude that Nietzsche's morality of breeding is utterly opposed to every form of eugenics that selects for comparatively defined identities, traits, or abilities. Far from being compatible with ethically dangerous forms of eugenics, it provides us with a decisive critical basis for their rejection.

12

An "Other Way of Being"

The Nietzschean "Animal": Contributions to the Question of Biopolitics

MÓNICA B. CRAGNOLINI

> To make out of the remains of our animality the most precious gem: in the same way that, after her metamorphosis, there remained of Isis only her lunar horns.
>
> **—Nietzsche, *KSA* 9:17[6]**

The text of the epigraph refers to Isis and her metamorphoses: transformed into a cow by Horus (and into other animals, according to the various myths), the goddess, who was able to resurrect her brother-husband Osiris, preserved something of the animal in her manifestation. In some way, the mode of "being human" implies a continuous "transformation" of the living animal for the sake of "humanization." The process of culture, understood as "spiritualization," means not only moving away from the living animal but above all, to dominate it, to enslave it, to gain usufruct over it, to "mechanize" it, to negate it. Starting from the consideration that the place of animality in Nietzsche's thought, especially in *Zarathustra*, is crucial to understanding the transition to the *Übermensch*, I will analyze the possibility of thinking the animal in this direction, that is to say, beyond any "humanist" assumption. The aim of this chapter is to seize some of the possibilities that the question of that "other way of being" opens for contemporary thought: the way of being of the living nonhuman in Nietzsche, and what this problematic can contribute to contemporary biopolitical debates.

Life as Will to Power and the Animal

In order to think the question of animality in Nietzsche, a question that has to do with the problematic of life, one must take into account the operation of the will to power, its movement of forces that create and destroy, agglutinate and disperse.[1] Giorgio Agamben notes in *Means Without End*[2] the intimate relationship between life and forms of life in the case of the living human. For Agamben, a "form-of-Life" characterizes and defines a way of life whose acts are not "facts," but "possibility," considering that the forms of life of man escape biological necessity. In this sense, the forms of human life are "political life."

In Nietzsche's conception of the will to power, the forms "that life gives to itself" are part of this will, and not something "alien to it." That is to say, the relation between life and forms of life should be thought not only with respect to "human" life, but rather in all that concerns life. Life is a constant self-overcoming and it generates its "own" architectures that are not "impositions" on life, but a process of life itself. In this sense, will to power as a plurality of forces in constant movement is *Selbstüberwindung* (self-overcoming), hence the forces that disperse are "stronger," because they allow for such self-overcoming.

The synthetizing character of the forces is connected with a "densification" of their becoming, which limits the chaos and, as Nietzsche says, "organizing a small fragment of the world" (*KSA* 12:9[60]). So that forces may seek their excedence, these "syntheses" must be submitted to a process of destruction or dispersal. Perhaps one could characterize decadent nihilism as the stagnant densifications of the forces that, in the preservation of conservation, try to annul the movement of life and wind up making this movement into a mechanism of death.

In the notion of the ideal ascetic, Nietzsche thought the question that contemporary biopolitics addresses in terms of "immunization."[3] In the fourth part of *Thus Spoke Zarathustra*, the supposed superior man, in the guise of the scientist, says to the Persian prophet that "spirit is the life that itself cuts into life" (*Z* IV "The Leech"). The Third Essay of the *Genealogy of Morals* is also dedicated to this question, translated into terms of "necessity" for life. The priest makes visible the process through which religion operates by contrasting life with life, starting from the valorization of another form of superior life. Religion is protection of life, as Derrida shows in "Faith and Knowledge,"[4] but the value judgments regarding the good or desirable life impose strata and differences that make it inevitable, if life is to aspire to other levels of the desirable, that life turns against itself. The ascetic life is life turned against itself, but what must be kept in mind is that this "hostility" concerns life itself (and is not only a myth of asceticism, busy with the construction of worlds that lie beyond life):

> It must be a necessity of the first rank, which makes this species continually grow and prosper when it is *hostile to life,—life itself must have an interest* in preserving such a self-contradictory type. For an ascetic life is a self-contradiction: here an unparalleled *ressentiment* rules, that of an unfulfilled instinct and power-will which wants to be master, not over something in life, but over life itself and its deepest, strongest, most profound conditions; here, an attempt is made to use power to block the sources of the power; here, the green eye of spite turns on physiological growth itself, in particular the manifestation of this in beauty and joy; while satisfaction is *looked for* and found in failure, decay, pain, misfortune, ugliness, voluntary deprivation, destruction of selfhood, self-flagellation and self-sacrifice. This is all paradoxical in the extreme: we are faced with a dissidence [*Zwiespältigkeit*] which *wills* itself to be dissident [*zwiespältig*], which *relishes* itself in this affliction and becomes more self-assured and triumphant to the same degree as its own condition, the physiological capacity of life, *decreases*. (*GM* III: 11)

From a political point of view, the previous passage suggests that life needs the ascetic ideal, and cannot eliminate this ideal, or return to "more natural ways of life." Instead it becomes essential to think of another way of confronting this aporia.[5]

Nietzsche believes one must take advantage of this knowledge of the inversions of perspectives and valorizations. Objectivity is needed here, but not understood as "disinterested contemplation"; rather as the capacity to know "the pros and cons" of each perspective and of the diversity of perspectives. Why is this objectivity necessary? Keeping in mind that life itself requires this hostility is conducive to thinking of modes of relating to the living that do not transform life into a material to be mastered by a resentful spirit. In terms of the contemporary biopolitical debate, this objectivity about perspectives makes it possible to think of the relation to the living in a way that is no longer thanatopolitical.

Considered physiologically, the expression "life *against* life" (*Leben gegen Leben*) is nonsense for Nietzsche (*GM* III: 13). In order to analyze the question of the ascetic ideal, therefore, he points out the fact that "*the ascetic ideal springs from the protective and healing instincts of a degenerating life*" (*GM* III: 13) intent on preserving itself. The struggle between instincts, in which the healthiest forces fight against the extenuated forces that desire to preserve themselves, is in practice nothing but a process of autoimmunization. The ascetic ideal is thus "a trick for the *preservation* of life" (*GM* III: 13).

The predominance of the ascetic ideal in distinct epochs of history demonstrates the sickened condition of man: "the ascetic priest is the incarnate wish for being otherwise, being elsewhere" (*GM* III: 13): but precisely this wish ties the priest to life itself, to life down here, since it obligates him to create better conditions for the life of men in their worldly existence: "this ascetic priest, this apparent enemy of life, this *negative man,*—he actually belongs to the really great forces in life which *conserve and create the positive*" (*GM* III: 13).

The human being is the most ill and insecure of animals, but precisely from its "no's," from the wounds it inflicts upon itself, it obligates itself to live. That is, the negation of "this" life nevertheless preserves this life: the ascetic ideal is a kind of wound to life that encourages living. It is as if life were "using" the forms of the ascetic ideal (that it itself produces) in order to preserve itself. It cannot be any other way, since the sick condition of the human being is the "norm" (*GM* III: 14), meaning the sickest and the weakest are present in various areas of culture, giving everything "something like the air of the mad-house and hospital" (*GM* III: 14).

It is true that the weak undermine life, generating resentment: "Here, the worms of revenge and rancor teem all around; here, the air stinks of things unrevealed, and unconfessed; here, the web of the most wicked conspiracy is continually being spun" (*GM* III: 14). Weak human beings are those who always desire being hangmen, making everyone else atone, those who "put their wrecked sensuality on the market, swaddled in verses and other nappies, as 'purity of the heart'" (*GM* III: 14). They know how to find torturous ways to become tyrants to the healthy: sick life generates mechanisms of domination that sacrifice what is healthy. The doctors of the sick are themselves sick, and this is the task of the ascetic priest, who in order to be a doctor must first wound (*GM* III: 14). And his shrewdness consists in the fact that while he soothes the pain of the wound, he poisons it at the same time. This is why the ascetic priests maintain the resentment of the herd at a level in which it will not explode—that is to say, he redirects resentment to keep things together rather that separating them. In this operation of the ascetic priest, it is the "healing instinct of life" that is acting (*GM* III: 15).

The priest resorts to a variety of means in order to palliate the pain of existence, among them "*mechanical activity*," (*GM* III: 17) the "blessing of work." In work, the patient separates from his suffering, and "that narrow chamber" that is conscience is occupied by doing: regularity, selecting a form of life sheltered in "impersonality" and in lasting choice, obedience, all these allow suffering to be left aside. This is "stimulated" by the priest who incites the love of one's neighbor as the "pleasure of giving pleasure." That is to say, the ascetic priest prescribes a "small dose" of the most affirmative aspect of the will to power, in order to somehow prevent the weak from harming one another out of resentment. "The *formation* of a herd" thus becomes a mechanism for assuring that those who suffer experience do not develop an aversion toward themselves. As Nietzsche indicates, the strong tend to disassociate themselves (this is why the force that disperses is stronger), while the weak need to be together. The "non-culpable" means of the priest in his battle against displeasure are, then, socialization, the fomenting of love for one's neighbor, the little joys, mechanical activity, all aided by the stifling of the feeling of life. The sacrificial machinery of the ascetic ideal functions by regularizing diversity and unifying difference in sameness. This presupposes the use of "animality," since the priest makes use of "the *whole* pack of wild hounds in man," (*GM* III: 20) since the "animal" bad conscience is only cruelty turned against oneself. This is why bad conscience is a "horrible animal [*schreckliche Thier*]," as Luther suggested: guilt manages to "sacrifice" that animality by way of torment, asceticism, discipline, fear. Pain is no longer a reason to complain but rather to desire; the herd *wants* to suffer so as to overcome fatigue: "life became *very* interesting again: awake, eternally awake, sleepless, glowing, burned out and yet not tired" (*GM* III: 20).

Confronted by this machinery, Nietzsche asks, "Where is the *counterpart* to this closed system of will, goal, and interpretation?" (*GM* III: 23). And in fact, it is difficult to respond to this question as neither science nor philosophy, despite the fact that they negate the transcendental character of existence, represent something other than the ascetic ideal; they are modes of this ideal.[6] The ascetic ideal functions by giving meaning to suffering, converting it into guilt and interpreting it in virtue of a goal. In this way, in this "poisoning of life," it expresses a "hatred of the animal" (*GM* III: 28). The priest (or any other representative of the ascetic ideal) is in the service of thanatological mechanisms: he takes care of degenerating life by generating death. Conserving a type of life (the other life, the superior life), he considers necessary the sacrifice of certain ways of life—above all, animal life, either the life of corporality in man (the flesh that must be submitted) or the life of the animal that is used up in its flesh, in its work force, in its life itself.

The Rests of Our Animality: Res(is)tance

What, then, are those rests of animality that Nietzsche would like us to turn into gems, as Isis did? What is the remainder of the process of "humanization"? Is it the subjected portion of corporality that "has resisted" subjection? The "interior animal" of bad conscience, shut in the cages of the interior world? Is it a matter of "liberating the repressed," or is it something altogether different? The expression "rests of animality" does not refer to a "liberation of the wild beast" once modern subjectivity has been deconstructed, but rather to a confrontation with subjectivity "*en restance.*" The expression *restance* refers to Derrida, and alludes to a movement of thought by which all dialectical or totalizing closure becomes impossible.[7]

Developing the idea of the remainder in its contraposition to the notion of resistance in psychoanalysis, Derrida argues that Freud preserves in this notion a certain nuance of the secret. The secret is postulated as unattainable, and yet maintains a certain homogeneity with the order of the analyzable, insofar as it "has a meaning." Analysis is a sort of *póleros*: a relation of forces that manifests itself as a union between *pólemos* and *eros*. This *póleros* entails that to "analyze anything whatsoever, anyone whatsoever, for anyone whatsoever, would mean saying to the other: choose my solution, prefer my solution, take my solution, love my solution; you will be in the truth if you do not resist my solution."[8]

This psychoanalytic notion of resistance assumes "a reserve of meaning that still awaits us."[9] With respect to such a reserve of meaning, Derrida, taking the idea of the *omphalós*, the navel of the dream, the "impenetrable, unfathomable, unanalyzable,"[10] thinks the remainder as the unanalyzable *omphalós*. The Derridean remainder is an *omphalós* that is not waiting to be deciphered, but remains as something other than meaning.

The term "*restance*" (remainder) takes up the notion of "*reste*" (rest or remainder) in the sphere of the syntagm "neither/nor" that characterizes deconstruction, insofar as it indicates a middle voice, neither active nor passive. The remainder is closely related to other Derridean notions such as the trace, which demonstrates, on the one hand, the absence of an origin, and on the other, iteration ("the trace of the trace"), which strives against full presence. The remainder, in writing, is the untranslatable that resists as textual excess: "res(is)tance." Referring to the notion of the messianic rest (the remainder of the Jews that would be left after the destruction of the temple, but that had always already been there), that absence of full presence has been characterized by Bensussan as "displacement that displaces without return the universal circle of integrating reappropriation."[11] The remainder, insofar as it is untranslatable, is what resists appropriation, what impedes ontologization with its topologizing location of places of possible meaning.

The "remainders" of animality, from this point of view, refer to this excess of life that destroys its own forms in a constant transgression of the limits it imposes on itself: self-overcoming means going beyond self-imposed limits.

The Fourth Part of *Thus Spoke Zarathustra*: Animal Resistance

It is undeniable that the transition to the overhuman presupposes a new mode of thinking animality. If *Thus Spoke Zarathustra* is the work that announces the overhuman, that other "way of being" with respect to the human, the question to ask is why the text concludes with the laughing lion and the flock of doves. Although *Zarathustra* is full of animals, the fourth part of the work, in which the prophet confronts the higher men who could be his disciples, constantly refers back to the question of the animal. Zarathustra receives the superior men and sends them off to his cave, so that they can be close to the strangeness of the animal that is not the "domestic animal," but rather something altogether different.

Since I have analyzed in detail elsewhere this passage through animality in the fourth part of *Zarathustra*,[12] here I would simply like to point out, in relation to the notion of remainder, that the superior men, despite the constant cautions of Zarathustra, appear to connect with animality in a regressive or restorative sense. In fact, while Zarathustra constantly instructs the "higher" men to "speak" and be with their animals, in his cave "with holes for thousands of animals," what the superior men end up doing is to get on their knees before an ass. Zarathustra's harsh response to this, and the final flight of the "higher" men before the lion and the flock of doves, indicates that there is something in the passage through animality that these men are incapable of dealing with. When they come up with a sort of "return to nature" (in the veneration of the animal), the only one who apparently interprets this occurrence as parody is the ugliest of men, the one who, because of his monstrosity, is closest (in the eyes of the others) to the plurality of forces that is the animal.

The entire fourth part of *Zarathustra* can be interpreted as a text that signals the passage from the "higher" man to the overman. This passage is rendered more difficult by the way of being of the "higher" man, who cannot relate to the problem of the animal outside the traditional ways. The fact that, at the end of this fourth part, the "higher" men flee from the animals (the lion that laughs and the flock of doves) indicates the human rejection (because of the fear it generates) of the living animal's way of life.

If one reads *Thus Spoke Zarathustra* not as a text seeking to unveil the "substantial truth" about human beings and their future, but instead as a writing built on passages and dedicated to opening up routes,[13] it is clear that the fourth part of the work addresses the problem of the "passage" through animality, a passage announced in Zarathustra's introduction of the *Übermensch* in the "Prologue." The announcement of the *Übermensch* does not refer to a "superior" way of being human, but rather to a different happening, to an "ultrahuman" way, insofar as it presupposes "another way of being" than that of humanity. The routes in the work are announced as "twilight" and "declining" continuums: Zarathustra does not come to announce a "superman man," but rather to indicate a "beyond" the human. Thus, the human way of thinking about its way of being needs to decline. This declining way of being is what humanism has forged, turning the human being into the center of all of reality, culminating in the subjectivity of modern philosophy.

From the point of view of animality, that way of being human implies the subjection and appropriation of animality. The ipseity of the modern subject appropriates its selfhood precisely through the "domination of its own animality (its body, its passions, its desires) and the animality of others (the body of others, which is a body "subjected" in the dispositifs of ordering, normalizing, governing). The "superiority" of this way of being human becomes visible in this possibility of domination: in the case of animals, domination is expressed through the usufruct of the animal, and in putting the animal "at the disposal" of the human being. The animal is thus transformed into an exploitable "resource," which can be used and sacrificed in virtue of the "superior ends" of humanity.

In the face of this mode of thinking the animal question (the animal as what can be dominated and mastered), *Thus Spoke Zarathustra* manifests the strangeness of animality, the aspect of animality that impedes and "resists" all domination. Zarathustra is "inhabited" by animality, because the work begins with his solitude "accompanied" by animals, and it ends in a similar manner. Zarathustra's descent from the mountain traces a path through "humanity," which entails coming into contact with diverse ways of being human: from the human saint who does not know of the death of God, to the last man, who feels entirely satisfied with his own existence in the world of the market; from the adventurers of the islands to the "superior men" who come to his cave in the fourth part of the work. In the end, Zarathustra is alone once again, fed up with "humanity" because his peregrinations have shown him that the ways of "being human" cannot bear the announcement of the overman. The announcement of the overman is given by signs that already appeared in the third part of the work: the laughing lion with the flock of doves (*Z* III "On Old and New Tablets" 1). The passage "to another way of being" different from the way of being human presupposes an "encounter" with animality. And that encounter turns out to be unbearable for the superior men, who flee before these animals because they continue being "men," and cannot imagine any way of being (an overhuman way of being) different from that which they live. That is, the superior men can admit the death of God (who appears in different guises: the Pope: the personal God of the Christian faith; kings: the God present in the idea of government; the scientist: the God of the truth of science; and so on for the rest of the superior men), but they cannot bear the "decline" of humanity because that decline implies, among other things, another way of thinking animality. And that is what they cannot do, and this is why they flee.

The animals that "signal" the overman are not domestic animals, they are not "humanized" like "companion animals" or "pets." Nor are they placed at the disposal of man's table as food, but they are rather something different: the lion, the wild animal, and the flock of doves, the multiplicity of the pack that escapes domination. Zarathustra had actually announced in some manner the necessity of "another way of being" in the face of the human in the speech "On the Higher Man" (*Z* IV "On the Higher Man" 4). There he indicated that the love in question is love for the remote, which is love for the overman (and not for the human being as we know him). Loving the overman presupposes loving in the human being what is passing and the twilight of decline (*Übergang, Untergang*), what is no longer human, and is undergoing transformation.

In this process of transformation, it would appear that the insistent presence of the animal in the fourth part of the work indicates that the passage toward the overman must traverse animality. But that passage is not a "return" to the animal (as though the animal were the "original" lost in "humanization"). It is something altogether different. It is not a matter of "recuperating" forces made dormant (or subjected) by culture.[14]

That They Don't Speak Does Not Mean That They Have Nothing to Say: Abnormal Animal Anomalies

As Foucault points out, the discourse on abnormality condemns the abnormal to the status of objects of scientific knowledge, without a voice; one could say it has done the same with animals. Of the three groups of abnormal figures that Foucault mentions, the "human monster" refers most directly to the question of animality. Although both the "individual in need of correction" and the onanist also refer to the animal question, insofar as they represent the necessity of disciplining the body that does not obey the dictates of the norm,[15] it is the monster who best shows the human-beast mixture, the combination of "the impossible and the forbidden." The question of abnormality has permitted the social and moral justification of techniques of identification, classification, and intervention of what is considered abnormal. At the same time, it has given rise to the organization of an institutional network fulfilling double function: while "defending society" from the abnormal, it also strives to protect and help them. Abnormal is whoever is reduced to silence; as an object of study, others will speak "for" them. Recent struggles of resistance, especially those conducted within the framework of the biopolitical organization of the world, have brought back the problem that corporality reduced to silence. The animal in man is reduced to silence, by a long tradition that says that "it" does not speak.

But Nietzsche has pointed out that "*It* thinks" (*Es denkt*) (*BGE* 24). That someone—or something—does not speak does not mean that it has nothing to say: perhaps the question one ought to be asking revolves around what the body-animal says, as well as the body of the animal, in resistance. Modern thought has reduced the animal—in the human being and outside of her—to the fixity of instinct, permitting, thereby, the justification of the cruelty of sacrifice. The remainder of animality to which Nietzsche alludes indicates that the "It" that thinks (or the *Selbst*)[16] is a plurality that accounts for the excess that is life, an excess that the "ego" (*Ich*) in vain attempts to stop. And this is why life is always in the mode of *restance*. Assuming animality as *restance* presupposes acknowledging, from the political point of view, and in relation to the ascetic ideal, the "resistance" as mode of struggle.

The "party of life" (*Partei des Lebens*, an expression which has given Nietzsche's interpreters so many problems) announced in the posthumously published texts written immediately prior to Nietzsche's madness (December 1888–January 1889), seeks the annihilation of that "which corrupts, envenoms, calumniates" (*KSA* 13:25[1]) life, and speaks of the war between rise and decline, "between will to life and thirst for revenge against life" (*KSA* 13:25[1]). In doing so, perhaps it thematizes modes of resistance to thanatopolitcs. In this sense, the so-called "superior species of human beings" would no longer be any form of humanity at all, but rather that part of humanity which is moving toward posthumanity in the form of the overman.

The passage toward the overman entails giving up the "way of being human" according to which life that is not human can be sacrificed. That sacrifice is made possible by the hegemonic role acquired by the ascetic ideal in culture. By converting its forces into an interior animal that is subtle and vengeful, life tortures itself and enjoys this torture: that is, the pleasure generated by cruelty toward the living (in oneself and in the other). One could say that humanism is the epochal configuration of forces in which the ascetic ideal as sacrifice of the living torments animality in the cruelest manner (and experiences pleasure in this cruelty). Humanism, by placing man in the center of reality, and by defining the "human" virtues as a function of the idea of the "rational animal," stifles the life of the "flesh." The overman requires the twilight and decline of humanism in order to think itself as a promise-to-come, and given the necessity for life of the ascetic ideal, the overman cannot but establish another kind of relationship to the living animal.

It is not a matter of negating the ascetic ideal, but rather of thinking about a "change of perspectives" in the resistance to the empire of the thanatological. If the ascetic ideal was itself a desire to be otherwise, which ultimately became fixated on the habit of sacrificing other nonhuman life, then what is at stake with the overman is thinking about the living otherwise than as sacrificial flesh.

It is true that thinking the animal as "being otherwise" is frightening, just as the sign of the flock of birds and the laughing lion scared the superior men in *Thus Spoke Zarathustra.* Thinking about the animal according to sacrificiality allows for the dominion of the human over all of reality because it presupposes the dominion of what is most indomitable: life itself.

In his seminar *La bête et le souverain*[17] Derrida shows this need for dominating the animal in the process that connects modes of knowledge with modes of power; seeing, being able to, knowing, and having (*voir, pouvoir, savoir, avoir*) presuppose a relation with the living animal according to which wanting to know is wanting-to-be-able (*vouloir-pouvoir*), like wanting-to-see *(vouloir-voir*) and wanting-to-have *(vouloir-avoir*).[18] The human wanting-to-know is appropriative of the way of being animal, and implies the availability (*vouloir-avoir*) of the animal for human beings. This availability is demonstrated in the autopsy as the model of "the objectifying inspection of a knowledge that precisely inspects, sees, looks at the aspect of a *zoon,* the life and force of which had been neutralized either by death or by captivity, or quite simply by objectification that exhibits there before, to hand, before the gaze, and de-vitalizes by simple objectification."[19]

The autopsy (of the living animal, of the animal in man) as the model of knowledge facilitates the disposal of life and domination over what terrifies. The autopsy exposes on the dissection table, before the eyes of knowledge, the dead body of a living being, be it animal or human. This is why Derrida establishes an analogy between the zoo and psychiatric institutions, since both are governed by and developed from *curiositas*, that desire to know but also to take care of (domestic cure, hospital cure). The "epistemophilic autopsy,"[20] as Derrida calls it, is what permits having under one's care that which one wishes to understand. After the French Revolution, zoos were transformed into sites for the exercise of that neutralizing curiosity—under the guise of caretaking—about vitality.

In the nineteenth century both zoos and insane asylums generated, from within confinement, an ecosystem that implied "a better way of life" for animals and the mentally ill. This ecosystem, in the case of the zoos, was "economic" in the most general sense of the term, but also in the narrower, capitalist sense since zoos generated income for businessmen who provided the spectacle of animals in captivity to the *curiositas* of human beings. *Oiko-nomia* means the law (*nomos*) of the household (*oikos*); this law organizes the life of the animal (by breaking it in, training it, raising it), giving it a habitat with certain characteristics. Through the actions of capturing, confining, hunting, and raising, the living animal is placed under the law of the household. The animal thus becomes object of ipseity that "appropriates" the life of the other according to its own law. The autopsy is "autoptical": it puts "on stage," spotlighting, for everyone to see the animal, the animal's cadaver.[21] The "dead" animal on the vivisection table is also already dead in the other ways of knowing and disposing, which are generated by this autoptic: the disposable animal as figure of recreation in circuses and zoos, the farm animal, usable as meat for feeding, are not interesting insofar as they are "alive" but only because they are at one's disposition. To appropriate the animal means "dominating" the living part of it, submitting it to "the economy itself."

Thus the scene of life's "representation" comes about: the animal as object of knowledge and of *curiositas*, becomes an "object" on the stage of consciousness, the stage that lies at the disposal of the subject, who in turn can appropriate all of reality by appropriating its "mental contents" (its *cogitationes*) as "its own." The law of "one's own" home (the *ipseity* of the *ipse*) organizes the knowledge of life insofar as this knowledge submits to the law of the "autoptical (*autoptique*)."

In this analogy Derrida establishes between insane asylums and zoos—confinement stands out in both cases (whether of human animals or of living animals)—as what makes possible the idea of "treatment": "an experience of treatment, or even trade [*la traite*] (and the white slave trade obeys an analogous logic), of treatment, tractation, or trade without contract, which consists, precisely, in a strange and equivocal economy, a strange and equivocal ecology, that consists in expropriating the other, appropriating the other by depriving the other of what is supposed to be proper to him or her, the other's proper place, proper habitat, *oikos.* And time, Celan would say."[22] It is a culture of well-being that implies having at one's disposal the "displacement" of other living beings, having the power to circumscribe their movements in the name of a "treatment."

Earlier, I mentioned Foucault's work on the abnormal in order to show how the routes to "normalization" try to silence the strangeness of the animal (that we are). Animals and abnormals confined for the purposes of treatment put "on stage" the attempt to submit the life of the living to the *oikonomía* of human ipseity. Nonetheless, life cannot be silenced.

The Animal and *Res(is)tance*

Thus Spoke Zarathustra shows the importance of traversing the question of animality in terms of strangeness. The different animals that populate Zarathustra's cave deconstruct any *oikonomía* of that cave—as *domus*—in terms of appropriation, since they cannot be dominated by the law of ipseity. This is why the "higher" men flee before these animals that present themselves as not appropriable, and in that gesture the "higher" men continue to be "human beings."

The "higher men" cannot be hospitable to the animal, as Zarathustra is, because they cannot assume animality in its strangeness; they need to dominate it, convert it into a spectacle (the festival of the ass), or into an object of knowledge (as the scientist does with the brain of the leech). Being hospitable means refraining from transforming alterity into sameness (whether in knowledge or in the spectacle). When Nietzsche refers to hospitality,[23] he points out that "the meaning of the usages of hospitality is the paralyzing of enmity in the stranger. Where the stranger is no longer felt to be first and foremost an enemy, hospitality decreases; it flourishes as long as its evil presupposition flourishes" (*D* 158). One can be hospitable only when hostility is maintained, that is, when one preserves the strange character of the other, which prevents appropriation or homologization of that radical difference that is alterity in the sameness of the self. Nietzsche thinks of this hospitality-hostility ("hostipitality," Derrida says) in the figure of the friend, the one who maintains the tension between nearness and distance, preventing familiarity from turning into appropriation of the other. There is, then, a "hostipitality" with the living animal that, far from wanting to appropriate it into the autoptic of knowledge that sees, masters, and makes use of, thinks animality (our animality) in terms of remainder, of the inappropriable. Earlier, I referred to biopolitics and to the possibility of resisting thanatological mechanisms by thinking of these mechanisms as a function of the desire to elude (or master) the inappropriable remainder in and through a radicalization of immunity (a process of autoimmunity).

When Derrida poses the question of religion in the Capri seminar, he suggests that religion takes care of the "unscathed that is safe and sound," the pure, the uncontaminated.[24] Religions, in general, concern themselves with life and its preservation (the commandment "thou shalt not kill" is the premise of many modes of religiosity). Nevertheless, the religious care for life requires distinguishing between distinct ways of life, some more valuable than others. This distinction generates a "terrifying but fatal logic of the *auto-immunity of the unscathed*."[25] In biology, the immune reaction is the preservation of unscathedness by generating antibodies as a reaction to the other (the strangeness that threatens life). But the life that protects itself, by protecting itself from its own self-protection, can also destroy its own immune system. In terms of institutions, these are the autoimmune mechanisms that become thanatological in the age of biopolitics: if the aim of politics is the administration of life, then autoimmunitary religious "care" of life tends to generate a "politics of death." This is the same dynamic that Nietzsche had seen exacerbated in the ascetic ideal, which turns against life itself, attempting to destroy it.

Derrida believes that "auto-immunity haunts the community and its system of immunitary survival like the hyperbole of its own possibility. Nothing in *common*, nothing immune, safe and sound, *helig* and holy, nothing unscathed in the most autonomous living present without a risk of auto-immunity."[26] In terms of what I am suggesting here regarding animality, the conversion of the living animal into an object of domination, manipulation, experimentation, is a kind of autoimmunization, whereby "humanity" considers the "animality" that it itself is as something strange, dangerous, and thus confinable, normalizable.

I indicated earlier that Derrida uses the term "*res(is)tance*" to refer to, among other things, the fact that some remainder of the textual excess always resists translation. The resistance to the thanatological that I propose here (the non-autoptical hostipitality with strangeness) *resists* and *remains* in the listening to the voice of those who do not speak but who have so much to say: the animal in us, and the animal, the other.

PART V

Purification and the Freedom of Death

13

Nietzsche and the Transformation of Death

EDUARDO NASSER

The Reinterpretation of Death

"Death needs to be reinterpreted (Der Tod ist umzudeuten)!" This is what Nietzsche demands in a posthumous fragment from the fall of 1881 (*KSA* 9:11[70]). Our senses tell us that the so-called dead world (*tote Welt*) is something external, indifferent, and immovable. However, this conclusion is flawed (*KSA* 9:11[70]). One can identify in Nietzsche three claims justifying his rejection of the typical understanding of death: the first involves the forces operating in the so-called dead world; the second concerns the eternity of the so-called dead world; and the last addresses the impossibility of error in the so-called dead world. I shall discuss each in turn.

Nietzsche's hypothesis of the "will to power" allows him to claim that matter is far from extension without qualities. In the first place, for Nietzsche, empty space does not exist. Three-dimensional space is merely a representation (*KSA* 11:6[413]) because "'force' and 'space' are two different expressions and ways of considering the same thing" (*KSA* 11:26[431]). Is it more fitting, then, to conclude that there is no separation between space and matter? The question is undoubtedly more complex than that. Nietzsche rejects the idea of the "infinitely extensive" (*KSA* 11:38[12]), showing his sympathy for the campaign against substantialism promoted by the physicist Roger Boscovich.[1]

Nietzsche endorses Boscovich as an ally in, along with Copernicus, rejecting "materialistic atomism." "Boscovich taught us," says Nietzsche, "to forswear the belief in the last firm piece of earth, the belief in 'substance,' in 'matter,' this residue and particle of the Earth, the atom: the biggest triumph over the senses ever obtained on earth" (*BGE* 12). In *A Theory of Natural Philosophy*, Boscovich displays his Leibnizian inheritance, suggesting that notions such as extension and mass are inappropriate to explain the constitution of matter. According to him, there are inextensive and discrete material points (*punctas*), whose impenetrability is created by the energy exerted at a distance by the forces of attraction and repulsion.[2] However, if it is right to say that Nietzsche borrows Boscovich's critique of matter, it is also true that Nietzsche radicalizes it. Despite Boscovich's remarkable originality, his project remains trapped within the conventional explanation of matter[3]: he does not identify matter with forces and is, thus, still attached to mechanicism.[4] Nietzsche, on the other hand, clearly states that "matter" does not exist, and that "forces" should be used instead (Letter to Peter Gast, 20 March 1882 [Letter Nr. 213, *KSB* 6:182f; *KSA* 11:26[432]; *BGE* 12). The concept of force represents the definitive triumph over the conception of matter as an immovable, purely quantitative world, in favor of a dynamic and qualitative world (*KSA* 12:2[157]). "[F]orce is, as a magnitude, stable, while its essence is fluctuating, a product of tensions" (*KSA* 11:35[54]). In other words, the world is comprised of a measurable quantity of forces that do not increase or decrease. However, it is important to note that according to their "essence," forces are not magnitudes, but qualities. Nietzsche attributes an "interior dimension" (*innere Welt*) to the force he calls "will to power" (*KSA* 11:36[31]). What assigns quality to forces is the value judgment of whether they are "more" or "less" strong (*KSA* 12:2[94]). This means that the world of forces is not homogeneous and immovable mass, because it is governed by a constant struggle for a *surplus* of power. Hierarchies are formed between commanders and commanded. These hierarchies undergo continuous modifications; a force that is subjected in a struggle will never cease to resist, always aspiring to gain strength, and this dynamic results in ceaseless changes between what commands and what obeys. Consequently, the inorganic level is made up by forces in combat (*KSA* 11:36[22]). Nietzsche often addresses the fluidity of "chemical qualities" that make unfeasible the existence of precise and strict "laws." Considering the uninterrupted becoming brought about by the relations of forces, for instance, the proportion of "9 oxygen parts to 11 hydrogen parts" is flawed. Such proportion cannot be maintained because "the oxygen is never the same as in the previous instant" (*KSA* 9:11[149]; *KSA* 11:36[18]).

I now pass to the second claim, having to do with the eternity of the so-called dead world. Nietzsche's identification of matter with force is valid both at the inorganic and the organic levels (*KSA* 11:34[247]; *KSA* 11:36[22]). For Nietzsche, the world is an "immensity of forces" (*KSA* 11:38[12]), which "seen from inside" is "will to power and nothing else" (*BGE* 36). Therefore, there is no difference in nature between the world of organic life and the world of inorganic, "dead" matter. Such a distinction, warns the philosopher, can only be applied to the "world of phenomena" (*Erscheinungswelt*) (*KSA* 11:25[356]). Strictly speaking, everything that is "dead" was, at some point, "alive" and vice versa. There is a circular movement between death and life that is assured by the "eternity of duration" (*ewige Dauer*) (*KSA* 11:11[84]). Time, which belongs to the "essence" of force, impedes the exhaustion of becoming (*KSA* 11:35[55]). A finite quantity of forces in an infinite amount of time necessarily implies the eternal recurrence of the same (*KSA* 9:11[202]). However, this permutation of life and death must be carefully analyzed, particularly since Nietzsche holds, against Caspari, that the "whole" is not an organism.[5] In his polemic against Thomson, Caspari rejects the mechanicist perspective of the universe because of the absence of a final state in an infinite time. Considering that such a state has not been reached, the universe can only be akin to an organism, so long as one excludes any intervention from a *deus ex machina.*[6] Nietzsche frequently employs similar arguments in order to oppose proponents of thermodynamic theories. As Nietzsche sees it, if it were conceivable that the world of forces would reach an equilibrium point, given infinite duration, this would have already happened (*KSA* 9:11[148]; *KSA* 9: 11[245]). However, Nietzsche formulates his argument such that its conclusions oppose Caspari's. For Nietzsche, "if the whole could be an organism, it would already have been one" (*KSA* 9:11[201]). The hypothesis that the world is a living being leads to other obvious problems as well. For example, it would have to feed on something, grow, and ultimately, perish. This representation, then, is inconsistent with the hypothesis of the universe's eternity.[7] What Nietzsche can admit, instead, is that "whatever is alive is only a variety of what is dead," and, he adds, "a very rare variety" (*GS* 109). Organic life is a "derived," "late," and inessential modality of the universe (*GS* 109). The universe is fundamentally inorganic: "The inorganic completely conditions us: water, air, the sun, the Earth's configuration, electricity, etc." (*KSA* 9:11[210]). The protoplasm understood as a "plurality of chemical forces" (*KSA* 11:35[58]) is a good illustration of the "completely false view" (*KSA* 9:11[70]) that the external world is a "dead world."

If there is no difference in nature between life and death, and moreover, if life is a variation of what is dead, what demarcates these domains? This question leads me to Nietzsche's third claim, according to which the so-called dead world knows of no error. For Nietzsche, organic beings are complexes of forces in combat, in such a way that an organ cannot be explained by its utility. The usefulness of an organ is always in the service of something irreducible to utility itself. It is not enough to interrogate an organ's use in order to understand what an organ really is; one must first ask "useful for what?" (*KSA* 12:7[25]). In this way, Nietzsche argues that "value judgments" condition organic functions (*KSA* 11:26[72]). For example, the eye is not "intended" or "made" for seeing, nor is the hand "made" for manipulating objects, because the meanings inherited by such organs are due to their being used by a will to power. Consequently, the "use" of an organ is always subject to new adjustments in meaning related to the "subjugation" and "overpowering" that comprises the organic world (*GM* II: 12). However, if the meaning of each organ corresponds to an interpretation given to it by a will to power, and if these meanings are continuously being modified, how is an organism possible? According to Nietzsche, an organism only arises through "compassion" (*Mitleid*) among "different organs" (*verschiedenen Organen*) (*KSA* 11:25[431]). This means that a uniformity of senses is an indispensable condition for the interrelation of organs for the sake of survival. One force must overpower the others and neutralize the most primitive sense of "hierarchy" in reducing differences, for the whole organism assumes "the representation and belief in what is identical to itself, and persistent" (*KSA* 9:11[329]). The organism would not be conserved unless a synthetic activity intervened so as to enable unawareness of original becoming (*KSA* 11:26[294]). "The ultimate truth about the flux of every thing (*die lezte Wahrheit vom Fluss der Dinge*) is unbearable to be *incorporated*, our (vital) *Organs* are in themselves consequences of such error" (*KSA* 9:11[162]). Everything that is alive depends upon "error" (*Irrthum*) (*KSA* 11: 40[39]). The same error, however, is not found at the inorganic level, in which exactitude contrasts with the "indetermination" (*Unbestimmtheit*) and "appearance" (*Schein*) that prevails in the organic world. In the inorganic world, Nietzsche says, "'truth' prevails (*da herrscht 'Wahrheit'*)!" (*KSA* 11:35[53]). In the inorganic world, "the error, and the perspectival limitation [*die perspektivische Beschränktheit*] are absent," for there is an exact perception of "the values, forces, and power relationships" (*KSA* 12:1[105]; *KSA* 11:35[59]). In the inorganic world, perspective and perception coincide, as a force center perceives the other forces from the perspective of its own level of power. That is exactly why Nietzsche considers dying a "feast." When the living being is freed from its life, it dismisses the errors that cause its suffering, and it "reconciles with the actual" (*versöhnen mit dem Wirklichen*), that is, with the world of "force against force" (*KSA* 9:11[70]; *KSA* 9:11[125]). In a sense, then, the transition from organic to inorganic represents a remarkable advancement (*KSA* 11:4[177]).[8]

Freedom to Death

What are the consequences of Nietzsche's reinterpretation of death for human beings, or, how is the relationship between human beings and death affected by this reinterpretation? Before attempting to answer this question, it is important to emphasize that, for Nietzsche, human beings experience death in two opposed ways: there is a "coward's death" (*Feiglings Tod*) or "non-free death" (*unfreier Tod*), and there is a "voluntary death" (*freien Tode*) or the "freedom to death" (*Freiheit zum Tode*).

A "cowardly" death may be defined as the experience of death as a "chance" event, in which the immediate effect is the desire to die. In this case, death is desired because it occurs. Life's finitude is enough for some to advocate that it should be abandoned. Nietzsche calls advocates of this standpoint "preachers of death." They are the ones who, when seeing "a diseased, or old man, or a corpse, say promptly: 'life is refuted' [*das Leben ist widerlegt*]" (*Z* "Of the Preachers of Death"). Nietzsche here has in view "the miserable and terrible comedy Christianity has made of the moment of death" (*TI* "Skimishes" 36). Christianity is "the religion that, among all of the hours of human life, considers the last as the most important" (*UM* II: 8). The hope of the Christians, or the "preachers of death" is that by renouncing this life, "assaulted" by death, a path will be opened to another life, an "eternal life" (*Z* I "Of the Preachers of Death"). For Nietzsche, this hope is a will to nothingness.

The preachers of death aspire to leave this life because death comes unexpected, because "death sneaks in like a thief." And so they hope, "clenching their teeth," for death to come "at the wrong time" (*ein Tod zur unrechten Zeit*) (*Z* I "On the Preachers of Death"; *Z* I "On Free Death"; *TI* "Skirmishes" 36). However, why do these "preachers" view death as a "thief" stealing life? Because they interpret time as a father who devours his own children; that is, as an irreversible outflow directed toward death. According to Nietzsche, human beings, as opposed to other animals, are characterized by a capacity to remember the "it was" that lies at the root of all human suffering. The "'it was' is what gives all the teeth-clenching and the most solitary angst," for a will cannot will backward in time. The "it was" is not only a type of past, alongside present and future, but it is time itself in its totality,[9] which makes every happening seem like a "horrific chance." Time as "it was" frustrates the freedom of the will, which cannot do anything about what is "not anymore." Powerless against the past, human beings recognize themselves as immersed in a time that does not flow backward and feel like a victim of its "passage" (*Z* II "On Redemption"). Unfree death, then, is a logical consequence of the captive will before the passage of time, for this is the only way death can be seen as an accident that assaults human beings from outside. The time when one dies as a coward is always the wrong time because time itself is understood as the source of incompleteness (*TI* "Skirmishes" 36). Death thus arises as a fatality that must be feared. Finally, the anger against death comes hand in hand with the anger against time. The spirit of revenge, in condemning time for preventing man from fully realizing who he is, condemns inevitable death by saying: "everything perishes, everything, therefore, deserves to perish! (*Alles vergeht, darum ist Alles werth zu vergehn!*)." In this sense, human anger directed at the inescapable finitude caused by time is reflected—and this could not be otherwise—in a rejection of death, the most radical chance.

The "free death," by contrast, is the one that comes at the "right time" (*rechten Zeit*) because "I want it." In this case, one does not wish death because death occurs, but one desires death in order to affirm oneself. Death is not imagined as a stranger who steals my life because it is always "my" death, that is, something inherent to my own being (*Z* I "On Free Death"). An excessive attachment to longevity becomes condemnable. According to Nietzsche, when it is no longer possible to live "proudly," one should choose to "die proudly," and not continue to live indecently, relying on doctors and medical treatments. In any case, this apparent apology for suicide should be taken with a grain of salt. The point is that any death, whether natural or not, is a suicide, for we invariably perish because of our own deeds. Only those who enjoy a coward's death have the (equivocal) impression of death being "someone else's deed" (*TI* "Skirmishes" 36).

The "freedom to death" is attained when one "dies in time." For those who die at the "wrong time," death always comes either too late or too early, because "how could someone who does not live in time, die in time"? Thus the way to move from a will coerced by death to a death freely willed requires a fundamental modification in the perception of time. For those convinced that time passes, life haunted by the "it was"—inaccessible to the will—is never complete, so death can only occur by chance, that is, at the "wrong time." The will that says "but I will it thus" to the "it was" is the will that is able to affirm its own death, which can only come at the "right time." In assenting to the "it was," the will is free from its captivity and reconciled with time. Will becomes, therefore, free (*Z* I "On Redemption"). However, it is not enough to affirm the time that has gone by. It is also essential to wish that time return for all eternity. Nietzsche submits human beings to a crucial test: before proposing that they triumph over the spirit of revenge by reconciling with time, he suggests that redemption can only be consummated with the transformation of time itself. Time is no longer something that "goes by" if one desires to relive life "countless times," including "each pain, and each pleasure, and each sigh, and each thought, and everything that is indescribably great and small" (*GS* 341). The "it was" only exists for those who believe that everything happens by chance. The doctrine of the eternal recurrence of the same provides the transition from the successive time to the instant (*Augenblick*), which in its eternity (*Ewigkeit*) does not know the passage of time (*Z* III "On the Vision and the Riddle"; *Z* IV "At Noon"). Consequently, with the incorporation of this teaching, the "thought of death" is annulled. The death that steals, violates, attacks, frustrates, limits is a morbid symptom of those human beings who consider time as a father who eats his own children. In adhering to the eternity of the instant, one becomes complete, and death "never arrives."

It should now be clearer that the interpretation of death as something external, inanimate, and hostile to life is directly linked to a certain way of devaluing existence. Nietzsche's reinterpretation of death is, first, a psychological exercise with the objective of preparing the human will to affirm death by neutralizing the sovereignty of the "it was." Second, Nietzsche's proposed reinterpretation of death is far from being solely a psychological trick. It implies a reconnection with the world as it is, where there is no separation between life and death, or, where life is only a variety of death. This accounts for Zarathustra's equation of the love for the Earth with the desire to die. Free from denial and the fear of death, and assured that dying is a "feast," Zarathustra tells us: "I want to become earth again, that I may have peace in her who bore me" (*Z* I "On Free Death").

The Problem of Death in Nietzsche and the History of Philosophy

After this brief and somewhat schematic presentation of the problem of death in Nietzsche's texts, I propose investigating the repercussions of this problem within the modern philosophical tradition. This analysis will serve as a preamble for a more general question: how to place the Nietzschean argument about death in the history of philosophy?

One cannot rely here on Nietzsche's interpreters, who, in the last hundred years, have given little importance to the subject. With the exception of the contributions of Andler,[10] Moles,[11] and, above all, Mittasch,[12] the problem of death has not occasioned more general, systematic investigations. Nor has it appeared in the inventory of the most studied of Nietzschean concepts, which, since Heidegger's reading, remains practically unaltered.[13] However, even relegated to the status of secondary issue by his interpreters, Nietzsche's approach to the problem of death had an enormous, and unexpected, influence in philosophical discussions in the twentieth century, at least according to Sean Ireton in his article "Heidegger's Ontological Analysis of Death and Its Prefiguration in Nietzsche."[14] Ireton's main thesis is that a part of Heidegger's *Sein und Zeit*, the so called *Todesanalytik*, owes much to Nietzsche's discussions of death—specifically his discussions of the *Freiheit zum Tode*, as it appears in *Also sprach Zarathustra*—revealing not only a "rich connection in thought, but a substantial debt" to Nietzsche.[15] Ireton finds two main justifications to support this thesis. The first is more circumstantial: Heidegger employs the concept, created by Nietzsche, of *Freiheit zum Tode*, and throughout the argument, refers, even though in an obscure manner, to Nietzsche by name.[16] More significant, however, is the other justification, based on the argumentative affinities between Nietzsche and Heidegger. Such affinities are formally present in the existential focus on death by both philosophers, as well as in their considerations of the ambiguous relationship of human beings to death, which oscillate between authenticity and inauthenticity in Heidegger and between the categories of *freiwilliger/vernünftiger* and *unfreiwilliger/natürlicher Tod* in Nietzsche.[17] Ireton concludes that the "speech from the first part of *Also Sprach Zarathustra* clearly anticipates Heidegger's project of an authenticating free and self-determined death" and that the "ideas raised in Zarathustra's pronouncements even correspond in detail to several important aspects of the *Todesanalytik*."[18]

Ireton's detailed study is, without a doubt, very important in establishing Nietzsche as the main influence behind Heidegger's thinking about death. However, if Ireton is correct, and Nietzsche does provide death with a similar, or analogous, treatment to the one given by Heidegger, then his philosophy has to be understood in the light of a long tradition—of which Heidegger is perhaps one of the main representatives—that views death as the engine of philosophical activity. But is this interpretation truly faithful to the Nietzschean vision of death?

Throughout its development, Western culture has been accompanied by a fixation on death. If one turns to the Greek epic poems, it is evident that death was an object of great fascination and terror to the Greeks. The dilemma of Achilles—to have either the imperishable glory of the warrior in his youth or a long existence without glory—defined the essence of that culture.[19] This obsession with death prevailed—with an unmatched intensity[20]—in the Late Middle Ages, when the problem of the decomposing human body invades the popular imaginary and is widely considered in the fine arts, as well as in clerical and popular literature.[21] In the Western world, then, death has been on the horizon of various human productions, and philosophy, of course, is no exception.

Apparently, Western philosophical discourse is not only intimately tied to death at its origin, but also seems utterly unintelligible without death. In Plato's *Phaedo*, Socrates says "those who apply themselves correctly to the pursuit of philosophy are in fact practicing nothing more nor less than dying and death."[22] Schopenhauer, in *Die Welt als Wille und Vorstellung*, is inspired by Socrates' speech and claims that "death is the true inspiring genius, or the muse of philosophy" and that "without death, man will scarcely philosophize."[23] In the twentieth century, this scenario continues unabated—it is perhaps precisely during this period, with the German "philosophies of existence,"[24] led by Jaspers and, above all, Heidegger,[25] that this entanglement between death and philosophy is presented in a more incisive manner.[26] In his work *An Introduction to Philosophy* Jaspers writes, "if to philosophize is to learn to die, then we must learn how to die in order to lead a good life. To learn how to live and to learn how to die are one and the same thing."[27] Gloeckner, in describing a conversation with a philosopher—probably Heidegger—reproduces the interlocutor's speech: "We made the surprising discovery that man is, since the first moment of life, a dying man. This is the discovery that impregnates and inseminates our philosophy."[28] Why, then, does death deserve such great importance in these philosophers of existence, to the extent of defining the practice of philosophy?

These existentialist philosophers have distinct answers to this question. For Jaspers, death is one of the "limit-situations," which, along with "fright" and "doubt," compose the indispensable conditions that give rise to philosophy. Death concerns the Stoic moment of self-consciousness in anyone devoted to the knowing of things.[29] For Heidegger, death is an indispensable component of the problem of being and his response—the philosophical question par excellence.[30] Given that "fundamental ontology" depends on the "existential analytic of the '*Dasein*,'"[31] it is death that discloses the "meaning of being of *Dasein*'s whole-being"[32]; death discloses for Dasein a "non-entity," that is, Being.[33] Both philosophers give this philosophical treatment to death only insofar as it is seen as an "existential death"—only, that is, insofar as it is the "true death." Scheler had already shown that death is not a generic concept, deduced from the observation of the progressive collapse of the organism. Even if human beings were the only beings on earth, they would always know that death awaits them; it is death that offers direction to life; it is the principle that organizes and builds existence.[34] Heidegger says that it is from the point of view of *Das Man*, or inauthenticity, that death is seen as an empirical certainty. In the ordinary, everyday world, death is no more than a "fact of experience," an accident that affects all and no one in particular—"death comes certainly, but not yet." Of course, this is one possible way to relate to death, but it is a "false" one, driven by the concealment of "being-toward-death" (*Sein-zum-Tode*)—death as the "*possible being at every instant*."[35] In brief, for the philosophers of existence, death only has relevance insofar as it is beyond generalization, that is, when it is experienced in a free, authentic, and personal manner.

Despite its brevity, this general presentation of the tie between philosophy and death—with particular focus on the German philosophies of existence—provides a background for a few considerations around this theme in Nietzsche's philosophy. I shall start with an integral quote from a paragraph of *The Gay Science*, entitled "The Thought of Death":

> It gives me a melancholy happiness to live in the midst of this jumble of lanes, needs, and voices: how much enjoyment, impatience, desire; how much thirsty life and drunkenness of life comes to light every moment of the day! And yet things will soon be so silent for all these noisy, living, life-thirsty ones! How even now everyone's shadow stands behind him, as his dark fellow traveler! It's always like the last moment before the departure of an emigrant ship: people have more to say to each other than ever; the hour is late; the ocean and its desolate silence await impatiently behind all the noise—so covetous, so certain of its prey. And everyone, everyone takes the past to be little or nothing while the near future is everything; hence this haste, this clamor, this outshouting and out-hustling one another. Everyone wants to be the first in this future—and yet death and deathly silence are the only things certain and common to all in this future! How strange that this sole certainty and commonality barely makes an impression on people and that they are farthest removed from feeling like a brotherhood of death! It makes me happy to see that people do not at all want to think the thought of death! I would very much like to do something that would make the thought of life [*Gedanken an das Leben*] even a hundred times more *worth being thought* to them. (*GS* 278)

The scenario described by Nietzsche in this paragraph is that of an ignorant, common-sense view of death. Always in a hurry, noisy and thirsty for life, the ordinary human being lives as if the immediate future were all there was; as if death simply did not apply to him. The ordinary human being, then, does not die—a finding Heidegger would explore years later. However, unlike Heidegger, Nietzsche does not identify an inauthenticity in the commonsense discourse about death, or even a behavior that should be corrected. The fact that the certainty of death does not generally disturb thought is not a reason for lamentation but for rejoicing. From here, the central thesis of the passage: thinking about life is a thousand times more valuable than thinking about death. But how can this resistance of thinking about death be understood? Two possible answers come to mind: either the problem of death, as opposed to the problem of life, cannot be exhausted by thought; or, death, as opposed to life, is not truly a problem. Death is not worth thinking about because it is only the thought of nothing.

The first answer leads to the idea that death exceeds the intellectual domain, a hypothesis that is in part similar to Heidegger's argument: death is not a "presence-at-hand [*Vorhandenheit*]," and can only be authentically understood by a very particular state of being or mood (*Stimmung*): anxiety. It is by way of anxiety that *Dasein* faces "the nothingness of the possible impossibility of its existence."[36] To Nietzsche, however, this would not be an adequate understanding of death, since thought is not separate from sensation (there is only the think-feel-want, *BGE* 19), and is not even a faculty. The second answer suggests that the Nietzschean argument on death has a certain Epicurean undertone, which would lead one to surmise that Nietzsche is very far from being one of those philosophers who see death as the premise of the philosophical practice.

Although many philosophers regard death with enormous solemnity, viewing it less as an end and more as a beginning of thought, another philosophical tradition also existed, no less influential, which strived to minimize, and even discard, death from the philosophical horizon. This philosophical tradition can be called, in a general (and naturally imprecise) sense, "Epicurean." Epicureanism was the school of thought that made the following principle popular: "death is nothing to us."[37] In his *Letter to Menoeceus*, Epicurus claims, "death is nothing to us, because good and evil consist in sensation, and death is the removal of sensation."[38] "Most people shrink from death as the greatest of evils, or else extol it as a release from the evils of life. Yet the wise man does not dishonor life (since he is not set against it) and he is not afraid to stop living (since he does not consider that to be a bad thing)."[39] It is not about annulling the fear of death by "thinking constantly about death"—as Seneca would later preach[40]—but about recognizing that death is neither a good nor an evil:

it just "is not." "It is nothing to those who live (since to them it does not exist) and it is nothing to those who have died (since they no longer exist)."[41]

Epicureanism inaugurated a class of argument about death that would reappear (directly or indirectly, with eventual and obvious modifications) periodically in the history of philosophy—revisited, above all, from the point of view of its consequences, namely, that only life matters. It is in this spirit that Renaissance thinkers such as Petrarch opposed the importance given to death by the Catholic Church—which infused human beings with the constant imperative to remember their mortality, the *memento mori*, the ultimate moment in which the demons make their last investment in the soul—by exalting the *memento vivere*. Influenced by the ancient philosophers, in particular by Aristotle and Lucretius, Petrarch maintains that death is the total annihilation of the individual, whence the removal of the agony before death—in reality, an agony connected to eternal damnation—and the reencounter with the joy of living.[42] Along the same lines, Montaigne, who, despite the progressive adjustment of his argument on death in the *Essays*—at first staunchly Stoic, ultimately embracing Epicureanism[43]—essentially condemns any permanent state of alertness before death.[44] Likewise Spinoza in the *Ethics*: "A free man thinks of nothing less than death; and his wisdom is a meditation on life, not on death."[45] Although any association with Epicureanism at this point is doubtful[46]—since this is less about a confrontation with death itself than with the fear of death—the fact is that Spinoza puts forth a motto that philosophy does not revolve around death. "The *Ethics* does not prepare man to die; but to live throughout eternity thanks to the adequate knowledge and union with God."[47]

Is it this "Epicurean" tone that underlies Nietzsche's argument on death? Nietzsche was certainly familiar with the Epicurean argument that death is nothingness, and especially the Lucretian variant, which he reproduces in a posthumously published piece, through the reading of Dühring's *Der Werth des Lebens* (*KSA* 7:9[1]), even expressing sympathy for this line of thought. For example, in *The Dawn*, Nietzsche compliments the recent scientific achievements that refute the possibility of an afterlife, and ratify the anti-Christian perspective of Epicurus (*A* 72).[48]

However, any identification of Nietzsche with Epicureanism is problematic. If Nietzsche thought that death was nothing, that is, that death posed no problem, how, then, should one understand the considerations discussed previously regarding death? Nietzsche does not judge death to be an unintelligible subject; he presents demonstrative and extremely lucid arguments with respect to death, ultimately treating death as a concept.

Although it might be hasty to hint at a kind of aporia, the point is that the claim that death is nothing carries with it a subtle ambiguity, sheltering another possible reading: death, as it was *commonly understood*, is not a problem, and it is this *other* notion of death that is not worthy of being thought. As Nietzsche emphasizes elsewhere, how one dies or even the dying man's attitude at the time of death does not matter, but "how a man thinks about death during his fullest life" does (*WS* 88). It is not, then, the thought of death *as such* that should be eradicated or condemned, but a specific way of thinking about death. As I have already illustrated, death in Nietzsche is perfectly worthy of being thought about in terms of a theory of forces and will to power; that is, when he is talking about a "re-interpreted death." Death only becomes unworthy of being thought about when it is identified with annihilation, nothingness, matter, or as a passage to a distinct reality, something independent from life—unworthy of being thought because unthinkable.

At this point I am in a position to advance some conclusions. First, it does not seem adequate to classify the Nietzschean argument on death as "Epicurean," given that even if this seems reasonable at some points of his writings, it turns out that the Epicurean motifs serve only a critical function, and precede the introduction of his "true" thoughts on death. At the same time, the Nietzschean argument is different from the discourse on death found in Heidegger and Jaspers, and, in a more general sense, that found in the whole of the philosophical tradition, for which death was not just a problem but the crucial problem for the practice of philosophy. The point is that if Nietzsche encourages thinking about death, it is precisely to diminish the exaggerated importance that it is given elsewhere. This is the meaning of "freedom to death": it is an interiorization of death through a correction of the notion of temporality and, more important, through a transvaluation of all values, leading to an acknowledgement that *we are already death*. Unlike Ireton, then, I do not think that there is a parallel here with "freedom to death" as understood by Heidegger. For the latter, being free to die is directly related to the emancipation of *Das Man* and the singularization of *Dasein*, while for Nietzsche, this "freedom" says less about a process of subjectivity than it does about a kind of exteriorization; death is the moment in which human beings are freed from "errors" of life in order to enter into a cosmic totality where a continuity between life and death prevails. In this way, one can say that Nietzsche constructs an argument on death that connects with the arguments developed by those philosophers who privileged cosmology, such as Giordano Bruno. For Bruno, the attenuation of the fear of death follows from the revelation of the infinite universe, where nothing really perishes except in appearance.

In the universe, even though all is subject to becoming, there is no death as dissolution.[49] One can also refer to the Stoics and Heraclitism in general. In the *Meditations*, Marcus Aurelius recommends "waiting for death with a cheerful mind, as being nothing else than a dissolution of the elements of which every living being is compounded. But if there is no harm to the elements themselves in each continually changing into another, why should a man have any apprehension about the change and dissolution of all the elements? For it is according to nature, and nothing is evil which is according to nature."[50] This is said in the same spirit of Heraclitus's Fragment XCIII (*D* 88): "The same . . . : living and dead, and the waking and the sleeping, and young and old. For these transposed are those, and those transposed again are these."[51]

14

Becoming and Purification
Empedocles, Zarathustra's Übermensch, *and Lucian's Tyrant*

BABETTE BABICH

> Das Leben suchst du, suchst, und es quillt und glänzt
> Ein göttlich Feuer tief aus der Erde dir,
> Und du in schauderndem Verlangen
> Wirftst dich hinab, in des Aetna Flammen.
>
> —**Hölderlin, *Empedocles***

> You look for life, you look and from deeps of Earth
> A fire, divinely gleaming wells up for you,
> And quick, aquiver with desire, you
> Hurl yourself down into Etna's furnace.
>
> —**Hölderlin, *Empedocles***

Introduction

"Who is Nietzsche's Zarathustra?" Heidegger once asked, reminding us as he sought to pose this question that qua advocate,[1] Zarathustra takes the part of, or speaks on behalf of, others. Heidegger's question permits us to ask about Zarathustra's style as a "rhetor," an orator, a speaker. When we read *Thus Spoke Zarathustra*, what does it mean that Nietzsche tells us that his Zarathustra *speaks*? What does it mean that he tells us that Zarathustra conscientiously, deliberately speaks "otherwise" to his disciples and to the general public than he does to himself (*Z* II "On Redemption")? And what is the role of the advocate in philosophy? For the most part, such questions exceed what we can do here but are important to keep in mind if we wish to read *Thus Spoke Zarathustra* in terms of Zarathustra's teaching of both the overhuman—that is literally: the *Übermensch*—and the eternal return.

In an effort to address both themes, I will undertake to read Nietzsche's *Zarathustra* with reference to Empedocles.

The pre-Socratic, or as Nietzsche would say, the pre-Platonic Empedocles was a paradigmatic speaker and, according to Aristotle, the first of the orators. And in addition to *Thus Spoke Zarathustra*, Nietzsche (like Hölderlin) composed several drafts entitled *The Death of Empedocles*. Significantly for the title *Thus Spoke Zarathustra*, the first lines of the fragments usually presented as the *Katharmoi*[2] begin with an exemplification of Empedocles' "speakerly" prowess,[3] as Empedocles presents himself in his writings.[4] Nietzsche's Zarathustra as stylistic orator or rhetorician may also be compared to Empedocles in terms of style, native and nonnative, just as the Sicilian Empedocles may be compared to the Syrian Lucian of Samosata who wrote in a form of Greek said to have been purer than a native's own. Critically, comparatively, Nietzsche commanded his own special expertise on the writings of the Sicilian chronologist and contemporary of the second-century Lucian: Diogenes Laërtius.[5]

Nietzsche's Zarathustra echoes Empedocles as a speaker and political or moral advocate as he teaches self-overcoming. A parallel to Empedocles is also suggested by Zarathustra's apparent flight into the volcano and his elusive death (as both Lucian and Diogenes Laërtius foreground *conflicting* reports of Empedocles' death). Thus tracing a parallel between Nietzsche's Empedocles and Hölderlin's Empedocles, I read Nietzsche's *Thus Spoke Zarathustra* as a parodic echo of Empedocles' *Purifications*. Like Empedocles' call for reform and for the transfiguration of humanity, Zarathustra's speech to the crowd teaches the overhuman, calling as it would seem for humanity's self-overcoming.

This call includes what may be called the politics of kingship or "revolution," as this political dimension appears in Hölderlin's *Empedocles*. It is important to explore this revolutionary spirit alongside Nietzsche's own discussion of princes, economics, and politics in *Thus Spoke Zarathustra*. This undertaking is especially challenging, not only because of the difficulties attendant upon reading Hölderlin in general, but also because of the complex question of the role of tragedy. Nietzsche argues that tragedy commits suicide at its own hand, implicating Euripides and Socrates but also the New Comedy. He also reminds us that the satirical is always part and parcel of the tragic world view.

The complex question of the relation between tragedy and parody (or Lucianic Menippean satire) spans Nietzsche's works from *The Birth of Tragedy* to *Thus Spoke Zarathustra* to *Ecce Homo*'s "What I Owe the Ancients." And we read in his preface to the 1886 second edition of *The Gay Science*[6] the self-referential warning: "'*Incipit tragoedia*' we read at the end . . . Beware! Something downright wicked and malicious is announced here: *incipit parodia*, no doubt" (*GS* 1; see *GS* 342). Here we may recall that comedy, seen from the perspective of Nietzsche's classical antiquity, is an all-too typical word for life itself. Thus we read Nietzsche's provocative and wondrous allusion to Aeschylus's "waves of uncountable laughter" together with his reflection that "*in the long run* every one of those great teachers of a purpose (of existence) was vanquished by laughter, reason, and nature; the short tragedy always gave way again and returned into the eternal comedy of existence" (*GS* 1; see *GS* 36, 67). The tonality—for those of us who look to beginnings—is indeed already at work in Nietzsche's initial questioning of the usual, that is, the classically scholarly valuation of the epic poet Homer *and* the lyric and bawdy Archilochus. He reminds his readers that the ancients ranked these two poets together (*BT* 5). Nietzsche's reflection on *The Birth of Tragedy Out of the Spirit of Music* does not permit us to see tragedy, comedy, and parody as contradictions—an insight already expressed in the sublime coincidence of opposites in Hölderlin's short verse *Sophocles*:

> Many strove in vain the highest joy, joyfully to say, Here finally it speaks to me, here in sorrow expressed.[7]

Nietzsche's Sketches for the *Death of Empedocles*

Scholars observe that in 1870–1872 Nietzsche planned a drama on the model of and bearing the same title as Hölderlin's several drafts of the *Death of Empedocles*.[8] Like Hölderlin's project, Nietzsche's drafts are not brought to fruition. Here it is important to recall that compositions and letters imitating ancient authors was part of a classical formation whereby, recalling Aristotle's emphasis, Empedocles may arguably be regarded as a signifier for this classical tradition.[9] Thus Plutarch writes or composes a text after the fashion of Empedocles,[10] as does Cicero. As does the student Nietzsche, infamously borrowing his words to do so—and note that our modern conviction that he was "plagiarizing" would not have been his own understanding of his practice. Nor would his teacher, as I have elsewhere argued,[11] have been unaware of the source and thus would hardly have been duped. One learns, very traditionally, through imitation.

In a section titled, "The Philosophers of the Tragic Age revealed, the world as tragedy" (*KSA* 7:21[16]), Nietzsche sketches "the tragic human being," outlining three acts of his plan for the "death" of Empedocles. The parallel with Zarathustra at this stage is patent to the extent that both Empedocles and Zarathustra can be compared with the divine, and both present themselves as such. At the same time, both are imbued with mortality;

thus Empedocles names himself an outcast in these terms: "Of these I too am now one, an exile from the gods and a wanderer, having put my trust in raving strife."[12] While Zarathustra teaches the death of God and can be compared to divinity only in this context owing to the Judeo-Christian God, Empedocles attains his reputed elevation to a divinity among or alongside the gods by means of a dramatic death, whether self-elected as suicide or else self-arranged or staged as such or, as Diogenes Laërtius writes, "otherwise unknown."[13] Lucian, in his account of Empedocles, plays on this "staging" by presenting it as the unexpected and so comic device of an updraft (hereby reversing the usual workings of the *deus ex machina*, which lowered the god to the stage and into public view). Thus, in Lucian's *Icaro-Menippus*, our hero meets Empedocles on the moon, wafted there, as we are told, from the volcano's updraft and where, as Lucian's Empedocles reports to his bastard-winged visitor (sporting one wing from an eagle and one from a vulture—yet another touch that could not help but appeal to the one-time Wagnerian Nietzsche), he has since survived on "dew."[14]

As many scholars have argued, Zarathustra is about death. And the afterlife, as Nietzsche tells us, is the epitome of the rejection of the becoming of life, which is why Nietzsche emphasizes the universal disinclination of human beings even to think "*The Thought of Death*"—"nothing is further from their minds than the feeling that they form a brotherhood of death" as the inspiration for his desire "to do something that would make the thought of life even a hundred times more appealing to them" (*GS* 278). And Nietzsche gives this theme of the refusal of becoming and death pride of place in the first section of his "'Reason' in Philosophy" in *Twilight of the Idols* (*TI* "Reason" 1). Writing here against traditional philosophers, Nietzsche argues that "nothing real has escaped their hands alive . . . death, change, and age, like reproduction and growth, are for them objections—refutations even" (*TI* "Reason" 1). Nietzsche had earlier reflected on the meaning of life in a *Gay Science* aphorism entitled *What Is Life?* "Life—that is: continually shedding something that wants to die" (*GS* 26). It only adds to this point to note, as David Allison and others tell us, that Nietzsche's plans for the text initially included Zarathustra's literal death. Indeed, I argue that this same event had already transpired in the schema of the text from the start, just where Zarathustra succumbs to a snake bite under a fig tree (shades of Pierre Courcelle's attention to the conventional trope of the image of Augustine under his fig tree, allegorically, hermeneutically, *figuratively* speaking): "'Your way is short,' the adder said sadly; 'my poison kills'" (*Z* I "On the Adder's Bite"). The bitten Zarathustra then commands the adder take back his poison, and the adder falls upon his neck a second time. The second bite is the bite of fantasy, the articulation of Zarathustra's remonstration against the past, against what has been—the command that it not have been, that it be *as if it had never been.* And on this reading, the entirety of *Thus Spoke Zarathustra* would be a dream before dying—another philosopher's dream to be added to the array of such and the interpretation of the same.

So read, the beginning of Zarathustra's downgoing—usually (and informatively) read as an allusion to Plato's *Republic*—acquires a different aspect in concord with the many allusions to death. These allusions begin already at the start of *Thus Spoke Zarathustra* with the not-yet transmitted tale of the death of God to the old hermit in the forest and with the tightrope walker who falls to his death and whose corpse Zarathustra carries with him only to leave him in a hollow tree (an archaically, typically Greek burial place). The general concern with the "this-wordly" versus the "otherworldly" continues with the invocation of the *Isles of the Blest*, as well as the uncanny (and Lucianic) *Tomb Song* in addition to Zarathustra's flight into the volcano into hell. This can be explored with reference to Lucian's dialogues of the dead and his mocking of the traditional accounts of the afterlife but also the philosophers and the gods of the Romans and the Greeks, the Christians and the Jews alike.

Here we may recall the section "On Free Death," invoking "the death that consummates" with Zarathustra's twice-repeated remonstration "'Die at the right time'" (*Z* I "On Free Death"). Zarathustra thus describes death as a "festival," echoing the esoteric dimension of Empedocles' teaching. In association with this, we may add Nietzsche's most explicit echo of Lucian's *True Story* (*Alethe Diegemata*), whereby he titled a section "On the Isles of the Blest" (just as Lucian did—thereby following Hesiod, Pindar, and Plato). If today's readers are inclined to think of the Caribbean or Tahiti for such "blessed isles," Nietzsche refers to a classicist's vision of the afterlife where Zarathustra describes himself as "a wind to ripe figs," emphasizing that rather than salvation or redemption or eternal life, it is "of time and becoming that the best parables should speak: let them be a praise and a justification of all impermanence" (*Z* II "On the Isles of the Blest"). It is here, too, that Zarathustra echoes Empedocles who first proposed the teaching of eternal recurrence: "Verily, through a hundred souls I have already passed on my way, and through a hundred cradles and birth pangs. Many a farewell have I taken; I know the heartrending last hours" (*Z* II "On the Isles of the Blest"). But Nietzsche's Zarathustra affirms "thus my creative will, my destiny, wills it. Or, to say it more honestly: this very destiny: my will wills" (*Z* II "On the Isles of the Blest")—and it is Empedocles' teaching of rebirth that echoes in the language of the "nuptial ring of rings, the ring of recurrence" (*Z* III "The Seven Seals").

Zarathustra teaches the *Übermensch* as the above-human or overhuman as both the transition to and the eternal recurrence of the same. Speaking of what his posthumous notes from 1887 describe as "*ein Hiatus zwischen zwei Nichtsen*" (*KSA* 12:10[34]), Nietzsche's Zarathustra describes the human being as "a rope over an abyss" (*Z* "Prologue" 4)[15] and begins with what reads as a sermon delivered against the backdrop of a dynamic tableau of life and death, a living *biblia pauperum* taking place above and behind him as he speaks. Thus, as Zarathustra begins to speak, we read that the tightrope walker, mistaking his cue, "began his performance" (*Z* "Prologue" 4), a doubling of the play or mise-en-scène. This explains the patience of Zarathustra's audience as he begins speaking (an important point as they did not come to hear him) and simultaneously works—literally above and below—to illustrate Zarathustra's talk of the human as "a dangerous across, a dangerous on-the-way, a dangerous looking-back, a dangerous shuddering and stopping" (*Z* "Prologue" 4).

The reference to life and death is doubled once again inasmuch as Zarathustra's sermon is all about what he calls the "rainbow bridge" of life:

> I love those who do not know how to live, except by going under, for they are those who cross over.
>
> I love the great despisers because they are the great reverers and arrows of longing for the other shore.
>
> I love those who do not first seek behind the stars for a reason to go under and be a sacrifice, but who sacrifice themselves for the earth, that the earth some day become the overhuman's . . . I love him whose soul squanders itself, who wants no thanks and returns none: for he always gives away and does not want to preserve himself (*Z* "Prologue" 4).

The reference here is commonly taken to echo the Christian teaching of dying to the life of the world or of the body. Yet Nietzsche's Zarathustra teaches the "great reason" of the body, and a self that "wants to create beyond itself" (*Z* I "On the Despisers of the Body"). He affirms not only the "rainbows and bridges of the overhuman" (*Z* I "On the New Idol"), but also declares "I love him who wants to create over and beyond himself and thus perishes" (*Z* I "On the Way of the Creator").

In this way, the notion of self-overcoming—of going under, conceiving life itself as that which always and inevitably overcomes itself—also teaches what Zarathustra names the great noon. Like the great year of the ancient philosophers, the great noon is the turning to the new associated with fire and with the sun as a consummation: "that is the great noon when man stands in the middle of his way between beast and overhuman and celebrates his way to evening as his highest hope: for it is the way to a new morning" (*Z* I "On the Gift-Giving Virtue" 3).

Inasmuch as Zarathustra teaches what all classical philosophy teaches, that is, the art of living, Zarathustra teaches the overhuman as "the meaning of the earth," a teaching that includes the conception that the "human is something that shall be overcome" (*Z* "Prologue" 3). The point is literal: the art of living, as we have needed the efforts of the late Pierre Hadot[16] and others to remind us, is also the art of dying, the art, once again as Nietzsche's Zarathustra teaches, of dying in the right way and, indeed: for the right reason, and even, if one would be perfect, "at the right time" (Z I "On Free Death").

Nietzsche's Zarathustra, Nietzsche's Empedocles

> Happy and blessed one, you shall be a god instead of a mortal.
>
> Empedocles[17]

I have suggested that Nietzsche's *Thus Spoke Zarathustra* offers a parodic retelling of Empedocles' esoteric and poetic *Katharmoi*. With this claim, I join those many scholars who argue that Nietzsche's Zarathustra is parodically modeled on something[18]—whether it be the Bible, or Plato's *Republic*, or Wagner's *Ring*. And I think there are intrinsic limitations to such parallels, but here let's see, if only experimentally, how far it takes us to look not only to Empedocles but also, as I argue rather radically, Lucian's comedies/parodies. We limit ourselves to Nietzsche's own Zarathustra, again, only to sketch out the plausibility of *beginning* such a reading, but it is important to note that by simply invoking Zarathustra as such, Nietzsche already invokes a prophetic figure of considerable, if disputed, antiquity.[19] Thus, as I argued earlier, taking Zarathustra as a Heideggerian "advocate" (*ein Fürsprecher*)[20] is to take him as an Empedoclean figure. Claiming, as Heidegger does, that "Zarathustra speaks on behalf of life, suffering, and the circle,"[21] we do not depart from Empedocles, especially as Heidegger defines life, suffering, and the circle as "the selfsame," and defines the solid circle (in similarly Hölderlinian terms) as the ring-dance of love, as the wedding dance. In this manner, Heidegger echoes Empedocles' sphere: "'Circle' is the sign of the ring that wrings its way back to itself and in that way always achieves recurrence of the same."[22] For Empedocles, who emphasizes the συνέχεια, that which conjoins the disjoint, the "wheel-shaped Sphere is held fast in the close obscurity of Harmonia, exulting in its joyous solitude".[23]

Thus Nietzsche's Zarathustra teaches that the "human being is something that shall be overcome" (*Z* "Prologue" 3) and that "What is great in man is that he is a bridge and not an end: what can be loved in man is that he is an overture and a going under" (*Z* "Prologue" 4). This is followed (as suggested earlier) by a string of metaphors for death and perishing: "Life itself confided this secret to me: Behold it said I am that which always overcomes itself . . . where there is perishing, a falling of leaves, behold, there life sacrifices itself—for power" (*Z* II "On Self-Overcoming"). This always-self-overcoming is the becoming of life, and it is the Dionysian meaning of the will to power.

To address any of these questions requires that we turn our attention to the spirit of rhetoric as it were. Thus we ask again: what is it to be a *Fürsprecher*, to be an advocate or an orator? Empedocles begins the *Katharmoi* fragments (as these are typically gathered together by editors) with what is thus conventionally the most striking address of any of the ancient philosophers. We have the perfect (and perfectly literal) rhetorical *topos*: thus Empedocles addresses his audience as citizens of a specific city, while yet telling only the tale of the speaker:

> Ὦ φίλοι, οἳ μέγα ἄστυ κατὰ ξανθοῦ Ἀκράγαντος
> ναίετ' ἀν' ἄκρα πόλιος,
>
> Ye friends who dwell in the mighty city along the yellow Acragas,
> hard by the Acropolis . . .[24]

Thus beginning, "O friends," Ὦ φίλοι—Empedocles continues to say *I*: ἐγὼ δ' ὔμμιν θεὸς ἄμβροτος . . . But unto ye I walk as god immortal now, no more as a man, On all sides honored fittingly and well, crowned both with fillets and with flowering wreaths."[25]

Thus Spoke Empedocles.

Friends—dwelling—high cities—not merely self-aggrandizement but—apotheosis—honors—with all the trappings of a festival.

Literally so, as *he writes*, as *he* tells us.

It is as rhetorician, as a speaker, that one first attends to Empedocles and this same speaker's element manifestly characterizes *Also Sprach Zarathustra*. Nietzsche begins his inaugural lecture in Basel on "Homer and Classical Philology" by noting the critical importance of the person both in antiquity and as it persists as an issue in the themes of then-current scholarship. He thereby highlights the objective or substantive as well as the rhetorical role of style.[26] He also emphasizes this same rhetorical strategy in *Human, All Too Human,* where he offers a philological explanation of how to write a book (his model is the *New Testament*) for everyone and consequently, as Nietzsche here emphasizes: for no one.[27] And if Empedocles is engaged in what the classicists rather flat-footedly call self-presentation, it is important that Nietzsche, by contrast, and even as Zarathustra, masks or dissembles himself. In other words, Nietzsche lies *and* takes care to tell us that he does so, like the rhetors, orators, poets, and most especially like the Menippean Lucian from whom, as already noted, he borrows more than a few allusions.[28]

Yet we recall again from Nietzsche's *Philosophy in the Tragic Age of the Greeks* as from his inaugural lecture: the key to antiquity is personality, and this key also seems to fit the case of Nietzsche's Zarathustra (speaking on the model of Diogenes Laërtius on Empedocles).

Who Is Nietzsche's *Übermensch*?

Emphasizing both catharsis and nemesis in his conception of the *Übermensch*, Nietzsche derives the term *Übermensch* not from Aristotle's conception of the great-souled man, *megalopsychos* (though this surely resonates in it), but from Lucian of Samosata's *hyperanthropos* ('υπεράνθρωπος) as it appears in Lucian's parodic dialogue *ΚΑΤΑΠΛΟΥΣ*, *The Downward Journey*. Lucian's alternative subtitle—*Η ΤΥΡΑΝΝΟΣ*, or *The Tyrant*—offers the account of the tyrant as "overman," that is: as a superior man of wealth and power who in this worldly life towers *above* others regarded in this same life as inferior or "lesser" human beings. Lucian's parody transposes the same putatively "higher" man, the *hyperanthropos*, escorted by Hermes and ferried by Charon or Death into the afterlife of the Greek underworld—hence the title reference to a descent from high to low: *Kataplous* or *Downward Journey*.

More important, although the derivation of Nietzsche's *Übermensch* from Lucian's *hyperanthropos* is hardly news to scholars (it is, indeed, a source scholarship cliché), no one has reviewed the substance of this source with specific reference to the substance of Zarathustra's teaching of the *Übermensch*.

In general, it is common to assume that we know what Nietzsche means by the *Übermensch* and that it corresponds, more or less coincidentally, more or less historically, to Hitler's fantasy: the evolutionary apex of human development. And this is the force of the argument claiming Nietzsche's advanced support of the transhuman condition;[29] Nietzsche's ideal of the overman is thus taken as being a superior human being (and that is also to say, with Plato and Aristotle and even Alasdair MacIntyre, a superior warrior or perfect soldier): born of science or at least *good breeding*, by which one means a family of a certain economic wherewithal, thereby heir to a certain "good" education, nutrition, environment, travel, and so on.[30]

The whole of technologically oriented society via the fantasy of genetic engineering and associated technologies as well as the fantasy life that is the Internet and mass media in general presupposes an identical vision of humanity as supreme, as "higher," as Nietzsche might have said. And if we are hardly eager to endorse the Nazi vision of the master-race, we nonetheless await the phantom du jour of transhuman or cyborg or whatever might be still expected under the now slightly aging rubric of "the singularity."[31]

Any rank ordering presupposes a developmental progression, but Empedocles also invokes a kind of evolution, if not a progressive one: a dispersal in time, an abandonment or expulsion, as expiation—and here we recall the ethical parallel with Anaximander—for a crime, for the bloody violence of dealing death and eating meat.

> When anyone sins and pollutes his own limbs with bloodshed, who by his error makes false the oath he swore—spirits whose portion is long life—for thrice ten thousand years he wanders apart from the blessed, being born throughout that time in all manner of forms of mortal things, exchanging one hard path of life for another. The force of the air pursues him into the sea, the sea spews him out onto the floor of the earth, the earth casts him into the rays of the blazing sun.[32]

Empedocles' vision of evolution and change also assumed that ours is the age of extinction—that is to say, the time of strife or hatred—precisely because of the killing that we cannot seem to stem and our aversion or abuse of the bonds or constraints of love.

We eat the flesh of animals, the beings we seduce into docility or breed for the purpose of domestication, caring for them from birth—we feed and succor our prey. This we name animal husbandry and the shepherd's love for his flocks is by no means coincidentally a metaphor for both human and divine love. Perversely, we are the only animals who use love's bonds, those ties of affection and caring, as Empedocles spoke of love, to draw animals to us in order, so tamed, to have easy access to them for slaughter at our convenience. This deception and its great efficiency is one of the reasons we can kill as many animals as we do, as systematically as we do. Thus we kill beings, living beings like ourselves, whom we can have known since the moment of their birth in order to cut slices from their bodies and limbs to roast and boil or steam them and sometimes even to eat them raw, and sometimes (both eggs and fetuses) before they are born. Most of us dress in the skins or fur or hair of animals (this animal hair is what we call wool and cashmere, the skin is leather, and so on). Most of us eat animal flesh for no other reason than that we like the taste (this, so it has been popularly argued, is the biggest counter-argument contra vegetarianism along with habit, convention, or sociability). The bandwagon argument: everyone is doing it, fuels an industry to supply animal body parts, whether via mechanized agriculture or hunted down in the wild or dredged in unimaginable amounts from the sea for the purpose of human consumption and use: the restaurant industry, the street food industry, the supermarket industry, nothing other than an apocalypse for every animal that had previously dwelled on the face of the earth in formerly "undeveloped" as in cultivated lands.

Wild or domestic, we kill them all. All this is unchanged since Empedocles' day:

> The father lifts up his own son changed in form and slaughters him with a prayer, blind fool, as he shrieks piteously, beseeching as he is killed. But he deaf to his cries slaughters him and makes ready in his halls an evil feast. In the same way son seizes father and children their mother, and tearing out life they eat the flesh of those they love.[33]

Classicists are fond of linking Empedocles' prohibition of carnivorism with metempsychosis. Thus one reads again and again that it is Empedocles' reasoning that one ought not eat meat just because one might thereby unknowingly consume one's recently deceased brother or father (assuming the situation applies in the first place). Yet the anthropological (incest or consanguinity) prohibition is inadequate here. The animal for Empedocles is brother to you—not in a limited, but an unlimited or universal way: universal in the way that Schiller's poem *An die Freude*, the "Ode to Joy," urges the Christian idealist vision for all humanity as brothers under heaven: *Alle Menschen werden Brüder*. Simone de Beauvoir concludes *The Second Sex* by speaking, to the great annoyance of feminists all over the world, of *fraternité* in just the same sense.

Empedocles is speaking, as Nietzsche would speak (this is the ontological meaning of the will to power),[34] of the fundamental relatedness of all living things. We are not "other" than animals and we are certainly not—consider only what we do!—"higher." The animal you barbecue *is* your brother, physiologically, biologically speaking, not a one that *could be* in some spiritualist sense, your literal (that is, genetically human) brother or son.[35] This that you do to the least of your neighbors, the least of your brethren, this you do to the Christ. So we have heard from the man Nietzsche named the only Christian, the one who hung on the cross and—the one who died for the things he said.

Beyond Nietzsche's reading of Empedocles' carnivorism, the notion of the overhuman may be anything but a goal or an advance.[36]

And yet Nietzscheans and anti-Nietzscheans alike *believe* in the overhuman. In fact, in practice, we tend to assume that we are (already) the transhuman (these days we prefer this term) or overhuman or posthuman, at least potentially, at least in some sense, perhaps by comparison with ages gone by: we are the dominant species in comparison not only with the ape but every other living being on this earth. Thus if not yet by ordinary or natural evolutionary means, then certainly, as we suppose, some scientist must currently be developing some mechanism to transform us further, using the latest genetic or stem cell technology; a transformation (think of the already mentioned metaphor of the "singularity") which is "singular" in name only, inasmuch as it happens to take us in the same direction we already find ourselves going.[37]

The human, all-too-human will be or already is (depending, again, on how transhuman you already take yourself to be) the "overhuman."

Between Nietzsche's *Übermensch* and Lucian's ὑπεράνθρωπος

This work is Lucian's, who well knew
The foolishness of times gone by,
For things the human race finds wise
Are folly to th' unclouded eye.

Erasmus[38]

I noted earlier that every scholar knows that Nietzsche's *Übermensch* is a coinage taken or derived from Lucian. Every scholar *knows* this because Walter Kaufmann tells us so, and seemingly every account duly cites Kaufmann (the citation is easy to find, taking just one line on the first page of the chapter in question: "*Kataplous*, 16").[39] However, if one actually reads (as scholars manifestly do not read) the actual source itself, namely, Lucian's *Kataplous hè turannos* [*Tyrannus sive cataplus*] or *Voyage to the Underworld or The Tyrant*,[40] one gains an intriguing insight into the "overhuman." Lucian articulates this in the same comedic-parodic-satiric fashion Nietzsche alludes to in *The Birth of Tragedy* and *The Gay Science* and specifically invokes as Menippean satire at the conclusion of his *Ecce Homo*, "What I owe the Ancients."

Satirically, ironically (or as literary scholars are apt to say, following Bakhtin as they do: *serio-comically*), the notion of the *Übermensch* spans Nietzsche's career.[41]

For his own part, Lucian's dialogue plays upon the tyrant Megapenthes' literal downgoing to the underworld in the wake of his death. Like the scenes in Lucian's *Dialogues of the Dead*, Lucian's *Kataplous* articulates the instructive morality tale of those who seem in everyday life to be superior, or "upperclass" or "higher" human beings, only to be shown to be just (or merely) all-too-human as soon as they cross over into the underworld (or, in Lucian's text, as they are unwillingly dragged into the afterlife, just as the dwarf leaps after the tightrope walker or "overman" at the start of Zarathustra, and similarly threatens to drag him down into hell).

In Lucian's *Kataplous*: "The 'superman' [ὑπεράνθρωπός] is the superior man, a king among men, a man of power like a tyrant."[42] Note that these attributes are political ones on the basis of which the cobbler musing on his own past life had seen the tyrant as physically enhanced: the tyrant "appeared to me a superman, thrice-blessed, better looking and a full royal cubit taller than almost anyone else."[43] But, so Lucian's satire continues, "when he died and had to take off his trappings, not only did he look ridiculous to me, but I had to laugh at how ridiculous *I* was."[44]

Context makes all the difference, not just for Nietzsche but for Lucian. Thus Lucian's provocative contrast highlights the superficial vision of the higher man, the man of the upper or wealthy classes, and the same man once translated into the afterlife.

Parody and satire are one thing, so we think, Nietzsche's *Übermensch* seems to be another notion, a transcendent, evolutionary ideal, not at all parodic. We are speaking after all of the philosophy that is reputed to have inspired the National Socialist language of the master-race and a world war that went with it: the ideology of the *Übermensch* as opposed to the *Unter-Mensch*. And Nietzsche himself uses both terms. Yet here I have been arguing that Nietzsche's emphasis on the rhetorical importance of Menippean satire together with the Lucianic orgins of the notion of the *Übermensch* make it at least plausible that Nietzsche's Zarathustra be read as "teaching" the *Übermensch* in a *parodic* fashion. To say, however, that the *Übermensch* is a parodic or satiric notion does little to make its meaning clear. For to say that is parodic (or better: tragico-parodic) hardly means that Nietzsche's Zarathustra does not undertake to "teach" the *Übermensch*—of course he does. But it is easy to fail to note (certainly even many sophisticated and sensitive Nietzsche scholars do so) that the elusive doctrine of the eternal return, the doctrine that Zarathustra comes to teach, the teaching that the overhuman himself or herself is meant to be the passage toward, is the eternal return of the *same*. And this teaching is Empedocles' "truth" of rebirth. Thus Nietzsche's Zarathustra can teach that the human is charged to overcome or to get beyond or to get over the human.

Empedocles and Death—or Zarathustra's Descent into Hell

> From what high rank and from what a height of bliss . . .
>
> Empedocles[45]

To conclude this very provisional suggestion of a parallel between Zarathustra and Empedocles, by way of Lucian, we may summarize what we have seen so far. Here we recall that Nietzsche reminds us that

> Empedocles sought to impress the oneness of all life most urgently, that carnivorism is a sort of self-cannibalism (*Sichselbstverspeisen*), a murder of the nearest relative. He desired a colossal purification of humanity, along with abstinence from beans and laurel leaves. (*PPP* 109)

Purification is what matters, if one can understand this in terms of a classical ascesis or training or practice. And when it comes to Empedocles' purification—far more than his caution against carnivorism (here through Nietzsche read as a kind of self-devouring), more than his cosmological cycle (although both of these issues matter greatly to the Schopenhauerian Nietzsche)—it is the tableau of the volcano and of Empedocles' voluntary death that strikes us most powerfully.[46] And then we can also note the nicely dramatic detail of a single bronze sandal, tossed up and back to the land of the living by the same volcano. *Why just one?*[47] And still more important, why would it not have been vaporized or melted?[48]

We have already encountered the topos of *The Islands of the Blest* as the subtitle of Wilhelm Heinse's *Ardinghello,* to whom Hölderlin dedicated his poem "Bread and Wine." With Heinse offering the recollections of Ardinghello, a wanderer in Sicily, and Hölderlin those of Hyperion, the hermit in an idealized vision of modern Greece, the geographic contours of these two accounts is critical to both and both point to a locative longing for a phantom: the dream of Greece.[49] But this is the high air of allegory. More concretely, Jung refers to an account of Nietzsche's Zarathustra that echoes the constellation of death.[50] As his point of departure, Jung's discussion engages *The Isles of the Blest* and *Of Great Events* as these appear in Nietzsche's *Thus Spoke Zarathustra.*

Most of us will recall the Zarathustran passage in question: it's weird and not just because Jung says so, if Zarathustra scholars rarely remark upon this wackiness, and I remember reading it for the first time and for however many hundreds of times I have read it, but always without much sense. But it is worth thinking about such things, especially with reference to Nietzsche who spent his life engaged with oddities often unquestioned by supposedly critical scholarship.[51]

Together with the above reading of Lucian, and together with the suggestion that Nietzsche retells the purifications of Empedocles along with the death of Empedocles with his *Thus Spoke Zarathustra* (and I have been attempting here to make both claims), the constellation in question may begin to lose much of its oddness.

For Jung, Nietzsche would have had to have recognized this as the locus classicus of the Dorian city of Acragas although, as Jung reflects, Nietzsche's Zarathustran account does not allude to Empedocles. Nevertheless, Jung rightly remarks that the story "has a very peculiar ring."[52]

> It was so funny—the noontide hour and the captain and his men—what was the matter with that ship that they go to shoot rabbits near the entrance of hell? Then it slowly came to me that when I was about eighteen, I had read a book from my grandfather's library, *Blätter aus Prévorst* by Kerner, a collection in four volumes of wonderful stories, about ghosts and phantasies and forbodings, and among them I found that story. It is called "An extract of awe-inspiring import from the log of the ship 'Sphinx', in the year 1686 in the Mediterranean."[53]

It's hard to argue with Jung's psychoanalytic insight here, for Nietzsche does indeed seem to "channel" Justinius Kerner's short account.[54]

Let us recall the passage from the section entitled "On Great Events."

> There is an island in the sea—not far from the Blissful Islands of Zarathustra—upon which a volcano continuously smokes; the people, and especially the old women among the people, say that it is placed like a block of stone before the gate of the underworld, but that the narrow downward path which leads to this gate of the underworld passes through the volcano itself. (*Z* II "On Great Events")

The passage could not be more obviously related to Lucian, but it is just as useful to note that it also echoes the spirit or sense of Rohde's broader constellation of his exploration into *Psyche: The Cult of Souls and the Belief in Immortality Among the Greeks*.[55] Inasmuch as both Nietzsche and Rohde shared the same background familiarity (and our reading above of Lucian helps us here), reading Rohde gives us access to terminology Nietzsche took for granted, some of which we seem no longer to take as convention, beginning with the language of "The Isles of the Blest," along with a certain expression of "translation" across the surface of the earth, and of dimensionality high and low, above and below the earth.

The relevant bit from Nietzsche's account in *Thus Spoke Zarathustra* is as follows:

> it happened that a ship dropped anchor at the island upon which the smoking mountain stood; and its crew landed in order to shoot rabbits. Towards the hour of noon, however, when the captain and his men were reassembled, they suddenly saw a man coming towards them through the air, and a voice said clearly: 'It is time! It is high time!' But as the figure was closest to them—or flew quickly past, however, like a shadow, in the direction of the volcano—they recognized, with the greatest consternation, that it was Zarathustra. (*Z* II "On Great Events")

Jung goes on to cite Kerner's original text for his students' sake.[56] For Jung, inasmuch as Nietzsche's account reproduces Kerner's ghost story, it would seem that Nietzsche would have had to have read the story in his youth (as Jung recognized to the extent that he was a near contemporary), a surmise he checks with Elisabeth Förster Nietzsche, who confirms that she and her brother found this book in the library of their own "grandfather, Pastor Oehler."[57]

In addition to Jung's (repeated) invocation of this story as a demonstration not of Nietzsche's conscious plagiarism but rather of the working power of the unconscious (and hence as an argument for the existence of the same agency),[58] Jung notes that "such stories are recorded because they are edifying"—and here we note that this edification resonates in turn with Lucian. In the case of Kerner's ghost story, so Jung explains: "The two gentlemen from London were big merchants and evidently they were not quite alright, because they are painted with the colors of hell which express sinfulness; one is black and the other grey, whereas they should be wearing white shirts which is court dress in heaven."[59]

The ghostly dimension of Zarathustra's witch-like flight, as should now be evident given our earlier reference to Lucian's underworld setting and now still more with our recollection of the context of Rohde's *Psyche*, is literal enough.[60] Most commentators similarly fail to note that Zarathustra's shadow, the *shade* in question, corresponds for the ancient Greek to the flattened dimensionality that is the only thing that remains of us after death, presuming here what Rohde characterizes as a "subterranean translation."

Hence with respect to the claim that it is, as Nietzsche's Zarathustra repeats, "high time," that it is therefore *late*—"it's time, it's time" as T. S.

Eliot calls, as Gadamer once spoke of age as including so many "warning shots across the bow"—so, too, Jung explains that "This is the secret, this is the key to the meaning of that descent into hell. It was a warning; soon you will go down into dissolution."[61]

There are numerous explorations of the meaning of the overhuman, and there is no doubt that it also has an ideal aspect.[62] But given the context of Lucian's *Kataplous*, I have argued that it may serve us to consider yet another rendering of the overhuman as an ironic and hence edifying construct. But then the didactic purpose of Zarathustra's "teaching" becomes more rather than less elliptical, and the overhuman also becomes something less than a consummation—whether transhuman or not.

PART VI

The Becoming of the Soul: Nomadism and Self-Experiment

15

"Falling in Love with Becoming"

Remarks on Nietzsche and Emerson

DIETER THOMÄ

One day, a certain Frank Bascombe overheard a colleague three cubicles away talking about his business behavior. She said: "I'm sure he would never do or say that." This remark somehow stuck with him when he "went off to sleep that night." Here is what he thought "of those words 'Mr. Bascombe would never . . .'":

> It occurred to me that even though my colleague . . . could say what Mr. Bascombe would never do, say, drive, eat, wear, laugh about, marry or think was sad, Mr. Bascombe himself wasn't sure *he* could. She could've said damn near anything about me and I would've had to give the possibility some thought . . . But very little about me, I realized—except what I'd *already* done, said, eaten, etc.—seemed written in stone, and all of that meant almost nothing about what I *might* do. I had my history, okay, but not really much of a regular character, at least not an inner essence I or anyone could use as a predictor. And something, I felt, needed to be done about that. I needed to go out and find myself a recognizable and persuasive semblance of a character. I mean, isn't that the most cherished pre-posthumous dream of all?"

This is a passage from the *The Lay of the Land*, Richard Ford's masterly novel, in which Bascombe, a real estate agent, goes on by saying:

> Some force in my life was bringing me hard up against what felt like my self . . . , presenting me, if I chose to accept it, with an imperative

> that all my choices in recent memory—volitions, discretions, extra beats, time spent offshore—hadn't presented me, though I might've said they had and argued you to the dirt about it. Here, for a man with no calculable character, was a hunger of *necessity*, for something solid, the thing "character" stands in for. . . . I set about deciding how I should put the next five to ten years to better use than the last five—progress being the ancients' benchmark for character.[1]

Richard Ford's hero is engaged in a quest for identity. I take it that Nietzsche's thought very much circles around the line "*Le style c'est l'homme même*" (even though this formula does not appear in his writings) or, to take Nietzsche's own wording, around the idea of giving "style to one's character" (GS 290). Thus Frank Bascombe's struggle with identifying character traits or shaping the trajectory of a life circles around a Nietzschean problem. Bascombe's fright of being immobilized is anticipated in Nietzsche's idea of living as "overcoming" oneself.

With his invocation of "overcoming," Nietzsche responds to the classical notion of formation as "progress" (Ford; see previous passage) and picks up on the idea of "perfectibility" that has already been conceptualized as an open-ended process in the eighteenth century. Nietzsche conceives "character" without relying on a core or kernel that would define personal identity and provide a guideline for its development. The motto for his attempt to rethink progress without having a preformatted origin or final aim could easily be a phrase from Emerson that, by the way, is also quoted in Richard Ford's novels *The Lay of the Land* and *Independence Day*.[2] Emerson says: "The soul *becomes.*"[3] In Nietzsche, this phrase is transformed to the "soul . . . falling in love with becoming" (*KSA* 10:20[10]).

Emerson's influence on Nietzsche can hardly be overrated. Direct and indirect quotes from Emerson's writings are to be found in many of Nietzsche's writings; his reading copy of Emerson's *Essays* is full of annotations. I do not intend to conduct a comprehensive comparison between the American philosopher of romantic individualism and Nietzsche.[4] Instead I focus on Emerson's and Nietzsche's idea of "becoming" that can serve as a building block for our understanding of living a life or, to put it in a more Socratic manner, as an answer to the question of "how to live."

Yet, before turning to "becoming," it is worthwhile considering its counterpart: stagnation or immobility. Richard Ford knows of such a condition; he calls it the "Permanent Period." "The Permanent Period is specifically commissioned to make you quit worrying about your own existence and how everything devolves on your *self*"[5]; it is supposed "to protect us from hazardous moments."[6] Frank Bascombe's intermittent longing for putting an end to this kind of hazard is not shared by his wife, Sally, who walks out on him as she begins "to fear permanence, to fear no longer *becoming*."[7] Most of the novel *The Lay of the Land* is about the "Permanent Period" and its discontents, about the hero's growing uneasiness with having reached saturation.

> Permanence can be scary. Even though it solves the problem of tiresome becoming, it can also erode optimism, render possibility small and remote, and make any of us feel that while we can't fuck up much of anything anymore, there really isn't much to fuck up because nothing matters a gnat's nuts; and that down deep inside we've finally become just an organism that for some reason can still make noise, but not much more than that. This you need to save yourself from, or else the slide off the transom of life's pleasure boat becomes irresistible and probably a good idea.[8]

What is envisaged for the period after the "Permanent Period" is mysteriously called the "Next Level."

Frank Bascombe's concern with becoming a mere "organism" very much reminds us of Friedrich Nietzsche's famous portrayal of the "last man."

> [The last men] have left the regions where it was hard to live: for one needs warmth. One loves his neighbors and rubs each other: for one needs warmth. . . . One is still working, for work is a form of entertainment. But one is careful lest the entertainment be too harrowing. . . . One has his little lust for the day and his little lust for the night; but one reveres health. "We have invented happiness"—say the last men and blink their eyes. (*Z* "Prologue" 5)

A close relative to this "last man," be it in Nietzsche's days only, are the "Chinese" who favor an immobile, feeble way of life and state of mind. Following Nietzsche, "China . . . is a country in which . . . the capacity for *change* ha[s] become extinct centuries ago; and the socialists and state idolaters of Europe with their measures of making life better and safer might easily establish in Europe, too, Chinese conditions and a Chinese 'happiness'" (*GS* 24).

In his critique of utilitarianism, Nietzsche polemicizes against "comfort" and "fashion" (*BGE* 228; *KSA* 11:27[6], *KSA* 11:35[34]); he loathes the "miserable ease" and "happiness of the greatest number," and rebuffs the core question of self-preservation: "How does the human being preserve itself the best, the longest and in the most comfortable way?" (*Z* IV "On the Higher Man" 3). Preservation is about maintaining something; its purpose is securing stability, not enabling change.

If we go back from Nietzsche to Emerson, we meet a predecessor of the "last man," who plays a leading role in what arguably is the most controversial passage in Emerson's work: his critique of pity or philanthropy. Emerson asks "Are they *my* poor?"—and he says: "I grudge the dollar, the dime, the cent, I give to such men." "I do not wish to expiate," to pay for some kind of appeasement, "but to live. . . . I wish [my life] . . . to be sound and sweet, and not to need diet and bleeding."[9]

> We want men and women who shall renovate life and our social state, but we see that most natures are insolvent, cannot satisfy their own wants, . . . and do lean and beg day and night continually. . . . We come to them who weep foolishly, and sit down and cry for company, instead of imparting to them truth and health in rough electric shocks . . . Welcome evermore to gods and men is the self-helping man.[10]

Opposed to the "self-helping man" are those natures that "weep" and "beg" day in and day out, and they, in turn, are forerunners of the "last man." Their main concern is self-preservation.

Grudging the dollar that I give to the needy—this attitude has attracted a lot of criticism, yet as numerous as Emerson's critics are his defenders. On the long list of those who have contributed to this controversy over the years are, among others, John Updike, Harold Bloom, Michael Sandel, Judith Shklar, George Kateb, and Stanley Cavell. I confine myself to giving some quotes from John Updike before turning to Stanley Cavell.

Updike claims that "a doctrine of righteousness is here propounded. The Biblical injunction 'Love thy neighbor as thyself' is conveniently shortened to 'Love thyself.'"[11] Updike claims that Emerson belonged to the school of "rugged individualism," cultivated the "art of relaxation and of doing what you wanted" and anticipated the Yippies' creed "If it feels good, it's moral" (ibid.). Updike goes on by saying:

> A social fabric, [Emerson] . . . did not seem quite to realize, . . . exists for the protection of its members . . . From the Over-soul to the *Übermensch* to the Supermen of Hitler's Master Race is a dreadful progression for which neither Emerson nor Nietzsche should be blamed; but Emerson's coldness and disengagement and distrust of altruism do become, in Nietzsche, a rapturous celebration of power and domination and the "'boldness' of noble races" and an exhilarated scorn of what the German called 'slave morality.' . . . The totalitarian leader is a study in self-reliance gone amok.[12]

This is a bit thick. Harold Bloom,[13] George Kateb,[14] Michael Sandel[15] and Judith Shklar[16] choose a different path, but I want to confine myself to a brief discussion of Cavell's[17] and look at the evidence in Emerson's texts themselves. It is true that Emerson says: "The worst of charity is, that the lives you are asked to preserve are not worth preserving."[18] But this is not meant to be disdainful, as he goes on by saying: "Masses! the calamity is the masses. I do not wish any mass at all, but honest men only, lovely, sweet, accomplished women only . . . When [government] . . . reaches its true law of action, every man that is born will be hailed as essential."[19]

> Generosity does not consist in giving money or money's worth. These so-called *goods* are only the shadow of good. To give money to the sufferer is only a come-off. It is only a postponement of the real payment, a bribe paid for silence . . . We owe to man higher succors than food and fire. We owe to man man. . . . You are to bring with you that spirit which is understanding, health, and self-help. To offer him money in lieu of these is to do him the same wrong as when the bridegroom offers his betrothed virgin a sum of money to release him from his engagements.[20]

In the light of these statements, it should be plain that John Updike was wrong and that Cavell is right. His defense of Emerson's is nourished by the same discontent that is voiced in Frank Bascombe's concerns about becoming an "organism" in the "Permanent Period." Cavell asks: "Is Emerson really so difficult to distinguish from those who may be taken as parodies of him?"—And he answers: "Not so difficult, it seems to me."[21] Part of his explanation runs as follows:

> A charitable dollar is wicked because it is given to unequals, because it supports what it is that keeps them down; which further suggests that when Emerson adds of the wicked dollar, 'which by and by I shall have the manhood to withhold,' he does not exactly mean that he will further harden his heart but that by and by he will live in a society that has achieved manhood, that one day human kind will not require the dole from one another.[22]

A "society that has achieved manhood" would be a society that has overcome the "Permanent Period." This would be a society in which the souls become.

A reading of life that stresses becoming or overcoming has its bearings on our understanding of a person's interaction with others. Another person's "becoming" runs against my insistence, in which I, for once, try to pinpoint the other. The other person whom I turn to is evasive, ephemeral. And if this other person seeks to get hold of me, she will not succeed either. A few lines from Emily Dickinson fit in nicely here:

> To pity those that know her not
> Is helped by the regret
> That those who know her, know her less
> The nearer her they get.[23]

Being familiar with somebody does not necessarily mean that you know the other in a way that could be called exhaustive. The very idea of "exhaustion" is suspicious if it comes to interaction, as a complete, exhaustive knowledge of the other may well lead to some kind of boredom, a lack of curiosity or a decrease of interest in the other, as he or she cannot come up with any surprises anymore. But according to Dickinson's poem, it is just not true that we really "know" the persons who are near to us in this manner. Their individuality still very much contains the promise of surprises, an open horizon of potentiality. A last pair of quotes from Emerson and Nietzsche may help establish a link between this notion of the individual and interaction.

Emerson says: "Dear to us are those who love us, the swift moments we spend with them are a compensation for a great deal of misery; they enlarge our life."[24] Concord is not only Emerson's hometown, but the ideal promoted in this sentence: concord or accordance with others. But if this love is confined to supporting and recognizing what I am doing, it does not entail the reaching out into the unknown. This is why Emerson goes on by saying: "But dearer are those who reject us as unworthy, for they add another life: they build a heaven before us, whereof we had not dreamed, and thereby supply to us new powers out of the recesses of the spirit, and urge us to new and unattempted performances."[25] According to Emerson, this kind of intervention works like a "nettle"[26] or a "cramp-fish."[27] This claim is supported by numerous contentions that run against saturation or satisfaction: "Character wants room; must not be crowded on by persons, nor be judged from glimpses got in the press of affairs or on few occasions."[28]

> The one thing which we seek with insatiable desire is to forget ourselves, to be surprised out of our propriety, to lose our sempiternal memory, and to do something without knowing how or why; in short, to draw a new circle. Nothing great was ever achieved without enthusiasm. The way of life is wonderful: it is by abandonment.[29]

Nietzsche heavily marks and partly excerpts (*KSA* 10:15[27]) this passage in his copy of the *Essays*; he picks up this line of thought in his musings about forgetfulness and happiness (*HL* 1) and in his early essay on "Fate and History," which is very much inspired by Emerson and elaborates on *Selbstentrücktsein*. In line with what Emerson says about interaction is the following quote from Nietzsche: "[Man] . . . is not only supposed to love his enemies, but to hate his friends" (*Z* I "On the Gift-Giving Virtue" 3). I take it that Nietzsche's "hate" is a slightly altered version of Emerson's "reject[ion]" of the other. Nietzsche experiments with an inversion between friend and fiend. He does not talk about hating enemies, but about hating those we hold dear. This hate turns out to be a love of a kind; it is a virtue among friends or something that you would call *Freundschaftsdienst* (service in the name of friendship) in German, which rather drily translates as a "friendly turn" or a "good turn" in English. What exactly could it mean, then, that my friends *owe* me hate, or what exactly do they hate if they hate me?

They hate my presence, or my being nothing but presence, my being reduced to the status quo. So their friendship or their love consists in demolishing my identification with the present and in pushing for what Emerson calls "abandonment" and Nietzsche calls *Selbstentrücktsein* (see previous passage). My friends' hate actually turns out to be love: the love of my future. Nietzsche: "Do I advise you to neighbor-love? Rather do I advise you to neighbor flight and to furthest love! Higher than love to your neighbor is love to the furthest and future ones" (*Z* I "On Love of the Neighbor"). I would reread this advice in a way that allows me to see the "furthest" and the "nearest," the "future one" and the "present one" not as two different people, but as aspects of the same person.

Friends of this kind do not push me to specific initiatives or seemingly promising "investments"; their peculiar hate provokes me to forget myself and to move in new directions. (Think of Emerson's reading of education as "provocation"[30] and of the literal meaning of the Latin *pro-vocare*) I encounter a kind of hate-love that is not necessarily self-defeating or neurotic.

My friends' attitude is complemented by an attitude that I cultivate myself: the attitude that combines self-reliance with abandonment (according to Emerson) or self-affirmation and overcoming the self (according to Nietzsche). What I see emerging here is exactly the life-form of the soul that "becomes." It is based on acknowledging what I am—and it entails the willingness or the courage to go through a process that transforms my personality. Emerson talks about the "courage to be what we are,"[31] and Nietzsche suggests that you should finally "become who you are" (*Z*

IV "The Honey Sacrifice"). This endeavor is no solitary task; it is bolstered by the support of others. "It is the individual's openness to the call of responsibility that confers on the individual life the possibility of augmenting its value and deepening its significance."[32] Being in love with becoming is encouraged by my friends' particular hate-love: an attitude that I adopt myself when my being who I am embraces the openness to who I will be. Stanley Cavell: "we become ashamed in a particular way of ourselves, of our present stance, and . . . , as a sign of consecration to the next self, . . . we hate ourselves . . . (bored with ourselves might be enough to say)."[33] This is in line with Nietzsche's question of how it could possibly "happen that we should ever *find* ourselves," and his claim that "we are necessarily strangers to ourselves," that "each is furthest from himself" (*GM* "Preface" 1).[34]

What does it mean to say that I am further away from myself than from anybody else? It should be noted that Nietzsche launches a full-fledged attack on a famous Latin proverb here: "I myself am closest to myself" (*Proxumus sum egomet mihi*). As a matter of fact, Nietzsche does not only subvert the creed of egotism, but also the creed of altruism, as "I myself am closest to myself" belongs to a pairing whose second half is the phrase "Love your neighbor as yourself [*Liebe deinen Nächsten wie dich selbst*]." When Nietzsche says "Each is furthest from himself," he not only destroys the basis of egotism, but also the premises of self-love which plays its part in the symmetry of neighborly, brotherly love, in a reconciliation of the love for myself and the love for the other. Proximity is not an option, neither in self-reflection nor in interaction. Nietzsche turns against self-reflection as intimate self-acquaintance, an idea that tends to make me feel comfortable or at least familiar with myself. Such acquaintance is delusive because the object of my knowledge is on the move and in the making.

The dual structure of the self consists of taking stock and moving on, or of knowledge and will. Many philosophical accounts of the self choose to stress one side of this dual structure only. Some state that identity is about figuring out who you are, as if your future behavior somehow emerged from your whereabouts: what you want is inferred from what you are. (This is what Schopenhauer argues for.) Others state that the self is not so much a matter of knowledge but of will. (Thus William James criticizes Schopenhauer and indulges in the "energy" that enables us to choose "between one of several equally possible future Characters."[35]) A combination of self-acquaintance and self-transformation is supported by the revised reading of interaction that has been proposed above. I am "surprised out of my propriety" by the intervention of others[36]; what I find in myself is strange to me, or "what one finds in oneself is a discovery as well of others."[37] Given that I experience strangeness within myself, I grow to feel more familiar with the strangers whom I meet in the outside world. Arthur Rimbaud's exclamation "*Je est un autre*"—"I is an other"—could be completed by the phrase "The other am I" or "The other is me." We have a chiasm here between me becoming the other and the other becoming me.

The concept of this chiasm is adumbrated by Nietzsche, but it is not laid out by Nietzsche himself in any consistent manner. He would not feel comfortable with the idea that self-overcoming requires symmetrical interaction. The quarrel about interaction and sociability puts Nietzsche scholars before an awkward alternative. *Either* they defend Nietzsche's individualism, which gives them a hard time when it comes to positively addressing social relations and tends to narrow the perspective to individual self-fashioning,[38] *or* they endorse the idea that self-overcoming is essentially a more comprehensive social endeavor, which makes them wary about patterns of domination and destruction in Nietzsche.[39] It seems to me that the chiasm of estrangement and familiarity helps to overcome this alternative, as it hints at the inherently social dimension of self-appropriation and makes the individuals raise their fellowmen to eye level. The chiastic structure of self-estrangement and growing familiar with others, or self-familiarization and the otherness as strangeness also has its bearings on the famous controversy on Nietzsche's aristocratism. It has been said that the equality of individuals stands against the highest individuals and their privileges.[40] Central to this controversy is the status of "exemplary" individuals,[41] which are in many ways preceded by Emerson's "Representative Men." The commonness of those exemplary individuals within any given social context comes to the fore when we think of these individuals as having their own hassle with inertia and as coping, like all others, with the dual structure of familiarity and estrangement.

The idea of me becoming the other and the other becoming me sounds like a plain exaggeration or even aberration, as I still remain distinct from the other. But there is a grain of truth to that chiasm that comes to the fore when we do not take it as a lofty experience of rapture, but as a plausible description of how my living my own life entails the experience of becoming a stranger to myself and how my living with others entails familiarity. The identification with the other does not overcome the confines of my bodily existence or my spatio-temporal identity, but it applies to the self-image in the sense of qualitative identity. Stating that I am farther from myself than from anybody else actually makes good sense in this perspective, as I feel the remoteness of certain "great escapes" of my mind much more vividly than those of other people. If every soul has an abyss, we are closer to the rim of our personal depths than to anybody else's.

Neither does my recognizing the other require the notion of a person as a source of agency equipped with a set of rational faculties. *Nor* is it linked to a personality shaped by a tradition that she belongs to and shares with members of her community. In opposition to these notions of sameness, which refer to us *either* as unencumbered rational beings *or* as socially embedded beings, we find ourselves and others entangled between sameness and otherness, self-affirmation and estrangement. We can thus take a step beyond Kantian morality *and* beyond communitarian *ethos*.

The experience of otherness-*within* corroborates what in Nietzsche is called "non-egotist ethics" ("*unegoistische Ethik*"; *KSA* 12:5[99]; [italics original]): an ethics that discovers the "multitude of persons . . . within one Ego" (*KSA* 11:26[73]) and is tired of the "accursed ipsissimosity" (*verfluchte Ipsissimosität*) (*BGE* 207). Nietzsche says: "Thus one participates in the lives and beings of many, as one does not deal with oneself as a stable, consistent, identical individual" (*HH* 618). Adorno daringly characterizes Nietzsche's philosophy as being "kind, gentle, unegoistic and open-hearted."[42]

This approach can be further explored by going back to the idea of "intellectual nomadism" introduced by Emerson and picked up by Nietzsche. In the second part of *Human, All Too Human*, Nietzsche links freedom as the "strongest drive of our mind" to the "ideal" of "intellectual nomadism" and puts it in opposition to a "bounded" and deeply "entrenched" mind (*AOM* 211). As of today, this "nomadism" is very much associated with the concepts of difference and deviation introduced by French readers of Nietzsche's. Yet his indebtedness to Emerson is particularly revealing here; based on this genealogy, we can cast some doubt on a reading of nomadism that indulges in the adventures of deviation.

In his German edition of the *Essays*, Nietzsche reads (I quote the English version):

> Some men have so much of the Indian left, have constitutionally such habits of accommodation, that at sea, or in the forest, or in the snow, they sleep as warm, and dine with as good appetite, and associate as happily, as in their own house. And to push this old fact still one degree nearer, we may find it a representative of a permanent fact in human nature. The intellectual nomadism is the faculty of objectiveness or of eyes which everywhere feed themselves. Who hath such eyes, everywhere falls into easy relations with his fellow-men. Every man, every thing is a prize, a study, a property to him, and this love smooths his brow, joins him to men and makes him beautiful

and beloved in their sight. His house is a wagon; he roams through all latitudes as easily as a calmuc."[43]

I could not think of a better way for expressing the movement of the self and the openness to the "other." Yet there is something strange about the passage just quoted. If one wanted to look it up in Emerson's *Essays*, one would not find it. To be sure, what I just quoted was an English version of the passage read by Nietzsche in his own German copy of the book. But this translation was based on the first edition of Emerson's *Essays* from 1841. When adopting "intellectual nomadism," Nietzsche was not aware of the fact that Emerson revised his description of it when he went through his essay "History" for the 1847 edition.

What is the outcome of this revision? He still talks about "intellectual nomadism," yet mitigates the idealization of movement. He discovers an "antagonism" between "the love of adventure" on the one hand, "the love of repose" on the other hand. Now it is said that "intellectual nomadism, in its excess, bankrupts the mind, through the dissipation of power on a miscellany of objects."[44] The "home-keeping wit" is not dismissed altogether, but is said to have "its own perils of monotony and deterioration, if not stimulated by foreign infusions."[45]

Digesting what Emerson has to say on nomadism in this final version of his argument is not easy. He seems to conduct a major recantation by revoking the unfettered celebration of movement (or "becoming") and by stating that nomadism could hit bankruptcy. Before examining the details of these changes and amendments, let me first stress the fact that "nomadism" is not a philosophical fancy, but a term with considerable historical "footing." With its many relatives, the vagrants and the "masterless" in the early modern age and today's representatives of mobility and flexibility, the figure of the "nomad" represents one of the major role models for modern individuals; it also attracts all kinds of criticisms, for example from Johann Gottlieb Fichte and Oswald Spengler (the former complains about the lack of a true "home" in modern times, the latter complains about the "new nomad" being "irreligious, intelligent, not fertile" and regards him as a "futureless . . . form of human existence"[46]).

But what about Emerson's own wariness about the "nomad"? Could it be said that the Nietzschean career of "nomadic thinking" was careless or inconsiderate, because it did not take Emerson's later concerns into account? Does this concept suffer from a lack of balance? To some extent, this concern is justified, at least if we look at the "French" readings of Nietzsche that lead from the nomad to the free-floating signifier. Deleuze links nomadism to a permanent dislocation of "intensities."[47] In line with

Emerson's early concerns, he wants to make us believe that there is an alternative between, on the one hand, a settlement organized bureaucratically and despotically, and, on the other hand, nomadic "adventures."[48] Yet eventually Emerson's pre-Nietzschean nomadism is balanced with the "love for repose," whereas Deleuze's post-Nietzschean nomadism continues to be at odds with settlement or, linguistically speaking, to "evade the codes."[49]

We could take that a step further and claim that the way to unfettered nomadism in this sense was paved by Nietzsche's adaptation of the first version of Emerson's *Essays* and by his *not* taking into account Emerson's critical afterthoughts. But this would be stretching things a little, at least as far as Nietzsche is concerned. Without any knowledge of Emerson's later amendments, Nietzsche himself comes to similar conclusions like his predecessor. One of Nietzsche's notes in his personal copy of Emerson's *Essays* reads as follows: "traveling, in every sense,/ being a 'fugitive and a vagabond'—for a time./ From time to time finding repose with your experiences, digest them (*reisen, in jedem Sinn/ "Unstet und flüchtig"—eine Zeit./ Von Zeit zu Zeit über seinen Erfahrungen ruhen, verdauen*)" (*KSA* 9:13[20]). "Fugitive" and "vagrant"—this is a quote from the bible: "a fugitive and a vagabond shalt thou be in the earth" (Genesis 4, 12).

Nietzsche actually endorses the idea of a balance between "being on the way" and "resting," which is laid out in Emerson's revised version of the *Essays.* Both thinkers take the same side, even though the editorial mishap hampered Nietzsche's knowledge of Emerson's *Essays*. This balance runs against Deleuze's reading of nomadism, but it does not run against intellectual nomadism altogether. The change between movement and repose rather reflects actual nomadic behavior as described by ethnologists: Even though nomads are vagrants, they very much rely on safe places where they take refuge. The knowledge of life-saving oases is precious. This fact is rather blurred than explained by Emerson's and Nietzsche's contention that the nomad has the ability to be "at home anywhere" or "everywhere." Nietzsche also underrates the sway of resting when he confines it to the process of digesting prior acquisitions. But with their comprehensive picture of the back and forth between movement and repose, Emerson as well as Nietzsche come close to a less stylized, ethnologically more accurate description of nomadism. Instead of mistaking Nietzsche as eulogizing nomadic movement, we should take nomadism as a metaphor for his own ambiguous stance between the urge of self-overcoming and the longing for timelessness that comes to the fore in his appraisal of the "moment" and also, in a more complicated manner, in his conception of eternal recurrence. It is safe to say though "that interpreters of Nietzsche who see men as constantly 'overcoming' themselves and rising higher and higher in a long succession of overmanliness miss the key point."[50]

Being-at-home is not something to be achieved by the sovereign behavior of a global player who takes the world to be a village that he knows like the back of his hand. The nomad's stance is much more fragile; he has to rely on favorable conditions that he cannot establish all by himself. Eventually this leads to a revision of Nietzsche's reading of the soul that "becomes": It cannot be conceptualized with the means provided by Nietzsche's theory of the "will" only. The sovereignty of the nomad is limited. While being on the move, nomads are exposed to the external world; their identity is situational. They do not only experience splendid adventures, but they face the experience of getting lost. Stanley Cavell identifies this critical situation as the experience of "exile,"[51] and rediscovers modes of such an exile whenever somebody does not know his way about, whenever somebody says, with Wittgenstein, "*Ich kenne mich nicht aus* [I do not know my way around]."[52] This kind of exile becomes a rather common experience. An exiled person suffers from her own "unknowingness," from her "incapacity either to know or to be known."[53] She experiences a loss of confidence. Exile is the "other face," as it were, of nomadism: A person is forced to be on the move, she suffers from insecurity, does not excel in volitions or power.

It is no coincidence that Cavell extends the perspective at this point and establishes a link between Emerson and Nietzsche on the one hand and Wittgenstein on the other hand. When in Emerson's and Nietzsche's balanced view nomadism comprises movement and repose, we find a similar structure in Wittgenstein. In his twofold picture there is a back and forth between "not knowing my way about" or exile on the one hand and situations marked by "*blind*" understanding[54] on the other hand. In these situations words have found what Wittgenstein calls their "Heimat" or their "original home."[55] Given that language games and life-forms coincide, a "Heimat" or "home" should be accessible to words as well as to human beings.

We should be well aware of the fact though that the counterpart to "Heimat" is not just chaos or a total loss of meaning. Like Emerson and Nietzsche, yet in a slightly less ecstatic mood, Wittgenstein acknowledges the creative or liberating mode of nomadism as well. Instead of creating a tension between "Heimat" and exile, he actually suggests that one could "feel at home" or "enjoy themselves" (*sich wohlfühlen*) while being exposed to "chaos,"[56] and talks about the "inconceivably waving totality of our language"[57]: "Life's infinite variations are essential to our life."[58] Wittgenstein's descriptions of being on the move and getting lost on the one hand, of being at "home" on the other hand are very much in line with Nietzsche's remarks on nomadism and the becoming of the soul.

A more elaborate account of Nietzsche's idea of "falling in love with becoming" would have to identify procedures or techniques that organize or shape this becoming. It seems to me that one term assumes a central role in such a setting: the term "experiment." When Emerson says: "Let me remind the reader that I am only an experimenter,"[59] Nietzsche says: "We are experiments: let us also want to be them!" (*D* 453). In *The Gay Science* Nietzsche says: "Everybody experiments with himself, improvises, makes new experiments, enjoys his experiments; and all nature ceases and becomes art" (*GS* 356). It is safe to say that the concept of "experimenting" and its German relatives "Versuch," "Versucher," and so on, are virtually omnipresent in Nietzsche's writings of all periods.

The word "experiment" seems to suggest that Nietzsche shifts the debate into a quasi-scientific framework, but a more detailed analysis of the idea of experimentation shows that it is by no means limited to an "experimental philosophy" in the sense of Francis Bacon. Nietzsche's experimentalism has been preferably discussed in the light of Kant's "experiment of reason"[60] or in relation to the natural sciences;[61] the "experiment" is also said to correspond to Nietzsche's aphoristic style.[62] More eclectic accounts of Nietzsche's experimentalism[63] still fail to systematically examine the practical viability of experimentalism and to properly situate Nietzsche within a fairly long history that includes, next to Emerson and many others, Montaigne's "Essais,"[64] Mill's "experiments in living,"[65] Dewey's "experimentalism," and the "essayism" described in Robert Musil's novel *The Man Without Qualities*.[66] It is striking to see, for instance, that John Dewey founds his "experimentalism" on a "process of becoming,"[67] for which he does not refer to Nietzsche but to Henri Bergson and to William James, who, in turn, was very much influenced by Emerson.

I cannot expand upon these issues here,[68] but it would be intriguing to compare the process of experimenting, with its moments of insecurity, expectation, anticipation, exhilaration, trial and error, evaluation and new beginnings to the forming of life as an ethical attitude, as a willingness to affirm the potentialities of a character, to encourage oneself and others to overcome their limits, and also as an attempt to carefully assess and evaluate the livability of these experiments.

This brings us back to Frank Bascombe, Richard Ford's hero, eventually. This time we meet him in a time of turmoil, he seeks bonding with his son Paul and drives up to the Baseball Hall of Fame in Cooperstown with him. While sitting in the back of the car, "Paul reads in a pseudo-reverent Charlton Heston voice," and he reads from Emerson's *Essays*, the book that his father has brought with him: “Conforming to usages . . . scatters your force. It loses your time and blurs the impression of your ‘character.’” And then Paul says: “Quack, quack, quack, quack.”—“Suddenly with his dirty fingers [he] rips out the page he’s just read from. . . . ‘I’ll keep it instead of remembering it,’” he says.[69] At another occasion he “snorts lustily, ‘You’re all about development’”—and his father feels offended, as this sounds “as if development meant something like sex slavery or incest. I knew he didn’t mean real estate development.”[70]

After some major incidents and accidents, the father says:

> Where Paul is concerned I’ve only just begun trying. And while I don’t subscribe to the “crash-bam” theory of human improvement, which says you must knock good sense into your head and bad sense out, yesterday may have cleared our air and accounts and opened, along with wounds, an unexpected window for hope to go free . . . “The soul becomes,” as a great man said, by which he meant, I think, slowly.[71]

16

"We Are Experiments"
Nietzsche on Morality and Authenticity

KEITH ANSELL-PEARSON

> Epicurus relates to the Stoics as beauty does to sublimity; but one would have to be a Stoic at the very least to catch sight of this beauty at all! To be able to be jealous of it!
>
> —**Nietzsche, *Nachlass* (*KSA* 10:7[151])**

Epicurus famously writes that the arguments of a philosopher that do not touch on the therapeutic treatment of human suffering are empty. The analogy is made with the art of medicine: just as the use of this art is to cast out sicknesses of the body, so the use of philosophy is to throw out suffering from the soul. It is in the texts of his middle period (1878–1882) that Nietzsche's writing comes closest to being an exercise in philosophical therapeutics, and in this essay I focus on *Dawn* from 1881 as a way of exploring this. I am interested in the way it revitalizes for a modern age ancient philosophical concerns, notably a teaching for mortal souls who wish to be liberated from the fear and anguish of existence, as well as from God, the "metaphysical need,"[1] and are able to affirm their mortal conditions of existence. In recent years *Dawn*, one of the most neglected texts in Nietzsche's corpus, has come to be admired for its ethical naturalism[2] and for its anticipation of phenomenology.[3] In this essay I explore the way in which the book resurrects a Hellenistic conception of philosophy in which the love of wisdom is intimately bound up with the promotion of eudaemonia or human happiness and flourishing, and show the extent to which Nietzsche's primary concern is a practical and pedagogical one, not simply a theoretical one. I also show that for Nietzsche the achievement of individual eudaemonia involves for modern-day free spirits the experimental search for an authentic mode of existence.

As a general point of inspiration I have adopted Pierre Hadot's insight into the therapeutic ambitions of ancient philosophy which was, he claims, "intended to cure mankind's anguish" (for example, anguish over our mortality).[4] This is evident in the teaching of Epicurus, which sought to demonstrate the mortality of the soul and whose aim was, "to free humans from 'the fears of the mind.'"[5] Similarly, Nietzsche's teaching in *Dawn* is for mortal souls. In the face of the loss of the dream of the soul's immortality, philosophy for Nietzsche has new consolations to offer in the form of new sublimities, which he explores in the final part of the text (book five).[6] The ultimate aim of this conception of philosophy is to promote joy in living and in one's own self (*WS* 86). As Nietzsche makes clear in *Dawn,* the main task is to translate into reason a strong and constant drive, one that yearns for "mild sunshine, clearer and fresher air, southerly vegetation, sea air" (*D* 553). For the greater part of its history, the human being has lived in a condition of fear and as a herd-conforming animal. Nietzsche's philosophy of the morning looks ahead to a new dawn in human existence in which individuals will have conquered this fear and cultivate their lives in a way that is conducive to themselves and beneficent to others. This at least is the hope—and the experiment. Nietzsche agrees with the Socratic schools and ancient sages of Hellenistic times that philosophy does indeed mean the love of wisdom (*philosophia*) and that it involves mastery of the affects; but he also appreciates that new types of knowledge are needed if we are to become the ones that we are: unique, singular, incomparable, self-creating, self-legislating (*GS* 335). "Physics"—knowledge and self-knowledge—and ethics (becoming the ones that we are) belong indissolubly together. The task is to secure individual eudaemonia but, as we shall see, traditional and typical formulations of morality prove to be a hindrance to it.

Nietzsche's thinking in *Dawn* contains a number of proposals and recommendations of tremendous value to philosophical *therapeia*, including (1) a call for a new honesty about the human ego and human relations, including relations of self and other and of love, so as to free us from certain delusions; (2) the search for an authentic mode of existence, which appreciates the value of solitude and independence; (3) the importance of having a rich and mature taste in order to eschew the fanatical; and (4) the promotion of the "rational death." In this essay I explore some of these aspects and focus on the opposition at work in the text between "morality" and "authenticity." The essay is structured as follows: first, an introductory section on the influence of Epicurus on Nietzsche; second, a section on morality in *Dawn*; third, a section, on authenticity in *Dawn*; fourth, a section on care of self; and finally, a section on Nietzsche's promotion of self-creation as an exercise in self-cultivation. Here I critically engage with Gianni Vattimo's interpretation of the significance of *Dawn.*

Introduction to *Dawn*: Nietzsche's Epicurean Moment

Dawn: Thoughts on the Prejudices of Morality was researched between January 1880 and March 1881 and published in the early summer of 1881. It is one of Nietzsche's "yes-saying" books, a work of enlightenment which, Nietzsche tells his readers, seeks to pour out "its light, its love, and its delicacy over nothing but bad things, giving back to these things the 'lofty right and *prerogative* of existence'" (*EH* "Books" *D* 1). The Indian motto from the Hymn to Varuna of the Rig Veda, "there are so many dawns that have not yet broken," lies inscribed on the door to the book (*EH* "Books" *D* 1). Nietzsche's amanuensis Peter Gast had written the motto on the title page while making a fair copy of the manuscript and this, in fact, inspired Nietzsche to adopt the new title and replace its original title of "The Ploughshare." In 1888 Nietzsche speaks of the book as amounting to a search for the new morning that ushers in a whole series of new days and he insists that not a single negative word is to be found in it, and no attack or malice either. In this book we encounter a thinker who lies in the sun, "like a sea creature sunning itself among rocks" (*EH* "Books" *D* 1)—and the book was largely conceived in the rocks near Genoa in solitude and where, so Nietzsche discloses, he "had secrets to share with the sea" (see also *D* 423 and 575). *Dawn* is a book that journeys into the future, and which for Nietzsche constitutes, in fact, its true destination: "Even now," he writes in a letter of 24 March 1881 to his old friend Erwin Rohde, "there are moments when I walk about on the heights above Genoa having glimpses and feelings such as Columbus once, perhaps from the very same place, sent out across the sea and into the future" (Letter Nr. 96, *KSB* 6:74f). Nietzsche's appeal to Columbus is figurative; he is, in fact, critical of the real Columbus (*D* 37). But as a figure of thought, Columbus the seafarer serves *Dawn* well; he denotes "the true experimenter, who may have an idea of where he thinks he is heading but is always prepared to be surprised by the outcome of his experiments."[7] The book concludes on an enigmatic note with Nietzsche asking his readers and fellow travelers whether it will be said of them one day that they too, "steering toward the west, hoped to reach an India" but that it was their fate to shipwreck upon infinity (*D* 575).

At this point in his writings "India" denotes for Nietzsche the path to self-enlightenment. Nietzsche holds that Europe remains behind Indian culture in terms of the progress it needs to make with respect to religious matters because it has not yet attained the "free-minded naiveté" of the Brahmins. The priests of India demonstrated "pleasure in thinking" in which observances—prayers, ceremonies, sacrifices, and hymns—are celebrated as the givers of all good things. One step further, he adds, and one also throws aside the gods—"which is what Europe will also have to do one day" (*D* 96). Europe remains distant, he muses, from the level of culture attained in the appearance of the Buddha (the teacher of self-redemption). Nietzsche anticipates an age when all the observances and customs of the old moralities and religions have come to an end. In a reversal of the Christian meaning of the expression "*In hoc signo vinces* [In this sign (cross) you will be the victor]," which heads *Dawn* (*D* 96), Nietzsche is suggesting that the conquest will take place under the sign that the redemptive God is dead. Buddha is a significant teacher because his religion is one of self-redemption, and this is a valuable step along the way of ultimate redemption from religion and from God. Instead of speculating on what will then emerge into existence, he calls for a new community of nonbelievers to make their sign and communicate with one another: "There exist today perhaps ten to twenty million people among the different countries of Europe who no longer 'believe in God'—is it too much to ask that they *give a sign* to one another?" (*D* 96). He imagines these people constituting a new power in Europe, between nations, classes, rulers and subjects, and between the un-peaceable and the most peaceable.

Dawn strikes me as a distinctly Epicurean moment in Nietzsche's development.[8] In *The Wanderer and his Shadow* (1879) Nietzsche confesses to being inspired by the example of Epicurus whom he calls the inventor of a "heroic-idyllic mode of philosophizing" (*WS* 295). We can follow Epicurus's example and learn to quiet ourselves by appreciating that it is not necessary to solve the ultimate and outermost theoretical questions; for example, if the gods exist, they do not concern themselves with us (*WS* 7).[9] In the letter to Menoeceus, Epicurus seeks to identify what the study of philosophy can do for the health of the soul and on the premise that, "pleasure is the starting-point and goal of living blessedly."[10] Epicurus stresses that he does not mean the pleasures of the profligate or of consumption; rather, the task, is to become accustomed to simple, non-extravagant ways of living. The key goal for Epicurus is to liberate the body from pain and remove disturbances from the soul. Central to his counsel is the thought that we need to accustom ourselves to believing that death is nothing to us; our longing for immortality needs to be removed: ". . . there is nothing fearful in life for one who has grasped that there is nothing fearful in the absence of life."[11] What appears to be the most frightening of bad things should be nothing to us, "since when we exist, death is not yet present, and when death is present, then we do not exist."[12] The wise human being "neither rejects life nor fears death. For living does not offend him, nor does he believe not living to be something bad."[13] If, as Epicurus supposes, everything good and bad consists in sense-experience, then death is simply the privation of sense-experience. The goal of philosophical training, then, is freedom from disturbance and anxiety in which we reach a state of *ataraxia* or psychic tranquility.[14]

According to Martha Nussbaum, Epicurus's teaching amounts to an inversion of Plato because for him truth is in the body and in contrast to Plato for whom the body is the main source of "delusion and bewitchment" and where the task is to purify ourselves of our bodily attachments through proper mathematical and dialectical training.[15] This "inversion" was well understood by Nietzsche and appreciated by him, and, like Epicurus, he tells us that he would rather have human beings think about life than death: "It makes me happy that human beings do not want at all to think the thought of death! I should like very much to do something that would make the thought of life even a hundred times more appealing to them" (*GS* 278).[16]

In *Dawn* Epicurus is portrayed as the enemy of the idea of punishments in Hell after death, which was developed by numerous secret cults in the Roman Empire and was taken up by Christianity.[17] For Nietzsche the triumph of Epicurus's teaching resounds most beautifully in the mouth of the somber Roman Lucretius, but comes too early. Christianity takes the belief in "subterranean terrors" under its special protection, and this foray into heathendom enables it to carry the day over the popularity of the Mithras and Isis cults, winning to its side the rank of the timorous as the most zealous adherents of the new faith (Nietzsche notes that because of the extent of the Jews' attachment to life, such an idea fell on barren ground). However, the teaching of Epicurus triumphs anew in the guise of modern science, which has rejected "any other representation of death and any life beyond it" (*D* 72; see also 150). Nietzsche is keen to encourage human beings to cultivate an attitude toward existence in which they accept their mortality and attain a new serenity about their dwelling on the earth, to conquer unjustified fears, and to reinstitute the role played by chance and chance events in the world and in human existence (*D* 13, 33, 36). As Hadot notes, for the Epicurean sage the world is the product of chance, not divine intervention, and this brings with it pleasure and peace of mind, freeing him from an unreasonable fear of the gods and allowing him to consider each moment as an unexpected miracle.[18] Each moment can be greeted with immense gratitude.

Not only does Nietzsche subscribe at this time to much of the teaching of Epicurus on cosmology and philosophy, he was also inspired by Epicurus's conception of friendship and the ideal of withdrawing from society and cultivating one's own garden.[19] In a letter to Peter Gast of 3 August 1883 Nietzsche writes that Epicurus, "is the best negative argument in favor of my challenge to all rare spirits to isolate themselves from the mass of their fellows" (Letter Nr. 446, *KSB* 6:417f). If philosophical therapeutics is centered on a concern with the healing of our own lives so as to return us to the joy of existing,[20] then in Nietzsche's texts of his middle period, including *Dawn*, can be seen to be an heir to this ancient tradition. The difference is that he is developing a therapy for the sicknesses of the soul under peculiarly modern conditions of existence of social control and engineering.[21] Like Epicurus, Nietzsche's philosophical therapy is in search of pupils and disciples: "What I envy in Epicurus are the *disciples* in his garden; in *such circumstances* one could certainly forget noble Greece and more certainly still ignoble Germany!" (Letter to Peter Gast, 26 August 1883, Letter Nr. 457, *KSB* 6:435f).

Dawn and Morality

I now want to explore how Nietzsche draws up an opposition between morality and authenticity in the book. I will attend to the senses of morality at work in it. Perhaps Nietzsche's fundamental presupposition in the book is that ours is an age of great uncertainty in which there are emerging individuals who longer consider themselves to be bound by existing mores and laws and are thus making the first attempts to organize and create for themselves a right. Hitherto such individuals have lived their lives under the jurisdiction of a guilty conscience, being decried as criminals, freethinkers, and immoralists (*D* 164). Although this development will make the coming century a precarious one (it may mean, Nietzsche notes, that a rifle hangs on each and every shoulder), it is one that Nietzsche thinks we should find "fitting and good" because it at least ensures the presence of an oppositional power that will admonish that there is any such thing as a single moral-making morality. The future belongs, then, to the "inventive and fructifying person" (*D* 164), and it is to this person that Nietzsche's therapy is addressed. Nietzsche does not intend to lay down precepts for everyone. As he writes, "One should seek out limited circles and seek and promote the morality appropriate to them" (*D* 194). Moreover, real and great success will be reserved for him who seeks to educate a single individual.

In the book, Nietzsche operates with a couple of critical conceptions of morality: (1) the ancient morality of custom, which characterizes eras that precede world history and are decisive for determining the character of humanity; here, "Every individual action, every individual way of thinking provokes horror" (*D* 9; see also 16, 18); (2) the modern emphasis on self-sacrifice in which it is supposed that we have defined the essence of the moral (*D* 132). In addition, he is keen to attack the view that everything that exists has a connection with morality and thus an ethical significance can be projected onto the world (*D* 3, 90, 100, 197, 563).[22] Nietzsche identifies attempts to define the goal of morality, such as it is the preservation and advancement of mankind. Nietzsche protests, however, that this is an expression of the desire for a formula and nothing more. We need to ask: preserving "of what"? Advancing "where"? He continues with this line of questioning:

> So what, then, can it contribute to instruction of what our duty is other than what passes, tacitly and thoughtlessly, as already established? Can one discern sufficiently from the formula whether we ought to aim for the longest possible existence for humanity? Or the greatest possible de-animalisation of humanity? How different in each case the means, in other words, practical morality (*Moral*), would have to be! Suppose one wanted to supply humanity with the highest possible degree of rationality: this would certainly not mean vouchsafing it is greatest possible longevity! Or suppose one thought of its "highest happiness" as the "What" and "Where": does that mean the greatest degree individual persons could gradually attain? Or a, by the way, utterly incalculable, yet ultimately attained average-bliss for everyone? (*D* 106)

He arrives at one of his principal insights, which is that morality (*Moralität*), "broadly speaking," has opened up "an abundance of sources of displeasure" and to the point that one can say that with every "refinement in morality" (*Sittlichkeit*), human beings have grown "*more and more dissatisfied* with themselves, their neighbor, and their lot . . ." (*D* 106). Nietzsche's hostility toward morality stems from what he regards as the anti-naturalism of moral concepts and thinking, as when he writes that what he wants is to stop making causes into sinners and consequences into executioners (*D* 208).[23] A moral interpretation of the body and its affects blocks off the securing of naturalistically informed self-knowledge and generates a psychical suffering peculiar to it, as when Nietzsche writes of Pascal who construed whatever proceeded from the stomach, the entrails, the nerves, the gall, and the semen—"the whole contingent nature of the machine we know so little!"—as a moral and religious phenomenon in which one could ask whether God or devil, good or evil, salvation or damnation was to be discovered in them (*D* 86).

For Nietzsche the principal prejudice that holds sway today in Europe is that the sympathetic affects and compassion define the moral, such as actions deemed to be congenial, disinterested, of general utility, and so on. Although Nietzsche mentions Schopenhauer and Mill as famous teachers of this conception of morality, he holds that they merely echo doctrines that have been sprouting up in both fine and crude forms since the time of the French Revolution (*D* 132).[24] Central to modernity, as Nietzsche perceives it, is the idea that the ego must deny itself and adapt itself to the whole and as a result the "individual" is debilitated and canceled: "one never tires of enumerating and excoriating everything evil and malicious, prodigal, costly, and extravagant in the prior form of individual existence . . . empathy (*Mitempfindung*) for the individual and social feeling (*sociale Empfinduing*) here go hand in hand" (*D* 132). Nietzsche contests the morality of self-sacrifice and looks ahead to a different morality—one that is in keeping with the spirit of the book as a whole. In contrast to a narrow, petty bourgeois morality a higher and freer manner of thinking will now look beyond the immediate consequences our actions have for others and seek to further more distant aims. Under some circumstances this will be at the expense of the suffering of others, for example, by furthering genuine knowledge: does not "free thinking" initially plunge people into doubt and distress? In seeking victory over ourselves we need "*to get beyond our compassion*" (*D* 146). The grief, despair, blunderings and fearful footsteps of individuals will form part of "a new ploughshare" that will "cleave the ground, rendering it fruitful for all . . ." (*D* 146).

The morality that humanity has cultivated and dedicated itself to is one of "enthusiastic devotion" and "self-sacrifice" in which it looks down from sublime heights on the more sober morality of self-control (which is regarded as egotistical). Nietzsche suggests the reason why morality has been developed in this way is owing to the enjoyment of the state of intoxication, which has stemmed from the thought that the person is at one with the powerful being to whom it consecrates itself; in this way "the feeling of power" is enjoyed and is confirmed by a sacrifice of the self. For Nietzsche such an overcoming of the self is impossible: "In truth you only *seem* to sacrifice yourselves; instead, in your thoughts you transform yourselves into gods and take pleasure in yourselves as such" (*D* 215; see also *D* 269).

Here Nietzsche is dealing with a problem that preoccupies him in his middle and late periods: the problem of fanaticism (*D* 57–58, 68, 298, 511; see also *AOM* 15; *GS* 347; *BGE* 10).[25] As he notes, such "enthusiasts" will seek to implant the faith in intoxication "as *the* life within life: a terrible faith!" (*D* 50). Such is the extent of Nietzsche's anxiety that he wonders whether humanity as a whole will one day perish by its "spiritual firewaters" and those who keep alive the desire for them. The "strange madness of moral judgments" is bound up with states of exaltation and "the most exalted language" (*D* 189). Nietzsche is advising us to be on our guard, to be vigilant against "the half-mad, the fantastic, the fanatical," including so-called human beings of genius who claim to have "visions" and to have seen things others do not see. We are to be cautious, not credulous, when confronted with the claims of visions, that is to say, "of profound mental disturbances . . ." (*D* 66). The problem with the consolations that have been offered to humanity by religions to date is that they have imparted to life the fundamental character of suffering: "the human being's greatest diseases grew out of the battle against its diseases, and the apparent remedies have, in the long run, produced something much worse than what they were supposed to eliminate" (*D* 52). Humanity has mistaken "the momentarily effective, anesthetizing and intoxicating means, the so-called consolations, for the actual remedies" (*D* 52). It is under the most "scandalous quackery" that humanity has come to treat its diseases of the soul.

Nietzsche appeals to Epictetus for an example of a non-fanatical mode of living and as a counterweight to modern idealists who are greedy for expansion. Epictetus's ideal human being, lacking all fear of God and believing strictly in reason, "is not a preacher of penitence" (*D* 546). Although this ancient thinker was a slave, the exemplar he invokes is without class and is possible in every class. Nietzsche notes, moreover, that while Christianity was made for a different species of antique slave (one weak in will and mind), Epictetus neither lives in hope nor accepts the best he knows as a gift but "possesses it, he holds it valiantly in his hand, and he would take on the whole world if it tries to rob him of it" (*D* 546). Epictetus is also admired by Nietzsche on account of his dedication to his own ego and for resisting the glorification of thinking and living for others (*D* 131). He serves as a useful contrast to Christian thinkers such as Pascal, who considered the ego to be something hateful:

> If, as Pascal and Christianity claim, our ego (*Ich*) is always *hateful*, how might we possibly ever allow or assume that someone else could love it—be it God or a human being! It would go against all decency to let oneself be loved knowing full well that one only *deserves* hate—not to mention other feelings of repulsion. — "But this is precisely the kingdom of mercy."—So is your love-thy-neighbor mercy? Your

> compassion mercy? Well, if these things are possible for you, go still one step further: love yourselves out of mercy—then you won't need your God any more at all, and the whole drama of original sin and redemption will play itself out to the end in you yourselves. (*D* 79)

In an aphorism on "pseudo-egotism" Nietzsche notes how most people do nothing for their ego, but rather live in accordance with the "phantom ego" (*ego*) that has been formed in the opinions of those around them. The result is that we live in a fog of impersonal or half-personal opinions and arbitrary evaluations: "one person always in the head of another and then again this head in other heads: a curious world of phantasms that nonetheless knows how to don such a sensible appearance!" (*D* 105). As Nietzsche notes, this fog of habits and opinions comes to live and grow independently of the people it envelops. Unknown to ourselves we live within the effect of general opinions about the "human being," which is a "bloodless abstraction" and "fiction" (*D* 105). Even the modern glorification of work and talk of its blessings can be interpreted as a fear of everything individual. The subjection to hard industriousness from early until late serves as "the best policeman" because it keeps everyone in bounds and hinders the development of reason, desire, and the craving for independence. It uses vast amounts of nervous energy, which could be given over to reflection, brooding, dreaming, loving and hating, and working through our experiences: ". . . a society in which there is continuous hard work will have more security: and security is currently worshipped as the supreme divinity" (*D* 173). Nietzsche claims that it is the moral fashion of a commercial society to value actions aimed at common security and to cultivate above all the sympathetic affections. At work here is a collective drive toward timidity, which desires that life be rid of all the dangers it might have once held: "Are we not, with this prodigious intent to grate off all the rough and sharp edges of life, well on the way to turning humanity into *sand*!" (*D* 174).

In place of the ruling ethic of sympathy and self-sacrifice, which can assume the form of a "tyrannical encroachment," Nietzsche invites individuals to engage in self-fashioning, cultivating a self that others can behold with pleasure, a "lovely, peaceful, self-enclosed garden . . . with high walls to protect against the dangers and dust of the roadway, but with a hospitable gate as well" (*D* 174). Before an individual can practice benevolence toward others, he has to be beneficently disposed toward himself, otherwise he is running from and hating himself, and seeking to rescue himself from himself in others (*D* 516).

Nietzsche is not, I would contend, advocating the abolition of all possible types or forms of morality. Where morality centers on "continual self-command and self-overcoming . . . in great things and in the smallest," he is a champion of it (*WS* 45). His concern is that "morality" in the forms it has assumed in the greater part of human history, right up to Kant's moral law, has opened up an abundance of sources of displeasure and with every refinement of morals the human being has only become more discontented with itself, its neighbor, and its lot (*D* 106).[26] The individual in search of happiness, and who wishes to become its own lawgiver, cannot be treated with prescriptions to the path to happiness simply because individual happiness springs from one's own unknown laws, and external prescriptions only serve to obstruct and hinder it: "The so-called 'moral' precepts are, in truth, directed against individuals and are in no way aimed at promoting their happiness" (*D* 108). Up to now, Nietzsche notes, the moral law has been supposed to stand above our personal likes and dislikes; we did not want to impose this law upon ourselves but preferred to take it from somewhere or have it commanded to us. If we examine what is often taken to be the summit of the moral in philosophy—the mastery of the affects—we find that there is pleasure to be taken in this mastery. I can impress myself by what I can deny, defer, resist, and so on. It is through this mastery that I grow and develop. And yet morality, as we moderns have come to understand it, would have to give this ethical self-mastery a bad conscience. If we take as our criterion of the moral to be self-sacrificing resolution and self-denial, we would have to say, if being honest, that such acts are not performed strictly for the sake of others; my own fulfillment and pride are at work and the other provides the self with an opportunity to relieve itself through self-denial. There are no moral actions if we assume two things: (1) only those actions performed for the sake of another can be called moral; (2) only those actions performed out of free will can be called moral (*D* 148).[27] If we liberate ourselves from these errors, a revaluation can take place in which we will discover that we have overestimated the value and importance of free and non-egoistic actions at the expense of unfree and egoistic ones (see also *D* 164). For Nietzsche we are fully integrated into the causal order, and the ego is ineradicably a feature of any and all human action. Neither of these theoretical commitments prevents Nietzsche from advising his reader on a path to authenticity, as we shall now see.

Dawn and Authenticity

What, ultimately, is it that drives Nietzsche's project in the texts of his middle period and as we encounter it in *Dawn*? I believe it is the search for an authentic mode of existence. In this section I want to outline some of its main features and qualities.

Nietzsche notes that we typically adopt out of fear the evaluations that guide our actions, and only pretend that they are our own; we then grow accustomed to the pretense that this ends up being our nature. To have one's own evaluation of things is something exceedingly rare (*D* 104). Our actions can be traced back to our evaluations, which are either "original" or "adopted." It is the latter that is the most common. We adopt them from fear, Nietzsche argues, and pretend that they are our own and accustom ourselves to this pretense, and over time this becomes our nature. An "original" evaluation is said to be one in which a thing is assessed according to the extent that it pleases or displeases us alone and nobody else, and this is something rare. We learn as children and then rarely learn to change our views: "most of us are whole lives long the fools of the way we acquired in childhood of judging our neighbors (their minds, rank, morality, whether they are exemplary or reprehensible) and of finding it necessary to pay homage to their evaluations" (*D* 104).

For Nietzsche it is necessary to contest the idea that there is a single moral-making morality; every code of ethics that affirms itself in an exclusive manner "destroys too much valuable energy and costs humanity much too dearly" (*D* 164). In the future, Nietzsche hopes, the inventive and fructifying person shall no longer be sacrificed and numerous new attempts at living life and creating community shall be undertaken. When this takes place we will find that an enormous load of guilty conscience has been purged from the world. Humanity has suffered for too long from teachers of morality who wanted too much all at once and sought to lay down precepts for everyone (*D* 194). In the future the care of truth will need to center on the most personal questions and create time for them: "what is it that I actually do? What is it precisely that I wish to accomplish thereby?" (*D* 196). Small individual questions and experiments are no longer to be viewed with contempt and impatience (*D* 547). We will grow and become the ones that we are, however, only by experiencing dissatisfaction with ourselves and assuming the risk of experimenting in life, freely taking the journey through our wastelands, quagmires, and icy glaciers. The ones who don't take the risk of life "will never make the journey around the world (that you yourselves are!), but will remain trapped within yourselves like a knot on the log you were born to, a mere happenstance" (*D* 343).

In the book Nietzsche makes numerous practical recommendations for how we might go about cultivating and practicing such an authentic existence. When we are tired and fed up with ourselves and require fresh stimulation the best practice is to sleep a lot, "literally and figuratively! That way one will also awaken again upon a new morning!" (*D* 376). An essential test to learn is the endurance of solitude (*D* 443). Solitude has the advantage of providing us with the distant perspective we need to think well of things: "On my own I seem to see my friends more clearly and more appealingly than when together with them; and at the time when I loved music most and was most sensitive to it, I loved at a distance from it" (*D* 485). We need solitude "so as not to drink out of everyone's cisterns" for amongst the many we simply do not think as an "I." Not only is such solitude of benefit to ourselves, but it also improves our relation to others; when we turn angry toward people and fear them, we need the desert to become good again (*D* 491).

Nietzsche seeks to counsel us in the wisdom of "slow cures" (*D* 462). He notes that chronic diseases of the soul, like those of the body, rarely emerge through one-time large offenses against the rationality of body and soul, but rather through countless undetected little acts of negligence. If this is the case, then the cure has to be equally subtle and entail countless little offsetting exercises and the unwitting cultivation of different habits:

> Many a person has a cold, malicious word to say for his environment ten times a day and doesn't think anything of it, especially since, after a few years, he has created for himself a *law* of habit that from now on *compels* him ten times every day to sour his environment. But he can also accustom himself to doing it a kindness ten times! (*D* 462)

If we are to grow as a species and attain a new human maturity, we need a new honesty about matters of love. Nietzsche wonders whether people speak with such idolatry about love—the "food of the gods"—simply because they have had so little of it. But would not a utopia of universal love be something ludicrous?—"each person flocked around, pestered, longed for not by one love . . . but by thousands, indeed by each and everyone" (*D* 147). Instead, Nietzsche wants us to favor a future of solitude, quietude, and even being unpopular. In addition, he proposes that individuals should be discouraged from reaching a decision affecting their life while in the state of being in love; marriage needs to be taken much more seriously and not allowed to grow on the basis of the whim of lovers (*D* 151; see also *D* 532). The imperatives of philosophies of universal love and compassion will serve only to destroy us. If we are tempted by them, we should put them to the test and stop all our fantasizing (*D* 137).

Finally, authentic life involves for Nietzsche choosing the "rational death" or "free death." In *The Wanderer and His Shadow* (*WS* 322) he suggests that the certain prospect of death could introduce into every life "a precious, sweet-smelling drop of levity," while in *The Wanderer and His Shadow* (*WS* 185) he writes explicitly in favor of the rational death. Where natural death is the suicide of nature, or the "annihilation of the rational being by the irrational to which it is tied," we can imagine, as one of those many new dawns on the horizon of human existence, and however immoral sounding at present, the "wise regulation and disposal of death" as belonging to a morality of the future. It is into such dawns that Nietzsche wishes his "free spirits"—since this is who he is writing for, not for "everyone"—to gaze with "indescribable joy" (*WS* 185).[28]

It goes without saying, perhaps, that Nietzsche's emphasis on the individual's self-cultivation entails a corresponding devaluation of economics and politics. He considers these to represent a squandering of spirit: "Our age, no matter how much it talks and talks about economy, is a squanderer: it squanders what is most precious, spirit" (*D* 179). Today, he holds, we are in a state of "colossal and ridiculous lunacy" with everybody feeling obliged to know what is going on day in and day out and longing at every instant to be actively involved to the point of abandoning the work of their own therapy. Here he has a number of concerns, which I shall only briefly mention. First, modern culture is defined by the "soul" of commerce, as the personal contest was for the Greeks and war and victory was for the Romans: "Commercial man understands how to assess the value of everything without having made it and, indeed, to assess it not according to his own, most personal need, but *according to consumer need*; 'who and how many will consume this?' is his question of questions" (*D* 175). This mode of appraisal then gets applied, Nietzsche notes anxiously, to everything, including the productions of the arts and sciences, of thinkers, scholars, artists, statesmen, and so on, so becoming the character of an entire culture. Second, we are today creating a society of "universal security" but the price being paid for it is, Nietzsche thinks, much too high: "the maddest thing of all is, moreover, that this behavior brings about the very opposite of 'national security' . . ." (*D* 179). Third, and finally, in this age of "grand politics" (*D* 189) we are developing not a politics of food or digestion, but one of "intoxication":

> Nations are so exceedingly deceived because they are always *seeking* a deceiver, namely, a stimulating wine for their senses. If only they can have *that*, they gladly put up with lousy bread. Intoxication is more important to them than food—this is the bait they will always go after! (*D* 188)

Care of Self

In this section I want to provide an indication of the wider set of concerns Nietzsche has with respect to a philosophical therapy of the self in his middle period, and so draw attention to the horizon of existence he thinks we would be wise to focus on as we devote ourselves to healing ourselves of our metaphysical and religious inheritance and the problems it has caused for us.

Ruth Abbey has drawn attention to the centrality of an ethics of care of self in the middle period.[29] This centers on a concern for quotidian minutiae, attention to individualized goods, and an awareness of the close connection between psyche and physique.[30] In *Dawn* Nietzsche draws attention to the intimately personal character of his philosophy and its search. He raises the suspicion that it may be little more than the translation into reason of a concentrated drive, "for mild sunshine, clearer and fresher air, southerly vegetation, sea air, transient digests of meat, eggs, and fruit, hot water to drink, daylong silent wanderings . . . almost soldierly habits," and so on (*D* 553). In short, is it a philosophy "that at bottom is the instinct for a personal diet" and hygiene, one that suits a particular idiosyncratic taste and for whom it alone is beneficial? (*D* 553). He continues:

> An instinct that is searching for my own air, my own heights, my own weather, my own type of health, through the detour of my head? There are many other and certainly more loftier sublimities [*höhere Erhabenheiten*] of philosophy and not just those that are more gloomy and more ambitious than mine—perhaps they too are, each and every one, nothing other than intellectual detours for these kinds of personal drives?—In the meantime [*Inzwischen*] I observe with a new eye the secret and solitary swarming of a butterfly high on the rocky seashore where many good plants are growing; it flies about, untroubled that it only has one more day yet to live and that the night will be too cold for its winged fragility. One could certainly come up with a philosophy for it as well: although it is not likely to be mine. (*D* 553)

Elsewhere in the text Nietzsche posits the philosopher's existence in terms of an "ideal selfishness" in which one freely gives away one's spiritual house and possessions to ones in need. In this condition of solitude the satiated soul lightens the burden of its own soul, eschewing both praise for what it does and avoiding gratitude, which is invasive and fails to respect solitude and silence. This is to speak of a new kind of teacher who, armed with a handful of knowledge and a bag full of experiences, becomes "a doctor of the spirit to the indigent and to aid people here and there whose head *is disturbed by opinions* . . ." (*D* 449). The aim is not to prove that one is right before such a person, but rather "to speak with him in such a way that . . . he himself says what is right and, proud of the fact, walks away!" (*D* 449).

For Nietzsche, as Abbey notes, the small, daily practices of care of self are undervalued.[31] In modern culture we can detect, Nietzsche writes, a "feigned disrespect for all the things which men in fact take most seriously, *for all the things closest to them*" (*WS* 5). As Abbey further notes, in devaluing the small, worldly matters Christian and post-Christian sensibility, "puts people at war with themselves and forbids a close study of which forms of care of the self would be most conducive to individual flourishing" (*WS* 5). As Nietzsche notes, most people see the closest things badly and rarely pay heed to them, while "*almost all the physical and psychical frailties* of the individual derive from this lack . . . being *unknowledgeable in the smallest and everyday things* and failing to keep an eye on them—this it is that transforms the earth for so many into a 'vale of tears'" (*WS* 6). Our understanding of existence is diverted away from the "smallest and closest things":

> Priests and teachers, and the sublime lust for power of idealists of every description . . . hammer even into children that what matters is something quite different: the salvation of the soul, the service of the state, the advancement of science, or the accumulation of reputation and possessions, all as the means of doing service to mankind as a whole; while the requirements of the individual, his great and small needs within the twenty four hours of the day, are to be regarded as something contemptible or a matter of indifference. (*WS* 6)

Nietzsche goes on to name here Socrates as a key figure in the history of thought who defended himself against this "arrogant neglect" of the human for the benefit of the human race (see also *D* 9).[32] In *Dawn* (*D* 435) Nietzsche notes that our greatness does not crumble away all at once, but through continual neglect:

> . . . the little vegetation that grows in between everything and understands how to cling everywhere, this is what ruins what is great in us—the quotidian, hourly pitifulness of our environment that goes overlooked, the thousand tiny tendrils of this or that small and small-minded feeling growing out of our neighborhood, our job, the company we keep, the division of our day. If we allow these small weeds to grow unwittingly, then unwittingly they will destroy us! (*D* 435)

The closest things are those things that are overlooked or even disparaged by priests and metaphysicians who devote all their time and energy to the care of the soul. They include things like eating and diet, housing, clothing, and social intercourse. These should all be made the object of constant impartial and general reflection and reform. Nietzsche argues: "Our continual offenses against the most elementary laws of the body and the spirit reduce us all . . . to a disgraceful dependence and bondage . . . on physicians, teachers and curers of soul who lie like a burden on the whole of society" (*WS* 5). All the physical and psychical frailties of the individual derive from a lack of knowledge about the smallest and most everyday things, such as what is beneficial to us and what is harmful to us in the institution of our mode of life, in the division of the day, eating, sleeping, and reflecting, and so on (*WS* 6).

Nietzsche's thinking aspires to be a practical philosophy. He writes in *The Gay Science*: "I favor any skepsis to which one can reply: 'let us try it!' I do not wish to hear anything of all those things and questions that do not permit any experiment" (*GS* 51). In *Dawn* he states that "we are experiments" and our task should be to *want* to be such. Here I take Nietzsche to be suggesting that our history of moral formation and deformation is a contingent one, and that the future will be quite different now that the "passion of knowledge" has become such an important drive for us and taken such deep root in our existence. We will live differently to previous human beings who have lived in fear and ignorance. In short, we will live "experimentally," and Nietzsche seems to see no other way forward for the human species. We are to build anew the laws of life and of behavior by taking from the sciences of physiology, medicine, sociology, and solitude the foundation-stones for new ideals, if not the new ideals themselves (*D* 453). Because these sciences are not yet sure of themselves, we find ourselves living in either a preliminary or a posterior existence, depending on our taste and talent, and in this interregnum the best strategy is for us to become our own *reges* (sovereigns) and establish little experimental states. He proposes the following as a principle of the new life: "life should be ordered on the basis of what is most certain and most demonstrable, not as hitherto on that what is most remote, indefinite, and no more than a cloud on the horizon" (*WS* 310; see also 350). Nietzsche promotes "purifying knowledge" over the ideals of metaphysics (*HH* 34). Nietzsche thinks that the impulse to want certainties in the domain of first and last things is best regarded as a "*religious after-shoot*" (*WS* 16). It is a hidden, and only apparently, skeptical species of what he calls, following Schopenhauer, the "metaphysical need." The first and last things refer to those questions of knowledge that concern themselves with the "outermost regions" (How did the universe begin? What is its purpose? and so on). It is only under the influence of ethical and religious sensations that these questions have acquired for us such a dreadful weightiness. They compel the eye to strain itself, and where it encounters darkness it makes things even darker. Where it has not been possible to establish certainties of any kind in our efforts to penetrate this dark region, an entire moral-metaphysical world has been displaced into it, the fantasies of which posterity is then asked to take seriously and for truth. This is why carrying out an inquiry into the sources and origins of our ethical and religious sensations are such important tasks. The main objective is a deflationary one. We do not require certainties with regard to the "first and last things"—what Nietzsche calls "the furthest horizon"—in order to live a "full and excellent human life" (*WS* 16). He proposes a fundamental rupture be affected with regard to customary habits of thinking. In the face of questions such as—what is the purpose of man? What is his fate after death? How can man be reconciled with God?—it should not be felt necessary to develop knowledge against faith; rather we should practice an indifference toward faith and supposed knowledge in the domains of metaphysics and religion.

The Subject in Question

In Nietzsche's conception of the (ethical) task, self-creation is self-cultivation and not a matter of creating *ex nihilo*.[33] If we are to take control of our lives and become a "self," which is what Nietzsche wishes us to do, then we need to know ourselves and engage in a severe kind of knowledge that is unflinching and unsentimental.[34] Nietzsche never pretends that learning to know ourselves, so as to become ourselves, is an easy task and he is not recommending it for everyone.

Self-cultivation in Nietzsche denotes a fundamental concern with oneself that aims at a rich and healthy "egoism": one has purified oneself of one's opinions and valuations—of what has merely been passed down and unconsciously assimilated—and learns to think and feel for oneself, practicing one's own arts of self-preservation and self-enhancement. For Nietzsche, there is a new drive that is becoming implanted in us and that makes the overcoming of "morality" possible: he calls this "the passion of knowledge" (*D* 429). In *Dawn* the emphasis is on "knowing one's circumstances" in their widest sense and as a means of knowing one's power: "One ought to think of oneself as a variable quantity and whose accomplishment can perhaps under favorable circumstances match the highest ever" (*D* 326). Nietzsche argues that we, therefore, need to reflect on the circumstances and "spare no diligence" in our contemplation or knowledge of them

(*D* 326). In a note from autumn 1880 he insists that the intellect is the tool of our drives; "it is *never free*" (*KSA* 9:6[130]). It sharpens itself in the struggle with various drives and thereby refines the activity of each individual drive. But he also insists that:

> The will to power [*der Wille nach Macht*], to the infallibility [*Unfehlbarkeit*] of our person, resides in our greatest justice and integrity [*Redlichkeit*]: skepticism just applies to all authority, we do not want to be duped, not even by *our drives*! But what does not *want*? A drive, certainly! (*KSA* 9:6[130])

At work in Nietzsche we see an ethic of "individualization" or becoming-individual which: (1) is a form of perfecting oneself through quite radical independence; (2) entails constant and intense self-observation and the circumstances and situations one finds oneself in.[35]

In a reading of *Dawn* Gianni Vattimo claims that Nietzsche's critique of morality is not conducted, "in the name of the free and responsible subject, for such a subject is likewise a product of neurosis, a thing formed in illness."[36] He contends that because there is an "inextricable connection" between internal or internalized conscience, *including the* "*individual in* revolt," and social morality, the appeal to freedom in Nietzsche cannot be made in the name of "the sovereignty of the individual."[37] While he rightly notes that Nietzsche unmasks morality as a set of principles not intended for the utility or the good of the individual on whom they are imposed but for the preservation of society, even to the detriment of individuals, he wrongly in my view infers from this that Nietzsche's aim is not to defend the individual against the claims of the group. The reason, he argues, is not because, metaphysically speaking, it is necessary to prefer the claims of determinism over the belief in freedom, "but simply because there is no subject of such actions. Not: the subject is not free, but simply: the subject is not."[38] It is difficult, I think, on the evidence of the reading I have presented here, to make sense of this view. Although it is the case that in the book Nietzsche holds the subject or self to be an assemblage of materially and historically conditioned drives and affects, this does not prevent him from outlining as an aspiration—a new dawn in effect—the attempt on the part of the ego to become self-determining, and this for him lies in a set of specific practices and techniques to do with self-discovery and self-fashioning: the self is to work on itself for the ends of self-cultivation and mastery of the affects. His objection to Christianity is that it inflames the affects when the task is to support philosophy in its cooling down of them and to practice rational control over them. This task requires at the very least some minimum degree of rational, self-determining agency. I appreciate there is a difficulty here: if the subject or self is nothing other than its drives and affects, what is the "agency" that brings about the transformation of the self in the direction of autonomy and authenticity? I have already indicated at the answer: it is things like "the passion of knowledge" and the intellectual conscience that for Nietzsche are to account for the new dawn in human existence and the restoration of good conscience to a healthy (and experimental) egoism. "We" will now practice knowledge in a way that hitherto "morality" has denied, and through this knowledge earn the right to self-experimentation. This is the idea of a "new ploughshare."

Moreover, could it not be said that while it is true that Nietzsche exposes the extent to which the I or ego is the subject *of* its drives and affects (it is not the master in its own house we might say, looking ahead to Freud), it is manifestly clear that he is *perturbed* by this fact, that is, troubled by the extent to which the self, as we know it to date, is little more than a contingency or mere happenstance? In *Dawn* (*D* 119) Nietzsche explores the drives and notes that no matter how much we struggle for self-knowledge, nothing is more incomplete to us than the image of the totality of our drives. It is not only that we cannot call the cruder ones by name, but also more worryingly that their number and strength, their ebb and flow, and most of all the laws of their alimentation remain completely unknown to us:

> This alimentation thus becomes the work of chance: our daily experiences toss willy-nilly to this drive or that drive some prey or other which it seizes greedily, but the whole coming and going of these events exists completely apart from any meaningful connection to the alimentary needs of the sum drives: so that the result will always be two-fold: the starving and stunting of some drives and the overstuffing of others. (*D* 119)

Our experiences, then, are types of nourishment; the problem is that there is a deficit of knowledge on our part as to the character of our experiences. The result is that we live as contingent beings:

> . . . as a consequence of this contingent alimentation of the parts, the whole, the fully-grown polyp turns out to be a creature no less contingent [*Zufälliges*] than its maturation. (*D* 119)

The task in Nietzsche, it would seem, is not to allow oneself to be this mere happenstance; indeed he often defines the "task" as one of becoming "necessary"[39] and even says that the task has to be felt as necessary (*HH* "Preface" 7).[40] Authenticity means for Nietzsche experiencing dissatisfaction with oneself and assuming the risk of experimenting in life, freely taking the journey through our wastelands, quagmires, and icy glaciers. The ones who don't take the risk of life will, to repeat, "never make the journey around the world (that you yourselves are!), but will remain trapped within yourselves like a knot on the log you were born to, a mere happenstance" (*D* 343). This is not to deny that the self or subject is not something contingent for Nietzsche: his whole point in *Dawn* is to show the contingencies of our moral formation and deformation and to disclose to the self that it is something other than what it takes itself to be (fixed and stable), and that it may become something more fluid and dynamic, in short, that it may cultivate a "becoming" of what it "is."

In the book Nietzsche stresses that once you have taken "the decisive step" and entered "upon the way which is called our 'own way' [*eigenen Weg*], a secret suddenly reveals itself to us: even all those with whom we were friendly and intimate—all have imagined themselves superior to us and are offended" (*D* 484). He continues:

> The best among them are lenient with us and wait patiently for us to rediscover the "right way"—they know it, of course! Others make fun and act as if one had gone temporarily batty or else point spitefully to a seducer. The more malicious declare us to be vain fools and attempt to blacken our motives . . . What's to be done? I advise is: we initiate our sovereignty [*Souveränität*] by assuring all our acquaintances a year's amnesty in advance for their sins of every kind. (*D* 484)

Nietzsche is not, I think, recommending self-withdrawal and isolation as the ultimate cure to one's predicament; rather, these are means or steps on the way to working on oneself so one can become genuinely beneficent toward others. We go wrong when we *fail* to attend to the needs of the "ego" and flee from it:

> Let's stick to the idea that benevolence and beneficence are what constitute a good person; only let's add: "provided that he is first benevolently and beneficently disposed *towards himself* !" For *without this*—if he runs from himself, hates himself, causes injury to himself—he is certainly not a good person. Because he is rescuing himself from himself *in others* . . . to run from the ego (*ego*) and to hate it and to live in others, for others—has, heretofore, been called, just as unreflectedly as assuredly, "*unegotistical*" *and consequently "good"*! (*D* 516)

To suppose, as Vattimo does, that the "subject" is by definition something "neurotic" is to fail to make a distinction between autonomy and heteronomy, and to rule out *tout court* the possibility of an ethic of self-cultivation, and it is this ethic that I see Nietzsche championing in *Dawn*. The focus will be on the cultivation of the drives, and an initial step on the path to self-enlightenment and self-liberation is to know that here we do enjoy a certain liberty:

> One can handle one's drives like a gardener and, though few know it, cultivate the shoots of one's anger, pity, musing, vanity as fruitfully and advantageously as beautiful fruit on espaliers; one can do so with a gardener's good or bad taste and, as it were, in the French or English or Dutch or Chinese style; one can also let nature have her sway and only tend to a little decoration and cleaning-up here and there; finally, one can, without giving them any thought whatsoever, let the plants, in keeping with the natural advantages and disadvantages of their habitat, grow up and fight it out among themselves—indeed, one can take pleasure in such wildness and want to enjoy just this pleasure, even if one has difficulties with it. We are free to do all this: but how many actually know that they are free to do this? Don't most people *believe in themselves* as completed, *fully-grown facts*? Haven't great philosophers, with their doctrine of the immutability of character, pressed their seal of approval on this *prejudice*? (*D* 560 [emphasis added])

In a note from 1881 Nietzsche expresses his admiration of the Chinese for cultivating trees that bear roses on one side and pears on the other—an exotic fruit that is the result of selective breeding indeed! (*KSA* 9:11[276]). This theme continues in the later notes, such as one from 1887 where Nietzsche demands that individuals be allowed to freely work on themselves as artist-tyrants. He adds an important qualification:

> Not merely a master-race, whose task would be limited to governing, but a race or people with *its own sphere of life*, with an excess of strength for beauty, bravery, culture [*Cultur*], manners to the highest peak of the spirit; an affirming race that may grant itself every great luxury . . . a hothouse for strange and exquisite plants. (*KSA* 12:9[153]; *WP* 898)

The concept for this non-average type of human being is "the superhuman" (*KSA* 12:10[17]; *WP* 866).

This particular conception of the "superhuman" stands in marked contrast to what we encounter in Vattimo who argues that the "overman" names the *dissolution* of the subject.[41] It is quite clear, I think, that for Nietzsche no future "subject" or ego is possible without ethical training and self-cultivation. But what he envisages is not, *pace* Vattimo, the dissolution of the subject but something more akin to a radical pluralism: the pluralization of subjects or types of egos. To his credit, Vattimo recognizes this when he describes the project of *Dawn* as one of "the liberation of plurality": "Recognition of this opens up the way to an 'experimental' vision of existence,"[42] as when Nietzsche himself declares: "numerous novel experiments shall be made in ways of life and modes of society" (*D* 164). However, for Vattimo this new pluralism does not, strangely, require an autonomous or authentic subject, but what he calls "dis-subjection."

A reading of *Dawn* must do justice to the double philosophy being unfolded in it: on the one hand, there is a story about the complexity of our affects and drives and the extent to which we are unknown to ourselves and fundamentally heteronomous[43]; on the other hand, there is what I have identified in the book as the path of authenticity consisting in self-enlightenment and self-liberation and involving the cultivation of a new rapport of the self focused on working on the drives, or the becoming-autonomous. The task is to employ knowledge in the service of practical ends and a practical philosophy; the goal is for us—the ones inclined or predestined to lead a free-spirited existence—to become the ones that we are. Nietzsche's therapy is one of slow cures and small doses:

> *Small doses.*—If you want to effect the most profound transformation possible, then administer the means in the smallest doses, but unremittingly and over long periods of time! What great things can be accomplished at one fell swoop! Thus we want to guard against exchanging head over heels and with acts of violence the moral condition we are used to for a new evaluation of things—no, we want to keep on living in that condition for a long, long time—until we, very late, presumably, become fully aware that the *new evaluation* has become the predominant force and that the small doses of it, *to which we will have to grow accustomed from now on*, have laid down in us a new nature. (*D* 534)

17

States and Nomads
Hegel's World and Nietzsche's Earth

GARY SHAPIRO

What is Nietzsche's concept of the earth? While "earth" is often taken in a general way to refer to embodied life, to *this* world rather than to an imaginary and disastrous *other* world, I propose that the term and concept also have a significant political dimension—a geophilosophical dimension—which is closely related to the radical immanence so central to Nietzsche's thought. I shall argue that he often and pointedly replaces the very term "world" (*Welt*) with "earth" (*Erde*) because "world" is tied too closely to ideas of unity, eternity, and transcendence. "World" is a concept with theological affiliations, as Nietzsche indicates in *Beyond Good and Evil*:

> Around a hero everything becomes a tragedy, around a demi-god everything becomes a satyr play; and around God everything becomes—what do you think? perhaps the "world"? (*BGE* 150)

This can be amplified when we recall Nietzsche's declaration that he was afraid we haven't gotten rid of God yet, because we still have faith in grammar, his speaking of the lingering shadow of God, and his thesis that with the disappearance of the "true world" the apparent one disappears as well. The trinity of God, man, and world is a common philosopheme and set of philosophemes. Perhaps one of the late arriving insights that follow in the slow mourning process that accompanies God's death has to do with the disappearance of that which we call "world." Like all metaphysical and theological concepts, *world* has a political import, one evident to Nietzsche in Hegel and those he considered Hegelians (for example, Strauss and Eduard von Hartmann); in *The Birth of Tragedy* he speaks contemptuously of "so-called world-history" and in his second *Unmodern Observations* he ridicules the fashionable notion of the *Weltprozess*—do we hear an anticipation of such notions as globalization there?—and exclaims "world, world, world!" in high exasperation (*UM* II:9). When Nietzsche comes to write of "great events," they are not exclusively tied to the state and world-history, as they are for the Hegelians, but (as the chapter "On Great Events" in *Zarathustra* makes clear) events of the earth. If for Hegel "the state is the march (*Gang*) of God through the world," for Nietzsche the earth is a human-earth of mobile multitudes that can prepare a way for the overhuman. In order to grasp Nietzsche's "great politics" of the earth more perspicuously, it is useful to see how in rhetoric and substance it constitutes a response to the theologico-political treatise that is Hegel's *Philosophy of World History* and to those Nietzsche saw as Hegelian epigones.

Since Nietzsche claimed that *Thus Spoke Zarathustra* was his most important work, let us begin by listening to some of Zarathustra's striking invocations of the earth there. He calls on his listeners to sacrifice themselves for the *Sinn der Erde*; though this phrase is typically translated as "meaning" or "sense," it could also be rendered as "direction." Where is the earth going? Where do we want it to go? Zarathustra requires his disciples (*Jünger*) to give their loyalty (*Treue*) to the earth, addresses the condition of the human earth (*Menschen-Erde*), and encourages his listeners to think with "an earthly head that creates a direction for the earth [*einen Erden-Kopf, der der Erde Sinn schafft!*]" (*Z* "Prologue" 3; *Z* I "On the Gift-Giving Virtue"; *Z* III "The Convalescent"; *Z* I "The Afterworldly"). The earth must be rescued from the threatened domination of the last human: "For the earth has now become small, and upon it hops the last human, who makes everything small" (*Z* "Prologue" 5). After *Thus Spoke Zarathustra*, Nietzsche's later works typically refer to a project of evaluating moralities, religions, and cultures as ways of being "on the earth": I hope to show that this is more than a conventional phrase.

Most critical engagements with Nietzsche's idea of earth take one of several forms, which tend to ignore or minimize the political, geographical, and geological relevance of the concept. One approach sees earth as designating the immanent, bodily, or this-worldly, as opposed to imaginary afterworlds of religious and transcendental traditions; while not inaccurate, this characterization remains somewhat vague.[1] A phenomenological interpretation emphasizes Nietzsche's poetics and metaphorics of the earth, sometimes enriched by recalling his experience as traveler, walker, and poet receptive to the beautiful, sublime, and picturesque in natural and artificial landscapes.[2] This approach includes Bachelard's celebration of Nietzsche's virtual flight (air as an earthly element) and Irigaray's disappointed love letter, lamenting his avoidance of the feminine, maternal sea.[3] Some readers focus on Nietzsche's adaptation of poetic and philosophical topoi from early Greek thinkers and poets, especially Empedocles, for whom Gaia retained features of the divine.[4] Inspired by Nietzsche's reading of Hölderlin and Heidegger's reading of both, this approach tends to stop short of articulating the way in which, thinking with his *Erden-Kopf,* Nietzsche conceives the *Sinn der Erde* against the background of Hegel's philosophy of history and doctrine of the state, or his noting the new paths developing in human geography, which highlighted human mobility: nomadism, migrations, and wanderings of peoples.[5]

Another important strand in this thought complex should be explored more thoroughly—one involving Nietzsche's sustained and critical dialogue with Hegel's idea of world-history and sensitive, as Nietzsche was, to emerging trends in human geography. Nietzsche read Hegel's lectures on *Weltgeschichte* as early as 1865.[6] To read Nietzsche as the anti-Hegel is not unusual; it is one of the main themes of Deleuze's Nietzsche book, which brilliantly explicates the differences between the negations involved in Hegel's dialectic of recognition and Nietzsche's discrimination of sovereign affirmation and the other-directed *ressentiment* of the base. Here I focus on another contrast, one Deleuze developed in part from his engagement with Nietzsche: that between states and nomads considered as forms of human organization and inhabitation associated with distinctive ways of thinking. It is Nietzsche's attention to such themes that leads Deleuze and Guattari to credit him as the inventor of geophilosophy. History and the history of philosophy belong to the state, geography and geophilosophy to the nomads.[7] Nietzsche, rather than Hegel, can help us think more perspicuously about themes on the contemporary philosophical agenda, which go by names like globalization, multiculturalism, diaspora, hybridity, and cosmopolitanism. (The Hegel whom Nietzsche confronts will strike some readers as a caricature, based on a selective reading of incomplete and questionable versions of his lectures. While more recent scholarship has given us a more subtle Hegel—actually, a choice among several versions of a more subtle Hegel—Nietzsche's Hegel is firmly based in the text of *The Philosophy of World History* that was available to him. The popular Hegelians of Nietzsche's day—for example Strauss and Hartmann—reinforced the caricature, if such it is, and made it a forceful presence in the 1870s and 1880s. Finally—but this is a point that I can suggest only briefly in what follows—I believe that much recent scholarship has been overly zealous in its attempt to provide a Hegel who would be more acceptable to a democratic, pluralistic era, even to the point of producing somewhat misleading translations of key titles and passages).

Recall a few features of Hegelian *Weltgeschichte* that led Nietzsche to sneer repeatedly at "so-called world-history" and to exclaim with disgust at Eduard von Hartmann's grotesque version of Hegel: "world, world, world!" (*D* 307; *UM* I: 9).[8] Why does he challenge the implicit political ontology and ideology of this mantra? The short answer is that he rejects Hegel's understanding of world-history as the story of freedom and as the history of states which embody and develop it. Nietzsche sees that story of freedom as vain narcissism, masking the animal nature and millennia of custom that shape human beings. He denies that the state is the realization of freedom, the eternal or highest attainable form of human organization (*WS* 12, *D* 18). Nietzsche contrasts "major history" (*Hauptgeschichte*) with *world*-history; *Hauptgeschichte* includes the many millennia of animal and customary life—the *Sittlichkeit der Sitte*—in addition to the recent history of states that feeds our vanity (*BGE* 32; *GM* III: 9; *D* 18).[9] In *Beyond Good and Evil* Nietzsche considers the possibility that the role left for us critical thinkers in the carnivalesque atmosphere of modernity, swimming in our knowledge of the past and trying on one costume or mask after another, is to be "parodists of world history" (*BGE* 223).[10]

Hegel's claim that history is the story of freedom is well known; I will not elaborate it at length here. World-history, in Hegel's system, is the highest development of objective spirit, a realm in which the state is the final realization of human freedom. Only with states is world-history possible, and world-history is *exclusively* concerned with states. Hegel's restrictive conception of world-history has been obscured by many commentators and translators; some of the latter blur the issues by translating *Weltgeschichte* as "universal history." But Hegel is clear:

> The state is the divine Idea as it exists on earth. In this sense the state is the precise object of world-history in general.[11]

> In world-history, however, we are concerned with "individuals" that are nations, with wholes that are states.[12]

For Hegel the concepts "world" and "world-history" are highly singular, unifying, and exclusive. In his most systematic account of the place of world-history in the *Encyclopedia* he describes the movement of spirit as demonstrating the realization of "the absolute final aim of the world" where spirit "becomes to the outward eye a universal spirit—a world-spirit."[13] World-history is the totality of states, and the succession of world-historical states is the home ground of Absolute Spirit—art, religion, and philosophy. Hegel famously compares the Oriental, Classical, and Germanic worlds in which one, some, or all are free—varying realizations of freedom all achieved through states. The life of states is contrasted with the existence of a "people" or "folk [*Volk*]," or, speaking more precisely, the state is the *telos* of a people, one sometimes achieved and sometimes not. Hegel insists that the mere *Volk* is not a subject of history: "A *Volk* with no state formation [a mere nation/*Nation*] has, strictly speaking, no history—like the *Völker* which existed before the rise of states and others which still exist as wild nations [*als wilde Nationen*]."[14] A word concerning Hegel's reference to "mere nations" and "wild nations" is in order. *Nation* is an adaptation of a Latin term, whose verbal root is *nascere*, to give birth. Nations *as such*, then, are nothing but human beings of common ancestry, linked by "natality," that is genealogical affiliation. Hegel's terminology suggests that a nation may be more than this; it may become a people, and a people, with some degree of cultural coherence, is on the way to focusing itself in the form of a state.[15]

Why are migrations and wanderings specifically excluded from world-history, and why do migrants and wanderers tend to remain in the status of mere or wild nations? The root intuition seems to be that a world-historical people must stay in its place. The state must have sovereignty over a given territory, which is the prerequisite for its crystallization of the spiritual meaning of its people. Without the state, there are simply wild nations living on the earth; there is as yet no world. Hegel could say of the "wild nations" what Heidegger said of animals, that they are *weltarm*, world-poor.[16] "World-historical peoples" are those that form and live in states. When English translations render *Weltgeschichte* as "universal history," I assume that the aim, as in Carl Friedrich's introduction to the Sibree translation of the *Philosophy of History*, is to downplay Hegel's political theology, his idea that "the state is God's march [*Gang*] through the world."[17]

Historical existence requires a state that has settled in a territory. Therefore, it initially seems strange that Hegel emphasizes that the Germanic world, which will see the full flowering of Spirit and state, begins with barbarous, wandering, predatory peoples—Goths, Visigoths, and so on. Yet Hegel implies that these groups are no different than any others; no *Volk* enters history until engaged in the process of state formation. Hegel makes German barbarism a virtue, claiming that it was the Germans' strength to begin by absorbing and appropriating, unlike earlier historical peoples who begin with an internal development:

> The Greeks and Romans had reached maturity within, before they directed their energies outwards. The Germans, on the contrary, began with self-diffusion—deluging the world, and overpowering in their course the inwardly rotten, hollow political fabrics of the civilized nations. Only then did their development begin, kindled by a foreign religion, polity, and legislation.[18]

The very being of the German people is their transformation through encounters with the other, so they are uniquely suited to confirm Hegel's concept of the true identity as the identity of identity and non-identity. They seize Rome and appropriate Christianity almost thoughtlessly, but—such is the cunning of history—they are transformed in the end by what they have captured. They are predatory *subjects* who will be transformed by their *object*. On Hegel's account, it is this heritage that allows the Germans, through the Reformation and the development of the modern state, to spiritualize the secular. Their wandering, migration, and nomadism become subordinated to the process of state formation in which religion is essential.

Now consider some of Nietzsche's encounters with those he saw as the reigning Hegelian thinkers of his time. The first of Nietzsche's "assassination attempts" (as he called them in *Ecce Homo*) was directed at David F. Strauss in the first *Untimely Meditations*. He pilloried Strauss as a representative of the "cultural philistinism" of the emerging Bismarck era. From our post-Kojèvian perspective, we can read Strauss as an "end of history" thinker, a predecessor of Kojève and Francis Fukuyama, who believed that the German state was consolidating a final realization of human potential. While Strauss sought to distinguish himself from Hegel, embracing Darwinism and rejecting Hegel's insistence on religion as a necessary legitimizing and unifying component of the state, Nietzsche sees that this old "young Hegelian" has deeper ties to the master he ostensibly repudiates. Strauss's criticism of republics and democracy, and his insistence on the necessity of monarchy to provide a principle of national unity are close to Hegel's views. When Hegel famously describes world-history as a "slaughter-bench," he is not speaking about the violence of some (prehistorical) state of nature, but about the destruction of republics, whether aristocratic or democratic (these include Greece, Rome, Italian city-states, the first French republic).[19] Hegel's examples of world-historical figures—like Caesar, Alexander, and Napoleon—are men whose mission was to transform republics into empires. Hegel's "world" is not only the world of states but, in its highest and final development, monarchical states with official forms of Protestant Christianity.

Strauss's description of the United States as a spurious union echoes a specific diagnosis Hegel offers in his *Lectures.* Hegel implies that the United States is not a genuine state and has only a starkly contractarian and atomistic parody of a real constitution. It must be one of those republics destined for the dustbin of history. Hegel sought to explain how this simulacrum of a state exists, because he cannot consistently dismiss gross and obvious facts as mere appearances. He argues that the territorial expansion of the United States serves as a safety valve through which the excesses of a state not grounded in a *Volk*, or given unity by monarchy and religion, can nevertheless continue.[20] Mobility and cultural indeterminacy, ordinarily enemies or predecessors of the Hegelian state, are here invoked to save the appearances, to explain a state that is not a true state. Forty years later, Strauss amplified this verdict, arguing that the United States Civil War and its aftermath had demonstrated the ontological instability of the United States. Hegel might have seen the United States' western move to Hawaii and Alaska as an understandable extension of the solar movement of world history and a continuation of its evasion of true statehood by territorial expansion. A contemporary Hegelian could explain the Alaskan secessionist movement and Sarah Palin's political ascent in 2008 as signs of the impossibility of the secular contractarian state. Such a theorist might go on to speculate that Palin's affiliation with an apocalyptic, territorial form of Christianity that reverts to prehistorical forms of animism and belief in witches demonstrates the collapse of the world-historical back into ahistorical geography. With the United States division into red states and blue states, along with current and brewing conflicts over energy, water, immigration, and the fundamentalist social agenda, the Hegel of the new millennium would ask whether this experiment of a self-designing, federal constitutional republic without a religion could be expected to continue indefinitely. Yet the persistence of a secular, multicultural republic, still not swept away by the movement of world-history should be an incentive to examining Nietzsche's interrogation of Hegel's intertwined conceptions of state and world.

Nietzsche, I am arguing, turned away from the prevalent Hegelian concept of world, entangled as it is with that of the state, and toward a notion of the earth as the most general site of human life. For a politics of the earth, the state will not be an essential constituent or ultimate goal, but one among a number of social and political forms whose genealogy can be traced and whose dissolution can be envisioned. Beginning in *Human, All Too Human*, Nietzsche explicitly moves toward such an analysis by arguing that the contemporary state is intrinsically unstable and introducing the contrast of state and nomad. Despite the noisy nationalism of the early Bismarck era, he argues that there is a real counter-movement to statism, with Europeans becoming increasingly mobile or "nomadic," leading to a loosening of traditional ties and identities. Nietzsche effectively repudiates Hegel's "so-called world-history," beginning as it does with the exclusion of wanderings and migrations. Nietzsche takes nomadism to be an indisputable facet of European modernity:

> Trade and industry, the post and the book-trade, the possession in common of all higher culture, rapid changing of home and scene, the nomadic life now lived by all who do not own land—these circumstances are bringing with them a weakening and finally an abolition of nations . . . (*HH* 475)

In contrast, Hegel marginalizes two significant geopolitical phenomena, involving human mobility: the contemporary rise of the United States and the seven or so centuries of the spread of Islam. He sets up a logical contrast between two roughly contemporaneous developments, the wanderings of the Germanic *Völker* and the spread of Islam. The *Völker* are merely *particular* in origin, tied to arbitrary, contingent events and traditions; in opposition, Islam is the rule of *abstract universality* and is especially suited to Arabs roaming the wide expanses of the desert, compared in a stock metaphor to the boundless sea. Here Hegel sees nothing but an episodic succession of wars, caliphates, and kingdoms where "nothing firm abides."[21] The moment of *individuality* comes with Charlemagne's empire, uniting various Germanic tribes, drawing a firm line with Islam, and instituting the outlines of a state. While Hegel did not claim to predict specific futures, he did exclude certain possibilities. He denies that the United States in its democratic, secular form, and Islam as a religious-political phenomenon, can be genuine players in the field of world-history. In this respect Hegel and his heirs are still in thrall to the principles of national sovereignty, territory, and religion laid out in the 1648 Peace of Westphalia.

For Nietzsche, since the nation state conceives itself as a population of common ethnic origins and culture, it finds itself in an intrinsically unstable position, as mobility and mingling contribute to forming a "mixed race" (*Mischrasse*). Nietzsche welcomes the process and sees no point in resisting the inevitable. While some mobility has to do with individuals seeking employment, opportunity, or freedom from old, restrictive traditions, Nietzsche is also thinking about the movements of families, subcultures, and groups. In his vocabulary, the nomadic generally designates a collective rather than an individual mode of inhabiting the earth. Nietzsche notes that the main factor retarding the transformation or abolition of the national state is its scare tactics, its exaggeration or fabrication of external or internal threats to the population's security; these furnish the excuse to declare a state of exception, in which constitutional or traditional liberties are overridden and the sovereign unity of the state is affirmed. Hegelian monarchy, with its theological affiliation, is being replaced by the national security state. Nietzsche speaks of a "*Not- und Belagerungszustand*," the equivalent of Carl Schmitt's *Ausnahmezustand* (*HH* 475). Fifty years later Schmitt was to define sovereignty in these terms: the sovereign is the one who declares the exception. Appropriately, from a Nietzschean perspective, Schmitt offered this definition in his book *Political Theology*, which argues for a fairly strict parallel between the sovereignty of God and the state.[22] Nietzsche could have taken the equation in a different sense: just as the famous passage on the death of God tells us that this news is still on the way, and scarcely comprehended, so the state is in a long-term process of dissolution. It is a shadow of God that still lingers after his disappearance (*GS* 125, 108).

Nietzsche foresees a long period of "transitional struggles," during which "the attitude of veneration and piety" toward the state will be undermined, and it will increasingly be seen in a pragmatic and utilitarian perspective (*HH* 472). Much of the work of government will be reassigned to "private contractors"—"outsourcing" is the current word—another sign of the gradual "decline and *death of the state*" (*HH* 472). This would surely entail the collapse of Hegel's state-centered world-historical narrative; on the post-state earth, "a new page will be turned in the storybook of humanity in which there will be many strange tales to read and perhaps some of them good ones" (*HH* 472). Just as the domination of the organizing principle of the racial clan gave way to the family and then to that of the state, so humanity will eventually hit upon "an invention more suited to their purpose than the state" (*HH* 472). (Again Nietzsche eschews the vocabulary of "world" and "so-called world-history," and speaks of the earth as the sphere of human activity, suggesting that "a later generation will see the state shrink to insignificance in various parts of the earth" [*HH* 472].)

In *Thus Spoke Zarathustra* the alternative proposed to life in the shrinking, globalized "world" of modernity is called loyalty to the earth. *Earth* is best understood in contrast to the *world* of Hegel's world-history. The earth of Nietzsche's phantasmatic landscape poem offers a rich variation of mountain, sea, islands, towns, and cities. It is there to be traversed and inhabited, rather than reterritorialized by states. Zarathustra teaches both himself and others not only by speaking, but by his travels and wandering on the earth, a meaningful itinerary that is too complex to be explored here in any depth. Consider the chapter "On Great Events" whose title apparently alludes to Hegel.[23] Hegel expressly confines "great events" to the state-centered and centering realm of world-history,[24] and the Hegelian writers of Nietzsche's day, as he emphasized throughout his *Untimely Meditations*, persisted in this association. Nietzsche's struggles with the idea of the "great event" are evident in his unmodern essay on Wagner. There, the "last great event" is said to be Alexander's joining of Europe and Asia, and Wagner is hailed as ushering in the next great event, which will be the definitive cultural expression and realization of Europe (*UM* IV:4). The chapter "On Great Events" questions the credibility of all so-called great events, and the so-called world history that they are thought to constitute. To his disciples—those who have sworn fidelity to the earth—Zarathustra recounts his dialogue with the fire-hound, an ego puffed up with an expansive desire for crude power, a rebel or revolutionary. Such fiery demagogues are at most "ventriloquists [*Bauchredner*] of the earth," producing the illusion of a politics that speaks from the ground of being.[25] They give the impression that it is the earth as reterritorialized by the state which constitutes a nation's true identity. The secret unknown by the fire-hound (and the state-philosophy he represents) is that "*the heart of the earth is gold*" (*Z* II "On Great Events"). This explicitly geographical and geological chapter insists that the resources of the *Menschen-Erde* are rich in possibility. It is constituted by passionate, mobile human bodies, their combinations, and transformations in, by, and through the earth.

At the end of his talk, Zarathustra informs his disciples that it was only his shadow or specter that they had seen flying into the mouth of a volcano, which led them to think he was descending to hell. Yet he puzzles over the specter's exclamation: "It is time! It is high time!" (*Z* II "On Great Events"). Time for what? For a great event involving the earth? This question hangs in the air. If it receives an answer, it is in Part III where Zarathustra emerges from his struggle with his "abysmal thought" of eternal recurrence, confessing that the human-earth had seemed to turn into a cave of death and decay. Earlier, Zarathustra had prophesied "Verily, a site of convalescence shall the earth yet become!" (*Z* I "On the Gift-Giving Virtue" 2). Convalescing from this *agon*, he accepts his animals' cheering news that the world awaits him as a garden (*Z* III "The Convalescent"), and goes on to sing his celebratory song of the earth, "The Seven Seals" (*Z* III "The Seven Seals"), which imagines an earth freed from boundaries and borders, a counter-apocalypse where the earth frees itself from the world. The figure of the garden is a frequent one in Nietzsche, and of course it recalls a long history of associations, beginning with Eden, of a transformed world. Traditional gardens were walled and enclosed spaces (as the

Persian source of the word "paradise" testifies). Yet the English landscape garden that emerged in the eighteenth century and came to dominate European garden style in the nineteenth sought to eliminate the appearance of enclosure and boundaries, if not their reality. Nietzsche's combination of the garden motif with that of a radical disappearance of boundaries in the final chapters of *Zarathustra* III should be read as a poetic anticipation of a transformed geoaesthetics and geopolitics.

Unlike Hegel, Nietzsche does not define Europe in terms of its supposed destiny to establish a certain kind of political state. Europe is in crisis—whether it knows it or not—as it struggles with the collapse of Christianity, the emergence of democratic attitudes and practices, the threat of nihilism, and the possible rule of the herd and the last man. In *Beyond Good and Evil* Nietzsche descries the emergence in Europe of "an essentially supra-national and nomadic type of person who physiologically speaking, is typified by a maximal degree of the art and force of adaptation" (*BGE* 242).[26] While this tendency may lead to homogeneity and the production of a type prepared for "*slavery* in the most subtle sense," other aspects of the development may point in different directions (*BGE* 242). Mixing, wandering, and migration also produce a variety of singular hybrids, higher humans like Napoleon, Goethe, Beethoven, Stendhal, Heine, Schopenhauer, and Wagner (*BGE* 256). These experimental anticipations of the European *Zu-kunft* embody diverse mixtures of traditions and lineages. Although Europe "*wants to become one*," the "truth" of this desire is, at least for now, the proliferation of singularities (*BGE* 256). Accordingly, in the concluding aphorism of "Peoples and Fatherlands," Nietzsche emphatically declares that "this is the century of the *multitude* [*Menge*]!" (*BGE* 256). It is ironic that Nietzsche's translators have not always been attentive to the pointers in *On the Genealogy of Morals* (*GM* I) that ask us to be careful in discriminating the terms that designate nuanced distinctions of human types, and have often rendered *Menge* as "masses." The *Genealogy*, which Nietzsche advertised as a text meant to be helpful in understanding *Beyond Good and Evil*, insists on an acutely sensitive philological and differential reading of terms for social and political categories.[27] The multitude is diverse, masses are relatively uniform. The multitude is formed by a mixing of races, cultures, ethnicities, and so on. This might result eventually in the formation of herds and masses, but it need not. Exemplary here is Nietzsche's discussion of the emergence of what we think of as the Greeks from a mixing of Mongols, Semites, and others (*KSA* 8:5[198]).[28] Mixing was the necessary precondition for creating the Greeks.

The chapter on "Peoples and Fatherlands" (*BGE*) should be read as a thorough critique of Hegel's *Weltgeschichte* in which Nietzsche challenges

Hegel on the state, human mobility on the earth, the persistence of national types, and even the supposed east to west movement of the *Weltgeist*, that ghost or phantom, which is dispersed by the rise of the multitude who will not stay put to observe its passage. We need look no further than the United States-Mexican border to see the pertinence of this reconfiguration of the Hegelian story in terms of a north/south axis which does not coincide with the rise of states.

For Hegel, the decisive event of the German world after its Christianization is the Reformation, seen as a necessary step in human freedom. Nietzsche despises the Reformation, and argues that it was possible in Germany only because the *masses* there could be given a direction from above, although he suggests this required the contingent fact of Luther's intransigent temperament (*GS* 149; *AOM* 226). Yet no reformation was possible in Greece because the Greek *Menge* consisted of diverse groups who were impervious to the best efforts of Empedocles, Pythagoras, and Plato to effect one. In *The Gay Science* (*GS* 149) Nietzsche repeatedly draws contrasts between the uniform *Masse* and the heterogeneous *Menge*, or multitude, a distinction that must be kept in mind in reading his declaration in *Beyond Good and Evil* that "this is the century of the *Menge*!" (*BGE* 256). We might speculate that certain modern states like the Soviet Union collapsed because they were unsuccessful in transforming their population into masses, and could not resist the entropy of the multitude, which was the unintended consequence of their policies.

Nietzsche's conception of the conjunction of the Reformation, Germany, and the modern form of the state then, is the antipode of Hegel's. For Hegel, the Reformation is crucial to the story of history as the achievement of freedom. The Reformation, according to Hegel, has allowed peoples to rally around "the banner of free spirit":

> Time, since that epoch, has had no other work to do than the formal imbuing of the world with this principle, in bringing the reconciliation implicit [in Christianity] into objective and explicit realization . . . States and laws are nothing else than religion manifesting itself in the relations of the actual world.
>
> This is the essence of the Reformation: man is in his very nature destined to be free.[29]

In this connection Hegel praises the uniformity, according to general principles, of "law, property, social morality, government, constitutions" as rational expressions of free will. Nietzsche, as we have seen, takes the very fact of Reformation as a sign that it has operated upon an unfree mass, and "where there are masses, there is a need for slavery" (*GS* 149). The *Auseinandersetzung* of the two thinkers extends to the issues of the corruption of the church and the analysis of the varying fates of the Reformation in different areas of Europe. For Hegel, the corruption of the Catholic Church was essential, and consisted in its recognizing God in a sensuous, external form. This leads, when the power of the Church is firmly established, to superstition, "slavish deference to authority," credulous belief in miracles, and finally to "lust of power, riotous debauchery, all the forms of barbarous and vulgar corruption, hypocrisy and deception."[30] In a sequence of aphorisms in *The Gay Science* devoted to the politics of religion, Nietzsche seems to agree with Hegel that the Reformation took hold in Germany because there the Church "was the least corrupt" (*GS* 148). Yet in a reversal of Hegel's valuations, Nietzsche maintains that the corruption of peoples and institutions should not be understood moralistically, but as signs of healthy diversity and harbingers of new creative life. The point is argued at length in *The Gay Science* (*GS* 23), "The signs of corruption." Even superstition—one of Hegel's key signs of corruption—must be transvalued. In a condition of corruption, superstition is "colorful" and emancipatory:

> As soon as corruption sets in anywhere, a colorful superstition takes over, and the previous common faith of a people becomes pale and powerless against it: for superstition is free-spiritedness of the second rank—whoever succumbs to it selects certain forms and formulas that appeal to him and allows himself some freedom of choice . . . superstition always appears as progress against faith and as a sign that the intellect is becoming more independent and demanding its rights . . . Times of corruption are those in which the apples fall from the tree: I mean the individuals, the seed-bearers of the future, the spiritual colonizers and shapers of new states and communities. (*GS* 23)

It could be said, then, that corruption is the element of the multitude, the *Menge*.

Hegel feels compelled to give an account of why the Reformation arose in Germany and had greater success in the north and west than in the south and east. In examining the case of "the Romanic nations"—Italy, Spain, Portugal, and (to some extent) France—he offers an explanation that could appeal to Nietzsche, at least in formal terms: the spirit of those countries' population was too diverse, lacking the resolute "inwardness" of the Germans:

> The Romanic nations . . . have maintained in the very depth of their soul—in their spiritual consciousness—the principle of disharmony: they are a product of the fusion of Roman and German blood, and still retain the heterogeneity resulting from that.[31]

We note that Nietzsche praises such fusion and multiplicity in the case of the Greek multitude, which resisted reformations led by those he considered vastly more gifted and talented reformers than Luther. Again, there is a minimal, formal agreement on the question of conditions, but an extreme opposition regarding the values of uniformity and diversity. Hegel's discussion of the modern post-Reformation world needs to be read alongside Nietzsche's analysis of "peoples and fatherlands" in *Beyond Good and Evil*, where he longs for creative rearrangements of north and south, east and west.

Nietzsche then emerges as a theorist of nomadism, migration, immigration, diaspora, cosmopolitanism, and hybridity. He is better equipped than Hegel to understand the demise or evisceration of the monarchical state with a state (Christian) religion. Nietzsche could see a self-described hybrid like Barack Obama as a paradigmatic voice of and for the multitude. We should also note that the *Menge* is not a universal class, but is conceived as an audience, which is not coextensive with the population at large (*BGE* 263, 269). In *Beyond Good and Evil* (*BGE* 256), which announces the century of the multitude, it is introduced as the audience of the higher humans (Napoleon to Wagner) listed there. Goethe constructs a dialogue about such a multitude in *Faust*'s "Prelude in the Theater," where the *Menge* is described as relatively educated, widely read, yet mixed in mood and background.[32] The century of the nomadic multitude, then, as it frees itself from peoples, fatherlands, and states, is not so far from the society of the spectacle, making allowances for technological innovations in its promulgation and marketing. The bad news is that the multitude can be an audience for "tyrants of all sorts, including the most spiritual" (*BGE* 242), and the good news may be that, at present, they are still sufficiently diverse to resist a powerful religious reformation like the German one that brought Europe such disaster, including religious wars and the modern state system (*AOM* 226). However shifting and unstable the earth's multitude may be, its very diversity may be sufficient—if we are lucky—to resist the more monolithic forces of assassins and crusaders with their unitary visions of the world.[33]

Much recent political thought focuses on questions having to do with the movement and mixing of peoples, the rise of new cultural configurations, and the constitution of a diverse population. Nietzsche saw that by marginalizing human mobility, Hegel made it difficult to think these phenomena to which he then gave names like nomadism, hybridity, and multitude. We may be wary about where Nietzsche is going with these analytical tools, but we may also find other uses for them as we struggle with concepts such as cosmopolitanism and multiculturalism.

Notes

1. The Optics of Science, Art, and Life: How Tragedy Begins
Tracy B. Strong

1. See Brian Leiter, "Nietzsche's Naturalism Reconsidered," in *The Oxford Handbook of Nietzsche*, eds. John Richardson and Ken Gemes (Oxford: Oxford University Press, forthcoming); Mathias Risse, "Nietzsche's 'Animal Psychology' versus Kantian Ethics," in *Nietzsche and Morality*, eds. Brian Leiter and Neil Sinhababu (Oxford: Oxford University Press, 2007), 57–82. See the discussion in Lee Kerckhove, "Re-Thinking Ethical Naturalism: Nietzsche's 'Open Question' Argument," *Man and World*, 27 (1994): 54–64.

2. All translations of citations from Nietzsche are mine.

3. It was not so much roundly attacked as ignored. See the discussion in Chapter Two of my *Politics without Vision. Thinking without a Banister in the Twentieth Century* (Chicago and London: The University of Chicago Press, 2012), 57–90.

4. For a more detailed analysis see my "Philosophy and the Project of Cultural Revolution," *Philosophical Topics* 33, 2 (2008): 227–247, reprinted in Nietzsche, ed. Tracy B. Strong (London: Ashgate, 2009), 423–444.

5. For instance see Debora Carter Mullen, "Art, Science, and Truth in Nietzsche and Heidegger," *International Studies in Philosophy* 26 (1994): 45–55, who argues that "truth takes over from life" (48).

6. "Prism" as in the Cambridge University Press translation introduces a notion of distortion that is not as strong as with "optic". See Friedrich Nietzsche, *The Birth of Tragedy and other Writings*, trans. Ronald Speirs (Cambridge: Cambridge University Press, 2000).

7. For a fuller discussion see Babette Babich, "Gay Science: Science and *Wissenschaft, Leidenschaft* and Music," in Companion to Nietzsche, ed. Keith Ansell-Pearson (Cambridge: Blackwell, 2006), 97–114.

8. Henry David Thoreau, *A Week on the Concord and Merrimack Rivers* (Princeton: Princeton University Press, 1980), 170, 285. See David M. Robinson, *Natural Life: Thoreau's Worldly Transcendentalism* (Ithaca, N.Y.: Cornell University Press, 2004).

9. Babette Babich, *Nietzsche's Philosophy of Science* (Albany: State University of New York Press, 1994), 131.

10. See Max Weber, "Science as a Vocation," The Vocation Lectures, edited D. Owen and T. Strong (Cambridge, MA: Hackett, 2004), 1–31.

11. R. W. Emerson. *Essays and Lectures* (New York: Library of America, 1983), 483.

12. I discuss this at length in *Politics without Vision*, Chapter Three, 91–136.

13. Φύσις refers nature (and also to growth). *In Walden ("Spring")* Thoreau gives magnificently paced vision of a world coming into being (H.D. Thoreau, *Walden, Civil Disobedience and Other Writings* [New York: Norton, 2008], 247–262).

14. Martin Heidegger, *Nietzsche vol. 1*, trans. David Farrell (San Francisco: Harper and Row, 1991), 215.

15. "Absolute" here refers to a concept of an art as having relation to nothing other than itself. It is exemplified by the well-known claim from Eduard Hanslick (who was to be parodied by Wagner as Beckmesser in *Die Meistersinger von Nürnberg*): "Music has no subject beyond the combinations of notes we hear, for music speaks not only by means of sounds, it speaks nothing but sound" (Eduard Hanslick, quoted by Wolfgang Sandberger (1996) in liner notes to Juilliard String Quartet, *Intimate Letters* (SONY Classical SK 66840). See Daniel Chua, *Absolute Music and the Construction of Meaning* (Cambridge: Cambridge University Press, 1999) and Carl Dahlhaus, *The Idea of Absolute Music* (Chicago: University of Chicago Press, 1991).

16. This and the next paragraph draws directly from Babette Babich, "Μουσικȩ τεκνφ: The Philosophical Practice of Music from Socrates to Nietzsche to Heidegger," in *Gesture and Word: Thinking Between Philosophy and Poetry*, eds. Massimo Verdicchio and Robert Burch (Evanston: Northwestern University Press, 2002), 171–180. See also her *Words in Blood, Like Flowers* (State University of New York Press, 2004) and my "The Tragic Ethic and the Spirit of Music," *International Studies in Philosophy* 35 (3) (2004): 79–100.

17. Thrasybulos Georgiades, *Musik und Rhythmus bei den Griechen. Zum Ursprung der abendländischen Musik* (Hamburg: Rowohlt, 1958), 52–53.

18. Warren D. Anderson, *Music and Musicians in Ancient Greece* (Ithaca, N.Y.: Cornell University Press, 1994), 143.

19. Plato, *Laches* 188D in Plato. *Platonis Opera*. Volume III (Oxford: Clarendon Press, 1903).

20. Robert Frost will write that "All revelation has been ours" (Last line of the poem "All Revelation"). Robert Frost, *Collected Poems, Prose and Plays* (New York: Library of America, 1995), 302.

21. This is remarkably like the picture that Hume gives in Book I, Chapter Six, "Of Personal Identity," in *A Treatise of Human Nature* (Oxford: Oxford University Press, 2011), 47.

22. See Martin Heidegger, *Nietzsche,* Vols. 3 and 4, trans. David Farrell (San Francisco: Harper and Row, 1987), 136–137. See Vanessa Lemm, "Justice and Gift-Giving in *Thus Spoke Zarathustra,*" in *Nietzsche's Thus Spoke Zarathustra: Before Sunrise,* ed. James Luchte (London: Continuum, 2008), 165–182.

23. Thomas Brobjer, *Nietzsche's Philosophical Context* (Urbana: University of Illinois Press, 2008), 108.

24. Wallace Stevens, "Esthétique du mal," in *Collected Poetry and Prose* (New York: Library of America, 1997), 277–86.

25. See Jean Granier, *Nietzsche et le problème de la vérité* (Paris: Seuil, 1966), 357–366.

26. I have argued this in relation to Hobbes *Leviathan.* See my "How to Write Scripture: Words and Authority in Thomas Hobbes," *Critical Inquiry* 1 (1993): 128–159, 172–178.

27. For an elaboration of the thoughts in this paragraph see my "Introduction: Hammers, Idleness and Music," in Friedrich Nietzsche, *Twilight of the Idols.* Cambridge, MA. Hackett. 1997, xvi–xix.

28. From Wallace Stevens, part iii of *Esthétique du mal.* See Harold Bloom, *Wallace Stevens: The Poems of Our Climate* (Ithaca, N.Y.: Cornell University Press, 1960), 230, where he writes that the "'evil in the self' is the instinct for the Sublime, or the defense of repression, an unconsciously purposeful forgetting that safeguards and aggrandizes the self."

29. Wallace Stevens, *Esthétique du mal,* section viii.

2. Nietzsche, Nature, and the Affirmation of Life

Lawrence J. Hatab

Portions of this essay are taken from my recent book, *Nietzsche's On the Genealogy of Morality: An Introduction* (Cambridge University Press, 2008).

1. I borrow the term "crossing" from John Sallis, *Crossings: Nietzsche and the Space of Tragedy* (Chicago: University of Chicago Press, 1991).

2. Even the idea of sheer becoming cannot be maintained, according to Nietzsche. Discernment of such becoming can only arise once an imaginary counterworld of being is placed against it (*KSA* 9:11[162]).

3. See Babette Babich, "A Note on *Chaos Sive Natura*: On Theogony, Genesis, and Playing Stars," *New Nietzsche Studies* 5, 3/4 and 6, 1/2 (2003/2004): 48–70. For an insightful treatment of Nietzsche's naturalism, see Christoph Cox, *Nietzsche: Naturalism and Interpretation* (Berkeley, CA.: University of California Press, 1999).

4. Homer, *Odyssey* 11, 301.

5. Aristotle, *Physics* 193b5ff.

6. Aristotle, *On the Soul* 412a20ff.

7. Aristotle, *Physics* 200b12.

8. Aristotle, *Physics* 192b10ff.

9. Aristotle, *Metaphysics* 1003a26–32.

10. Aristotle, *Nicomachean Ethics* 1139a11.

11. Aristotle, *Nicomachean Ethics* 1134b18–35; *Politics* 1332a4ff.

12. René Descartes, *Rules for the Direction of the Mind* in *Philosophical Essays and Correspondence*, ed. Roger Ariew (Indianapolis, IN: Hackett, 2000), 7–10; Immanuel Kant, *Metaphysical Foundations of Natural Science* in *Philosophy of Material Nature*, trans. James W. Ellington (Indianapolis, IN: Hackett), 6.

13. "Preface" to Isaac Newton, *Mathematical Principles of Natural Philosophy* (Berkeley, CA: University of California Press, 1960), xvii.

14. René Descartes, *Descartes: Philosophical Letters*, trans. Anthony Kenny (Minneapolis, MN: University of Minnesota Press, 1981), 94.

15. It can be argued that the *Meditations* is not primarily about the separability of mind and body, but simply the radical distinctness of thought and extension. See Marleen Rozemond, "Descartes' Case for Dualism," *Journal of the History of Philosophy* 33 1 (1995): 29–63. Thought and extension are principal attributes of mental and physical substance, which is the base of their modes. Individual bodies are modes of the principal attribute of extension. A substance has only one principal attribute, defining its essence and bearing its modes. So *res extensa* should not be called "body" but the core defining element of individual bodies. In other words, body can be *nothing other than* extension. This scheme allows the treatment of *all* bodies as subject to the singular analysis of mathematical relations, thus supplanting the Aristotelian view of qualitative differences among bodies, and justifying the reductive mechanism of the new physics of nature.

16. Aristotle, *Metaphysics* 1072a9.

17. Nietzsche talks of Dionysian and Apollonian forces as "artistic energies that burst forth from nature herself" (in natural creation and destruction, birth and death, and the emergence of dream states and frenzied abandon, which are not deliberately intended by humans). Human artistry is an "imitation" of these immediate forces in nature by way of forming and deforming cultural narratives in tragedy. Here we have a kind of "physics" drawn from the original sense of *phusis* as self-emerging living phenomena (from *phuō*, to grow or burst forth)—a physics different from both the mathematized physics in modern science and traditional "essentialist" conceptions of nature.

18. See my discussion in Chs. 2–6 of *Myth and Philosophy: A Contest of Truths* (Chicago: Open Court, 1990).

19. For an important study of the agonistic nature of will to power, see Wolfgang Müller-Lauter, *Nietzsche: His Philosophy of Contradictions and the Contradictions of His Philosophy*, trans. David J. Parent (Urbana, IL: University of Illinois Press, 1999).

20. For important discussions of this idea, see Paul van Tongeren, "Nietzsche's Greek Measure," *Journal of Nietzsche Studies* 24 (2002): 5–24; Herman W. Siemens, "Agonal Communities of Taste: Law and Community in Nietzsche's Philosophy of Transvaluation," *Journal of Nietzsche Studies* 24 (2002): 83–112. See also Christa Davis Acampora, "Of Dangerous Games and Dastardly Deeds: A Typology of Nietzsche's Contests," *International Studies in Philosophy* 34 3 (2002): 135–151.

21. See my discussion in Ch. 2 of *A Nietzschean Defense of Democracy: An Experiment in Postmodern Politics* (Chicago: Open Court, 1995).

22. For an important study, see Alan D. Schrift, *Nietzsche and the Question of Interpretation: Between Hermeneutics and Deconstruction* (New York: Routledge, 1990).

23. That is why we must engage Nietzsche's texts in their "addressive" function, because "reader response" is inseparable from the nature of a written text. Nietzsche's stylistic choices—hyperbole, provocation, allusions, metaphors, aphorisms, literary forms, and historical narratives not confined to demonstrable facts or theories—all show that he presumed a reader's involvement in bringing sense to a text, even in exploring beyond or against a text. Nietzsche's books do not presume to advance "doctrines" as a one-way transmission of finished thoughts. Good readers must be active, not simply reactive; they must think for themselves (*EH* "Clever" 8). Aphorisms, for example, cannot merely be read; they require an "art of exegesis" on the part of readers (*GM* "Prologue" 8). Nietzsche wants to be read "with doors left open" (*D* "Preface" 5). This does not mean that Nietzsche's texts are nothing but an invitation for interpretation. Nietzsche's *own* voice is central to his writings, and he frequently advances sharp convictions and disagreements; yet he would not presume to advance a case as indefeasible.

24. René Descartes, *Philosophical Essays and Correspondence*, ed. Roger Ariew (Indianapolis, IN: Hackett, 2000), 107.

25. René Descartes, *Philosophical Essays and Correspondence*, 107.

26. Francis Bacon, "Novum Organum," in *The Philosophical Works of Francis Bacon*, trans. Robert L. Ellis and James Spedding, ed. John M. Robinson (London: Routledge, 1905), 27.

3. Is Evolution Blind? On Nietzsche's Reception of Darwin

Virginia Cano

1. Martin Heidegger, *Nietzsche Volume III: The Will to Power as Knowledge and Metaphysics,* trans. Joan Stambaugh, David Farrell Krell, and Frank A. Capuzzi. (San Francisco: Harper & Row, 1987), 39.

2. Martin Heidegger, *Nietzsche,* 41. We should note here that Heidegger makes a distinction between "biology," understood as the science that deals with phenomena, processes, and laws of the living, and "biologism," which alludes to the mode in which biological thinking is extended beyond its limits and its own sphere. Besides this terminological precision, Heidegger will negate the biologicist

character of Nietzsche's thought by differentiating between science, including biology, and metaphysics.

3. Jean Granier, *Le problème de la vérité dans la philosophie de Nietzsche* (Paris: Éditions du Seuil, 1966), 406. Granier opposes a biologistic reading of life to the will to power. See "La Volonté de Puissance est-elle la lutte biologique pour la prééminence?" (Jean Granier, *Le problème de la vérité*, 404–409). Along these same lines, it is worthwhile recalling Moore's statement on this issue: "by reconstructing the historical debates in which Nietzsche participated, we can show that those aspects of his biologism, which have often been dismissed as having merely a rhetorical or metaphorical function . . . emerge as a coherent strand of his thought backed up by the science, or rather, pseudoscience, of his day," Gregory Moore, *Nietzsche, Biology and Metaphor* (Cambridge: Cambridge University Press, 2002), 14.

4. See Barbara Stiegler, *Nietzsche et la biologie* (Paris: Presses universitaires de France, 2001).

5. Timothy Lenoir, *The Strategy of Life: Teleology and Mechanics in Nineteenth-Century German Biology* (Chicago and London: The University of Chicago Press, 1989), ix.

6. Following André Pichot's argument in his *Histoire de la notion de vie* (Paris: Gallimard, 2004), we might say that the teleological and mechanistic visions represent the two privileged paradigms imposed on the notion of life throughout history and that find their utmost expressions in the positions of Aristotle and Descartes.

7. In a text from 1868, "Teleologie seit Kant," Nietzsche develops his (early) critique of teleology based on Kant. There he maintains: "The assumption of a unified teleological world would have been made only according to a human analogy: why can the purposive not be an unconscious creative power, i.e., which nature produces?" (*TSK*).

8. Nietzsche notes in this text two idiosyncrasies of philosophers: (1) their "lack of historical sense, their hatred of even the idea of becoming," and (2) "mistaking the last for the first." The last, based on forgetting and injustices, is that world of being that is postulated as *arkhé* and *télos*. See *TI* "Reason" 45–47.

9. Here we take up the metaphor proposed by Richard Dawkins, *The Blind Watchmaker: Why the Evidence of Evolution Reveals a Universe without Design* (New York: Norton, 1996). Dawkins emphasizes the neither designed nor teleological character of evolutionary theory by way of the metaphor of the blind watchmaker.

10. Charles Darwin, "A Biographical Sketch of an Infant," *Mind: A Quarterly Review of Psychology and Philosophy* 2 (1877): 285–294. Regarding evolutionary theory, this paper is only slightly relevant. Andler, meanwhile, believes that Nietzsche would have known of *The Descent of Man*. See Charles Andler, *Nietzsche –sa vie et sa pensée* (Paris: Gallimard, 1954). And according to Barbara Stiegler, one volume of *The Variations of Plants and Animals under Domestication* was found in Nietzsche's personal library.

11. Wilson Frezzatti Junior notes that Nietzsche's personal library also included the following texts: Friedrich Albert Lange, *Geschichte des Materialismus* (1866); Oscar Schmidt, *Descendenzlehre und Darwinismus* (1873), Carl Nägeli, *Entstehung und Begriff der Naturhistorischen Art* (1865). Also important are the writings of E. Haeckel, *Generelle Morphologie* (1866); Wilhelm Roux, *Der Kamft der Theile im Organismus. Ein Beitrag zur Vervollständigung der mechanischen Zweckmäßigkeitslehre* (1881); W. H. Rolph, *Biologishe Probleme zugleich als Versuch zur Entwicklung einer rationalen Ethik* (1882), y P. Ree *Der Ursprung der Moralischen Empfindungen.* (1877). See Wilson Frezzatti Junior, *Nietzsche contra Darwin* (Sao Paulo: discurso editorial, 2001).

12. Charles Darwin, *On the Origin of the Species by Means of Natural Selection* (London: John Murray, 1859), 79.

13. See Wolfgang Müller-Lauter, "L'organisme comme lute intérieure," in *Nietzsche. Physiologie de la Volonté de Puissance* (Paris: Editions Allia, 1998), 111.

14. Darwin does not exclude the possibility of thinking a struggle internal to individuals, but that notion of war is simply not functional for his explanatory theory of natural selection.

15. Jean Granier, *Le problème de la vérité,* 405.

16. Another of the "injustices" done Darwin by Nietzsche should be noted here, given that the sphere of death-loss (for example, of traits not favorable in the struggle for existence) is a part of Darwin's theory. Even so, in Darwin there is only space for the "measure" (of those traits and individuals that progress in the struggle for life) in accordance with the utility or futility of certain characters for preservation. On this point, Nietzsche reincorporates that value possessed by futility, atrophy—that which is not useful and which does not serve preservation—when thinking the phenomenon of the vital.

17. Charles Darwin, *On the Origin of the Species,* 63.

18. Charles Darwin, *On the Origin of the Species,* 411.

19. Nietzsche even ends up negating the instinct for self-preservation: "Es giebt keinen Selbsterhaltungstrieb" (*KSA* 9:6[145]). Even so, in the majority of cases, he considers it, along with adaptation, as a consequence or derived principle.

20. Wilson Frezzatti Junior, *Nietzsche contra Darwin,* 67.

21. Charles Darwin, *On the Origin of the Species,* 84.

22. The improvement in Darwin, we cannot but clarify, is always relative and refers to the adaptive advances within the same species. There is no absolute notion of perfection or progress.

23. Friedrich Albert Lange, "Darwinism and Teleology," in *The History of Materialism,* Vol. 3, trans. Ernest Chester Thomas. (New York: Harcourt, Brace & Company, 1925), 66–67.

24. "One counts on the struggle for existence, the death of the weaker creatures and the survival of the most robust and gifted; consequently one imagines a continual growth in perfection" (WP 684; *KSA* 13:14[133]).

25. The importance that the reading of Spencer had in Nietzsche's approach to Darwin should be emphasized. See María Cristina Fornari, "Nietzsche y el

darwinismo," *Estudios Nietzsche* 8 (2008): 100. Along the same interpretive lines, see Gregory Moore, "Nietzsche, Spencer, and the Ethics of Evolution," *Journal of Nietzsche Studies* 23 (2002): 1–20.

26. Friedrich Albert Lange, *The History of Materialism,* Vol. 3, 67–68.

27. See William Paley, *Natural Theology or Evidences of the Existence and Attributes of the Deity Collected from the Appearances of Nature* (New York: Oxford University Press, 2006).

28. Richard Dawkins, *The Blind Watchmaker*, 5.

29. Darwin, *On the Origin of the Species*, 81.

30. Peter Vorzimmer, *Charles Darwin: The Years of Controversy* (Philadelphia: Temple University Press), 44–45. The author points out that the idea of variation that operates in natural selection is the idea of "continuous variation," whereas the "discontinuous variations"—the "leaps" and "large variations that burst into the continuity between progeny and brood"—are not transmissible and, therefore, appear as irrelevant for natural selection.

31. The British economist establishes, in *An Essay on the principle of population* (1789), the principle according to which human population grows in geometric progression, while livelihoods proceed arithmetically.

32. In this point, we should emphasize that Darwin does not give the theory of evolution a predictive value. It is not possible to make exact predictions regarding which individuals, and therefore which species, must be preserved, which ones modified, and which ones annihilated. And this is so because it is not possible to anticipate all the variables involved in this process of natural selection. The evolutionist theory has, in this sense, a retrospective application: having knowledge of the important variables (knowledge of the variations in a given environment) allows finding "the" correct, true explanation of the genesis and developmental process of the variations and the species. Still, even if Darwin's theory does not have a projective character, which in turn is determined by the limited, epistemic capacities of the individuals, the explanation continues operating under the idea of a unique interpretation of the phenomenon of existence. It is an interpretation that finds its guide in the idea of a struggle for existence propelling the process of natural selection.

33. Charles Darwin, *On the Origin of the Species*, 414.

34. Charles Darwin, *On the Origin of the Species*, 428. It is important to note that even though the theory has no projective value, Darwin does attribute to it a prophetic value: "We can so far take a prophetic glance into futurity as to foretell that it will be common and widely-spread species, belonging to the larger and dominant groups within each class, which will ultimately prevail and procreate new and dominant species . . . [W]e may look with some confidence to a secure future of great length. And as natural selection works solely by and for the good of each being, all corporeal and mental endowments will tend to progress toward perfection" (Charles Darwin, *On the Origin of the Species*, 428).

35. See Richard Dawkins, *Climbing Mount Improbable* (London and New York: Norton, 1996).

36. Charles Darwin, *On the Origin of the Species,* 34. There they appear as distinctive notes of monstrosity that "differ greatly," constitute "leaps" and "exceptions" that represent "some considerable deviation of structure in one part, either injurious to or not useful to the species" (Charles Darwin, *On the Origin of the Species,* 33).

4. Nietzsche and the Nineteenth-Century Debate on Teleology
Mariana A. Cruz

1. Mario Ariel González Porta, "Zurück zu Kant Adolf Trendelenburg, la superación del idealismo y los orígenes de la filosofía contemporánea," *Doispontos* 2 (2005): 35–59.

2. Otto Liebmann, *Kant und die Epigonen* (Erlangen: Fischer, 1991).

3. Herbert Schnädelbach, *Philosophy in Germany (1831–1933)* (Cambridge: Cambridge University Press, 1984), 78. See also Friedrich Albert Lange, "Philosophical Materialism Since Kant," in *The History of Materialism,* Vol. II, trans. Ernest Chester Thomas (London: Kegan Paul, Trench, Trubner & Co, 1925), 246: "Into the place of Classicism as well as Romanticism Young Germany forced its way. The rays of materialistic modes of thought gathered themselves together."

4. Adolf Trendelenburg (1802–1872), historian of philosophy, professor of moral philosophy, of pedagogy, and secretary of the Prussian Academy of Sciences. He made important contributions not only in the areas under discussion in this chapter, but also served as a foundation for subsequent philosophy of logic and theory of language, and is recognized as a key figure in the development of contemporary analytic philosophy and hermeneutics. That both Frege and Husserl produced works also titled *Logische Untersuchungen* would suggest recognition of this fact.

5. I refer to the second edition, which was revised in 1862, Adolf Trendelenburg, *Logische Untersuchungen* (Leipzig: S. Hirzel, 1862). In cases where the reference is to the first edition, it is through the mediation of Andrea Orsucci, *Dalla biologia cellulare alle scienze dello spirito. Aspetti del dibattito sull'individualità nell'Ottocento tedesco* (Bologna: Società editrice di Mulino, 1992).

6. Andrea Orsucci, *Dalla biologia cellulare alle scienze dello spirito,* 32–33.

7. Mario Ariel Gonzales, "Zurück zu Kant. Adolf Trendelenburg, la superación del idealismo y los orígenes de la filosofía contemporánea," 7.

8. *Zweckmässigkeit* is also convenience, utility, opportunity, but I opt here for functionality, because it is the technical sense. Nevertheless, in order not to miss any of the other meanings connected with this concept, I use the German term throughout the essay.

9. It is worthwhile to note here that the second component of the term, *mässig,* has to do with measure, but is also moderate, regular, mediocre. This is important in the context of Nietzsche, given his critique of the characteristics of the herd instinct of human beings, where the concepts of moderation, regularity, and mediocrity recur with some frequency. In these reflections, as well, science that seeks out norms is said to be the instrument of the herd. See *TL.*

10. For more details regarding the Aristotelian theory of causes, among others, William David Ross, *Aristotle* (New York: Routledge, 1995) and more specifically connected with teleological causation and the explanation of organisms, Monte Ransome Johnson, *Aristotle on Teleology* (Oxford: Clarendon Press, 2005).

11. Johannes Peter Müller (1801–1858) was professor of biology to notable personalities in Germany, whose most significant contributions are in the fields of physiology, embryology, and zoology.

12. Using this term, Nietzsche distances himself from the usual denomination that establishes a dividing line between the pre- and post-Socratic philosophers, because for Nietzsche, Socrates should be considered among the pre-Platonic philosophers.

13. Ciano Aydin, "De substantie-ontologie als een ontoereikende duiding van de wordende werkelijkheid," in *Zijn en Worden. Nietzsches omduiding van het substantiebegrip* (Nederlands: Shaker Publishing, 2003), 112.

14. David Ross, *Aristotle*, 96.

15. Ciano Aydin, "De substantie-ontologie als een ontoereikende duiding van de wordende werkelijkheid," 112.

16. David Ross, *Aristotle*, 96.

17. It must be recalled that form or formal cause is the internal parallel to the object of final cause.

18. Ciano Aydin, "De substantie-ontologie als een ontoereikende duiding van de wordende werkelijkheid," 113.

19. I return to the critique of this logic of explanation in the section on Anaxagoras.

20. Adolf Trendelenburg, "Worte der Erinnerung an J. Müller," in *Monatsberichte der Königlichen Preussischen Akademie der Wissenschaften zu Berlin* (1859), 121–23, cited in Andrea Orsucci, *Dalla biologia cellulare alle scienze dello spirito*, 31.

21. Johannes Müller, *Handbuch der Physiologie des Menschen* (Hölscher: Coblenz, 1833–40, II), 505, cited in Andrea Orsucci, *Dalla biologia cellulare alle scienze dello spirito*, 32.

22. Volker Peckhaus, "Language and Logic in German Post-Hegelian Philosophy," *200 Years of Analytical Philosophy* 4 (August 2009): 5.

23. Volker Peckhaus, "Language and Logic in German Post-Hegelian Philosophy," 5.

24. See Volker Peckhaus, "Language and Logic in German Post-Hegelian Philosophy," 5.

25. See Andrea Orsucci, *Dalla biologia cellulare alle scienze dello spirito*, 36.

26. Adolf Trendelenburg, *Naturrecht auf dem Grunde der Ethik* (Leipzig: S. Hirzel, 1860), 24.

27. Karl Ernst von Baer, *Über Entwicklungsgeschichte der Thiere. Beobachtung und Reflexion* I–II, 1828–1837 (Könisberg: Bornträger), I, 147 in Andrea Orsucci, *Dalla biologia cellulare alle scienze dello spirit*, 39. Nevertheless, for him, interest-

ingly enough, final cause does not act in a regularly harmonious form, which is why he maintains that it is strange that there are not more deformed beings. Irregularity in fetal growth, which he observed, leads him to contest preformism, thus leading him to question the predominance of teleology that Trendelenburg would propose anew later on.

28. Karl Ernst von Baer, *Über Entwicklungsgeschichte der Thiere,* I, 207, in Andrea Orsucci, *Dalla biologia cellulare alle scienze dello spirit,* 41.

29. See Andrea Orsucci, *Dalla biologia cellulare alle scienze dello spirito,* 56.

30. Andrea Orsucci, *Dalla biologia cellulare alle scienze dello spirit,* 57.

31. Andrea Orsucci, *Dalla biologia cellulare alle scienze dello spirit,* 56.

32. Adolf Trendelenburg, *Logische Untersuchungen.* 1840, II, 26–27 in Andrea Orsucci, *Dalla biologia cellulare alle scienze dello spirit* 57–58. The reference is to Leibniz. Trendelenburg is one of the first to return to Leibniz around the mid-nineteenth century. See Volker Peckhaus, "Language and Logic in German Post-Hegelian Philosophy," 6.

33. This explains the distance often noted between the Nietzschean description of the pre-Platonic philosophers and the more usual description of them.

34. Curt Paul Janz, *Friedrich Nietzsche. I. Kindheit/Jugend/Die Basler Jahre* (Munich: Hanser, 1978).

35. The fragments from April/May 1868 published in *KGW* I/4 NF 62, p. 548–578] under the title "Philosophische Notizen zur Teleologie" correspond to what is known as *Die Teleologie seit Kant* or *Zur Teleologie.* The first draft on the question of teleologie can be found in *KGW* I/4, NF 58[46] from Autumn 1867–Spring 1868. The complete set of fragments on the question of teleologie reappear under the fragment number 62[1–58], April/May 1868.

36. Nietzsche deals with the problem of identifying logic with metaphysics in *PTA*, referring to Afrikan Spir and his concept of the unconditional, which demonstrates, perhaps, a continuity in the Nietzsche's interests regarding this topic reaching all the way back to 1868 See Sergio Sánchez, *Lógica, verdad y creencia: algunas consideraciones sobre la relación Nietzsche-Spir* (Córdoba: Universias, 2000).

37. As Nietzsche says this occurs with the origin of language, when information passes from one sphere to another, thereby generating a metaphor. See *TL*.

38. With regard to Anaxagoras's identification between the *nous* as cause, an interpretation that differs from Nietzsche's can be seen in the text cited above by Monte Ransom Johnson, *Aristotle on Teleology,* 112.

39. Rudolf Virchow, *Cellular Pathology as Based upon Physiological and Pathological Histology,* trans. Frank Chance (Philadelphia: J.B. Lippincott and Co., 1863), 321–322.

40. Interestingly, this same critical touch expressed in "taking refuge" will be taken up later by Nietzsche when he discusses the metaphysical philosophers—for example, in the section on Parmenides in *PTA*.

41. Virchow, Rudolf, *Cellular Pathology as Based upon Physiological and Pathological Histology*, 274.

42. Johann Wolfgang von Goethe, "Setting Forth a Morphology," in *Goethe on Science: A Selection of Goethe's Writings*, ed. Jeremy Naydler (Edinburgh: Floris, 1997), 47–63.

43. Andrea Orsucci, *Dalla biologia cellulare alle scienze dello spirito*, 66.

44. See Christian Gottfried Ehrenberg, *Die Infusionsthierchen als vollkommene Organismen* (Leipzig: Voss, 1838), 519, in Andrea Orsucci, *Dalla biologia cellulare alle scienze dello spirito*, 72.

45. Andrea Orsucci, *Dalla biologia cellulare alle scienze dello spirito*, 72.

46. See Friedrich Albert Lange, "Darwinism and Teleology," in *The History of Materialism*, Vol. III, trans. Ernest Chester Thomas (London: Kegan Paul, Trench, Trubner & Co, 1925), 37.

47. Georg Henrik von Wright, "Two Traditions," in *Explanation and Understanding* (Cornell, NY: Cornell University Press, 1971), 1–33.

48. Andrea Orsucci, *Dalla biologia cellulare alle scienze dello spirito*, 34.

49. Adolf Trendelenburg, *Logische Untersuchungen*, 22.

5. Nietzsche's Concept of "Necessity" and its Relation to "Laws of Nature"
Herman W. Siemens

1. Concerning references to Nietzsche's works, all emphases are original: underlining designates Nietzsche's own underlining; bolding designates his double-underlinings. Translations are mine, and square brackets are used in quotes for the original German words or interpolations of mine.

2. Forthcoming in *Das Nietzsche-Wörterbuch*, Nietzsche Online (http://www.degruyter.com/view/db/nietzsche). See Paul van Tongeren, Gerd Schank and Herman W. Siemens, eds., *Das Nietzsche-Wörterbuch*, Vol. 1: Abbreviatur—Einfach (Berlin & New York: De Gruyter, 2004).

3. See Jackson Herschbell and Stephen Nimis, "Nietzsche and Heraclitus," *Nietzsche-Studien* 8 (1979): 17–38; Thomas Busch, *Die Affirmation des Chaos. Zur Überwindung des Nihilismus in der Metaphysik Friedrich Nietzsches* (St. Ottilien: EOS Verlag, 1989), 271; Uve Hölscher, "Nietzsche's debt to Heraclitus," in *Classical Influences on European Culture Vol III: 1650—1870*, ed. R.R. Bolgar (Cambridge: Cambridge University Press, 1977), 339–348.

4. E.g., between *Wissenschaft* and early legislators (*KSA* 9:3[71]); between natural scientists and moralists (*D* 428); between knowledge and the organic (*KSA* 11:35[50]). See also *KSA* 9:7[66]; *KSA* 9:7[82]; *KSA* 11:26[36].

5. Or more bluntly: 'Fundamental principle: to be like nature': (*KSA* 11:25[309]). For Christianity as 'Widernatur der Moral' and 'widernatürliche Moral' and his counter-conception of "naturalism in morality," see *TI* "Morality" 4. For the formulation "Naturalismus der Moral" see *KSA* 13:15[5]; *KSA* 13:16[73].

6. For the body: *KSA* 10:7[150]. For the drives: *KSA* 10:7[76]. For conditions for existence: *KSA* 12:10[157]; *KSA* 13:14[158]; *KSA* 13:14[105]). See also: *KSA* 9:4[67]; *KSA* 11:25[460]; *KSA* 11:26[38]; BGE 188; *KSA* 12:9[86].

7. See also *KSA* 9:6[189]; AC 43.

8. See also *KSA* 10:4[99]; *D* 453; *KSA* 9:11[21]; *KSA* 9:11[54]; *KSA* 9:11[220]; *KSA* 11:25[309]; *KSA* 11:27[56].

9. *KSA* 12:9[8].

10. This expression is not used by Nietzsche, who does however write of "*ent*moralisiren" with reference to "the world": *KSA* 10:24[7]; *KSA* 13:16[16]. Also: (*GS* 109) on "[die] Natur zu vernatürlichen" and "Natur ganz entgöttlicht." For aspects of Nietzsche's naturalization of morality, see also: *KSA* 10:4[99]; *D* 453; *KSA* 11:25[309]; *KSA* 11:27[56]; *KSA* 9:11[21].

11. See e.g. *UM* I: 7 (*contra* Strauss): "an honest investigator of nature believes in the unconditional lawfulness of the world without, however, pronouncing anything at all about the ethical or intellectual value of these laws: in such pronouncements he would recognize the highly anthropomorphic behavior of a form of reason that does not hold itself within the limits of what is permissible." (*GS* 373): "an essentially mechanical world would be an essentially *meaningless* (*sinnlose*) world." Also *KSA* 9:7[226]; *KSA* 12:2[31]; see also *HH* 215 on music as the language of feeling or nature.

12. For an analysis of philosophical legislation on the model of taste see: Herman W. Siemens, "Agonal Communities of Taste: Law and Community in Nietzsche's Philosophy of Transvaluation," *Journal of Nietzsche Studies* 24 (2002): 83–112. This relation between philosophy and *Wissenschaft* is central to notebook 19 in *KSA* 7:19[27, 28, 35, 36, 41, 45, 64, 83]. See also: *KSA* 7:23[14]; *KSA* 7:23[45]; *KSA* 7:28[8]. But it is by no means confined to the early Nietzsche: see e.g. *GS* 373; *BGE* 211; *KSA* 11:26[407], *KSA* 11:38[13].

13. See also *BGE* 21, 22; *KSA* 11:23[427]; *KSA* 11:36[18]; *KSA* 11:40[55]; *KSA* 12:2[139]; *KSA* 12:2[142]; *KSA* 13:14[79]. See also *KSA* 9:11[311], [313].

14. On the critique of regularity in nature, see also *KSA* 12:2[142]; *KSA* 13:14[79].

15. *KSA* 11:36[31]. See also: *KSA* 12: 1[30]; *KSA* 12:7[9]; *KSA* 12:7[34]; *BGE* 36; *KSA* 12:2[39]; *KSA* 13:14[79]; and *KSA* 9:11[313].

16. Operational uses of "Gesetz" in the context of knowledge claims regarding nature or life include: with reference to the Will to Power: *KSA* 11:43[2] (see also *KSA* 9:11[21]; *KSA* 11:39[13]; *KSA* 11:25[314]); with reference to the inorganic (*das Unorganische*): *KSA* 11:26[36]; *KSA* 9:11[70] ("die todte Welt"); with reference to the organic (*das Organische*): *KSA* 10:16[76]); *KSA* 11:26[81]. Of particular importance for Nietzsche as a domain of *Gesetz* is physiology: for law and drives (*Triebe*) see *D* 108, 119; *KSA* 12:1[58]; for law and the feeling of pleasure/unpleasure (*Lust-/Unlust-Empfindung*) see *GS* 162; *KSA* 11:25[460]; *KSA* 9:11[334]. Perhaps most striking of all are Nietzsche's affirmative uses of "Gesetz" in the expressions "the law of life" (*Gesetz des Lebens*: *GM*: III, 27; *TI* "Morality" 6; *A* 57; *KSA* 13:14[92]; *KSA* 13:22[23] and the "law of development" or "evolution" (*Gesetz(e) der Entwicklung*: *A* 7; *KSA* 13:11[361]).

17. *KSA* 7:19[237]; *KSA* 7:29[8]. On Nietzsche's etymological thesis that man (*der Mensch*) as the measuring being (*der Messende*) imposes his measure (*Mass*)

on things and interprets the world according to his measure (*Maass*), see Hannes Böhringer, "Nietzsche als Etymologe. Zur Genealogie seiner Wertphilosophie," *Allgemeine Zeitschrift für Philosophie* 7 (1982): 41–57.

18. For the "'laws' of optics" ("'Gesetze' der Optik"): *KSA* 11:26[359]; *KSA* 9:6[441]. For "laws of perception" ("*Empfindungsgesetze*"): *KSA* 7:27[37]; also *GS* 162 ("*perspectivische Gesetz der Empfindung*"). For similar formulations ("Gesetze der menschlichen Empfindung," "Gesetze der Perspektive," "Gesetze dieser höchsten Optik") see *KSA* 7:27[77]; *KSA* 7:29[8]; *KSA* 7:29[12]; *KSA* 9:6[429]; *KSA* 9:6[433]; *KSA* 9:15[9].

19. *Existenzbedingungen*: see *KSA* 11:25[460]; *KSA* 12:6[8].

20. The German terms are: *Formel, Schema, Bild, Chiffrenschrift*. On laws as "formulae" (*Formel*), see: *KSA* 11:38[2]; *KSA* 12:2[142]; *KSA* 12:1[30]; *KSA* 13:14[79]. See also *KSA* 7:19[48]; *D* 121; comparison *D* 243; *KSA* 12:2[139].

21. See *BGE* 21; *KSA* 11:38[2]; *KSA* 11:26[227]; *KSA* 12:7[14]; *KSA* 13:14[79].

22. See Alwin Mittasch, *Friedrich Nietzsche als Naturphilosoph* (Stuttgart: Kröner Verlag, 1952), 27, 91.

23. E.g. *KSA* 11:40[53]; *KSA* 13:14[79]; *BGE* 21, 22.

24. AOM 9; *KSA* 12: 2[142]; *KSA* 13:14[79].

25. "Man soll da, wo etwas gethan werden *muß*, nicht von Gesetz reden, sondern nur da, wo etwas gethan werden *soll*. Gegen die sogenannten Naturgesetze und namentlich die ökonomischen usw" (*KSA* 8:44[6]).

26. The different meanings of "necessity" identified in the course of the paper will henceforth be designated as N1, N2, N3, etc. For quick reference they are listed in the appendix at the end of the paper.

27. Alwin Mittasch, *Friedrich Nietzsche als Naturphilosoph*, 101.

28. Alwin Mittasch, *Friedrich Nietzsche als Naturphilosoph*, 85.

29. See *KSA* 12:1[30]; *KSA* 12:7[9] and *KSA* 12:7[34]; *KSA* 13:14[79]; *KSA* 11:36[31]; *BGE* 36; also *KSA* 11:26[81] for the first formulation of the 'inner' in connection with law.

30. Nietzsche goes on to compare Heraclitus's world-view with the aesthetic human's, who sees in the creation of the art-work "how the conflict of the multiplicity can nonetheless bear law and right within it [. . .] how necessity and play, discord and harmony must couple for the (pro)creation of the art-work" (*wie der Streit der Vielheit doch in sich Gesetz und Recht tragen kann [. . .] wie Nothwendigkeit und Spiel, Widerstreit und Harmonie sich zur Zeugung des Kunstwerkes paaren müssen*). For immanent or absolute lawfulness in Heraclitus, see also *KSA* 7:19[114]; *KSA* 7:21[9]; *KSA* 7:23[35]; *KSA* 8:6[21]; *PTA* 19 for Nietzsche's Heraclitean interpretation of Anaxagoras. Also *KSA* 11:38[12] for a late Heraclitean vision.

31. See Albert Jungmann, *Goethes Naturphilosophie zwischen Spinoza und Nietzsche: Studien zur Entwicklung von Goethes Naturphilosophie bis zur Aufnahme von Kants "Kritik der Urteilskraft"* (Frankfurt am Main: Peter Lang, 1989), 179–182.

32. Jungmann, *Goethes Naturphilosophie zwischen Spinoza und Nietzsche*, 181 (emphasis added).

33. Although it falls outside the scope of this paper, the affinities with Goethe on immanent lawfulness call for research into possible affinities with his concept of necessity or *ananke* as well.

34. Werner Stegmaier, *Nietzsches "Genealogie der Moral"* (Darmstadt: Wissenschaftliche Buchgesellschaft, 1994), 86.

35. On Nietzsche's dynamic, relational concept of force (*Kraft*) and its sources, see: Günter Abel, *Nietzsche: Die Dynamik der Willen zur Macht und die ewige Wiederkehr* (Berlin and New York: De Gruyter, 1984), 6–27; Alwin Mittasch, *Friedrich Nietzsche als Naturphilosoph*, 102–113. On Nietzsche's concept of power (*Macht*), see also Volker Gerhardt, *Vom Willen zur Macht: Anthropologie und Metaphysik der Macht am exemplarischen Fall Friedrich Nietzsches* (Berlin and New York: De Gruyter, 1996), 155–161, 203–245, 285–309.

36. See e.g. *KSA* 12:2[142], where Nietzsche criticizes the concept of "lawfulness" as follows: "That something *always* occurs thus-and-thus [*immer so und so geschieht*] is interpreted here as if a being always acted thus-and-thus as a consequence of an obedience to a law or lawgiver: while it, disregarding the 'law', would have had freedom [*abgesehen vom 'Gesetz', Freiheit hätte*] to act otherwise."

6. Life and Justice in Nietzsche's Conception of History

Vanessa Lemm

1. On the *Entstehungsgeschichte* of Nietzsche's second untimely consideration, see Jörg Salaquarda,"Studien zur Zweiten unzeitgemässen Betrachtung," *Nietzsche-Studien* 13 (1984): 1–45.

2. The importance of self-knowledge is the guiding thread of Catherine Zuckert's reading of Nietzsche's untimely considerations. For Zuckert, self-knowledge culminates in the simultaneous creation of the true individual and the true order, Catherine Zuckert, "Nature, History and the Self: Nietzsche's Untimely Considerations," *Nietzsche-Studien* 5 (1976): 55–82.

3. In a note from the late *Nachlass*, Nietzsche identifies justice as the representative of life where justice is associated with the activities previously related to the monumental, antiquarian and critical mode of history: "The ways of freedom . . . *Justice* as a constructive [*bauende*] [*monumental*] eliminating [*ausscheidende*] [*antiquarian*] destructive [*vernichtende*] [*critical*] way of thought, based on value judgments [*Werthschätzungen*]: *the highest representative of life itself*" (*KSA* 11:25[484]). This note, as is well known, is central to Heidegger's interpretation of justice in Nietzsche as truth, Martin Heidegger, *Holzwege* (Frankfurt am Main: Vittorio Klostermann, 1980) and *Nietzsche*, vols. 1 and 2 (Stuttgart: Verlag Günter Neske, 1998). This note is also in a central position in Bertram's reading of justice in Nietzsche. He seems to have been the first to have commented on this note from the *Nachlass*, Ernst Bertram, *Nietzsche: Attempt at a Mythology* (Urbana and Chicago: University of Illinois Press, 2009). On truth and justice in

Nietzsche and Heidegger, see also the informative articles of Ullrich Haase, "Dike and Justicia, or: Between Heidegger and Nietzsche," *Journal of the British Society for Phenomenology* 38 (2007): 18–36 and "Nietzsche on Truth and Justice," *New Nietzsche Studies* 1/2 8 (2009/2010): 78–97 as well as Vanessa Lemm, "Política o Filosofía: Nietzsche y Heidegger sobre la justicia" in Vanessa Lemm, *Nietzsche y el pensamiento político contemporáneo* (Santiago de Chile: Fondo de cultura económica, 2013), 217–37, available also in English as "Nietzsche and Heidegger on Justice", *Graduate Faculty Philosophy Journal* 34/2 (2013): 439–455.

4. Zuckert argues that although Nietzsche rejects the idea of a natural order, he holds that nature should not be deprived of its normativity (Zuckert, "Nature, History and the Self: Nietzsche's Untimely Considerations," 81).

5. See also in comparison *HH* 64 where justice is understood as a sign of weakness.

6. On the importance of affect in the constitution of justice, see Lars K. Brunn, "Vergessen als der grösste Affekt: Affekt, Vergessen und Gerechtigkeit in *Vom Nutzen und Nachteil der Historie für das Leben*." in *Friedrich Nietzsche - Geschichte, Affekte, Medien*, eds. Renate Rescheke and Volker Gerhardt (Berlin: Akademie Verlag, 2008), 213–220.

7. See in comparison, *HL* 1; *KSA* 8:11[7]; *D* 404.

8. On the tension between action and justice, see also *HL* 2.

9. Interestingly, for Nietzsche, love is not only the link that ties justice to action but also constitutes the unifying bond between justice and truth (*KSA* 10:3[1]214). See also *HH* 291; *KSA* 9:12[75]; *KSA* 10:16[14]; *HH* 629; *HH* 314; *KSA* 10:5[29; *KSA* 9:6[67]; *HH* 55 and *KSA* 12:1[9] where Nietzsche defines justice as a loving comprehension (*liebevolles Begreifen*) an affirming appreciation (*Gutheißen*). On the relation between justice, love, and knowledge see Chiara Piazzesi, "Liebe und Gerechtigkeit. Eine ethik der Erkenntnis," *Nietzsche-Studien* 39 (2010): 352–381.

10. See also *KSA* 7:29[45]; *SE*: 6 (as a motive of the philistine).

11. See also *HL* 6 and *KSA* 7:29[153].

12. See also *D* 111.

13. See also *HL* 8 where Nietzsche claims that justice is an outrage against the blind force of facts and the tyranny of the real. On the inversion of the scientific meaning of objectivity, see also Robert Doran, "Nietzsche: Utility, Aesthetics, History," *Comparative Literature Studies* 36 3 (2000): 324–327.

14. This question is in many ways related to the question of how and on what ground forgetfulness (unhistorical) enables memory (historical). For a treatment of this question see my "Animality, Historicity and Creativity: A Reading of Friedrich Nietzsche's 'Vom Nutzen und Nachtheil der Historie für das Leben'," *Nietzsche-Studien* 36 (2007): 169–200.

15. See also *KSA* 9:6[416].

16. See also in comparison, *GS* 111 and *KSA* 9:6[130].

17. See also *HL* 9 on the idea of a republic of genius founded upon a group of higher human beings.

18. On imitation as a way of becoming inimitable see Lacoue-Labarthe, Philippe, "History and Mimesis," in *Looking After Nietzsche*, ed. Lawrence Rickels (State University of New York: Albany, 1990), 209–231 and Herman W. Siemens, "Agonal Configurations in the *Unzeitgemässe Betrachtungen*. Identiy, Mimesis and the Übertragung of Cultures in Nietzsche's Early Thought," *Nietzsche-Studien* 30 (2001): 80–106.

19. See in comparison also *GS* 297; *GS* 3 ("the eternal injustice of the noble"); *KSA* 8:28[57] (injustice in the work art rests on egoism [*Selbstlust*] and overestimation [*Überschätzung*] on the part of the artist); *GS* 2; *KSA* 10:7[16]; *AOM* 87; *KSA* 8:23[133]; *HH* 353; *AOM* 220.

20. "Die Starke messen die Vergangenheit an sich" (*HL* 5).

21. This appreciation for singularity is also reflected in the correct judgment (*gerechte Urtheil*) of the philosopher who wants to determine anew the value of existence. For this is and has been, according to Nietzsche "the proper task of all great thinkers to be lawgivers as to measure, stamp and weight of things" (*HL* 3). Such a philosopher knows how to make a valuable use of the past and reach a just verdict on the whole fate of man, for he considers the latter not simply by looking at what is shared and common to all (*durchschnittlich*) but by looking at what distinguishes the fate of a singular individual or of a singular people (*SE* 3).

22. See also in comparison: *AOM* 320; *D* 114 (on the justice of judgment); *KSA* 11:38[1] (Thinking as a kind of exercise and act of justice); *GS* 333 and *KSA* 11:26[119].

23. See also *KSA* 5:8[26]; GMD; ST.

24. See in comparison *AOM* 79; *AOM* 149; *HH* 268; *D* 240; *GS* 3. On justice as conditioned by the ability to understand, comprehend, and know, see *BT* 9; *BT* 17; *FEI* V and *KSA* 7:7[101].

25. "Origin of intemperateness [*Herkunft des schlechten Temperaments*].—The lack of just judgment and consistency [*das Ungerechte und Sprunghafte*] in the temperament of many people, the disorderliness [*Unordnung*] and immoderation [*Maasslosigkeit*] that characterizes them, is the ultimate consequence of the countless logical inaccuracies, superficialities, and rash conclusions of which their ancestors were guilty. Temperate people on the other hand, are the descendants of reflective [*überlegsamen*] and unsuperficial races [*gründlichen Geschlechtern*] who set great store by rationality—whether for praiseworthy or evil ends is of no great moment [*kommt nicht so sehr in Betracht*]" (*D* 247). See in comparison also *D* 488; *KSA* 8:27[23]; *KSA* 8:27[37]; *KSA* 10:1[42]; *GS* 99.

26. In other words that one has acquired the right temperament, something which, according to Nietzsche, women typically fail to cultivate. See *HH* 417; *HH* 416; *KSA* 8:22[63]; *HH* 425; *KSA* 11:37[17]; *KSA* 11:26[214]; *KSA* 11:26[215]; *Z* I "The Friend" and *BGE* 232 on the lack of a sense of justice in women.

27. See also *HH* 32 where Nietzsche claims that we are illogical and therefore unjust beings; and *KSA* 8:9[1]; *KSA* 9:4[34]; *KSA* 11:36[10]; *KSA* 10:4[133]; *KSA* 10:7[7]; *KSA* 10:1[32]; *KSA* 10:1[28]; *KSA* 10:6[1].

7. Life, Injustice, and Recurrence

Scott Jenkins

I am grateful to audiences at Diego Portales University and the University of Kansas for helpful comments on earlier drafts of this paper.

1. Here I set aside the question of exactly what sort of value this is. For a discussion of this topic, see John Richardson, *Nietzsche's New Darwinism* (Oxford: Oxford University Press, 2004), 67–132.

2. For a detailed account of the selection of drives see John Richardson, *Nietzsche's New Darwinism.*

3. By an estimation of value I mean any evaluative state, not necessarily an explicit judgment. This is the notion that Nietzsche has in mind when he asserts that "a drive without some kind of knowing evaluation of the worth [*Abschätzung über den Werth*] of its objective, does not exist in man" (*HH* 32).

4. Nadeem Hussain's account of evaluative injustice attributes to Nietzsche the claim that all evaluations of things involve the judgment that those things have value in themselves. See Nadeem Hussain, "Valuing for Nietzsche's Free Spirits," in *Nietzsche and Morality*, eds. Brian Leiter and Neil Sinhababu (Oxford: Oxford University Press, 2007), 162. Here I show only that we can make good sense of Nietzsche's remarks concerning injustice without appealing to this claim. But I take this to be a virtue of my approach because Nietzsche thinks injustice is present in all living beings, even those that lack a notion of the in-itself.

5. This point concerning historical explanation is familiar to any reader of *On the Genealogy of Morals*, but it appears already in Nietzsche's account of the senseless death of Greek tragedy in *BT* 11.

6. Perhaps more accurately, Nietzsche holds that valuation is in no way logical and thus not the sort of thing that can be done in a just manner. It is likely for the sake of shocking the reader that Nietzsche prefers to speak of ineliminable injustice. This is the intended effect of his assertion that knowledge originates in "error" (*GS* 110), or that logic originates in the "illogical" (*GS* 111). In these cases the point is that our standards of knowledge and inference cannot themselves be justified—not that they are contrary to some more basic standards.

7. I prefer to translate "*Ekel*" as "disgust" because disgust, unlike nausea, is clearly an intentional state. This difference is significant because the kind of *Ekel* that interests Nietzsche is not just an unpleasant feeling. It also involves an evaluation of an object. (On this point, I have been influenced by an unpublished paper by Gudrun von Tevenar).

8. Arthur Schopenhauer, *The World as Will and Representation*, vol. 2. (New York: Dover Publications, 1969), 350–351.

9. Arthur Schopenhauer, *The World as Will and Representation*, vol. 1, 312.

10. Arthur Schopenhauer, *The World as Will and Representation*, vol. 2, XLVI.

11. Nietzsche also emphasizes the theme of injustice in *Human, All Too Human* in his 1886 preface to the work (*HH* "Preface"6). In order to show that

Nietzsche retains his commitment to this sort of pessimism through the time he was writing *Z*, I would need to show that it appears in *GS* as well. I do not have the space here to make that argument, but I will note that in Nietzsche's account of Socrates as a pessimist in *GS* 340 he never states that Socrates' pessimism involved an error of any sort. He states only that he wishes Socrates had not expressed his pessimism to others.

12. Robert Gooding-Williams notes that the soothsayer's doctrine also recalls the claim in "Ecclesiastes" 1:9 that there is nothing new under the sun. See Robert Gooding-Williams, *Zarathustra's Dionysian Modernism* (Stanford: Stanford University Press, 2001), 183–268.

13. Here I assume that the doctrine of eternal recurrence is different from the doctrine of the essential injustice of life. This assumption is complicated by Nietzsche's claim, in *HL*, that the past and present are "identical in all that is typical [*typisch gleich*]" and that there exists "a motionless structure of value that cannot alter and a significance that is always the same [*ewig gleicher Bedeutung*]" (*HL* 1). Nietzsche's language anticipates his talk of eternal recurrence (*ewige Wiederkunft*) and the animals' attribution to Zarathustra of the thought "*ich komme ewig wieder zu diesem gleichen und selbigen Leben*" (*Z* III "The Convalescent" 2). To be sure, postulating an immutable structure of life commits one to the thought that there is nothing new under the sun, and that the future will be in this way a recurrence of what has been. But it is necessary to distinguish between the recurrence of particular individuals and the recurrence of the basic structure of life (as Nietzsche does in *HL*). The former notion is the doctrine of eternal recurrence found in *Z*, while the latter underlies the wisdom of the suprahistorical standpoint. Both Alexander Nehamas, *Nietzsche* (Cambridge: Harvard University Press, 1985), 146 and Robert Gooding-Williams, *Zarathustra's Dionysian Modernism*, 204, 251 recognize this general distinction, though their approaches to the broader issues I discuss are quite different. For a discussion of the relation between these two quite different notions of recurrence, see Paul Loeb, "The Thought-Drama of Eternal Recurrence," *The Journal of Nietzsche Studies* 34 (2007): 81.

14. Alexander Nehamas makes just this point. See "The Eternal Recurrence," *The Philosophical Review* 3 89 (1980): 336–337.

15. A passage from Nietzsche's notebooks also suggests this view: "Let us think this thought [of nihilism] in its most terrible form: existence, as it is, without meaning or goal, but inevitably recurring, without any finale into nothingness" (*KSA* 12:5[71]). Paul Loeb provides an insightful account of this passage. See Paul Loeb, "Suicide, Meaning, and Redemption," in *Nietzsche on Time and History*, ed. Manuel Dries (Berlin: De Gruyter, 2008), 161–188, here 181.

16. If the thought that results in Zarathustra's *Ekel* in "The Convalescent" is the thought that the small man recurs eternally, then it would be correct to say that Zarathustra's abysmal thought does involve the eternal recurrence—at least in this particular context. It is important to keep in mind, however, that the

recurrence still serves only to intensify Zarathustra's response to the injustice of life. By itself, the eternal recurrence is no abysmal thought.

17. Laurence Lampert notes the ease with which the animals discuss recurrence and concludes from this that the animals are very well disposed toward themselves and the whole of life. See Laurence Lampert, *Nietzsche's Teaching* (New Haven: Yale University Press, 1986), 220–222. This explanation is correct, but it leaves out the crucial fact that this attitude arises from a lack of wisdom. Life does not fathom itself in the animals (to use Goethe's talk of fathoming—*ergründen*—from the epigraph to *The World as Will and Representation*), and for this reason they see no objection to eternal recurrence. Their contentedness resembles that of the forgetful cattle described in the first section of *HL*.

18. Zarathustra does say that the dwarf could not bear Zarathustra's abysmal thought, which suggests that he's about to hear it (*Z* III "On the Vision and the Riddle" 2). But it is not at all clear that Zarathustra does relate his abysmal thought. After all, the dwarf has no trouble accepting the doctrine of recurrence. Perhaps this means that Nietzsche sees a difference between merely reciting the doctrine of recurrence, as the dwarf does, and really facing up to it. While plausible, I take the merits of this reading to be outweighed by the connections between *Z* and the remarks on injustice in *HL* and *HH*.

8. Heeding the Law of Life: Receptivity, Submission, Hospitality
Daniel Conway
I am grateful to Vanessa Lemm for her instructive comments on an earlier draft of this essay.

1. With the exception of occasional emendations, I rely throughout this essay on Walter Kaufmann's translations of Nietzsche's writings for Random House/Vintage Books. (In the case of his translation of *On the Genealogy of Morals*, Kaufmann enlists and acknowledges the assistance of R.J. Hollingdale).

2. Hatab rightly notes that the term *Schauspiel* calls to mind the theater, and he provides an instructive account of the *tragic* character of the demise of Christian morality and the ascetic ideal, see Lawrence J. Hatab, *Nietzsche's On the Genealogy of Morality: An Introduction* (Cambridge: Cambridge University Press, 2008), 168–171.

3. Nietzsche later reveals that he was the first to attain the "height, a view of distances, a hitherto altogether unheard-of psychological depth and profundity" that allow him to feel "*Christian* morality to be *beneath* him[self]" (*EH* "destiny" 6).

4. Robert B. Pippin, *Nietzsche, Psychology, and First Philosophy* (Chicago: University of Chicago Press, 2010), 4–12.

5. I am indebted here to Paul S. Loeb, "Suicide, Meaning, and Redemption," in *Nietzsche on Time and History*, ed. Manuel Dries (Berlin: De Gruyter, 2008) 170–71; and Paul S. Loeb, *The Death of Nietzsche's Zarathustra* (Cambridge: Cambridge University Press, 2010), 237–40.

6. I develop this interpretation at greater length in my "Life After the Death of God: Thus Spoke Nietzsche," in *The History of Continental Philosophy Volume II: Nineteenth-century Philosophy: Revolutionary Responses to the Existing Order*, eds. Alan D. Schrift and Daniel Conway (London: Acumen Press, 2010) 129–32. See also Robert B. Pippin, *Nietzsche, Psychology, and First Philosophy*, 52–59.

7. Here I follow the translation suggested by Clark and Swensen (*On the Genealogy of Morality*, trans. Maudemarie Clark and Alan J. Swensen [Indianapolis: Hackett, 1998]), 47. Nietzsche's use of the term *Selbstaufhebung* very likely would have put his German readers immediately in mind of Hegel, leading them to anticipate a Hegelian (that is, dialectical) solution to the historical problem posed by the ascetic ideal. His sensitivity to the (unwanted) influence of Hegel is evident in his "review" of *The Birth of Tragedy*, which, sixteen years later, "smells offensively Hegelian" to him (*EH* 1). Translating the main thesis of *The Birth of Tragedy* into mock-Hegelese, Nietzsche offers the following synopsis of his first book: "An 'idea' [*"Idee"*]—the antithesis [*Gegensatz*] of the Dionysian and the Apollinian—translated into the realm of metaphysics; history itself as the development [*Entwicklung*] of this 'idea'; in tragedy this antithesis is sublimated into a unity [*zur Einheit augehoben*]; and in this perspective things that had never before faced each other are suddenly juxtaposed [*gegenüber gestellt*], used to illuminate each other, and comprehended [*begriffen*]—opera, for example, and the revolution" (*EH* 1). As this satirical passage confirms, Nietzsche understood that his readers would recognize the term he uses in *GM* III: 27—*Selbstaufhebung*—as a staple of Hegelian philosophy and jargon.

8. Nietzsche also refers to the "law of life" in *TI* "Morality" 6.

9. See his review of *GM* in *EH*.

10. This paragraph and the next borrow (in revised form) several sentences from my "Life After the Death of God: Thus Spoke Nietzsche," 111.

11. I am indebted here to Aaron Ridley, *Nietzsche's Conscience: Six Character Studies from the "Genealogy"* (Ithaca, N.Y.: Cornell University Press, 1998), 19–20 and Mathias Risse, "The Second Treatise in On the Genealogy of Morality: Nietzsche on the Origin of the Bad Conscience," *European Journal of Philosophy* 1 9 (2001): 57–61.

12. Here I follow the interpretation outlined by Aaron Ridley, *Nietzsche's Conscience*, 98–99.

13. Here I follow David Owen, *Nietzsche's Genealogy of Morality* (Stocksfield: Acumen Publishing, 2007), 129.

14. The possibility of a link between the "sovereign individual" and the "scientific conscience" of Nietzsche and his readers is suggested by Aaron Ridley, *Nietzsche's Conscience*, 16–20.

15. See Loeb, "Suicide, Meaning, and Redemption," 171–74; and Loeb, *The Death of Nietzsche's Zarathustra*, 236–40.

16. Here we recall Nietzsche's observation, toward the close of Essay I, that "today there is perhaps no more decisive mark of a '*higher nature*,' a more spiritual

nature, than that of being divided in this sense [viz., between Rome and Judea] and a genuine battleground of these opposed values" (*GM* I: 16).

17. This section makes use of several paragraphs that originally appeared in Daniel Conway, *Reader's Guide to Nietzsche's On the Genealogy of Morals*, 144–45 and, in revised form, in Daniel Conway, "*Does That Sound Strange to You?: Education and Indirection in Essay III of On the Genealogy of Morals*," in *Nietzsche, Nihilism and the Future of Philosophy*, ed. Jeffrey Metzger (London: Continuum Books, 2009), 96–98.

18. In *GS* 357, from which Nietzsche imports his account of how "the Christian conscience" became the "scientific conscience," Nietzsche attributes to Schopenhauer the "honest and unconditional atheism" that he identifies here as the source of "the only air we breathe, we more spiritual men of this age" (*GM* III:27).

19. Words such as *versuchen*, *Versuch*, and *Versuchung* acquire a heightened importance for Nietzsche in the writings from the post-Zarathustran period of his career. A *Versuch* is an *experiment* or an *attempt*, but it also suggests a *temptation* or *enticement*. Nietzsche called his 1886 Preface to the new edition of *The Birth of Tragedy* "An Attempt at a Self-Criticism" (*Versuch einer Selbstkritik*). He also suggests *Versucher* as a name for the "new species of philosopher" that he sees "coming up" (*BGE* 42). The basic idea here is that a *Versuch* is possible only for those with an excessive health, such that they may survive and capitalize on the violence they direct against themselves.

20. On the possibility and desirability of such a critique, see Christopher Janaway, *Beyond Selflessness: Reading Nietzsche's Genealogy* (Oxford: Oxford University Press, 2007), 229–33.

21. As Janaway puts it, "Nietzsche appears here as the instrument of a process that morality is inflicting upon itself," Cristopher Janaway, *Beyond Selflessness: Reading Nietzsche's Genealogy*, 239.

22. As Aaron Ridley observes, "Thus, when it overcomes itself, the ascetic ideal doesn't merely vacate the playing field, it abolishes it as well" (Aaron Ridley, *Nietzsche's Conscience,* 124). See also David Owen, *Nietzsche's Genealogy of Morality,* 126–29; Cristopher Janaway, *Beyond Selflessness: Reading Nietzsche's Genealogy*, 237–39; Lawrence J. Hatab, *Nietzsche's On the Genealogy of Morality*: *An Introduction*, 166–71; and Paul S. Loeb, *The Death of Nietzsche's Zarathustra*, 234–40.

23. This section makes revised use of several sentences that originally appeared in Daniel Conway, "Does That Sound Strange to You?," 96–98.

24. Nietzsche also claims this role for his "we" in *D* "Preface" 4.

25. That is, they do not yet appreciate that he seeks the "*so-called* 'free spirits,'" whom he describes in *GM* III: 24.

26. In its original context, the passage imported from *GS* 357 is followed by a discussion of how "*Schopenhauer's* question immediately comes to us in a terrifying way: *Has existence* [*Dasein*] *any meaning* [*Sinn*] *at all*?" (*GS* 357).

27. I am indebted here to the interpretation developed by Lawrence J. Hatab, *Nietzsche's On the Genealogy of Morality*: *An Introduction*, 158–64.

28. While some scholars have speculated that Nietzsche recruits his most excitable readers as cannon fodder for his war against morality—see, for example, Stanley Rosen, *The Mask of Enlightenment: Nietzsche's Zarathustra* (Cambridge: Cambridge University Press, 1995), 56–60 and Geoff Waite, *Nietzsche's Corps/e: Aesthetics, Politics, Prophecy, or, the Spectacular Technoculture of Everyday Life* (Durham, NC: Duke University Press, 1996), 275–288—here he intimates that he regards his fellow warriors as neither disposable nor expendable. Of course, this too may be part of his ruse.

29. He does so, to be sure, via a rhetorical question.

30. Initially presented by Nietzsche as prone to "miscount" the "twelve trembling bell-strokes of . . . [their] being," his best readers are presumed here to have matured sufficiently that they may secure meaning [*Sinn*] for their "whole being" (*GM* III: 27).

31. In a telling revelation, Nietzsche allows that his friends are largely blind to the magnitude of his philosophical achievements: "I tell every one of my friends to his face that he has never considered it worthwhile to *study* any of my writings: I infer from the smallest signs that they do not even know what is in them. As for my *Zarathustra*: who among my friends saw more in it than an impermissible but fortunately utterly inconsequential presumption?" (*EH* 4). Unlike his real (but clueless) friends, the "*unknown* friends" for whom he writes will appreciate the urgency and gravity of what he invites them to do in his company.

32. As he explains in *Ecce Homo*, the completion of his *Zarathustra* led him to look around for "those *related* to [him]" (*Verwandten*) (*EH* 1 [emphasis added]), which suggests a degree of intimacy and mutual understanding that his anemic contemporaries would have been unlikely to muster and unable to sustain.

33. I develop this interpretation at greater length in Daniel Conway, "Does That Sound Strange to You?," 85–89. Hatab similarly emphasizes Nietzsche's likely reliance on devices of contention and contestation in overcoming the ascetic ideal, Lawrence J. Hatab, *Nietzsche's On the Genealogy of Morality: An Introduction*, 164–65.

34. See, for example, Lester Hunt, *Nietzsche and the Origin of Virtue* (London: Routledge, 1991), 21–24; Simon May, *Nietzsche's Ethics and His War on 'Morality'* (Oxford: Oxford University Press, 1999), 104–07; Brian Leiter, *Nietzsche on Morality* (London: Routledge, 2002), 161–63; Robert Solomon, *Living With Nietzsche: What the Great "Immoralist" Has to Teach Us* (Oxford: Oxford University Press, 2003), 124–128; Owen, *Nietzsche's Genealogy of Morality*, 69–73; Hatab, *Nietzsche's On the Genealogy of Morality: An Introduction*, 233–342.

35. See, for example, Lester Hunt, *Nietzsche and the Origin of Virtue*, 145–53.

36. Here I rely on, and generalize from, Loeb's interpretation of the dying Zarathustra, Paul S. Loeb, *The Death of Nietzsche's Zarathustra*, 76–81.

37. May helpfully observes that Nietzsche "wishes to be *more* truthful about the value of truth (to life-enhancement) than is the tradition that claims to value

it unconditionally" Simon May, *Nietzsche's Ethics and His War on 'Morality,'* 137; see also pages 177–182.

38. Young may be making a similar point when he remarks that "in the *Genealogy*, in sum, Nietzsche remains a communitarian," Julian Young, *Nietzsche's Philosophy of Religion* (Cambridge: Cambridge University Press, 2006), 155.

39. See also Paul S. Loeb, *The Death of Nietzsche's* Zarathustra, 226–34.

40. Leiter draws attention to this element of Nietzsche's critical project, Brian Leiter, *Nietzsche on Morality*, 159–161 and 180–181.

9. Toward the Body of the Overman

Debra Bergoffen

1. *Thus Spake Zarathustra*, trans. James Birx and Thomas Common (New York: Prometheus Books, 1993), 26.

2. Walter Kaufmann, *The Portable Nietzsche* (New York: Penguin Books, 1976), 115.

3. *Thus Spoke Zarathustra: A Book for Everyone and Nobody*, Graham Parkes, trans. (New York: Oxford, 2005).

4. *Thus Spake Zarathustra*, trans. James Birx and Thomas Common, 279.

5. Vanessa Lemm, "The Overhuman Animal," in *A Nietzschean Bestiary: Becoming Animal Beyond Docile and Brutal*, eds. Christa. D. Acampora and Ralph Acampora (New York: Roman and Littlefield, 2004), 220.

6. Vanessa Lemm, "The Overhuman Animal," 225.

7. Jeniffer Ham, "Circe's Truth: On the Way to Animals and Women," in *A Nietzschean Bestiary: Becoming Animal Beyond Docile and Brutal*, eds. Christa. D. Acampora and Ralph Acampora (New York: Roman and Littlefield, 2004), 194.

8. Simone de Beauvoir, *The Second Sex*, trans. Shelia Malovany-Chevallier and Constance Borde (New York: Alfred A. Knopf, 2009), 532.

9. Simone de *Beauvoir, The Second Sex*, 532.

10. Luce Irigaray, *Je, Tous, Nous: Toward a Culture of Difference*, trans. Alison Martin (New York: Routledge, 1993), 39.

11. Luce Irigaray, *Je, Tous, Nous: Toward a Culture of Difference,* 39.

12. Luce Irigaray, *Je, Tous, Nous: Toward a Culture of Difference,* 41.

13. Luce Irigaray, *I love to you: Sketch for a Felicity Within History* (New York, Routledge, 1996), 26.

14. Luce Irigaray, *Speculum of the Other Woman*, 183.

15. Luce Irigaray, *Speculum of the Other Woman*, 183.

16. Julia Kristeva, "Stabat Mater," in *Tales of Love* (New York: Columbia University Press, 1987), 183.

17. Julia Kristeva, "Stabat Mater," 183.

18. Julia Kristeva, "Motherhood According to Bellini," in *The Portable Kristeva*, ed. Kelly Oliver (New York: Columbia University Press, 1997), 301.

19. Julia Kristeva, "Motherhood According to Bellini," 301.

20. Robert Gooding-Williams, *Zarathustra's Dionysian Modernism* (Stanford, Stanford University Press, 2001), 121.

21. Robert Gooding-Williams, *Zarathustra's Dionysian Modernism*, 117.

22. Alan D. Schrift, "Foucault and Derrida on Nietzsche and the End(s) of 'Man,'" in *Exceedingly Nietzsche: Aspects of Contemporary Nietzsche-Interpretation*, eds. David Farrell Krell and David Wood (New York: Routledge, 1988), 144.

23. Jean Graybeal, "Ecco Homo: Abjection and 'the Feminine,'" in *Feminist Interpretations of Friedrich Nietzsche*, eds. Kelly Oliver and Marilyn Pearsall (University Park: The Pennsylvania State University Press, 1998), 162.

24. Jean Graybeal, "Ecco Homo: Abjection and 'the Feminine,'" 161.

25. Jean Graybeal, "Ecco Homo: Abjection and 'the Feminine,'" 161.

26. Luce Irigaray, *Marine Lover of Friedrich Nietzsche* (New York, Columbia University Press, 1991), 14.

27. Luce Irigaray, *Marine Lover of Friedrich Nietzsche*, 15.

28. Luce Irigaray, *Marine Lover of Friedrich Nietzsche*, 26.

29. Luce Irigaray, *Marine Lover of Friedrich Nietzsche*, 39.

30. Luce Irigaray, *Marine Lover of Friedrich Nietzsche*, 40.

10. Nietzsche's Synaesthetic Epistemology and the Restitution of the Holistic Human

Rainer J. Hanshe

1. Empedocles, *The Poem of Empedocles* (Toronto: University of Toronto Press, 1992), 105.

2. Michel Serres, *Angels: A Modern Myth* (Paris: Flammarion, 1995), 71.

3. There are only two studies devoted strictly to synaesthesia in Nietzsche's thought: Diana Behler, "Synaesthesia in Nietzsche's *Die Geburt der Tragödie* and Its Correlation to French and Russian Symbolism," *Carrefour de Cultures,* ed. Régis Antoine (Tübingen: Narr, 1993), 169–80; and Clive Cazeaux, "Sound and Synaesthesia in Nietzsche and Merleau-Ponty," *Proceedings of the Sound Practice Conference* (Dartington: Dartington College of Arts, 2001): 35–40. The former article focuses only on *BT* and suffers from a myopic understanding of the phenomenon, if not of Nietzsche; the latter, while brief and concerned strictly with *TL*, is still a rich and suggestive article, but Merleau-Ponty receives the lion's share of its focus. Though not referring to it as such, Sarah Kofman briefly addresses the concept (the first consideration of the topic to my knowledge) in her *Nietzsche et la métaphore* (Paris: Bibliothèque scientifique, 1972), while Babette Babich mentions it in one passage of her *Words in Blood, Like Flowers* (New York: State University of New York Press, 2006), 39. Hence, this essay is the first extensive overview of the synaesthetic aspect of Nietzsche's thought.

4. The two basic perspectives regarding the senses: (1) there are five senses that function independently; and (2) there is *one* sense organ with five *suborgans*. See Heinz Werner, "Unity of the Senses," in *Developmental Processes: Heinz Werner's Selected Writings*, Vol. 1, eds. Sybil S. Barten and Margery B. Franklin (New York: International Universities Press, 1978), 153–167.

5. One might add, *more noses* et al. too, especially when recalling Nietzsche's assertion that his "genius is in his nostrils!" (*EH* "Destiny" 1). On the use of the

term "perspectivalism" versus "perspectivism," see Babette E. Babich, *Nietzsche's Philosophy of Science: Reflecting Science on the Ground of Art and Life* (New York: State University of New York Press, 1994), 46–49.

6. Democritus, *The Atomists: Leucippus and Democritus: Fragments*, trans. and ed. by Christopher C.W. Taylor (Toronto: University of Toronto Press, 2010), 13 (frag. 125).

7. Lucretius, *De rerum natura*, trans. David R. Slavitt (Berkeley: University of California Press, 2008), 699–700.

8. Jonathan Barnes, *The Presocratic Philosophers* (London: Routledge, 1982), 248.

9. Jonathan Barnes, *The Presocratic Philosophers*, 248.

10. Heraclitus, *Fragments* (Toronto: University of Toronto Press, 1991), 55.

11. Heraclitus, *Fragments*, 101.

12. Heraclitus, *Fragments*, 107.

13. Gregory Vlastos, *Studies in Greek Philosophy: Volume I: The Presocratics*, Daniel W. Graham, ed. (Princeton: Princeton University Press, 1995), 156. In *Thus Spoke Zarathustra*, Nietzsche views the "professors of virtue" as equally somnambulistic figures, a condition due specifically to their type of virtue as opposed to Zarathustra's, which is a wide awake type of virtue. For an examination of this and its relation to the praxis of incubation, see Rainer J. Hanshe, "Zarathustra's Stillness: Dreaming and the Art of Incubation" in *Nietzsche's Therapeutic Teaching: For Individuals and Culture*, eds. Horst Hutter and Eli Friedland (London and New York: Bloomsbury, 2013), 141–156.

14. Simon Trépanier, *Empedocles: An Interpretation* (London: Routledge, 2004), 56.

15. Empedocles, *The Poem of Empedocles* (Toronto: University of Toronto Press, 1992), 77.

16. Simon Trépanier, *Empedocles: An Interpretation*, 56.

17. Jonathan Barnes, *Early Greek Philosophy* (London: Penguin Classics, 2001), 118.

18. Simon Trépanier, *Empedocles: An Interpretation*, 213.

19. Gregory Vlastos, *Studies in Greek Philosophy*, 157.

20. Peter Kingsley, *Reality* (Inverness: Golden Sufi Center, 2003), 514.

21. There may be some correlation between this and Ansell-Pearson's description of "superior" empiricism as that "in which we go beyond a synthesis of points within the field of appearance and attempt to discover the 'real articulation and individuality of things.'" See Keith Ansell-Pearson, *Philosophy and the Adventure of the Virtual* (London: Routledge, 2002), 121, and further, 12, 38, 139, 170.

22. See Kevin T. Dann, *Bright Colors Falsely Seen: Synaesthesia and the Search for Transcendental Knowledge* (New Heaven: Yale University Press, 1998), 20.

23. Jonathan Barnes, *Early Greek Philosophy*, xli.

24. If Nietzsche's view of Parmenides is a distortion, which some scholars argue, thinkers such as Sextus Empiricus had the same view, which is to say, this

is how Parmenides was interpreted by a large number of people: "Parmenides rejected opinionative reason [. . .] and assumed as criterion the cognitive—that is, the inerrant—reason, as he gave up belief in the senses." See *Sextus Empiricus: Against the Logicians*, Vol. 2, trans. Robert G. Bury (Cambridge: Harvard University Press, 1949), 57.

25. It is instructive to recall that not only did Nietzsche "write" while on vigorous walks, later transcribing into notebooks what he thought during those peripatetic moments, he also often *recited* his aphorisms aloud to amanuenses and had books read to him. Thus, reading and writing for him always had an auditory or oral dimension. Cf. *BGE* 246, 247.

26. For another passage on the coarsening or obstruction of the senses see *TL* 1.

27. See the "Preface to *Lyrical Ballads* (1802)," in *The Major Works*, William Wordsworth (Oxford: Oxford University Press, 2000), 599.

28. The German for brain-ventricles is *Hirnkammern*, a neologism Nietzsche created specifically to convey the idea of a brain possessing chambers as if it were also a heart.

29. For the evolution of the ear, see *D* 250.

30. On the "godlike feeling" Nietzsche calls true humaneness, see *GS* 337. This extraordinary and profound aphorism advances a conception of compassion that far supersedes the Christian notion of pity. What could be more sublimely thoughtful and magnanimous than the "godlike feeling" Nietzsche calls humaneness?

31. For a contemporary example, the Turkish painter Esref Armagan, who was born blind, asserts that he can see with his fingers: http://www.youtube.com/watch?v=8QUOy83po60.

32. For similar warnings, but from a poetic context, see "Au Lecteur (1857)," in Charles Baudelaire, *The Flowers of Evil* (New York: New Directions, 1989), 3, and the first canto in Comte de Lautréamont, "Les Chants de Maldoror (1869)," in *Maldoror and the Complete Works of the Comte de Lautréamont*, trans. Alexis Lykiard (Cambridge: Exact Change, 1994), 27–28.

33. Ernst Bertram, *Nietzsche: Attempt at a Mythology* (Illinois: University of Illinois Press, 2009), 300.

34. Ernst Bertram, *Nietzsche: Attempt at a Mythology*, 300.

35. Hofmannsthal may have Empedocles' notion in mind, too, or Nietzsche's, when he has Chandos state in his letter to Lord Bacon that "we could enter into a new, momentous relationship with all of existence if we began to think with our hearts." See "A Letter" in Hugo von Hofmannsthal, *The Lord Chandos Letter and Other Writings* (New York: NYRB Classics, 2005), 125.

36. See *BGE* 14 for a similar passage on the senses and the difference between the strength of the senses of those in Plato's time, or just of Plato himself, versus the degree of strength of the senses of those in Nietzsche's day and age, if not surely our own.

37. Greta Berman, "Synesthesia and the Arts," *Leonardo*, Vol. 1, No. 32 (1999): 15.

38. Cretien van Campen, *The Hidden Sense: Synesthesia in Art and Science* (Cambridge: MIT Press, 2008), 100.

39. Greta Berman, "Synesthesia and the Arts," 16.

40. Greta Berman, "Synesthesia and the Arts," 16.

41. See *BGE* 14 for another passage on exercising mastery of the senses. Also, for Kant, sense perception is passive whereas for Nietzsche, or in synaesthetic perception, it certainly is not.

42. Think here of Nietzsche's statement that "truths are illusions that we have forgotten are illusions; they are metaphors that have become worn out and have been drained of sensuous force" (*TL* 1).

43. Consider this similar passage: "I understand; I'll open my ears again (oh! oh! oh! and *close* my nose). Now I can really hear what they have been saying all along" (*GM* I: 14).

44. During that synaesthetic episode, Zarathustra learns from Life of the will to power; with that specific knowledge, he will "go on to solve the riddle" of the *hearts* of his disciples.

45. In *HH* II, Nietzsche speaks of words having odors: "Every word has its odor: there exists a harmony and disharmony of odors thus of words" (*WS* 119).

46. For another instance of being seen by objects, see Edward Casey, *The World at a Glance* (Bloomington: Indiana University Press, 2007), 29, *passim*. Casey speaks of objects witnessing us, of the sensation of feeling as if objects that we glance at are actually also glancing at us.

47. Zarathustra is also referred to as a roaring stream (*Z* II "The Child with the Mirror") and as a forest and a night of dark trees (*Z* II "The Dancing Song"). Also, earlier in the book, his "I" teaches him the new pride of carrying an *earthen* head that creates a sense for the earth (*Z* I "On Believers in a World Behind").

48. For a passage on how human endeavors have color, see *HH* 150, and for one on how significance has an odor, see *HH* 217.

49. In *Daybreak*, Nietzsche states that it is not the senses that deceive us, but *the habits* of our senses that weave us "into lies and deception of sensation: these again are the basis of all our judgments and 'knowledge'—there is absolutely no escape, no backway or bypath into the *real world!*" (*D* 117).

50. One can think here too of Nietzsche's discussion of the monumental column of Memnon which, when struck by sunlight, was said to produce a musical tone (*BT* 9). Cox claims that, "wary of the attempt to reduce sound to sight," when discussing Chladni and his sand figures, "Nietzsche insists that the visual and the auditory constitute separate spheres and that the relationship between the two can only ever be a matter of translation or metaphor." In my view, Cox misconstrues the passage on Chladni in *TL* and is incorrect about the crossing of senses as being only a matter of translation or metaphor, as the above passage should make quite clear. If language cannot fully convey "reality" or what one experiences, synaesthesia or the crossing of senses is not a matter of reducing one sense to another; instead, it is an *expansion* or *intensification* of our perceptual abilities.

See Christopher Cox, "Lost in Translation: Sound in the Discourse of Synaesthesia," *Art Forum International* (October 2005): 236–241.

51. For further related material, see the chapter on Heraclitus (PPP 60–63).

52. Peter Kingsley, *Reality*, 513.

53. See *UM* 9 for an earlier passage on the spiritualization of the senses.

54. Jill Marsden, "Sensing the Overhuman," *The Journal of Nietzsche Studies* 30 (2005): 114.

55. For an illuminating essay on the "great reason of the body," see Volker Gerhardt, "The Body, the Self, and the Ego," in *A Companion to Nietzsche*, ed. Keith Ansell-Pearson (Oxford: Blackwell Publishing, 2006), 273–296. See also Wayne Klein, *Nietzsche and the Promise of Philosophy* (New York: State University of New York Press, 1997), in particular 89–95.

56. Jill Marsden, "Sensing the Overhuman," 106.

57. Jill Marsden, "Sensing the Overhuman," 107.

58. Jill Marsden, "Sensing the Overhuman," 109.

59. Peter Kingsley, *Reality*, 523.

60. On the relation between breath and words as understood by the ancient Greeks, see the chapter "Archilochos at the Edge," in Anne Carson, *Eros the Bittersweet* (New York: Dalkey Archive Press, 1998), especially 48–50.

61. Peter Kingsley, *Reality*, 551.

62. Lampert refers to Empedocles only once and it is in a marginal footnote. See his *Nietzsche's Teaching* (Connecticut: Yale University Press, 1989), 319. Seung refers to Empedocles only twice in his book but does not address the similar use of agricultural metaphors either. See T.K. Seung, *Nietzsche's Epic of the Soul* (Lanham: Lexington Books, 2005), 88, 92. Although the relation between Empedocles and Zarathustra has been explored by numerous scholars (Janz, Krell, Babich, etc.), to my knowledge, no scholar has outlined this very specific correlation, which is illuminating and certainly significant.

63. Deane Juhan, *Job's Body: A Handbook for Bodywork* (New York: Station Hill Press, 2003), 43.

64. Peter Kingsley, *Reality*, 513.

65. Peter Kingsley, *Reality*, 513.

66. While in *Zarathustra* an uncanny *voice* functions as a curative tonic for the *sightless*, in the *Anti-Christ*, Nietzsche declares that his "voice reaches even the hard-of-hearing" (*A* 50) and that he "can write in letters which make even the blind see" (*A* 62). For an insightful analysis of these abilities, see "The Text as Graffito: Historical Semiotics (*The Antichrist*)" in Gary Shapiro's *Nietzschean Narratives* (Bloomington: Indiana University Press, 1989), 124–141.

67. As Empedocles illustrates, there is a deep philosophical import to synaesthesia and what one can acquire through it, which Kingsley discusses in this interview (see segment 15:00–17:31): http://www.youtube.com/watch?v=Ow-_G26lpOk. Last accessed on April 24, 2010.

68. According to neuroscientific research, all infants experience different modes of synaesthesia in the first several months of their lives. Thus, the condition

is considered "normal" and a stage of sensory development. See Daphne Maurer, "Neonatal Synaesthesia," in *Synaesthesia: Classic and Contemporary Readings*, eds. Simon Baron-Cohen & J.E. Harrison (Oxford: Blackwell Publishers, 1997), 182–207.

69. This is not to suggest that one cannot grasp Nietzsche's ideas unless one is synaesthetic, for one clearly can, but if the transfiguration of the human that Nietzsche seeks to instigate is to occur, it seems necessary to approach his *felt* texts in a more holistic manner, that is, synaesthetically.

11. Nietzsche's Naturalist Morality of Breeding: A Critique of Eugenics as Taming
Donovan Miyasaki

1. Although most commentators agree that Nietzsche endorses breeding, Julian Young, *Nietzsche's Philosophy of Religion* (Cambridge: Cambridge University Press, 2006), 168 and Thomas Brobjer, "The Absence of Political Ideals in Nietzsche's Writings: The Case of the Laws of Manu and the Associated Caste-Society," *Nietzsche-Studien* 27 (1999): 304, suggest that Nietzsche is critical of breeding, particularly in his discussion of the laws of Manu, while Vanessa Lemm argues that he is opposed to both breeding and taming as forms of civilization as opposed to culture, Vanessa Lemm, *Nietzsche's Animal Philosophy: Culture, Politics, and the Animality of the Human Being* (New York: Fordham University Press, 2009), 12 and 164. While it is true that Nietzsche does not fully endorse the laws of Manu, I believe it is a mistake to interpret his opposition to this individual example as opposition to breeding as such. Although Nietzsche does not explicitly endorse the morality of breeding in his contrast of breeding and taming, his commitment to a morality of this form is clearly implied by his repeated, consistently positive, use of *Züchtung* and *züchten* to indicate the positive task of future philosophers. See, for example, *A* 3: "The problem I raise here is . . . what type of human one ought to breed (*züchten*)"; *BGE* 61: "The philosopher as *we* understand him, we free spirits—as the man of the most comprehensive responsibility who has the conscience for the overall development of man kind . . . will make use of religions for his project of cultivation and education work (*Züchtungs- und Erziehungswerke*)"; and *BGE* 62: "one always pays dearly . . . when religions do not want to be a means of education and cultivation (*Züchtungs- und Erziehungsmittel*) in the philosopher's hand."

2. There is a wide consensus on at least one issue: if Nietzsche's notion of breeding is comparable to eugenics, it is certainly not aimed at racial purity, nor does it rely on race as a criterion of selection. See, for example, Jacqueline Scott "On the Use and Abuse of Race in Philosophy: Nietzsche, Jews, and Race," in *Race and Racism in Continental Philosophy*, eds. Robert Bernasconi and Sybol Cook (Bloomington: Indiana University Press, 2003), 53–73 and "The Price of the Ticket: A Genealogy and Revaluation of Race," in *Critical Affinities: Nietzsche and African American Thought*, eds. Jacqueline Scott and A. Todd Franklin (Albany: State University of New York Press, 2006), 149–173; Jacob Golomb and

Robert Wistrich, eds., *Nietzsche, Godfather of Fascism?* (Princeton: Princeton University Press, 2002); Gerd Schank, *"Rasse" und "Züchtung" bei Nietzsche* (Berlin: Walter de Gruyter, 2000) and "Nietzsche's 'Blond Beast': on the Recuperation of the Nietzschean Metaphor," in *A Nietzschean Bestiary: Becoming Animal Beyond Docile and Brutal*, eds. Christa Davis Acampora and Ralph Acampora (Oxford: Rowman and Littlefield, 2004), 140–155; Richard Schacht, *Nietzsche* (London: Routledge, 1983); Detlef Brennecke, "Die Blonde Bestie. Vom Missverständis eines Schlagworts," *Nietzsche-Studien* 5: (1976): 113–145; and Walter Kaufmann, *Nietzsche: Philosopher, Psychologist, Antichrist* (Princeton: Princeton University Press, 1968). For a detailed history of the misappropriation of Nietzsche by British racial eugenicists, see Dan Stone, *Breeding Superman: Nietzsche, Race, and Eugenics in Edwardian and Interwar Britain* (Liverpool: Liverpool University Press, 2005). Note that the author approaches the topic as a strict history of influence and does not address the question of correct interpretation of Nietzsche's work in this historical lineage.

3. For a contrary view, see Walter Kaufmann, *Nietzsche*, 304–306, who strongly downplays the biological in his commentary, frequently translating *Züchtung* as "cultivation" to emphasize this.

4. Contrast Ofelia Schutte, who emphasizes Nietzsche's literal usage, often relying on the *Nachlass*, which differs from the published writings in its greater focus on biological forms of breeding. See Ofelia Schutte, *Beyond Nihilism: Nietzsche Without Masks* (Chicago: University of Chicago, 1984).

5. English translations of Nietzsche's work are by Walter Kaufmann, *The Gay Science* (New York: Random House, 1974); *Thus Spoke Zarathustra* (New York: Viking Press, 1954); *Beyond Good and Evil* (New York: Random House, 1966); *On the Genealogy of Morals* (New York: Random House, 1967); *Ecce Homo* (London: Penguin Books, 1979) and R. J. Hollingdale, *Twilight of the Idols and the Anti-Christ* (London: Penguin Books, 1968).

6. As Bruce Detwiler has pointed out, this cultural aspect is consistent with many primary senses of the language of *Züchtung* since, in German as in English, "well-bred" refers to culture rather than nature, Bruce Detwiler, *Nietzsche and the Politics of Aristocratic Radicalism* (Chicago: University of Chicago Press, 1990), 111. Kristen Brown also notes that many words that are derivative of *Züchten* refer to concepts related to discipline and punishment, such as *Zucht* (discipline), *züchtig* (modest), *züchtigen* (to beat or flog) and *Züchthaus* (prison), Kristen Brown, *Nietzsche and Embodiment: Discerning Bodies and Non-Dualism* (Albany: State University of New York Press, 2006), 33.

7. Although there are many apolitical and liberal interpretations of Nietzsche's views, some commentators on the topic of breeding think Nietzsche endorses the use of political institutions as means. See, for example, Detwiler, *Nietzsche and the Politics of Aristocratic Radicalism*, 111 and Tracy B. Strong, *Friedrich Nietzsche and the Politics of Transfiguration* (Urbana: University of Illinois Press, 1975), 289. There is some textual support for this interpretation; however, it is often found in unpublished notes that cannot be viewed as Nietzsche's definitive views. While

there is also some support in the published writings, the majority of the relevant passages can be interpreted in a way that avoids any political commitment. Richardson points out, for example, that when Nietzsche speaks of a ruling philosophical elite, he need not mean a political one: "It might guide society merely by persuading the other members: perhaps only by teaching them their basic values," John Richardson, *Nietzsche's System* (Oxford: Oxford University Press, 1996), 177. Shaw argues that Nietzsche is strongly critical of the "predatory state" and explicitly endorses only ideological, not political, manipulation, Tamsin Shaw, *Nietzsche's Political Skepticism* (Princeton: Princeton University Press, 2007), 32–35 and 107. See also Julian Young, *Nietzsche's Philosophy of Religion*, 163.

8. As Kaufmann points out, Nietzsche sometimes describes Judeo-Christian morality as a form of breeding in this broader sense (Kaufmann, *Nietzsche*, 313)—for example, when he says that through Christian morality a "smaller, almost ridiculous type, a herd animal, something eager to please, sickly, and mediocre has been bred (*herangezüchtet ist*)" (*BGE* 62).

9. We might also distinguish these two different senses of "breeding" according to whether they refer to an end or means of moral improvement. The broader sense, which includes Judeo-Christian morality, is characterized by non-moral, non-voluntary *methods* of producing human types, such as sexual selection and cultural training, in distinction from moral education's emphasis upon rational reflection, understanding, and choice. In contrast, the narrower sense of breeding is distinguished according to its *ends*—the types that it seeks to breed. Breeding in this narrow sense uses non-moral, non-voluntary means to produce authentic types characterized by positive traits and abilities, in contrast to taming which, as I explain in more detail below, has as its aim the production of false types characterized by negative traits, a "counter-breeding" or "un-breeding" in the term's narrower sense. This distinction allows us to make sense of Nietzsche's consistently positive use of the language of breeding in his comments about the task of future philosophers (see footnote 1), while also recognizing Nietzsche's occasional critical remarks about breeding, for example, in his discussion of the laws of Manu (*TI* "Improvers" 3–5). I interpret his criticism of the laws of Manu as a rejection of two ends: first, that of the promotion of a priestly, ascetic type as moral ideal and, second, that of the active destruction of the Chandala—a case that, like Christianity, disguises a counter-breeding, a negation of traits and types through the intentional production of sickness and weakness (*TI* "Improvers" 3) as authentic breeding or the production of positive traits and types. Nietzsche's rejection of both *ends* is consistent with the endorsement of "breeding" as *means*: the non-voluntary production of types through sexual selection and social training.

10. For a starkly contrasting view, see Keith Ansell-Pearson, "On the Miscarriage of Life and the Future of the Human: Thinking Beyond the Human Condition with Nietzsche," *Nietzsche-Studien* 29 (2000): 153–177, who interprets breeding as an attempt to "put an end to Darwinian evolution" (171). Ansell-Pearson rightly suggests that the task of culture is to establish "conditions that are

favorable to the appearance of the unique, singular, and the incomparable" (Keith Ansell-Pearson, "Miscarriage," 171). However, he mistakenly sees this task as directly opposed to the natural order, in which "it is the weak and mediocre that prevail in the actual course of evolution" (Keith Ansell-Pearson, "Miscarriage," 162). This excessively teleological interpretation of natural selection as heavily favoring mediocrity is questionable (indeed, Nietzsche's critique of morality would be rather pointless if it is evolution that is the primary cause of human decline), and it is far from evident that either Darwin or Nietzsche must accept it. But even granting it, Ansell-Pearson's view overlooks the fact that the relative prevalence of the mediocre is entirely compatible with the promotion of the relative frequency and duration of "higher" types, so breeding still need not be directly opposed to natural selection.

11. Consequently, a "naturalist morality" does not abstractly affirm nature by refusing to select, simply accepting the accidental products of natural selection. And, consequently, breeding should not be interpreted in contrast to the natural—as, say, a form of "playing God" or as an "unnatural" intervention into natural processes. Although breeding rejects the accidental quality of natural selection, Nietzsche believes moral selection can be performed in a way consistent with, or opposed to, a basic affirmation of the natural world. In this respect, I disagree with Richardson's suggestion that in breeding "we take a new kind of control . . . *away* from natural and social selection" or that breeding amounts to "redesigning" our drives and purposes, John Richardson, *Nietzsche's New Darwinism* (Oxford: Oxford University Press, 2004), 195. As part of my claim that Nietzschean breeding is not a form of eugenics, I will argue that it selects from among, and preserves, naturally selected forms. It does not "redesign," because it protects given forms, rather than producing new ones or actively eliminating existing ones.

12. While it might be thought that natural selection, which depends principally upon extinction for the development of species, is a de-selection and breeding out of traits, this is misleading because natural selection, as accidental adaptive advantage, actively preserves well-adapted traits from extinction, rather than, as taming does, actively eliminating maladapted ones. Put another way, survival of the adapted is a necessary consequence of natural selection, extinction of the maladapted an accidental one.

13. Peter Sloterdijk rightly emphasizes this fact: Nietzschean breeding is not to be opposed to conventional morality as an alternative means of human improvement, but as a counter-breeding, the overturning of a *previous* project of breeding: "From Zarathustra's perspective, modern men are primarily profitable breeders who have made out of wild men the Last Men. It is clear that this could not be done with humanistic education alone," Peter Sloterdijk, "Rules for the Human Zoo: A Response to the *Letter on Humanism*," *Environment and Planning D: Society and Space* 27 (2009): 22. However, like Ansell-Pearson, Sloterdijk also questionably conceives of this project as one that aims "beyond" the human in a substantial sense that suggests a project against natural selection: "This is the root

of the basic conflict Nietzsche postulates for the future: the battle between those who wish to breed for minimization and those who wish to breed for maximization of human function, or, as we might say, a battle between humanists and superhumanists" (Peter Sloterdijk, "Rules for the Human Zoo," 22). Even if we assume—and it is a questionable assumption, given Nietzsche's suspicions about the "improvers of mankind"—that Nietzsche's conception of the "overman" is intended as an ideal to be actualized through the morality of breeding, the "human, all too human" to which Nietzsche's overman is opposed may be better understood, not as the natural category of the "human" and the natural development from which it originates, but rather as one specific conception and moral ideal of humanity—namely, the anti-natural, false conception of human nature that underlies the Christian moral tradition. The project of breeding overcomes only a false interpretation of humanity: "to translate man back again into nature; to master the many vain and fanciful interpretations and secondary meanings which have hitherto been scribbled and daubed over the eternal original text, homo natura" (*BGE* 230). Nietzsche may, then, in one sense, be considered a "humanist"—provided our conception of "humanity" is one continuous with the natural—unlike the traditional one that divorces humanity from the natural world with its metaphysics of the soul and the will, but also unlike the "superhumanist" one that allows humanity to conduct a process of breeding independently of and against natural selection, a divorce of humanity and nature that we might suspect also disguises an unacknowledged metaphysical foundation for that divide. My view, which I expand upon below, is that Nietzsche's notion of breeding is compatible with the rejection of "improvement" precisely because it seeks, not to realize and enhance an alternative ideal or type, but instead to preserve naturally occurring higher types from the active de-selection of the morality of taming. Nietzschean breeding maximizes not "human function" but the diversity of human types and, with that diversity, the frequency and success of "well-turned out" types.

14. This does not mean, of course, that disability is necessarily a bad thing. If there are intrinsically bad abilities, then a morality that disables may be beneficial or justified. Similarly, if some disabilities have concomitant benefits that equal or exceed any benefits lost, then intentionally allowing or causing some disabilities may be morally justifiable.

15. For this reason, I disagree with those commentators who characterize breeding as a positive imposition of form and order into animal life, a direct enhancement, rather than the preservation of natural enhancements. See, for example, Vanessa Lemm, *Nietzsche's Animal Philosophy*, 12 and 139 and Ralph Acampora, *Corporeal Compassion: Animal Ethics and the Philosophy of the Body* (Pittsburgh: University of Pittsburgh Press, 2006), 68. I argue below that taming is effected through the elimination of traits: a removal of form rather than the production of types. Consequently, breeding, as a counter to taming, does not actively create alternate types, but instead protects the diversity of natural forms from the destructive effects of taming. This is its decisive difference from eugen-

ics, which actively enhances positive traits or actively eliminates negative ones, rather than simply preserving naturally given traits from active cultural destruction.

16. See also *A* 51: "Making sick is the true hidden objective of the church's whole system of salvation procedures." *The Antichrist* constantly reiterates this connection between anti-natural morality and sickness—a connection downplayed in Hollingdale's English translations by his tendency to translate *krank* as the more psychologically inflected "morbid."

17. This important, and often overlooked, connection between the method of breeding, Nietzsche's rejection of free will, and the interest in types over individuals, has been helpfully emphasized by Brian Leiter, *The Routledge Philosophy Guidebook to Nietzsche on Morality* (London: Routledge, 2002), 226–27.

18. Mark Warren notes that Nietzsche initially uses *Züchtung* and *Bildung* (education, cultivation) interchangeably, but in later years prefers "breeding" because it emphasizes the "organic and intrinsic functions of culture, rather than *Bildung* with its more liberal and extrinsic connotations," Mark Warren, *Nietzsche and Political Thought* (Cambridge: MIT Press, 1988), 262. Strong, *Friedrich Nietzsche and the Politics of Transfiguration*, 273 and Fredrick Appel, *Nietzsche contra Democracy* (Ithaca, N.Y.: Cornell University Press, 1999), 107 have made similar points about Nietzsche's preference for *züchten* over *erziehen* (to educate). While I agree, I think the principal reason for Nietzsche's later avoidance of the language of *Bildung* and *Erziehung* is their close ties to metaphysical freedom, their voluntaristic connotation that one can, by heeding the moral and cultural values of one's upbringing, choose and determine what one will become. The distinctive feature of Nietzsche's idea of breeding, we will see, is its indirect method: breeding does not *form* (*bilden*) but selects from among naturally given forms, and it does not select by actively producing or making, but by protecting and maintaining. For this reason, I do not think the contrast of breeding and taming is analogous, as Warren suggests, to that of sublimation and repression. Warren identifies breeding as the work of culture to "discipline, improve, and sublimate the 'animal' man" (Warren, *Nietzsche and Political Thought*, 264). However, Nietzsche's appeal to breeding—as opposed to voluntaristic forms of human improvement—implies a recognition of the limitations, even impossibility, of substantial change through "sublimation," through the voluntary moderation and redirection of drives. As Richardson points out (Richardson, *Nietzsche's New Darwinism*, 195), the goal of breeding is not to change the subject's relation to its drives but to change the constitution of the subject at the level of the drives, thus making sublimation unnecessary.

19. Lemm makes a similar point about Nietzsche's conception of culture, suggesting it is a form of cultivation that "reflects a desire to embrace life in all its forms . . . The practice of cultivation is, in this sense, a practice of hospitality, receiving and giving life. Rather than imposing one universal form on life, culture as cultivation is directed toward the pluralization of forms of life that are inherently singular and are irreducible to each other" (Lemm, *Nietzsche's Animal*

Philosophy, 12). Don Dombowsky has argued, to the contrary, that Nietzsche's celebration of a rich diversity of types is unconvincing, since "the typology he ultimately produces is not pluralistic but dualistic: there is master (or noble) morality and slave morality," Don Dombowsky, *Nietzsche's Machiavellian Politics* (New York: Palgrave Macmillan, 2004), 49. However, this view is questionable. First, it fails to recognize that the slave is an "anti-type" rather than a true type, constituted by the negation of traits, instincts, and behaviors. Thus it misses Nietzsche's emphasis upon the distinction of positive qualities in the production of higher types. Second, it confuses Nietzsche's human typology with his moral typology. Nietzsche's willingness to categorize forms of morality in this way does not commit him to an equally reductive understanding of human types. Indeed, since Nietzsche's distinction of noble and slave morality is one of form rather than content—a noble morality is grounded in a positive conception of the good rather than one reducible to the negation of an evil—the content of a noble morality is not fixed. Even if we accept a basic distinction of noble and slavish human types, we might imagine the content of a noble character is equally content-variable: there need not be any limit to the possible variations of character within the "noble" as a general human type.

20. This may indicate, in contrast to the quantitative language of *Grösse* and *Vergrößerung*, an additional, more qualitative sense of *Erhöhung* or "heightening": the heightening of one's *feeling* of well-being relative to particular environmental conditions, rather than the quantitative comparison of individuals' traits or abilities independent of subjective conditions. I develop a qualitative interpretation of enhancement as the heightened subjective feeling of power in "The Equivocal Use of Power in Nietzsche's Failed Anti-Egalitarianism" (forthcoming in *Journal of Moral Philosophy*).

21. Compare Nietzsche's claim that the modern age is not more moral than previous eras. His claim that modern humaneness is symptomatic of physiological weakness is meant, not to praise earlier, more vigorous eras as absolutely "higher," but rather to reject any absolute evaluation of human values and types, any evaluation that abstracts from historical conditions: "If we think away our delicacy and belatedness, our physiological aging, then our morality of 'humanization,' too, loses its value at once—no morality has any value in itself" (*TI* "Expeditions" 37).

22. For similar reasons, we might question the common view, held by John Rawls, *A Theory of Justice* (Cambridge, Mass.: Harvard University Press, 1971); Stanley Cavell, *Conditions Handsome and Unhandsome: The Constitution of Emersonian Perfectionism* (Chicago: University of Chicago Press, 1990) and Thomas Hurka, "Nietzsche: Perfectionist," in *Nietzsche and Morality*, eds. Brian Leiter and Neil Sinhababu (Oxford: Oxford University Press, 2007), 9–31, among others, that Nietzsche's morality is a "perfectionist" one. For the contingent nature of individual "excellence"—the accidental fit of individual traits with each other and with the individual's environment—suggests that there cannot be any universal criteria of human excellence, since "perfection" exists only relatively to

individual and environment. Consequently, there may not be traits that universally promote or diminish the perfection of every person. It follows not only that such a morality would be practically empty, since it provides no universal goals or criteria of moral merit, but also, more important, that it would lose the moral force of the value it places upon excellence: namely, the universal value of the development of a given ability as the perfection of humanity, its necessary connection to the human good. If, on the contrary, the perfection of a given trait has value only contingently and only to the well-being of a given individual, it is not clear that there is any specifically *moral* merit in its cultivation. Continuing the previous analogy to natural selection, moral perfectionism may be as deep a misunderstanding of Nietzsche as Social Darwinism is of natural selection. For an alternate approach to the critique of Nietzschean perfectionism, one that draws on Nietzsche's conceptions of culture and responsibility, see Vanessa Lemm, "Is Nietzsche a Perfectionist? Rawls, Cavell, and the Politics of Culture in Nietzsche's *Schopenhauer as Educator*," *Journal of Nietzsche Studies* 34 (2007): 5–27.

23. Daniel Conway makes a similar claim in *Nietzsche and the Political*, 35. Note that in this respect Social Darwinism is both anti-Nietzschean and anti-Darwinian: under contingent environmental conditions, both the promotion of Nietzsche's "higher types" and the promotion of fitness require proliferation and variation, rather than reduction or extinction, of human types.

24. Note that both objections can also be applied to interpretations of Nietzschean breeding as a production of a superhuman ideal type. See for example, Sloterdijk, "Rules for the Human Zoo" and Ansell-Pearson "Miscarriage."

25. We can also, consequently, reject Detwiler's claim that Nietzsche is "suggesting (with evident approval) that all moral impediments to policies of human annihilation have been removed" (Detwiler, *Nietzsche and the Politics of Aristocratic Radicalism*, 109). Detwiler sees Nietzsche's positive moral philosophy as a form of aestheticism, claiming that "in Nietzsche's hands the question of annihilation becomes an artist's question." However, on my reading Nietzsche's moral philosophy is a naturalistic one, and so *amor fati*'s incompatibility with violence is not an aesthetic prejudice, but a non-obligating norm (something like a physician's advice) grounded in factual claims about the natural well-being of the human species—specifically, claims about the role of variation and proliferation as conditions for the production of higher human types (see above, section 4).

26. For an excellent discussion of the compatibility of Nietzsche's critical and affirmative projects, see Herman W. Siemens, "*Umwerthung*: Nietzsche's 'War Praxis' and the Problem of Yes-Saying and No-Saying in *Ecce Homo*," *Nietzsche-Studien* 38 (2009): 183–206.

27. Siemens makes this point very effectively, arguing that Nietzsche "is concerned, not with persons, but with the philosophical problems they name . . . Nietzsche's pathos of aggression and his demand that we transvalue our values respond to a *cultural* problematic. They are not leveled at individuals, as if they were the motors of change; the principles of agency are located at the level of cultural mores—collective schemas or regimes of evaluation forming types

according to specific bodily economies" (Siemens, "*Umwerthung*: Nietzsche's 'War Praxis' and the Problem of Yes-Saying and No-Saying in *Ecce Homo*," 193).

28. Conway makes a similar point about breeding as a production and destruction of types rather than individuals, when he emphasizes that breeding produces the "preconditions . . . from which rare and exotic specimens are likely to emerge" (Conway, *Nietzsche and the Political*, 35). However, he does not clarify, as I will try to do, the central role that negatively determined character types play in the destruction of those conditions.

29. Compare the third of Nietzsche's four rules governing his "practice of war": "I never attack persons; I merely avail myself of the person as a strong magnifying glass that allows one to make visible a general but creeping and elusive calamity" (*EH* "Wise" 7). He points out, for example, that his attacks on David Strauss and Wagner are attacks on a false *culture* (*Bildung*) "the success of a senile book with the 'cultured' people of Germany" in the former case and "the falseness, the half-couth instincts of our 'culture'" in the latter (*EH* "Wise" 7). The individual then is attacked or "destroyed" as a type representing an entire anticulture, a false set of values, practices, and forms of life.

30. Schank hints at this indirect, negative form of destruction when he stresses that breeding is not an active construction of new forms of humanity, but rather an unmaking, a reversal of the taming of man: "the undoing of his 'hypermoralization' . . . the undoing of the process of his 'civilization,'" Gerd Schank, "Nietzsche's 'Blond Beast': On the Recuperation of the Nietzschean Metaphor," in *A Nietzschean Bestiary: Becoming Animal Beyond Docile and Brutal*, eds. Christa Davis Acampora and Ralph Acampora (Oxford: Rowman and Littlefield 2004), 149. Most commentators, in contrast, describe breeding as a strong positive eugenics that actively chooses, instills, and develops traits, as a creative and formative action, rather than, as Schank rightly sees it, a *restoration*. Contrast the positive conceptions of breeding in, for example, Strong, *Friedrich Nietzsche and the Politics of Transfiguration*, 273–74 and Richard Schacht, *Nietzsche*, 335.

31. I should clarify the apparently inconsistent suggestion that breeding can be *literal* destruction without being *authentic* destruction. It is literally destruction as the intended abolition of certain ideas and types. But it is not *authentic* destruction because it abolishes negatively determined ideas and types, which does not require the destruction of any *actually existing* beings. It destroys ideals in the defense of realities. This interpretation of Nietzschean destruction as that of negatively determined types through the preservation of positively determined ones offers an alternative resolution to the paradox of yes and no-saying, destruction and affirmation, that Siemens so effectively poses. Destruction is compatible with the total affirmation of all things if it is directed only against values and practices that are directly aimed at the elimination of traits and types. This allows for the agonistic pluralism Siemens rightly emphasizes, provided we recognize that true pluralism consists of positively defined types. Although Nietzsche's critical philosophy destroys fictional ideas and values rather than realities, the weakening of abilities rather than authentic abilities, and degeneration of forms of life

and character rather than positively determined forms, this does not amount to a negation of life. In contrast, Siemens resolves the conflict by weakening Nietzsche's claims of "destruction" to limitation: "Nietzschean critique seeks, not to destroy the ideals it attacks, but to *place a limit or measure on their tyranny*, so as to make room for competing ideals" (Siemens, "*Umwerthung*: Nietzsche's 'War Praxis' and the Problem of Yes-Saying and No-Saying in *Ecce Homo*," 194). This emphasis upon limitation—presumably the continued existence but practical failure of these ideals—not only dismisses Nietzsche's intentional and repeated emphasis upon the language of destruction, but it also leads to internal incoherence: he cannot consistently affirm a limited form of nihilistic value-systems, if those value-systems endorse the *unlimited* destruction of other forms of life and value—for to will the failure of values that consist of nothing more than negation is indistinguishable from willing their destruction simply. Nietzsche can affirm the existence of *passive* forms of nihilism, but not active forms. While Siemens is surely right that "Nietzschean *Umwerthung* is a philosophical war-praxis that serves, not to establish victory or a personal hegemony over his opponents," it does not follow that destruction has been completely reduced to limitation (Siemens, "*Umwerthung*: Nietzsche's 'War Praxis' and the Problem of Yes-Saying and No-Saying in *Ecce Homo*," 197). Nietzsche can consistently preserve the open-ended agonistic struggle of forms of life while still seeking to eradicate those forms that have the direct denial of others as their essential content.

32. While my argument is limited to one form of positive eugenics, I believe this includes all forms suspected of intrinsic ethical harm. Among those who see Nietzschean breeding as a form of eugenics (Julian Young, *Nietzsche's Philosophy of Religion*; John Richardson, *Nietzsche's New Darwinism*; Gregory Moore, *Nietzsche, Biology and Metaphor*), there is disagreement about whether it includes both positive and negative forms—both the active introduction of valuable traits and the elimination or prevention of negative traits. Moore insists Nietzsche is primarily interested in the negative form (Moore, *Nietzsche, Biology and Metaphor*, 136). Richardson, on the contrary, has pointed to Nietzsche's unpublished comments in favor of selective marriage as evidence of "positive eugenics," of "inducing the valuable to reproduce more, and with valuable others" (Richardson, *Nietzsche's New Darwinism*, 197). While true, this is an attenuated sense of "positive eugenics," comparable to any form of marital custom or individual sexual selection, so not a sense relevant to the contemporary eugenic ethical debate, which focuses on the genetic engineering of traits.

33. I am stipulatively defining perfectionist eugenics to include the promotion of only comparative traits, though I believe a case could be made that all forms of liberal eugenics concern comparative traits. As a kind of test for this form of trait-value, one might ask: would a parent choose to give a child this trait if *every* child were mandated to receive it to an equivalent degree? Such a test would likely exclude the most commonly debated real and imaginary cases, such as the genetic engineering of intelligence, talent, and beauty—perhaps even apparently

non-comparative traits such as height or hair color or facial features, which bear value in part due to their distinctiveness or rarity.

12. An "Other Way of Being." The Nietzschean "Animal": Contributions to the Question of Biopolitics

Mónica B. Cragnolini

1. For a systematic treatment of the question of the animal in Nietzsche, see Vanessa Lemm, *Nietzsche's Animal Philosophy* (New York: Fordham University Press, 2009). Lemm argues that for Nietzsche there exists a continuity among human, animal, and plant life. She conceives of politics in relation to the problem of animal life. In this way, she interprets an "aristocratic society of the future" in terms of the struggle for the overcoming of domination.

2. Giorgio Agamben, "Form-of-Life," in *Means without End: Notes on Politics,* trans. Vicenzo Binetti and Cesare Casarino (Minneapolis: University of Minnesota Press, 2000), 3–11.

3. Roberto Esposito, *Immunitas. Protezione e negazione della vita.* (Torino: Einaudi, 2002) and *Terms of the Political* (New York: Fordham University Press, 2012).

4. Jacques Derrida, "Faith and Knowledge," in *Acts of Religion* (London: Routledge, 2001), 40–101.

5. It is also interesting to note that Nietzsche suggests that the problem evoked by this ideal is fundamentally concerned with the pleasure taken from the same, hence the expression "lewd ascetic conflict" (*lüsternen Asketen–Zwiespältigkeit*) (*GM* III: 12).

6. Nietzsche suggests as antidote "art, in which *lying* sacrifices itself" (*GM* II: 12).

7. See my text entitled "El resto, entre Nietzsche y Derrida," in *Derrida, un pensador del resto* (Buenos Aires: La Cebra, 2007), 137–156.

8. Jacques Derrida, *Resistances of Psychoanalysis,* trans. Peggy Kamuf, Pascale-Anne Brault and Michael Naas (Stanford: Stanford University Press, 1998), 9.

9. Jacques Derrida, *Resistances of Psychoanalysis,* 10.

10. Jacques Derrida, *Resistances of Psychoanalysis,* 11.

11. Gérard Bensussan, "Le dernier, le reste," in *Judéités. Questions pour Jacques Derrida,* eds. Joseph Cohen and Raphael Zagury-Orly (Paris: Galilée, 2003), 43–58, here 48.

12. See Mónica B. Cragnolini, "Los animales de Zarathustra: Heidegger y Nietzsche en torno la cuestión de lo viviente animal," *Estudios Nietzsche,* 10 (2010): 53–66.

13. For more on this topic, see my article "De Bactriana y el Urmi a la montaña y el ocaso. A modo de introducción *a Así habló Zarathustra,*" *Revista de Filosofía* LV–LVI (2000): 39–56. When I speak of "passages" I am thinking of the textuality of the work as a "force field" that takes into account, at the same time, the consideration of life in terms of forces that are interwoven with each other, and not of substances.

14. This was one of the common interpretations, particularly around the turn of the century, of Nietzsche's thought. That is to say, to argue that, in the face of the critique of "humanization," Nietzsche would advocate a "return" to the animal, for example, in the model of the "blond beast." Affirming that "return" presupposes ignoring that Nietzsche does not signal an inversion of meanings and values, but rather a "subversion" of these, that is to say, a transformation of the very schema of valorization and attribution of meaning (and not an "exchange" of some values and some meanings for others).

15. Michel Foucault, *Abnormal: Lectures at the Collège de France 1974–1975* (New York: Picador, 2003).

16. I cannot develop this theme further here but have done so elsewhere. I remit this theme/issue that I cannot develop here to: "Ello piensa: la otra razón, la del cuerpo," in *El problema económico. Yo-ello-super yo-síntoma,* ed. Juan Carlos Cosentino (Buenos Aires: Imago Mundi, 2005), 147–158.

17. Jacques Derrida, *The Beast & The Sovereign,* vol. I, trans. Geoffrey Bennington (Chicago: University of Chicago Press, 2009).

18. Jacques Derrida, *The Beast & The Sovereign*, 280.

19. Jacques Derrida, *The Beast & The Sovereign*, 296.

20. Derrida frames this question of the autopsy as a model of knowing with his commentary regarding the scene Ellenberger narrates, citing Loisel: the presence of Louis XIV attending, in 1681, in his *ménagerie* at Versailles, the dissection of an elephant. See Jacques Derrida, *The Beast & The Sovereign*, 296.

21. Jacques Derrida, *The Beast & The Sovereign*, 287.

22. Jacques Derrida, *The Beast & The Sovereign*, 299.

23. I develop this idea of hostipitality in Mónica B. Cragnolini, "Nietzsche hospitalario y comunitario: una apuesta extraña," in *Modos de lo extraño: subjetividad y alteridad en el pensamiento postnietzscheano* (Buenos Aires: Santiago Arcos, 2005), 11–27.

24. Jacques Derrida, "Faith and Knowledge," 72.

25. Jacques Derrida, "Faith and Knowledge," 80.

26. Jacques Derrida, "Faith and Knowledge," 82.

13. Nietzsche and the Transformation of Death

Eduardo Nasser

1. Nietzsche most likely discovers Boscovich in 1873, after having read Theodor Fechner's *Über die physikalische und philosophische Atomlehre*, and Friedrich Lange's *Geschichte des Materialismus* (Karl Schlechta and Anni Anders, *Friedrich Nietzsche. Von den verborgenen Anfängen seines Philosophierens* [Stuttgart-Bad Cannstatt: Frommann Verlag, 1962], 128); Georg Stack, *Lange and Nietzsche* (Berlin and New York: De Gruyter, 1983), 226. Despite the fact that the dialogue with Boscovich intensified during the 1880s, some interpreters believe that the influence of Boscovich is noticeable in the young Nietzsche, mainly in the posthumously published writings of 1873, generally referred to as the *Zeitatomlehre* (Karl Schlechta and Anni Anders, *Friedrich Nietzsche. Von den verborgenen*

Anfängen seines Philosophierens, 140; Greg Whitlock, "Examining Nietzsche's 'Time Atom Theory' Fragment from 1873," *Nietzsche-Studien* 26 [1997]: 350–360, in particular p. 350. This would prove that Boscovich had always been present in Nietzsche's thinking and played a significant role in his philosophy (Greg Whitlock, "Roger Boscovich, Benedict de Spinoza and Friedrich Nietzsche: The Untold Story," *Nietzsche-Studien* 25 [1996]: 200–220, in particular pp. 202 and 206.

2. Ruggero Boscovich, *A Theory of Natural Philosophy*, trans. J.M. Child (Boston: MIT Press, 1966), 20 and 134.

3. Ruggero Boscovich, *A Theory of Natural Philosophy*, 10.

4. Mary B. Hesse, *Forces and Fields* (Endinburgh: Dover, 1962), 201.

5. Michel Haar believes that Nietzsche's critique of the world's organicity targets the Stoic model of the universe as a "Great Living Being" (Michel Haar, *Nietzsche and Metaphysics* [Albany, NY: State University of New York Press, 1996], 114–5). This is a controversial statement, particularly after the contributions to Nietzsche studies by Paolo D'Iorio. See Paolo D'Iorio, "Cosmologie de l'eternel retour," *Nietzsche Studien* 24 (1995): 62–123, and "O eterno retorno. Gênese e interpretação," *Cadernos Nietzsche* 20 (2006): 69–114. Based on a thorough investigation of Nietzsche's library, D'Iorio suggests that the criticism of the world as a living being is inserted into the discussion of the thermal death of the universe, manifestly objecting to Otto Caspari (Paolo D'Iorio, "Cosmologie de l'eternel retour," 99–111; D'Iorio, "O eterno retorno. Gênese e interpretação," 76–100).

6. Paolo D'Iorio, "Cosmologie de l'eternel retour," 100–101.

7. Paolo D'Iorio, "Cosmologie de l'eternel retour," 111.

8. "Organic creatures may be seen not as an advance over the inorganic forms, but as a degeneration of them," Alistar Moles, *Nietzsche's Philosophy of Nature and Cosmology* (New York: Peter Lang, 1990), 156.

9. "Nietzsche considers revenge to be 'the recalcitrant will against time and its 'it was." This definition does not unilaterally emphasize an isolated character of time, neglecting the two others, but rather characterizes the fundamental aspect of time in its own absolute essence," *Ensaios e Conferências*, trans. Emmanuel Carneiro Leão, Gilvan Fogel and Márcia Sá C. Schulback (Petrópolis: Vozes, 2002), 101.

10. Charles Andler, *Nietzsche. Sa vie et sa pensée* (Paris: Gallimard, 1979), 446–447.

11. Alistar Moles, *Nietzsche's Philosophy of Nature and Cosmology*, 140–183.

12. Alwin Mittasch, *Friedrich Nietzsche Stellung zur Chemie* (Berlin: Verlag Chemie, 1944), 72–78; Alwin Mittasch, *Friedrich Nietzsche als Naturphilosoph* (Stuttgart: Alfred Kröner Verlag, 1952), 259–261.

13. "'The will to power,' 'nihilism,' 'the eternal recurrence of the same,' 'the Overman,' 'justice' are the five fundamental expressions of Nietzsche's metaphysics," Martin Heidegger, *Nietzsche,* vol. 2, (Stuttgart: Neske Verlag, 1961), 233.

14. Sean Ireton, "Heidegger's Ontological Analysis of Death and Its Prefiguration in Nietzsche," *Nietzsche Studien* 26 (1997): 405–20.

15. Sean Ireton, "Heidegger's Ontological Analysis of Death and Its Prefiguration in Nietzsche," *Nietzsche Studien* 26 (1997): 407 and 420.

16. Sean Ireton, "Heidegger's Ontological Analysis of Death and Its Prefiguration in Nietzsche," *Nietzsche Studien* 26 (1997): 413.

17. Sean Ireton, "Heidegger's Ontological Analysis of Death and Its Prefiguration in Nietzsche," *Nietzsche Studien* 26 (1997): 415 and 419.

18. Sean Ireton, "Heidegger's Ontological Analysis of Death and Its Prefiguration in Nietzsche," *Nietzsche Studien* 26 (1997): 407.

19. See Jean Pierre Vernant, *L'individu, la mort, l'amour* (Paris: Gallimard, 2005), 41–89. In his treatise *Wie die Alten den Tod Gebildet*, Lessing suggests that the Greeks did not feel threatened by death. Evidence indicates, however, that this suggestion is controversial. Schelling, Rohde, and Cornford emphatically defend the thesis that the Greeks did not even maintain an ambiguous relationship with death—they simply hated it. It is possible that this latter interpretation is the most adequate, above all if one considers the period of the tragedies, in which laments to death prevailed. See Jacques Choron, *La mort et la pensée occidentale*, trans. Monique Manin (Paris: Payot, 1969), 23, 33.

20. "No other era if not the Middle Ages, in its decadence gave so much emphasis and pathos to the idea of death. The appeal to the *memento mori* echoes incessantly, throughout life," Johan Huizinga, *Le déclin du Moyen Age* (Paris: Payot, 1967), 164. Translation from the passage into English: Eduardo Nasser.

21. John Huizinga, *Le déclin du Moyen Age* (Paris: Payot, 1967), 167.

22. Plato, *Complete Works* (Indianapolis: Hackett, 1997), 56. Choron suggests that when Plato, in *Theaetetus*, states that "philosophy starts with a fright," perhaps this "fright" is caused precisely by the discovery of death. See Jacques Choron, *La mort et la pensée occidentale*, 40.

23. Arthur Schopenhauer, *Die Welt als Wille und Vorstellung*, vol. 3 (Stuttgart/Frankfurt: Suhrkamp, 1986), 249.

24. "In the twentieth century, death has been rediscovered as a philosophical idea and problem. It is in fact with the contemporary German existentialists, Karl Jaspers and Martin Heidegger, near the center of their interpretation of reality and human existence" (. . .) "I shall be dealing chiefly with the two German existentialists because they have emphasized this theme much more than have Kierkeggard, Sartre, and the minor figures of this school of thought," Glenn J. Gray, "The Idea of Death in Existentialism," *Journal of Philosophy* 45, 5 (1951): 114. It is important, nevertheless, to remember the beginning of the *Myth of Sisyphus* by Camus: "There is but one truly serious philosophic problem, and that is suicide" (Albert Camus, *The Myth of Sisyphus and Other Essays* [New York: Vintage, 1991], 3).

25. "But if existentialism is widely associated not merely with extreme experiences in general but above all with death, this is due primarily to Heidegger who discussed death in a crucial 32-page chapter of his influential *Being and Time*," Walter Kaufmann, "Existentialism and Death," *Chicago Review* 2 13 (1959): 75.

26. According to Kaufmann, it is likely that the experience of the First World War heightened in this generation of philosophers the fascination with death. Kaufmann bases his suspicion on two essays by Freud ("Timely Thoughts on War and Death" and "Our Relation to Death"), in which the psychoanalyst calls attention to a change in behavior of human beings toward death in the interwar period: if before the vision that death did not concern human beings was predominant, now it was part of everyone's life. See Walter Kaufmann, "Existentialism and Death," 81–82.

27. Karl Jaspers, *Way to Wisdom. An Introduction to Philosophy* (New Haven: Yale University Press, 1954), 126.

28. See Jacques Choron, *La mort et la pensée occidentale*, 194–195.

29. Karl Jaspers, *Way to Wisdom*, 22–26.

30. Martin Heidegger, *Sein und Zeit* (Tübingen: Max Niemeyer Verlag, 1986), 11–12.

31. Martin Heidegger, *Sein und Zeit*, 13.

32. Martin Heidegger, *Sein und Zeit*, 237–241.

33. See Henri Charles Tauxe, *La notion de finitude dans la philosophie de Martin Heidegger* (Lausanne: L'age d'homme, 1971), 62.

34. Max Scheler, "The Meaning of Suffering" in *On Feeling, Knowing, and Valuing*, ed. Harold Bershady (Chicago: University of Chicago Press, 1992), chapter 5 passim.

35. Martin Heidegger, *Sein und Zeit*, 252–254.

36. "In ihr befindet sich das Dasein vor dem Nichts der möglichen Unmöglichkeit seiner Existenz," Martin Heidegger, *Sein und Zeit*, 266.

37. Everything indicates that this formula had already been used by the Cynics. See Jean Salem, *Tel un dieu parmi les homes* (Paris: J. Vrin, 1994), 204.

38. Epicure cited from new translation of *Letter to Menoeceus* by Peter Saint-Andre, last cited 2/8/2013 from: http://www.monadnock.net/epicurus/letter.html.

39. Epicure cited from new translation of *Letter to Menoeceus* by Peter Saint-Andre, last cited 2/8/2013 from: http://www.monadnock.net/epicurus/letter.html.

40. See Jacques Choron, *La mort et la pensée occidentale*, 61.

41. Epicure cited from new translation of *Letter to Menoeceus* by Peter Saint-Andre, last cited 2/8/2013 from: http://www.monadnock.net/epicurus/letter.html.

42. Jacques Choron, *La mort et la pensée occidentale*, 81–85. See Michel Vovelle, *La mort et l'occident* (Paris: Gallimard, 1983), 201.

43. See Jean Salem, *Tel un dieu parmi les homes*, 214–217.

44. Jacques Choron, *La mort et la pensée occidentale*, 87–90.

45. Benedict Spinoza, *A Spinoza Reader. The Ethics and Other Works,* trans. E Curley (Princeton: Princeton University Press, 1994), *Ethics*, Part IV, prop 67.

46. See Jean Salem, *Tel un dieu parmi les homes*, 226–227; Chantal Jaquet, *Sub Specie Aeternitatis* (Paris: Kimé, 1997), 78.

47. Chantal Jaquet, *Sub Specie Aeternitatis*, 78.

48. It is important to remember here that Epicurus figured in the list of the four pairs of thinkers (Epicurus and Montaigne, Goethe and Spinoza, Plato and Rousseau, Pascal and Schopenhauer) on whom Nietzsche "fixes his eyes." See *WS* 408.

49. Jacques Choron, *La mort et la pensée occidentale*, 91–95.

50. Marcus Aurelius, *The Meditations, Second Meditation*. Trans. George Long. Last cited on 2/8/2013 in: http://classics.mit.edu/Antoninus/meditations.2.two.html

51. Charles Kahn makes an interesting observation about this fragment: "Maybe the biggest surprise that awaits us at death is that, then, things won't be so different once we are and have always been used to the experience of continuously dying and being born," Charles H. Kahn, *The Art and Thought of Heraclitus* (Cambridge: Cambridge University Press, 1979), 220ff.

14. Becoming and Purification: Empedocles, Zarathustra's *Übermensch*, and Lucian's Tyrant

Babette Babich

1. Martin Heidegger, *Nietzsche*, vol. 2, trans. David Krell (San Francisco: Harper, 1991), 211.

2. Empedocles, Frag. 399 in *The Presocratic Philosophers*, eds. Geoffrey S. Kirk, John E. Raven, and Malcolm Schofield (Cambridge: Cambridge University Press, 2007), 313ff.

3. Regarding Empedocles, one cannot but be struck by his style of self-presentation as we have already noted and as the classicist Eva Stehle emphasizes. See Stehle, *Performance and Gender in Ancient Greece: Nondramatic Poetry in its Setting* (Princeton: Princeton University Press, 1997), 210ff.

4. Many classicists who write on Empedocles mock him, asserting that ancient authors did so as well, but this reading may tell us more about the classicists in question or our modern/Christian aversion to saying "I" (See Nietzsche's allusion to this "lyrical" tradition with regard to Archilochus in *BT* 5).

5. Jonathan Barnes invokes Nietzsche's characterization of Diogenes Laërtius as "the porter who guards the gate of the Castle of Ancient Philosophy. Scholars may scorn him; but they must pass by him and cannot pass him by." Jonathan Barnes, "Review of *Diogenes Laërtius. Vitae Philosophorum* by M. Marcovich," *The Classical Review, New Series*, 52 1 (2002): 8.

6. Composed after the publication of *Thus Spoke Zarathustra*, but also after the addition of the fifth book to *The Gay Science* and following the private circulation in 1885 of the fourth part of *Zarathustra*.

7. Friedrich Hölderlin, *Gedichte* (Stuttgart: Reclaim, 1990), 50.

8. Discussions of Nietzsche and Empedocles have been part of the tradition of Nietzsche interpretation from the outset. See for example and among others, Johann Piatek, *Nietzsches Empedokles-Fragmente* (Stryj: Progr. Gymn., 1910) and Raymond Furness, "Nietzsche and Empedocles," *Journal of the British Society for*

Phenomenology 2 2 (1971): 91–94. For further references, see also Anke Bennholdt-Thomsen, *Nietzsches Also Sprach Zarathustra als literarisches Phänomen* (Frankfurt: Athenäum Verlag, 1974), 151–152. For a recent contemporary or mainstream reading, but lacking the contextual dimensions noted here, see Glenn Most, "The Stillbirth of a Tragedy: Nietzsche and Empedocles," in *The Empedoclean Kosmos: Structure, Process and the Question of Cyclicity*, ed. Apostolos. L. Pierris (Patras: Institute for Philosophical Research, 2005), 31–44. Given the constraints of Most's reading, Walther Kranz, *Empedokles: Antike Gestalt und romantische Neuschöpfung* (Zürich: Artemis, 1949) remains invaluable, particularly as it includes Hölderlin, as does Karl Reinhardt's review/reflection on Kranz in Karl Reinhardt, *Vermächtnis der Antike*: *Gesammelte Essays zur Philosophie und Geschichtsschreibung* (Göttingen: Vandenhoeck & Ruprecht, 1966). See also: David Farrell Krell, *Postponements: Woman, Sensuality and Death in Nietzsche* (Bloomington: Indiana University Press, 1986) as well as for additional bibliographical references, Jürgen Söring, "Nietzsches Empedokles-Plan," *Nietzsche Studien* 19 (1990): 176–211.

9. David Sedley adverts to Cicero's conventional characterization of Lucretius's *De rerum natura* by comparing in terms of its opening style, comparing it to a version of Empedocles by "a certain Sallustius" in the first chapter "The Empedoclean Opening," *Lucretius and the Transformation of Greek Wisdom* (Cambridge: Cambridge University Press, 2003), 1.

10. Jackson P. Hershbell, "Plutarch as a Source for Empedocles Re-Examined," *The American Journal of Philology*, 2 92 (1971): 156–184.

11. See Babette Babich, "Between Hölderlin and Heidegger: Nietzsche's Transfiguration of Philosophy," *Nietzsche-Studien*, 29 (2000): 267–301.

12. Empedocles, Fr. 404 in *The Presocratic Philosophers*, 315.

13. Diogenes Laërtius is our first source for the traditional conflicting array of different deaths Empedocles was said to have died: "καὶ ταῦτα μὲν περὶ τοῦ θανάτου καὶ τοσαῦτα (Thus and thus much of his death)," Diogenes Laërtius, *Lives of the Eminent Philosophers*, Books VI–X, trans. Robert D. Hicks (Cambridge: Harvard University Press, 1925), 388–389.

14. The debate about Empedocles' death is longstanding but it also includes the debate about his godlike status, the best way for a mortal to ascend to the status of the immortals is to die. Thus Nietzsche reminds us of "the old German saying, all gods must die" (*KSA* 7:5[115]).

15. See with reference to the contextualization of humanity and animality, and a discussion of the transitional relation between "the animal, the human, and the overhuman," Vanessa Lemm, *Nietzsche's Animal Philosophy: Culture, Politics, and the Animality of the Human Being* (New York: Fordham University Press, 2009), 2.

16. See Pierre Hadot, *Philosophy as a Way of Life*, trans. Michael Chase (Chicago: University of Chicago Press, 1995) and see more broadly here, Horst Hutter, *Shaping the Future: Nietzsche's New Regime of the Soul and its Ascetic Practices* (Lanham, MD: Lexington Books, 2005), especially but not only chapter one.

17. Empedocles, Frag. 400, *The Presocratic Philosophers*, 314.

18. One usually speaks of parodies in this general sense. See for further references in English, Peter Wolfe, "Image and Meaning in *Also Sprach Zarathustra*," *Modern Language Notes* 5 (1964): 546–552 as well as Anke Bennholdt-Thomsen, *Nietzsches Also Sprach Zarathustra als literarisches Phänomen* (Frankfurt: Athenäum Verlag, 1974) for useful references to an array of German and French literature that is increasingly forgotten, and see, too the references in the note to follow.

19. See Emil Abegg, "Nietzsches Zarathustra und der Prophet des alten Iran" in *Nietzsche. Conférences prononcées à Genève sous les auspices de la Fondation M. Gretler* (Erlenbach-Zürich, 1945), 64–82. There are ongoing disputes regarding the age of the historical Zoroaster (some scholars say roughly 750 years by contrast with ancient authors who date Zoroaster some 5,000 years before the current era). For although Zoroaster had been dated in antiquity as extremely ancient, modern historians tend to set him in the seventh century BCE owing to accounts that he had met with Pythagoras (572–497 BCE); otherwise his flourishing may be rounded back to about 1700. See Farhang Mehr, *The Zoroastrian Tradition, An Introduction to the Ancient Wisdom of Zarathustra* (Rockport, MA: Element Inc., 1991) or those who, philologically enough, dispute the etymology Nietzsche gives us of his name, duly telling us that the name Zarathustra has naught to do with stars or brightness or the sun or anything at all, but only golden camels. Even the usually iconoclastic David Allison repeats this debunking exposition of Zarathustra's name. See Allison's reference to Janz's remark that "Creuzer's *Symbolik und Mythologie der alten Völker* had mistakenly given alternate etymologies for Zoroaster, namely 'Zeretoschtro-Zeratuscht' which he translated as 'Golden Star'—'Star of Light' or 'Shining Gold'" in David Allison, *Reading the New Nietzsche* (New York: Rowman and Littlefield, 2001), 282. Charles Andler by contrast emphasizes the oriental relevance of both the historical Zoroaster and Buddha, and Bennholdt-Thomsen draws upon both Andler and Schlechta and notes that Zarathustra's laughter may derive from the legend, detailed by Pliny, that Zoroaster laughs on the day of his birth. Bennholdt-Thomsen, *Nietzsches Also Sprach Zarathustra als literarisches Phänomen*, 88 refers to Abegg, "Nietzsches Zarathustra und der Prophet des alten Iran," 68.

20. Martin Heidegger, *Nietzsche*, vol. 2, 211.

21. Martin Heidegger, *Nietzsche*, vol. 2, 212.

22. Martin Heidegger, *Nietzsche*, vol. 2, 213.

23. Empedocles, Frag. 358, *The Presocratic Philosophers*, 295 (trans. modified). I follow John Curtis Franklin's translation and see Franklin for a discussion of "Harmony in Greek and Indo-Iranian Cosmology," *The Journal of Indo-European Studies*, 1 and 2 30 (2002): 1–25. If I had more time here I would undertake to argue this wheel-shaped sphere is Zarathustra's golden ball.

24. Empedocles, Frag. 399, *The Presocratic Philosophers*, 313ff.

25. Empedocles, Frag. 399, *The Presocratic Philosophers*, 313ff.

26. I discuss this in the context of classical philology in Babette Babich, "Nietzsche's Philology and Nietzsche's Science: On the 'Problem of Science' and 'fröhliche Wissenschaft," in: *Metaphilology: Histories and Languages of Philology*, ed. Pascale Hummel (Paris: Philologicum, 2009), 155–201.

27. See the introduction and the first third in general of Babich, *Words in Blood, Like Flowers: Philosophy and Poetry, Music and Eros in Hölderlin, Nietzsche and Heidegger* (New York: State University of New York Press, 2005), vii–xii, 3–116. I develop this in Babich "Zu Nietzsches Stil," in *Eines Gottes Glück, voller Macht und Liebe* (Weimar: Bauhaus Universitätsverlag, 2009), 9–27.

28. Thus Lucian expounds upon his own prevarication as a variation upon the traditional lies of others in his "True Stories" [*Alethe Diegemata*]. Thus he pleads "I too have turned to lying—but a much more honest lying than all the others. The one and only truth you'll hear from me is that I am lying. By frankly admitting that there isn't a word of truth in what I say, I feel I am avoiding the possibility of attack from any quarter." Lucian, "A True Story," in *Selected Satires of Lucian*, ed. and trans. Lionel Casson (New York: Norton, 1968), 15. See *BGE* 22. Lucian could not make his warning plainer: "Well then I am writing about things I neither saw nor heard of from a single soul, things which don't exist and couldn't possibly exist. So all readers beware, don't believe any of it" ("A True Story," 15).

29. See for discussion and a range of further references, pro and contra, Babette Babich, "Nietzsche's Post-Human Imperative: On the "All-too-Human" Dream of Transhumanism," *The Agonist*. Vol. IV, Issue II (2012). Online publication: http://www.nietzschecircle.com/AGONIST/2011_08/Dream_of_Transhumanism.html.

30. Michael Allen Gillespie, "Slouching Toward Bethlehem to Be Born': On the Nature and Meaning of Nietzsche's Superman," *The Journal of Nietzsche Studies* 30 (2005): 49–69 and see too Lawrence Lambert, *Nietzsche's Teaching: An Interpretation of "Thus Spoke Zarathustra"* (New Haven: Yale University Press, 1989).

31. See Ray Kurzweil, *The Singularity is Near: When Humans Transcend Biology* (New York: Viking, 2006) and for further discussion and other references, Babette Babich, "*O, Superman!* or Being Towards Transhumanism: Martin Heidegger, Günther Anders, and Media Aesthetics," *Divinatio* (January 2013): 83–99.

32. Empedocles, Frag. 401, *The Presocratic Philosophers*, 315.

33. Empedocles, Frag. 415, *The Presocratic Philosophers*, 319.

34. See Babette Babich, "Ontologie," in *Nietzsche-Lexikon*, ed. Christian Niemeyer (Darmstadt: Wissenschaftliche Buchgesellschaft, 2009), 257–260.

35. Like the duck that *could be* somebody's mother in the popular song of my grandparent's era in the states.

36. It is not that it has never occurred to anyone that the *Übermensch* might be a parodic concept: Keith Ansell-Pearson has argued that Nietzsche lays out a

potentially parodic path in his 1886 preface to *Human, All Too Human*. "Toward the *Übermensch:* Reflections on the Year of Nietzsche's Daybreak," *Nietzsche-Studien* 23 (1994): 128–30. Richard Perkins sees these figures as the lover, the knower, and the creator: "How an Ape Becomes a Superman: Notes on a Parodic Metamorphosis in Nietzsche," *Nietzsche-Studien* 15 (1986): 180. Without underscoring the parodic dimension, Marie-Luise Haase sees the figures of the *Übermensch* as saint, philosopher, and artist: "Der Übermensch in Also Sprach Zarathustra und im Zarathustra Nachlass, 1882–1885," *Nietzsche-Studien* 13 (1984): 236. Eugen Fink argues for the genius, the free spirit, and Zarathustra himself, *Nietzsches Philosophie* (Stuttgart: Kohlhammer, 1960), 72ff.

37. At the same time, this also means that Ray Kurzweil's *The Singularity is Near* illustrates the contemporary face of evolutionary triumpalism or millenarism. See, by contrast, Babette Babich, "Ex aliquo nihil: Nietzsche on Science and Modern Nihilism," *American Catholic Philosophical Quarterly. Special Issue on Nietzsche* 84–2 (Spring 2010): 231–256, and on the postmodern fascination with the redemptive promise of electronic media, Babich, "Thus Spoke Zarathustra, or Nietzsche and Hermeneutics in Gadamer, Lyotard, and Vattimo," in *Consequences of Hermeneutics: 50 Years After Gadamer's Truth and Method*, eds. Jeff Malpas and Santiago Zabala (Evanston: Northwestern University Press, 2010), 218–243.

38. After Christopher Robinson, *Lucian and his Influence in Europe*, citing the epigram to Aldine edition of Erasmus, *In Praise of Folly* (Chapel Hill: The University of North Carolina Press, 1979), 191.

39. This citation, "*Kataplous*, 16" reproduces Kaufmann's footnote in its entirety. See Walter Kaufmann, *Nietzsche, Philosopher, Psychologist, Antichrist* (Princeton: Princeton University Press, 1974), footnote 1, 307. The footnote itself clarifies Kaufmann's main text: "The *hyperanthropous* is to be found in the writings of Lucian in the second century AD and Nietzsche as a classical philologist had studied Lucian and made frequent references to him in his philologia," (Walter Kaufmann, *Nietzsche, Philosopher, Psychologist, Antichrist*, 307). Joseph Erkme, *Nietzsche im "Zauberberg"* (Frankfurt am Main: Klostermann, 1996) duly cites Kaufmann in his notes before going on to detail the earlier appearances of the term *Übermensch* as such in German (Joseph Erkme, *Nietzsche im "Zauberberg,"* 271ff). But prior to Kaufmann, see the entry in Rudolf Eisler's *Handwörterbuch der Philosophie* (Berlin: Mittler und Sohn, 1913) as well as Ernst Benz, "Das Bild des Übermenschen in der Europäischen Geistesgeschichte," *Der Übermensch. Eine Diskussion* (Stuttgart: Rhein-Verlag 1961), 19–16. Similar details, drawn from Kaufmann, appear in Karen Joisten, cited below, and so too with reference to anthropology and the social sciences Jyung-Hyun Kim, *Nietzsches Sozialphilosophie: Versuch einer Überwindung der Moderne im Mittelpunkt des Begriffes Leib* (Würzburg: Königshausen and Neumann, 1995), 198ff. See for a politicized overview, Ulrich Busch, "Vergessene Utopien: Friedrich Nietzsches Vision vom Übermenschen," *Utopie kreativ*, 151 (2003): 460–667.

40. Lucian's *Kataplous* is included in several collections of Lucian's dialogues, appearing as the first dialogue in the Loeb edition of *Lucian*, Volume II, trans. A. H. Harmon (Cambridge: Harvard University Press, 1915), 2–57 and including the Everyman library edition, translated by Lionel Casson, *Selected Satires of Lucian,* 175–193.

41. But Northrop Frye had already laid the ground rules or gone to the grounds, or, still better: to the underground for English readers, explaining in a section of his *Anatomy of Criticism* entitled "Theory of Myths"—just because and rhetorically and given the distance between our own time and Lucian and Menippus, but also Nietzsche himself, it really *needs* explaining—that "whenever the 'other world' appears in satire, it appears as an ironic counterpart to our own, a reversal of accepted social standards. This form of satire is represented in Lucian's *Kataplous* and *Charon*, journeys to the other world in which the eminent in this one are shown doing appropriate but unaccustomed things, a form incorporated in Rabelais, and in the medieval *danse macabre.* In the last named the simple equality of death is set against the complex inequalities of life," [Herman] N. Frye, *Anatomy of Criticism: Four Essays* (Princeton: Princeton University Press, 1957), 232.

42. Lucian, "The Downward Journey," *Volume II,* Trans. A. H. Harmon (Cambridge: Harvard University Press, 1915), 34–35.

43. Lucian, "The Downward Journey," 34–35. See Lucian's "Dialogues of the Dead" where Croesus complains to Pluto that Menippus is giving them a hard time in hell. Menippus replies: "True enough, Pluto: I hate them; they're low scoundrels, not content with having led bad lives but even in death they remember their past and cling to it. That's why I enjoy tormenting them," Lucian, *Volume VII,* trans. M. D. Macleod (Cambridge: Harvard University Press, 1961), 17. To which Pluto replies "You shouldn't; they mourn great losses." Menippus is adamant, and Croesus cries "Isn't this outrageous?" to which Menippus retorts: "No, the outrageous thing was your behavior when you expected people to worship you, treated free men with contempt, and forgot all about death. That's why you're going to lament the loss of all those things,"" Lucian, *Volume VII,* 17–19. See *AOM* 408 und Erwin Rohde, *Der griechische Roman und seine Vorläufer* (Leipzig: Breitkopf und Härtel, 1900). For Lucian's influence, see further Herbert Hunger, *Die hochsprachliche profane Literatur der Byzantiner; Teilbd. 2: Philologie, Profandichtung, Musik, Mathematik und Astronomie, Naturwissenschaften, Medizin, Kriegswissenschaft, Rechtsliteratur* (München: Beck, 1978), 151f., as well as Christopher Robinson, *Lucian and his Influence in Europe* (London: Duckworth, 1979) and more broadly, Werner von Koppenfels, *Der andere Blick. Das Vermächtnis des Menippos in der europäischen Literatur* (Munich: C.H. Beck, 2007). A rewarding treatment is Francis G. Allinson, *Lucian: Satirist and Artist* (Boston: Marshall Jones Company, 1926) who for his own part refers to Rohde's studies and to Swift's objectly "Lucianic" debt to Lucian.

44. "Imagine—I had stood in awe of that trash and had jumped to the conclusion that he was divinely happy on the basis of the smells from his kitchen

and the color of his robes" Lucian, *Volume VII*, 17–19. And Lucian goes on to mock the moneylenders, and so on (and on).

45. Empedocles, Frag. 404, *The Presocratic Philosophers*, 316.

46. This fascination remains even where Diogenes Laertius begins with a veritable catalogue of the various ways Empedocles was said to have exited this world. This indeed is the point of departure for the classicist Eva Chitwood's monograph, *Death by Philosophy: The Biographical Tradition in the Life and Death of the Archaic Philosophers Empedocles, Heraclitus, and Democritus* (Ann Arbor: University of Michigan Press, 2004).

47. Bracht Branham notes that the single sandal would have counted as a classical signifier: "Must this not be an allusion to Jason's singular footwear? Pelias is warned by an oracle to beware a man with one sandal (Pindar). Of course it's also a comic image. The evocation of Jason might have something to do with metempsychosis, suggesting a connection between the heroic 'healer' (Jason) and Empedocles." (Personal communication with the author.) This suggestion is illuminating but the question regarding the particular significance of such signifiers here remains to be answered. What does it mean that one sandal was tossed back? And did it mean that Empedocles, wherever he was going, went there wearing just one? The Derveni Krater's one-sandal shod figure only underscores this question.

48. This point is the most Lucianic inasmuch as recollecting Lucian's account, Empedocles survived the leap into the volcano as the man in the moon, living on gathered dew. But also to the extent that ancient bronze differs from the kind we know today in many ways and there were many kinds and much ancient bronze had a lower melting point: one of the reasons for its ubiquity and appeal and not less its utility. In Babette Babich, "Die Naturkunde der Griechischen Bronze im Spiegel des Lebens: Betrachtungen über Heideggers ästhetische Phänomenologie und Nietzsches agonale Politik," in *Internationales Jahrbuch für Hermeneutik*, ed. Günter Figal (Tübingen: Mohr Siebeck, 2008), 127–189, I argue that this labile character may serve to explain the abundance of life-size statues in antiquity by suggesting that portrait statues may have served as identifying place-holders of bronze to be quickly forged as armor on demand and handy in the absence of personal storage space given what we know of Greek domestic architecture.

49. There are a number of studies of this theme, beginning with Eliza Butler's *The Tyranny of Greece over Germany: A Study of the Influence Exercised by Greek Art and Poetry Over the Great German Writers of the of the Eighteenth, Nineteenth and Twentieth Centuries* (London: Cambridge University Press, 1935), but see for a recent account, Constanze Güthenke, *Placing Modern Greece: The Dynamics of Romantic Hellenism, 1770–1840* (Oxford: Oxford University Press, 2008), 70ff and Walter Seitter, "Der Deutsche Griechen-Komplex," in *Die Glücklichen sind neugierig Zehn Jahre Kolleg Friedrich Nietzsche*, eds. Julia Wagner and Stefan Wilke (Weimar: Bauhaus Universitätsverlag, 2009), 232–253.

50. Whether self-willed or not (and therefore an image of death in life, at least as set together with Lucian's *Kataplous*), Jung himself does not explore. Nevertheless, Jung glosses the account in question as the descent of Zarathustra into Hades

in his seminar from 4 May 1938. "There is the volcano and the fire underneath, the entrance to the interior of the earth, the entrance to the underworld—there is even old Cerberus, the fire dog—and Zarathustra is now going down into all this. Psychologically it would mean that after all that great talk, there is an underworld and down there one has to go. But if one is so high and mighty, why not stay up there? Why bother about this descent? Yet the tale says inevitably one goes down—that is the *enantiodromia*—and when one gets down there, well one will be burned up, one will dissolve." James L. Jarrett, ed., *Jung's Seminar on Nietzsche's Zarathustra* (Princeton, NJ: Princeton University Press, 1988), 2116–2117.

51. In general, when scholars say they are puzzled, they are usually halfway to dismissing the issue. The scholarly epoché brackets what does not make sense. Nietzsche's *Birth of Tragedy*, by contrast, attempts to revive questions usually taken for granted, and in this case, fairly striking questions: why tragedy? Why the delight in the tragic; that is: why the enjoyment of tragic music drama?

52. James L. Jarrett, ed., *Jung's Seminar on Nietzsche's Zarathustra*, 2117.

53. James L. Jarrett, ed., *Jung's Seminar on Nietzsche's Zarathustra*, 2117. In his text, Jung refers to Kerner's *Blätter aus Prevorst*, a series of volumes edited by Kerner and entitled *Blätter aus Prevorst; Originalien und Lesefrüchte für Freunde des innern Lebens, mitgetheilt von dem Herausgeber Der Seherin Aus Prevorst*. Erste Sammlung (Karlsruhe: Gottlieb Braun, 1831). See for a discussion, John R. Haule, "From Somnambulism to the Archetypes: The French Roots of Jung's Split With Freud," *The Psychoanalytic Review* 71/4 (1984): 635–659. This is an arena that calls for further research (Robin Small has emphasized the actual or literal historical elements of the account with respect to English history) but especially in connection with Nietzsche but also Hölderlin. This collection of spiritualist, mesmerist, and magnetic tales inspired by Erika Hauffe, the subject of *Die Seherin von Prevorst. Eröffnungen über das innere Leben der Menschen und über das Hereinragen einer Geisterwelt in die unsere*, was compiled over a number of years Justinius Kerner (1786–1862), a Suabian poet. As a medical student, Kerner had helped care for Hölderlin during his clinical confinement in Tübingen and was influential in arranging the publication of Hölderlin's collected works. The reference given by the compiler of Jung's Zarathustra seminar is to *Seeress of Prevorst*. Although Jung was in the habit of citing the two together, the citation he gives here is "Volume IV, page 57" (James L. Jarrett, ed., *Jung's Seminar on Nietzsche's Zarathustra*, 2117), can only refer to the *Blätter aus Prevorst*, which was indeed issued serially, although in this case the indicated page reference refers to this specific (first) collection of different writings, included together with a set of aphorism (from Professor Eschenmauer) and a selection of Kerner's own poems. I am grateful to Robin Small for drawing my attention to the need to clarify this. The story is also repeated (here citing the *Blätter aus Prevorst* rather than the *Seeress of Prevorst*) in Jung, "Approaching the Unconscious" in Jung, ed., *Man and His Symbols*, (New York: Random House, 1968), 24, citation in the note to page 24 and 389. For Jung who included an illustration of the unconscious influence of advertising on the previous page, the story demonstrates the actuality of uncon-

scious processes in Nietzsche's recollection, as in musical compositions where a composer reprises a folksong from his youth, "an idea or an image moves from the unconscious to the conscious mind," (Jung, "Approaching the Unconscious," 25). I add here that Robin Small in his *Nietzsche and Reé* (Oxford: Oxford University Press, 2005) also refers to Jung as well as to Kerner.

54. Justinius Kerner, *Die Seherin von Prevorst. Eröffnungen über das innere Leben der Menschen und über das Hereinragen einer Geisterwelt in die unsere* (Stuttgart: J. F. Steinkopf, 1963 [1829]). In English as *The Seeress of Prevost*, trans. Catherine Crowe (New York: Partridge & Brittan, 1855).

55. See Erwin Rohde, *Psyche: The Cult of Souls & The Belief in Immortality Among the Greeks*, trans. W. B. Hillis (London: Routledge & Kegan Paul, 1925). Originally published in 1894, Thomas Mann owned and annotated a copy of Rohde's *Psyche: Seelencult und Unsterblichkeits Glaube der Griechen* (Tübingen: Mohr, 1907).

56. "The four captains and a merchant, Mr Bell, went ashore on the island of Stromboli to shoot rabbits. At three o'clock they called the crew together to go aboard, when, to their inexpressible astonishment, they saw two men flying rapidly over them through the air. One was dressed in black, the other in grey. They approached them very closely, in the greatest haste; to their greatest dismay they descended amid the burning flames into the crater of the terrible volcano, Mt. Stromboli. They recognized the pair as acquaintances from London," James L. Jarrett, ed., *Jung's Seminar on Nietzsche's Zarathustra*, 1217–1218.

57. James L. Jarrett, ed., *Jung's Seminar on Nietzsche's Zarathustra*, 2118. In accord with the fetishism that seems to attend the search for Nietzsche's sources (whether to prove or disprove his originality), commentators can be expected to be quick to wonder whether Elisabeth was lying but the popularity of the book and the very coincidence of which Jung speaks between his own access to the book and the young Nietzsche and his sister's access suggest that this is not something it would served purposes to lie about. Indeed, the coincidence is plausible enough even without Elisabeth's confirmation and Bennholdt-Thomsen notes, following Jung, that Nietzsche concerns himself with Kerner between the ages of 12 and 15.

58. The story was one Jung had been telling since his inaugural dissertation, published two years after Nietzsche's death in 1902.

59. James L. Jarrett, ed., *Jung's Seminar on Nietzsche's Zarathustra*, 2118. I thank the anthropologist and Hölderlin scholar, Annette Hornbacher for noting that Jung's invocation of this color distinction and significance is itself taken from Kerner.

60. If Gary Shapiro is right to point to the geological significance of the contrast of this passage with the *Isles of the Blest* where Zarathustra "appears mysteriously on a volcanic island (where his Shadow seems to fly into the volcano itself)," Gary Shapiro, "Beyond Peoples and Fatherlands: Nietzsche's Geophilosophy and the Direction of the Earth," *Journal of Nietzsche Studies*, 35–36 (2008): 13. Restoring this emphasis however, an emphasis Shapiro conscientiously avoids,

exposes us once again to what he identifies as the risks and dangers of "reading Nietzsche through the prism of Hölderlin's Greek and German earth, in a Heideggerian mode, risks what Foucault called the return and retreat of the origin and the nostalgia and site fetishism that mar Heidegger's thought," Gary Shapiro, "Beyond Peoples and Fatherlands," 10.

61. James L. Jarrett, ed., *Jung's Seminar on Nietzsche's Zarathustra*, 1224).

62. In addition, again, to numerous English readings in German studies as well as in philosophy, Rudolf Eisler's *Handwörterbuch der Philosophie* repays reading with regard to the question of the *Übermensch* as a philosophical notion in particular connection with Nietzsche. For a general overview, see Ernst Benz, "Das Bild des Übermenschen in der Europäischen Geistesgeschichte" in his *Der Übermensch. Eine Diskussion* (Stuttgart: Rhein-Verlag, 1961), 19–161 as well as Karen Joisten, *Die Überwindung der Anthropozentrizität durch Friedrich Nietzsche* (Würzburg: Königshausen und Neumann, 1994), 172ff.

15. "Falling in Love with Becoming": Remarks on Nietzsche and Emerson

Dieter Thomä

1. Richard Ford, *The Lay of the Land* (New York: Alfred A. Knopf, 2006), 52–54; italics original.

2. Richard Ford, *The Lay of the Land*, 200 and Richard Ford, *Independence Day* (New York: Vintage, 1996), 377.

3. Ralph W. Emerson, *Essays and Lectures* (New York: Library of America, 1983), 271 (italics original).

4. See Vivetta Vivarelli, "Nietzsche und Emerson: Über einige Pfade in Zarathustras metaphorischer Landschaft," *Nietzsche-Studien* 16 (1987): 227–263; Stanley Cavell, *This New Yet Unapproachable America: Lectures after Emerson after Wittgenstein* (Albuquerque: Living Batch Press, 1989); Georg Stack, *Nietzsche and Emerson: An Elective Affinity* (Athens: Ohio University Press, 1992); David Mikics, *The Romance of Individualism in Emerson and Nietzsche* (Athens: Ohio University Press, 2003); Benedetta Zavatta, "Nietzsche, Emerson und das Selbstvertrauen," *Nietzsche-Studien* 35 (2006): 274–297; Dieter Thomä, "Jeder ist sich selbst der Fernste: Zum Zusammenhang zwischen personaler Identität und Moral bei Nietzsche und Emerson," *Nietzsche-Studien* 36 (2007): 316–343; Dieter Thomä, "Das werdende Selbst: Identität, Alterität und Interaktion nach Emerson, Nietzsche und Cavell," in *Happy Days: Lebenswissen nach Cavell*, eds. Kathrin Thiele and Katrin Trüstedt (Munich: Wilhem Fink, 2010), 171–186.

5. Richard Ford, *The Lay of the Land*, 73 (italics original).

6. Richard Ford, *The Lay of the Land*, 379.

7. Richard Ford, *The Lay of the Land*, 249 (italics original).

8. Richard Ford, *The Lay of the Land*, 76.

9. Ralph W. Emerson, *Essays and Lectures*, 262–263 (italics original).

10. Ralph W. Emerson, *Essays and Lectures*, 274, 276.

11. John Updike, "Emersonianism," in: *Odd Jobs* (New York: Knopf, 1991), 159.

12. John Updike, "Emersonianism," 159–163.

13. Harold Bloom. *Poetics of Influence* (New Haven: Henry R. Schwab, 1988), 310, 319.

14. George Kateb, *The Inner Ocean: Individualism and Democratic Culture* (Ithaca, N.Y.: Cornell University Press, 1992), 225–226.

15. Michael Sandel, *Democracy's Discontent: America in Search of a Public Philosophy* (Cambridge, MA: Harvard University Press, 1996), 17.

16. Judith Shklar, *Redeeming American Political Thought* (Chicago/London: University of Chicago Press, 1998), 50–51.

17. Stanley Cavell, *Conditions Handsome and Unhandsome* (Chicago/London: University of Chicago, 1990), 134–137.

18. Ralph W. Emerson, *Essays and Lectures*, 1081.

19. Ralph W. Emerson, *Essays and Lectures*, 1081.

20. Ralph W. Emerson, *Complete Works* (Boston/New York: Houghton Mifflin, 1904), Vol. VII: *Society and Solitude*, 114–115 (italics original).

21. Stanely Cavell, *Conditions Handsome and Unhandsome*, 137.

22. Stanely Cavell, *Conditions Handsome and Unhandsome*, 137.

23. Emily Dickinson, *The Poems* (Cambridge, MA: Harvard University Press, 1979), 971.

24. Ralph W. Emerson, *Essays and Lectures*, 604.

25. Ralph W. Emerson, *Essays and Lectures*, 604.

26. Ralph W. Emerson, *Essays and Lectures*, 350–1.

27. Ralph W. Emerson, *Essays and Lectures*, 650–651 (here he uses one of the epithets given to Socrates by Plato).

28. Ralph W. Emerson, *Essays and Lectures*, 505.

29. Ralph W. Emerson, *Essays and Lectures*, 414; see on "abandonment," Stanley Cavell, *In Quest of the Ordinary* (Chicago/London: University of Chicago Press 1988), 132.

30. Ralph W. Emerson, *Essays and Lectures*, 79.

31. Ralph W. Emerson, *Essays and Lectures*, 1096; see Stanley Cavell, *Conditions Handsome and Unhandsome*, 16.

32. Vanessa Lemm, "Is Nietzsche a Perfectionist? Rawls, Cavell, and the Politics of Culture in Nietzsche's 'Schopenhauer as Educator,'" *Journal of Nietzsche Studies* 34 (2007): 12.

33. Stanley Cavell, *Conditions Handsome and Unhandsome*, 16.

34. See Stanley Cavell, *This New Yet Unapproachable America: Lectures after Emerson after Wittgenstein*, 24–25; Stanley Cavell, *Cities of Words: Pedagogical Letters on a Register of The Moral Life* (Cambridge, MA: Harvard University Press, 2004), 392.

35. William James, *The Writings: A Comprehensive Edition* (Chicago/London: University of Chicago Press, 1977), 73.

36. Ralph W. Emerson, *Essays and Lectures*, 414 (see above).

37. Stanley Cavell, *The Claim of Reason: Wittgenstein, Skepticism, Morality, and Tragedy* (Oxford: Oxford University Press, 1979), 459.

38. See Alexander Nehamas, *Nietzsche: Life as Literature* (Cambridge, MA: Harvard University Press, 1985).

39. See Daniel Conway, "Life and Self-Overcoming," in *A Companion to Nietzsche*, ed. Keith Ansell Pearson (Oxford: Blackwell Publishing, 2006), 532–547.

40. See, for example, Vanessa Lemm, "Is Nietzsche a Perfectionist? Rawls, Cavell, and the Politics of Culture in Nietzsche's 'Schopenhauer as Educator'" on the controversy between John Rawls and Stanley Cavell.

41. James Conant, "Nietzsche's Perfectionism: A Reading of 'Schopenhauer as Educator'," in *Nietzsche's Postmoralism*, ed. Richard Schacht (Cambridge: Cambridge University Press, 2000), 181–257.

42. Theodor W. Adorno, *Minima Moralia: Reflections on a Damaged Live* (London and New York: Verso, 2005), 97.

43. Ralph W. Emerson, *The Collected Works*, Vol. II: *Essays: First Series* (Cambridge, MA, and London: Harvard University Press, 1979), 272.

44. Ralph W. Emerson, *Essays and Lectures*, 247; Ralph W. Emerson, *The Collected Works*, Vol. II, 272.

45. Ralph W. Emerson, *Essays and Lectures*, 247.

46. Johann Gottlieb Fichte, *Der geschloßne Handelsstaat* (Hamburg: Meiner, 1979), 126; Oswald Spengler, *Der Untergang des Abendlandes* (Munich: Deutscher Taschenbuch Verlag, 1991), 45–6.

47. Gilles Deleuze, "Nomad Thought," in *The New Nietzsche*, ed. David B. Allison (Cambridge, MA: Rowman and Littlefield Publishers, 1985), 146, 148.

48. Gilles Deleuze, "Nomad Thought," 148.

49. Gilles Deleuze, "Nomad Thought," 149.

50. Tracy B. Strong, *Friedrich Nietzsche and the Politics of Transfiguration* (Urbana: University of Illinois Press, 2000), 266.

51. Stanley Cavell, *This New Yet Unapproachable America: Lectures after Emerson after Wittgenstein*, 36.

52. Ludwig Wittgenstein, *Philosophische Untersuchungen—Philosophical Investigations* (Oxford: Blackwell, 1953), 49.

53. Stanley Cavell, *The Claim of Reason: Wittgenstein, Skepticism, Morality, and Tragedy*, 369.

54. Ludwig Wittgenstein, *Philosophische Untersuchungen—Philosophical Investigations*, 85 (italics original).

55. Ludwig Wittgenstein, *Philosophische Untersuchungen—Philosophical Investigations*, 48.

56. Ludwig Wittgenstein, *Culture and Value* (Oxford: Blackwell, 1980), 65.

57. Gordon Baker, ed. *The Voices of Wittgenstein—The Vienna Circle: Ludwig Wittgenstein and Friedrich Waismann* (London and New York: Routledge, 2003), 66.

58. Ludwig Wittgenstein, *Culture and Value*, 73.

59. Ralph W. Emerson, *Essays and Lectures*, 412.

60. Friedrich Kaulbach, *Nietzsches Idee einer Experimentalphilosophie* (Cologne and Vienna: Böhlau 1980), 144; Hans Seigfried, "Nietzsche's radical experimentalism," *Man and World* 22 (1989): 489, 493–494.

61. Walter Kaufmann, *Nietzsche: Philosopher, Psychologist, Antichrist* (Princeton: Princeton University Press, 1974), 89; Georg Stack, *Lange and Nietzsche* (Berlin and New York: De Gruyter, 1983), 252.

62. Karl Löwith, *Nietzsches Philosophie der ewigen Wiederkehr des Gleichen* (Hamburg: Meiner, 1986), 15–21; Kaufmann, *Nietzsche: Philosopher, Psychologist, Antichrist*, 87.

63. Volker Gerhardt, "Experimental Philosophy—An Attempt at a Reconstruction," in *Nietzsche: Critical Assessments*, eds. Daniel W. Conway and Peter S. Groff (London: Routledge, 1998), Vol. III, 79–94.

64. Stephen Toulmin, *Cosmopolis: The Hidden Agenda of Modernity* (Chicago and London: Chicago University Press, 1990).

65. John S. Mill, "On Liberty," in *Collected Works*, Vol. XVIII (Toronto and Buffalo: University of Toronto Press, 1977), 281.

66. Dieter Thomä, "Das gesprochene Wort verliert seinen Eigensinn: Die Spuren der Sprach- und Lebensphilosophie Ralph Waldo Emersons im Werk Robert Musils," *Deutsche Vierteljahrsschrift für Literaturwissenschaft und Geistesgeschichte* 80 (2006): 456–485.

67. John Dewey, *German Philosophy and Politics* (New York: H. Holt, 1915), 125–126; John Dewey, *Philosophy and Civilization* (New York: Minton, Black and Company, 1931), 25.

68. See Martin Jay, *Songs of Experience: Modern American and European Variations on a Universal Theme* (Berkeley and Los Angeles and London: University of California Press, 2005); Kwame Anthony Appiah, *Experiments in Ethics* (Cambridge, MA: Harvard University Press, 2008).

69. Richard Ford, *Independence Day*, 291.

70. Richard Ford, *The Lay of the Land*, 120.

71. Richard Ford, *Independence Day*, 430.

16. "We Are Experiments": Nietzsche on Morality and Authenticity

Keith Ansell-Pearson

1. In a note from the autumn of 1880 Nietzsche maintains that the metaphysical need is not the source of religion, as might be supposed, but rather the aftereffect of its decline: the "need" is a result and not an origin (*KSA* 9:6[290]). See also *GS* 151 where Nietzsche makes it clear that he is arguing contra Schopenhauer on this point. For Schopenhauer on the "metaphysical need," see Arthur Schopenhauer, *The World as Will and Representation*, vol. 2, trans. Eric F. J. Payne (New York: Dover Press, 1966), 160–191.

2. Maudemarie Clark and Brian Leiter, "Introduction," in *Daybreak: Thoughts on the Prejudices of Morality*, Friedrich Nietzsche, trans. R. J. Hollingdale (Cambridge: Cambridge University Press, 1997), viii–xxxiv.

3. Rüdiger Safranski, *Nietzsche, A Philosophical Biography*, trans. Shelley Frisch (New York: Norton 2002), 207–219.

4. Pierre Hadot, *Philosophy as a Way of Life* (Oxford: Basil Blackwell 1995), 265–266. In a letter to Heinrich von Stein of December 1882 Nietzsche says he "would like to take away from human existence some of its heartbreaking and cruel character" (Letter Nr. 342, *KSB* 6:286f).

5. Catherine Wilson, *Epicureanism at the Origins of Modernity* (Oxford: Oxford University Press 2008), 7. See also "Epicurus" in *The Epicurus Reader*, eds. Brad Inwood and Lloyd P. Gerson (Indianapolis: Hackett, 1994), 29: "For there is nothing fearful in life for one who has grasped that there is nothing fearful in the absence of life . . . the wise man neither rejects life nor fears death." As Porter notes: ". . . in Epicureanism *love of life is love of a mortal life* and not a love of life as abstracted from death, much less of immortal life," James I. Porter, "Epicurean Attachments: Life, Pleasure, Beauty, Friendship, and Piety," *Cronache Ercolanesi* 33 (2003): 212.

6. I have discussed these "sublimities of philosophy" in Keith Ansell-Pearson, "For Mortal Souls: Philosophy and Therapeia in Nietzsche's *Dawn*," *Philosophy and Therapeia. Royal Institute of Philosophy Supplement* 66 (2010): 137–165. We can note that Nietzsche confesses to not fearing death himself in a note of 1878: "A prominent quality: a more refined heroism (which, by the way, I recognize in Epicurus). In my book there is not a word against the fear of death. I have little of that" (*KSA* 8:28[15]). There are several places in his published writings where Nietzsche writes in praise of the rational and voluntary death, and in a note from 1888 he writes of the need to "convert the stupid psychological fact" of death "into a moral necessity. So to live that one can also *will at the right time to die!*" (*KSA* 12:10[165]; *WP* 916).

7. Duncan Large, "Nietzsche and the Figure of Columbus," *Nietzsche-Studien* 24 (1995): 174.

8. This has also been noted by Julian Young who construes *Dawn* as practicing an Epicurean-inspired conception of the goal of philosophy, which involves "happiness-promoting 'wisdom'" rather than knowledge-promoting theory or theory for the sake of theory. He describes *Dawn* not as a theoretical treatise but as a "spiritual *resource*," by which he means a book for meditation and rumination rather than instant consumption. He rightly adds that the book does not aim to fulfill this purpose in the manner of Eastern philosophy where the aim is to put the intellect out of action. As he puts it, "the basis for the work is the use, even the passionate use, of reason." See Julian Young, *Friedrich Nietzsche. A Philosophical Biography* (Cambridge: Cambridge University Press, 2010), 297, 299.

9. Melissa Lane has suggested that from *The Gay Science* (1882) on, that is, after *Dawn*, Nietzsche's preoccupation with Epicurus and Epicureans evaporates and that his subsequent remarks on them are almost relentlessly negative. She also argues that the late Nietzsche favors Stoicism over Epicureanism, Melissa Lane, "Honesty as the Best Policy: Nietzsche on Redlichkeit and the Contrast between Stoic and Epicurean Strategies of the Self," in *Histories of Postmodernism*, eds.

Mark Bevir, Jill Hargis, and Sara Rushing (London: Routledge, 2007), 25–53. On her reading the difference is that whereas for Nietzsche Epicureanism is fatally flawed as a cognitive stance, the Stoics steel themselves cognitively and emotionally so as to confront reality, and in the process they expand their knowledge to the whole of nature. Where the one restricts knowledge the other acknowledges reality in terms of a non-consolatory, non-delusional cognitive attitude toward it. Nietzsche's later appraisal of Epicurus is complex because he is identifying in him *both* a will to knowledge (in the form of knowledge of our actual mortal conditions of existence) and the denial of such a will (in the form of 'decadent' attempt to escape from the pain and tragic lot of human existence). In *GM* (1887) Nietzsche refers to the super cool but "suffering Epicurus" as one who may have been hypnotized by the "feeling of nothingness" and the "repose of deepest sleep," that is, the *absence* of suffering (*GM* III: 17). In *NCW* (1888) Nietzsche notes that Epicurus may well have worn a *mask* and so may have been superficial out of profundity: "Profound suffering makes you noble; it separates.— One of the most refined forms of disguise is Epicureanism, and a certain showy courage of taste that accepts suffering without a second thought and resists everything sad and profound. There are "cheerful people" who use cheerfulness because it lets them be misunderstood:—they *want* to be misunderstood" (*NCW* 3). For further insight into Nietzsche's reading of Epicurus, see also Howard Caygill, "The Consolation of Philosophy or Neither Dionysus nor the Crucified," *Journal of Nietzsche Studies* 7 (1994): 113–140 and Richard Bett, "Nietzsche, the Greeks, and Happiness (with special reference to Aristotle and Epicurus)," *Philosophical Topics* 33 2 (2008): 45–70.

10. Inwood and Gerson, *The Epicurus Reader*, 30.

11. Inwood and Gerson, *The Epicurus Reader*, 29.

12. Inwood and Gerson, *The Epicurus Reader*, 29.

13. Inwood and Gerson, *The Epicurus Reader*, 29.

14. For further insight into *ataraxia* in Epicurus see James I. Porter, "Epicurean Attachments: Life, Pleasure, Beauty, Friendship, and Piety," *Cronache Ercolanesi* 33 (2003): 205–227. Porter describes it as "stable (katastematic) pleasure" (James I. Porter, "Epicurean Attachments," 214), and, furthermore, as the "basal experience of pleasure" on account of it being the criterion of all pleasure (James I. Porter, "Epicurean Attachments," 218). In this sense, then, it is more than a condition of simple or mere happiness: "it seems to operate as life's internal formal principle, as that which gives moral sense and shape to a life that is lived . . ." (James I. Porter, "Epicurean Attachments," 218).

15. Martha Nussbaum, *The Therapy of Desire: Theory and Practice in Hellenistic Ethics* (Princeton: Princeton University Press, 1994), 110. Nussbaum also offers imaginative insight into Epicurus's Garden (Martha Nussbaum, *The Therapy of Desire*, 119).

16. Nietzsche was a close reader of Plato's *Phaedo*, which depicts the last days of Socrates and the last words of the dying Socrates; the "image of the dying Socrates" runs throughout Nietzsche's writings, with one notable presence in *GS*

340. For an instructive attempt to bring together Plato, Epicurus, and Nietzsche on life and death, the soul and the body, see Howard Caygill, "The Consolation of Philosophy or Neither Dionysus nor the Crucified," *Journal of Nietzsche Studies*, 7 Spring (1994): 113–140.

17. In *D* 202 Nietzsche encourages us to do with away with the concepts of "sin" and "punishment": "May these banished monsters henceforth live somewhere other than among human beings, if they want to go on living at all and do not perish of disgust with themselves!" In *D* 208 entitled "Question of Conscience" he states what he wishes to see changed: "We want to cease making causes into sinners and consequences into executioners." In *D* 53 he notes that it is the most conscientious who suffer so dreadfully from the fears of Hell: "Thus life has been made gloomy precisely for those who had need of cheerfulness and pleasant pictures . . ."

18. Pierre Hadot, *Philosophy as a Way of Life*, trans. Arnold Davidson (Oxford: Blackwell Publishing 1995) 252.

19. Catherine Wilson neatly lays out the central tenets of the Epicurean system in her recent study. They include: the denial of supernatural agency engaged in the design and maintenance of the world; the view that self-moving, subvisible particles acting blindly bring about all growth, change, and decline; and the insistence that the goal of ethical self-discipline, which involves asceticism, is the minimization of mental and physical suffering. Catherine Wilson, *Epicureanism at the Origins of Modernity* (New York: Oxford University Press 2008), 37. It is on this last point that Nietzsche will come to later criticize Epicureanism and describe Epicurus as a "typical decadent." See *A* 30. In the same text Epicurus is once again prized on account of his battle against "the *subterranean* cults, the whole of latent Christianity, his fight against the 'corruption of the soul' through notions of guilt, punishment, and immortality" (*A* 58).

20. Pierre Hadot, *Philosophy as a Way of Life*, 87.

21. In a note from 1881 Nietzsche states that he considers the various moral schools of antiquity to be "experimental laboratories" containing a number of recipes for worldly wisdom or the art of living and holds that these experiments now belong to us as our legitimate property: "we shall not hesitate to adopt a Stoic recipe just because we have profited in the past from Epicurean recipes" (*KSA* 9:15[59]).

22. See also *D* 141 and 146 on Nietzsche's opposition to "picturesque morality" and "petty bourgeois morality." In *D* 432 Nietzsche speaks of his "audacious morality (*verwegenen Moralität*)."

23. See Carl Sachs, "Nietzsche's *Daybreak*: Toward a Naturalized Theory of Autonomy," *Epoché* 13 1 (2008): 88.

24. In his sketch of modern European thought since the French Revolution Nietzsche fails to acknowledge, of course, the extent to which Mill is a champion of individual liberty and autonomy. In the chapter on "Individuality, as one of the elements of well-being" in his *On Liberty* Mill writes: "but the evil, is that individual spontaneity is hardly recognized by the common modes of thinking,

as having any intrinsic worth, or deserving any regard on its own account. The majority, being satisfied with the ways of mankind as they now are (for it is they who make them what they are), cannot comprehend why those ways should not be good enough for everybody . . .", John Stuart Mill, *On Liberty* (Oxford: Oxford University Press, 1991), 63.

25. At this time Nietzsche is reading Voltaire's *Mahomet* (see *HH* 221) and recommending to people, including his sister Elisabeth, that they read it (see letter to her dated 13 February 1881, Letter Nr. 82, *KSB* 6:62). However, we need to read carefully here since there is the danger of turning Nietzsche's championing of the Enlightenment against forces of reaction into an all-too timely position against Islam. To avoid this requires a careful analysis of Nietzsche's comments on different religions. In *GS* 347, for example, it is not Islam but Christianity and Buddhism that he describes as teaching fanaticism. In *D* 68 Saint Paul is described as a fanatic whilst in *D* 546 Epictetus is presented as an example of a non-fanatical person. For further insight into Nietzsche on fanaticism, see Bernard Reginster, "What is a Free Spirit? Nietzsche on Fanaticism," *Archiv für Geschichte der Philosophie* 85 1 (2003): 51–85.

26. Nietzsche considers Kant an important figure because he stands outside the movement within modernity that places the stress on the sympathetic affects (*D* 132). The problem is that his conception of the rational moral law conceals a remnant of ascetic cruelty (*D* 338; see also *D* 187, 207).

27. In *Daybreak* Nietzsche does not spell out his reasons for rejecting "free will" or make clear in what sense he intends the notion. But see *WS* 9–11 for what might be the necessary set of insights; see also *D* 112 and 128.

28. Nietzsche continues to affirm the rational death in his subsequent writings. See, for example (*TI* "Skirmishes" 36): "For love of *life*—one ought to want death to be different, free, conscious, no accident, no ambush . . . ."; and *WP* 916, where Nietzsche says that the task is to transform a "stupid, psychological fact" into a "moral necessity": "So to live that one can also *will at the right time to die*!"

29. See also Michael Ure, *Nietzsche's Therapy: Self-Cultivation in the Middle Works* (Lanham: Lexington Books, 2008).

30. Ruth Abbey, *Nietzsche's Middle Period* (New York: Oxford University Press, 2000), 102.

31. Ruth Abbey, *Nietzsche's Middle Period*, 99.

32. For further insight into the different depictions of Socrates we find in Nietzsche, see Alexander Nehamas, *The Art of Living: Socratic Reflections from Plato to*

Foucault (Berkeley and London: University of California Press, 1998), 128–156. See also Pierre Hadot, *Philosophy as a Way of Life*, 147–79. In *D* 9 Socrates is said to be one of those (rare) moralists who offer the individual a morality of self-control and temperance and as a means to their own advantage or a personal key to happiness.

33. See Julian Young, *Friedrich Nietzsche. A Philosophical Biography* (Cambridge: Cambridge University Press, 2010), 306. For further insight into

Nietzsche on an ethics of self-cultivation, see Michael Ure, *Nietzsche's Therapy* and Horst Hutter, *Shaping the Future: Nietzsche's New Regime of the Soul and Its Ascetic Practices* (Lanham: Lexington Books, 2006).

34. Julian Young, *Friedrich Nietzsche*, 305.

35. See Carl B. Sachs "Nietzsche's *Daybreak*: Toward a Naturalized Theory of Autonomy," 91.

36. Gianni Vattimo, *Dialogue with Nietzsche* (New York: Columbia University Press, 2006), 164. This essay by Vattimo was originally published in Italian in 1979.

37. Gianni Vattimo, *Dialogue with Nietzsche*, 162–163.

38. Gianni Vattimo, *Dialogue with Nietzsche*, 161.

39. I have in mind the well-known passages in *Twilight of the Idols*: "The Individual is a piece of fate from top to bottom, one more law, one more necessity for all that is to come and will be" (*TI* "Morality" 6), and: "One is necessary, one is a piece of fate . . ." (*TI* "Errors" 8).

40. Speaking of the *task* that wants to become incarnate and enter the world, Nietzsche writes of the free spirit: "The secret power and necessity of this task will rule among and in his particular destinies like an unconscious pregnancy—long before he has glimpsed this task itself and knows its name" (*HH* "Preface" 7). As Simon May has noted, freedom presupposes, as its condition—as "fate" or "necessity"—"the reality of our nature, nurture, and life-circumstances, and hence of our individual past . . . 'Freedom of the will'—which, for him, means mastery of ourselves and thus of circumstances—is unattainable without maximally expressing what he calls the 'necessity' of our own nature," Simon May, *Nietzsche's Ethics and His War on Morality* (Oxford and New York: Oxford University Press, 1999), 21.

41. Gianni Vattimo, *Dialogue with Nietzsche*, 160. Vattimo's claim is that the dawn heralded in Nietzsche's book is the "overman": "The elements of dissolution—of the ego, of culture, of 'form'—which the avant-garde embraced and sought to push further and which also constitute the key to Nietzsche's work as 'critic of culture,' are not pure symptoms of decadence and disintegration, but neither are they simply the preparatory phase for a subsequent 'positive' construct. 'Dissolution' is what *positively* characterizes the overman" (Gianni Vattimo, *Dialogue with Nietzsche*, 160). Consider also the following: "The overman is not coming in the future, after this process of dissolution, after this farewell to the subject. He is precisely this depotentiated subject, no longer consigned to his own decisions and to pathos, able to live a superficial existence without anguish. The individual without a center—or even: the individual without qualities—is not an intermediate stage, a transit zone toward the construction of the new man" (Gianni Vattimo, *Dialogue with Nietzsche*, 165). For Vattimo, then, liberation from power, which requires subjects over which to dominate, comes about from a process of "dis-subjection" or from ceasing to be a subject altogether.

42. Gianni Vattimo, *Dialogue with Nietzsche*, 165.

43. Sachs defines heteronomous subjectivity as the internalization of domination, "a subjectivity that has been structured through social practices which one has not reflectively revised and endorsed as one's own," Carl B. Sachs, "Nietzsche's *Daybreak*: Toward a Naturalized Theory of Autonomy," 93.

17. States and Nomads: Hegel's World and Nietzsche's Earth
Gary Shapiro

1. For example Robert Gooding-Williams, *Zarathustra's Dionysian Modernism* (Stanford: Stanford University Press, 2001), 65.

2. For example Adrian Del Caro, *Grounding Nietzsche's Rhetoric of Earth* (New York: de Gruyter, 2004).

3. Gaston Bachelard, *Air and Dreams*, trans. Edith and C. Frederick Farrell (Dallas: Dallas Institute Publications, 1988); Luce Irigaray, *Marine Lover*, trans. Gillian Gill (New York: Columbia University Press, 1991).

4. See David Farrell Krell, *Postponements: Woman, Sensuality, and Death in Nietzsche* (Bloomington: Indiana University Press, 1986); Graham Parkes, introduction and notes to his translation of *Thus Spoke Zarathustra* (New York: Penguin, 2005).

5. In the 1880s Nietzsche was a careful reader of Friedrich Ratzel's *Anthropo-Geographie* (Stuttgart: J. Engelhorm, 1882), which argues—against Kant, Hegel, and others—that mobility rather than permanent attachment to territory is the most general characteristic of humans' relation to territory. See Stephan Günzel, *Geophilosophie: Nietzsches philosophische Geographie* (Berlin: Akademie Verlag, 2001), Stephan Günzel "Nietzsche's Geophilosophy," *The Journal of Nietzsche Studies* 25 (Spring 2003): 78–91; Gary Shapiro, "Territory, Landscape, Garden: Toward Geoaesthetics," *Angelaki* 9 2 (2004): 103–116; Gary Shapiro, "Nietzsche on Geophilosophy and Geoaesthetics" in *A Companion to Nietzsche*, ed. Keith Ansell Pearson (New York: Blackwell, 2006), 477–494 and "Beyond Peoples and Fatherlands," *Journal of Nietzsche Studies* 35–36 (2008): 9–27.

6. See letter to Hermann Mushacke 1865, Nr. 480, *KSB* 2:85. Before that, he took several courses at Schulpforta based on textbooks on world-history, which appear to be indebted in a general way to Hegel. Johann Figl, *Nietzsche und die Religionen* (Berlin: de Gruyter, 2008), 52–66.

7. Gilles Deleuze and Claire Parnet, *Dialogues* (New York: Columbia University Press, 1988), 30–31. For further considerations of Nietzsche's geophilosophy, see Gilles Deleuze and Félix Guattari, *What Is Philosophy?* trans. Hugh Tomlinson and Graham Burchell (New York: Columbia University Press, 1994), 102 and the entire chapter on "Geophilosophy." Stephan Günzel, *Geophilosophie: Nietzsches philosophische Geographie* (Berlin: Akademie Verlag, 2001) is a very comprehensive study of Nietzsche's geophilosophy illuminated both by the philosophy of Deleuze and Guattari and a careful attention to Nietzsche's extensive reading in nineteenth century geographical studies, including theoretical ones. See also Günzel "Nietzsche's Geophilosophy," *The Journal of Nietzsche Studies* 25

(Spring 2003): 78–91 and Sebastian Posth, *Der meteorologische Komplex bei Nietzsche* (Bochum: Germanistisches Institut, 2002).

8. In a letter of 29 March 1871 to Rohde, Nietzsche speaks with obvious irony of the "so-called world history of the last ten months," that is Prussian victory over France and the founding of the German Reich (Letter Nr. 130, *KSB* 3:190). A few months later Nietzsche writes (*BT* 15) that "we must regard Socrates as the nub and turning point of so-called world history." Here he seems torn between using the concept and casting a cold eye on both "*Hegelei*" in general and the more specifically contemporary triumphalism that he attacked in *UM* I, against David F. Strauss.

9. This late formulation in *GM* cites and recapitulates *D* 18, indicating the continuing importance for Nietzsche of this topic.

10. For a sampling of additional passages, see *BT* 7, 15; *AOM* 33, 94; *A* 24.

11. Georg W. F. Hegel, *Introduction to the Philosophy of History*, trans. Leo Rauch (Indianapolis: Hackett, 1988), 42.

12. Georg W. F. Hegel, *Introduction to the Philosophy of History*, 16.

13. Georg W. F. Hegel, *Encyclopedia of the Philosophical Sciences*, trans. William Wallace and A.V. Miller (Oxford: Oxford University Press, 1971), 549.

14. Georg W. F. Hegel, *Encyclopedia of the Philosophical Sciences*, 549; Hegel makes similar claims in the lectures: Georg W. F. Hegel, *Introduction to the Philosophy of History* 16, 42, 50.

15. Nietzsche is well aware of the complex textual and linguistic history of *Nation*, *Volk*, and related terms. In *GS* 146 he notes that "the names of *Völker* are usually terms of abuse," and goes on to remark: "The 'Germans': this originally meant 'heathen' [*die Heiden*]; that is what the Goths after their conversion named the great mass of their unbaptized kindred tribes [*die grosse Masse ihrer ungetauften Stammverwandten*], in accordance with their translation of the Septuagint in which the heathens were designated with a word that in Greek means 'the peoples' [*Völker*]; see Ulfilas." The original term in the Hebrew scriptures is *goy*, used often in the singular to refer to the Jewish nation or people (see *Genesis* 12:2), but in the plural *goyim* referring to non-Jews or Gentiles. While the term has a neutral sense in this context it has taken on a pejorative one in later usage, and Luther typically translates it as "heathens." The Latin Vulgate uses *gens*, the Septuagint *ethnos*. Revised versions of Luther's Bible generally substitute *Nationen* for *Heiden*.

16. Martin Heidegger, *The Fundamental Concepts of Metaphysics*, trans. William McNeill and Nicholas Walker (Bloomington: Indiana University Press, 1995).

17. Georg W. F. Hegel, *Introduction to the Philosophy of History*, 42.

18. Georg W. F. Hegel, *The Philosophy of History*, trans. John Sibree (New York: Dover, 1956): 341.

19. Georg W. F. Hegel, *Introduction to the Philosophy of History*, 24.

20. Georg W. F. Hegel, *Introduction to the Philosophy of History*, 89–90.

21. Georg W. F. Hegel, *The Philosophy of History*, 358.

22. Carl Schmitt, *Political Theology*, trans. George Schwab (Chicago: University of Chicago Press, 2005).

23. Alain Badiou claims that this is the book's most decisive chapter in line with his own concept of the event, but does not mention Hegel in this connection. See "Who Is Nietzsche?," *Pli* 11 (2001): 1–10.

24. Georg W.F. Hegel, *Encyclopedia of the Philosophical Sciences*, trans. William Wallace and A.V. Miller (Oxford: Oxford University Press, 1971), 549.

25. See *Z* I "The Afterworldly" where Zarathustra suggests that we may be led away from the earth by ventriloquists of being, with variations and plays on the term *Bauchredner* (ventriloquist).

26. For a fuller discussion see Gary Shapiro, "Beyond Peoples and Fatherlands," *Journal of Nietzsche Studies* 35–36 (2008): 9–27.

27. For example, both the first and most recent translations of *BGE*, by Helen Zimmern and Judith Norman (Cambridge: Cambridge University Press, 2002), translate *Menge* in *BGE* 256 (and occasionally elsewhere) as "masses." Other problematic English translations of *Menge* abound, R. J. Hollingdale's version of *Human, All Too Human* 472 (Cambridge: Cambridge University Press, 1986). See *Menge* in Grimm's *Wörterbuch*:

http://germazope.uni-trier.de/Projects/WBB/woerterbuecher/dwb/wbgui

Another crucial passage employing the distinction: "Statistics prove that there are laws in history. Indeed, it proves how common and disgustingly uniform the mass [*Masse*] is. You should have tried statistical analysis in Athens for once! The lower and more non-individual the mass [*Masse*] is, the statistical laws are that much stronger. If the multitude [*Menge*] is finer and nobler, the law goes to the devil" (*KSA* 7:29[41]; see *Z* "Prologue" 5; *KSA* 7:5[98]; *KSA* 9:11[57]; *KSA* 12:2[76]).

28. Yirmiyahu Yovel says that "there is a marked lacuna in (Nietzsche's) thinking—the lack of a positive philosophy of the 'multitude.' Politics is not about the happy few but about those ordinary people, the modern mass or 'herd,' which Nietzsche did not care about and did not make the topic of any positive philosophical reflection." Yovel goes on to say that this political lacuna left (and still leaves) Nietzsche open to abuse by Fascists, Nazis, and the like. Yovel conflates multitude, herd, and mass in "Nietzsche and the Jews: The Structure of an Ambivalence," in *Nietzsche and Jewish Culture*, ed. Jacob Golomb (New York: Routledge, 1997), 132. On what could be called Nietzsche's affirmative concept of the multitude or *Menge*, see Hubert Cancik, "'Mongols, Semites, and the Purebred Greeks': Nietzsche's Handling of the Racial Doctrines of his Time," in *Nietzsche and Jewish Culture*, ed. Jacob Golomb (New York: Routledge, 1997), 55–75; and Shapiro "Beyond Peoples and Fatherlands."

29. Georg W. F. Hegel, *The Philosophy of History*, 416–417.

30. Georg W. F. Hegel, *The Philosophy of History*, 417.

31. Georg W. F. Hegel, *The Philosophy of History*, 420–421.

32. Johann Wolgang Goethe, *Faust*, trans. W. Kaufmann (New York: Anchor, 1962), 68–81 (lines 33–242); see also Faust's speech in the Easter scene (Goethe, *Faust,* 180–82) (lines 903–40), which emphasizes the variety and energy of the *Menge.*

33. See Gary Shapiro, "Assassins and Crusaders: Nietzsche After 9/11," in *Nietzsche at the Margins*, eds. Steven V. Hicks and Alan Rosenberg (West Lafayette, IN: Purdue University Press, 2007), 186–204.

Contributors

Keith Ansell-Pearson holds a Personal Chair in Philosophy at the University of Warwick. He is the author and editor of books on Nietzsche, Bergson, and Deleuze. In 2013/14 he is Visiting Fellow in the Humanities at Rice University and is researching a book on philosophy and the sublime.

Babette Babich is Professor of Philosophy at Fordham University in New York City. She is the author of *The Hallelujah Effect: Philosophical Reflections on Music, Performance Practice, and Technology* (2013); *La fin de la pensée? Philosophie analytique contre philosophie continentale* (2012); *Nietzsche's Philosophy of Science* (1994, in Italian 1996, and in German 2011); and *Words in Blood, Like Flowers: Philosophy and Poetry, Music and Eros* (2006). Editor of eight book collections and the journal *New Nietzsche Studies*, she writes on continental philosophy, specializing in continental philosophy of science and technology as well as aesthetics and critical theory.

Debra Bergoffen is Professor Emerita of Philosophy at George Mason University, USA, and the Bishop Hamilton Lecturer of Philosophy at American University. She is the author of *The Philosophy of Simone de Beauvoir: Gendered Phenomenologies; Erotic Generosities* (New York: SUNY Press, 1997); and *Contesting the Politics of Genocidal Rape: Affirming the Dignity of the Vulnerable Body* (Routledge, New York, 2012). She is also the author of numerous articles on Beauvoir, Nietzsche, human rights and French feminist theory. Bergoffen has co-edited anthologies on women and human rights, existentialism and phenomenology, and special issues of *New Nietzsche Studies* and *Hypatia*.

Virginia Cano teaches ethics and metaphysics in the Department of Philosophy at the University of Buenos Aires, Argentina. She received her PhD in Philosophy from the same University in 2010. Currently, she is an Assistant Researcher at CONICET (National Scientific and Technical Research Council) and focuses her work on gender and sexuality from a post-structuralist perspective. She has published numerous articles in the field and edited with M. L. Femenías and P. Torricella the book *Judith Butler, su filosofía a debate* (Buenos Aires: Editorial de la Universidad de Buenos Aires, Facultad de Filosofía y Letras, in press).

Daniel Conway is Professor of Philosophy and Humanities at Texas A&M University. He is the author of *Nietzsche's Dangerous Game* (Cambridge University Press, 1997), *Nietzsche and the Political* (Routledge, 1997), and *Nietzsche's "On the Genealogy of Morals": A Reader's Guide* (Continuum, 2008). He is the editor of the four-volume series *Nietzsche: Critical Assessments of Leading Philosophers* (Routledge, 1998) and the co-editor of *Nietzsche und die antike Philosophie* (*Wissenschaftlicher Verlag*, 1992); *Nietzsche, Philosophy, and the Arts* (Cambridge University Press, 1998); and *The History of Continental Philosophy*, Volume II (Acumen, 2010). He is a member of the Executive Committee of the Friedrich Nietzsche Society and a former Executive Editor of the *Journal of Nietzsche Studies.*

Mónica B. Cragnolini (PhD, Universidad de Buenos Aires) is Director of the Master in Interdisciplinary Studies of Subjectivity and professor in Metaphysics, in the Faculty of Philosophy and Letters of the University of Buenos Aires. She is a researcher of the Consejo Nacional de Investigaciones Científicas y Técnicas (CONICET). She is the author of *Razón imaginativa, identidad y ética en la obra de Paul Ricoeur* (Almagesto, 1993); *Nietzsche: camino y demora* (EUDEBA, 1998; 2nd ed.: Biblos, 2003); *Moradas nietzscheanas. Del sí mismo, del otro y del entre* (La Cebra, 2006, 2d ed.: Universidad Autónoma Ciudad de México, 2009); and *Derrida, un pensador del resto* (La Cebra, 2007). She has edited *Entre Nietzsche y Derrida. Vida, muerte, sobrevida* (La Cebra, 2013); *Extrañas comunidades. La impronta nietzscheana en el debate contemporáneo* (La Cebra, 2009); *Por amor a Derrida* (La Cebra, 2008); and *Modos de lo extraño. Subjetividad y alteridad en el pensamiento postnietzscheano* (Santiago Arcos, 2005). With G. Kaminsky, she edited *Nietzsche actual e inactual, vols. I y II* (Universidad de Buenos Aires, 1996), and with R. Maliandi, *La razón y el minotauro* (Almagesto, 1998). She is the director of the journal *Instantes y Azares. Escrituras nietzscheanas (ex Perspectivas Nietzscheanas).*

Mariana A. Cruz is an Assistant Professor at the Faculty of Psychology at the National University of Córdoba, Argentina, where she teaches in the area of epistemological problems. She holds a PhD degree in Philosophy from the same university. Her PhD thesis addresses questions about teleological explanations for natural organisms in the posthumously published early works by Nietzsche. She collaborated in the publication on epistemological questions derived from these works, especially on teleology in the context of nineteenth century's biological theories in Germany and its contemporary assessment, as well as issues about complexity, adaptive systems, neo-Kantianism, and related subjects.

Rainer J. Hanshe is a novelist and the founder of Contra Mundum Press. He co-founded and served as the director of the Nietzsche Circle, establishing two journals while there: *The Agonist* and *Hyperion: On the Future of Aesthetics*. For two years he worked as an assistant to Nan Goldin, which culminated in *The Devil's Playground*, her major exhibition at the Centre Pompidou in Paris. Hanshe is the author of *The Acolytes* (2010) and *The Abdication* (2012) and is now working on two other novels, *Now, Wonder* and *Humanimality*. Most recently, he edited Richard Foreman's *Plays with Films*. Other texts of his have appeared in *Jelenkor, Asymptote, Quarterly Conversation, ChrisMarker.org*, and elsewhere. Hanshe's second novel, *The Abdication*, is currently being translated into Italian, Turkish, and Slovakian.

Lawrence J. Hatab is Louis I. Jaffe Professor of Philosophy and Eminent Scholar at Old Dominion University. He has published over fifty articles, mostly on Nietzsche and Heidegger. His books include *Nietzsche's On the Genealogy of Morality: An Introduction* (Cambridge University Press, 2008); *Nietzsche's Life Sentence: Coming to Terms with Eternal Recurrence* (Routledge, 2005); *Ethics and Finitude: Heideggerian Contributions to Moral Philosophy* (Rowman & Littlefield, 2000); and *A Nietzschean Defense of Democracy: An Experiment in Postmodern Politics* (Open Court, 1995). He is currently writing a book on language.

Scott Jenkins is Associate Professor of Philosophy at the University of Kansas, USA. He is the author of numerous articles on post-Kantian European philosophy.

Vanessa Lemm is Professor of Philosophy at the School of Humanities and Languages at the University of New South Wales, Sydney, Australia. She is the author of *Nietzsche's Animal Philosophy: Culture, Politics, and the Animality of the Human Being* (New York: Fordham University Press, 2009), *Nietzsche y el pensamiento politico contemporáneo* (Santiago: Fondo de cultura económica, 2013) and several articles on Nietzsche, biopolitics, and contemporary political theory. She has also edited volumes on Hegel and Foucault.

Donovan Miyasaki is Associate Professor of Philosophy at Wright State University, Dayton, Ohio. His research focuses on moral psychology and political philosophy in nineteenth- and twentieth-century European philosophy, particularly in the works of Nietzsche, Heidegger, the Frankfurt School, and Freud. He is the author of several articles on Nietzsche, appearing in *Journal of Moral Philosophy, History of Philosophy Quarterly*, and *Nietzsche-Studien*.

Eduardo Nasser holds a Doctor of Philosophy from the University of São Paulo, Brazil. He is the author of various articles and book chapters on Nietzschean philosophy, such as "The Criticism of the Conception of Substance in Nietzsche" and "The Romanticism in Nietzsche as a Temporal, Aesthetic, and Ethical Problem." He is also a member of the Study Group Nietzsche (Grupo de Estudos Nietzsche—GEN) and The International Nietzsche Research Group (Groupe International de Recherches sur Nietzsche—GIRN).

Gary Shapiro is Tucker-Boatwright Professor of Humanities and Philosophy, Emeritus, at the University of Richmond. He has published the books *Nietzschean Narratives* (1989); *Alcyone: Nietzsche on Gifts, Noise, and Women* (1991); *Earthwards: Robert Smithson and Art After Babel* (1995); and *Archaeologies of Vision: Foucault and Nietzsche on Seeing and Saying* (2003). He is also the author of many articles on aesthetics, the history of philosophy, and other topics. Shapiro has recently published articles on Thoreau, J. M. Coetzee, and the aesthetics of the picturesque. He is completing a book on Nietzsche's political thought.

Herman W. Siemens teaches modern philosophy at Leiden University in the Netherlands and is president of the Friedrich Nietzsche Society of Great Britain. He is a chief editor and contributor to the ongoing "Nietzsche Dictionary" project, based at Radboud University of Nijmegen and Leiden. He has published widely on Nietzsche, including concept studies and articles on his main areas of interest: art, law, the agon, and its political implications. He is co-editor of the 2008 volume *Nietzsche, Power and Politics* (de Gruyter) and directs a research program funded by the Netherlands Organization for Scientific Research: "Between Deliberation and Agonism: Rethinking Conflict and Its Relation to Law in Political Philosophy." He is a Research Associate of the Universidad Diego Portales (Chile), the University of Pretoria (South Africa) and the Universidade de Lisboa (Portugal).

Dieter Thomä is Professor of Philosophy at the University of St. Gallen, Switzerland. He is the author of seven books, among them a monograph on Heidegger, *Die Zeit des Selbst und die Zeit danach* (*The Time of the Self and the Time Afterward*, Frankfurt: Suhrkamp, 1990); *Vom Glück in der Moderne* (*Of Happiness in Modern Times*, Frankfurt: Suhrkamp, 2003); and *Totaliät und Mitleid* (*Totality and Sympathy*, Frankfurt: Suhrkamp, 2006). He has also edited a Heidegger handbook and published numerous articles on Nietzsche, critical theory, and political philosophy.

Tracy B. Strong is Distinguished Professor at the University of California, San Diego, and Professor of Political and Social Thought at the University of Southampton. He has published on Nietzsche, Rousseau, Hobbes, Carl Schmitt, and Max Weber among others. His most recent book is *Politics without Vision: Thinking without a Banister in the Twentieth Century* (Winner of the David Easton Prize in 2013).

Index

Perspectives in Continental Philosophy

John D. Caputo, series editor

John D. Caputo, ed., *Deconstruction in a Nutshell: A Conversation with Jacques Derrida.*

Michael Strawser, *Both/And: Reading Kierkegaard—From Irony to Edification.*

Michael D. Barber, *Ethical Hermeneutics: Rationality in Enrique Dussel's Philosophy of Liberation.*

James H. Olthuis, ed., *Knowing* Other-*wise: Philosophy at the Threshold of Spirituality.*

James Swindal, *Reflection Revisited: Jürgen Habermas's Discursive Theory of Truth.*

Richard Kearney, *Poetics of Imagining: Modern and Postmodern.* Second edition.

Thomas W. Busch, *Circulating Being: From Embodiment to Incorporation—Essays on Late Existentialism.*

Edith Wyschogrod, *Emmanuel Levinas: The Problem of Ethical Metaphysics.* Second edition.

Francis J. Ambrosio, ed., *The Question of Christian Philosophy Today.*

Jeffrey Bloechl, ed., *The Face of the Other and the Trace of God: Essays on the Philosophy of Emmanuel Levinas.*

Ilse N. Bulhof and Laurens ten Kate, eds., *Flight of the Gods: Philosophical Perspectives on Negative Theology.*

Trish Glazebrook, *Heidegger's Philosophy of Science.*

Kevin Hart, *The Trespass of the Sign: Deconstruction, Theology, and Philosophy.*

Mark C. Taylor, *Journeys to Selfhood: Hegel and Kierkegaard.* Second edition.

Dominique Janicaud, Jean-François Courtine, Jean-Louis Chrétien, Michel Henry, Jean-Luc Marion, and Paul Ricoeur, *Phenomenology and the "Theological Turn": The French Debate.*

Karl Jaspers, *The Question of German Guilt.* Introduction by Joseph W. Koterski, S.J.

Jean-Luc Marion, *The Idol and Distance: Five Studies.* Translated with an introduction by Thomas A. Carlson.

Jeffrey Dudiak, *The Intrigue of Ethics: A Reading of the Idea of Discourse in the Thought of Emmanuel Levinas.*

Robyn Horner, *Rethinking God as Gift: Marion, Derrida, and the Limits of Phenomenology.*

Mark Dooley, *The Politics of Exodus: Søren Kierkegaard's Ethics of Responsibility.*

Merold Westphal, *Overcoming Onto-Theology: Toward a Postmodern Christian Faith.*

Edith Wyschogrod, Jean-Joseph Goux, and Eric Boynton, eds., *The Enigma of Gift and Sacrifice.*

Stanislas Breton, *The Word and the Cross.* Translated with an introduction by Jacquelyn Porter.

Jean-Luc Marion, *Prolegomena to Charity.* Translated by Stephen E. Lewis.

Peter H. Spader, *Scheler's Ethical Personalism: Its Logic, Development, and Promise.*

Jean-Louis Chrétien, *The Unforgettable and the Unhoped For.* Translated by Jeffrey Bloechl.

Don Cupitt, *Is Nothing Sacred? The Non-Realist Philosophy of Religion: Selected Essays.*

Jean-Luc Marion, *In Excess: Studies of Saturated Phenomena.* Translated by Robyn Horner and Vincent Berraud.

Phillip Goodchild, *Rethinking Philosophy of Religion: Approaches from Continental Philosophy.*

William J. Richardson, S.J., *Heidegger: Through Phenomenology to Thought.*

Jeffrey Andrew Barash, *Martin Heidegger and the Problem of Historical Meaning.*

Jean-Louis Chrétien, *Hand to Hand: Listening to the Work of Art.* Translated by Stephen E. Lewis.

Jean-Louis Chrétien, *The Call and the Response.* Translated with an introduction by Anne Davenport.

D. C. Schindler, *Han Urs von Balthasar and the Dramatic Structure of Truth: A Philosophical Investigation.*

Julian Wolfreys, ed., *Thinking Difference: Critics in Conversation.*

Allen Scult, *Being Jewish/Reading Heidegger: An Ontological Encounter.*

Richard Kearney, *Debates in Continental Philosophy: Conversations with Contemporary Thinkers.*

Jennifer Anna Gosetti-Ferencei, *Heidegger, Hölderlin, and the Subject of Poetic Language: Toward a New Poetics of Dasein.*

Jolita Pons, *Stealing a Gift: Kierkegaard's Pseudonyms and the Bible.*

Jean-Yves Lacoste, *Experience and the Absolute: Disputed Questions on the Humanity of Man.* Translated by Mark Raftery-Skehan.

Charles P. Bigger, *Between* Chora *and the Good: Metaphor's Metaphysical Neighborhood.*

Dominique Janicaud, *Phenomenology "Wide Open": After the French Debate.* Translated by Charles N. Cabral.

Ian Leask and Eoin Cassidy, eds., *Givenness and God: Questions of Jean-Luc Marion.*

Jacques Derrida, *Sovereignties in Question: The Poetics of Paul Celan.* Edited by Thomas Dutoit and Outi Pasanen.

William Desmond, *Is There a Sabbath for Thought? Between Religion and Philosophy.*

Bruce Ellis Benson and Norman Wirzba, eds., *The Phenomenology of Prayer.*

S. Clark Buckner and Matthew Statler, eds., *Styles of Piety: Practicing Philosophy after the Death of God.*

Kevin Hart and Barbara Wall, eds., *The Experience of God: A Postmodern Response.*

John Panteleimon Manoussakis, *After God: Richard Kearney and the Religious Turn in Continental Philosophy.*

John Martis, *Philippe Lacoue-Labarthe: Representation and the Loss of the Subject.*

Jean-Luc Nancy, *The Ground of the Image.*

Edith Wyschogrod, *Crossover Queries: Dwelling with Negatives, Embodying Philosophy's Others.*

Gerald Bruns, *On the Anarchy of Poetry and Philosophy: A Guide for the Unruly.*

Brian Treanor, *Aspects of Alterity: Levinas, Marcel, and the Contemporary Debate.*

Simon Morgan Wortham, *Counter-Institutions: Jacques Derrida and the Question of the University.*

Leonard Lawlor, *The Implications of Immanence: Toward a New Concept of Life.*

Clayton Crockett, *Interstices of the Sublime: Theology and Psychoanalytic Theory.*

Bettina Bergo, Joseph Cohen, and Raphael Zagury-Orly, eds., *Judeities: Questions for Jacques Derrida.* Translated by Bettina Bergo and Michael B. Smith.

Jean-Luc Marion, *On the Ego and on God: Further Cartesian Questions.* Translated by Christina M. Gschwandtner.

Jean-Luc Nancy, *Philosophical Chronicles.* Translated by Franson Manjali.

Jean-Luc Nancy, *Dis-Enclosure: The Deconstruction of Christianity.* Translated by Bettina Bergo, Gabriel Malenfant, and Michael B. Smith.

Andrea Hurst, *Derrida Vis-à-vis Lacan: Interweaving Deconstruction and Psychoanalysis.*

Jean-Luc Nancy, *Noli me tangere: On the Raising of the Body.* Translated by Sarah Clift, Pascale-Anne Brault, and Michael Naas.

Jacques Derrida, *The Animal That Therefore I Am.* Edited by Marie-Louise Mallet, translated by David Wills.

Jean-Luc Marion, *The Visible and the Revealed.* Translated by Christina M. Gschwandtner and others.

Michel Henry, *Material Phenomenology.* Translated by Scott Davidson.

Jean-Luc Nancy, *Corpus*. Translated by Richard A. Rand.
Joshua Kates, *Fielding Derrida*.
Michael Naas, *Derrida From Now On*.
Shannon Sullivan and Dennis J. Schmidt, eds., *Difficulties of Ethical Life*.
Catherine Malabou, *What Should We Do with Our Brain?* Translated by Sebastian Rand, Introduction by Marc Jeannerod.
Claude Romano, *Event and World*. Translated by Shane Mackinlay.
Vanessa Lemm, *Nietzsche's Animal Philosophy: Culture, Politics, and the Animality of the Human Being*.
B. Keith Putt, ed., *Gazing Through a Prism Darkly: Reflections on Merold Westphal's Hermeneutical Epistemology*.
Eric Boynton and Martin Kavka, eds., *Saintly Influence: Edith Wyschogrod and the Possibilities of Philosophy of Religion*.
Shane Mackinlay, *Interpreting Excess: Jean-Luc Marion, Saturated Phenomena, and Hermeneutics*.
Kevin Hart and Michael A. Signer, eds., *The Exorbitant: Emmanuel Levinas Between Jews and Christians*.
Bruce Ellis Benson and Norman Wirzba, eds., *Words of Life: New Theological Turns in French Phenomenology*.
William Robert, *Trials: Of Antigone and Jesus*.
Brian Treanor and Henry Isaac Venema, eds., *A Passion for the Possible: Thinking with Paul Ricoeur*.
Kas Saghafi, *Apparitions—Of Derrida's Other*.
Nick Mansfield, *The God Who Deconstructs Himself: Sovereignty and Subjectivity Between Freud, Bataille, and Derrida*.
Don Ihde, *Heidegger's Technologies: Postphenomenological Perspectives*.
Suzi Adams, *Castoriadis's Ontology: Being and Creation*.
Richard Kearney and Kascha Semonovitch, eds., *Phenomenologies of the Stranger: Between Hostility and Hospitality*.
Michael Naas, *Miracle and Machine: Jacques Derrida and the Two Sources of Religion, Science, and the Media*.
Alena Alexandrova, Ignaas Devisch, Laurens ten Kate, and Aukje van Rooden, *Re-treating Religion: Deconstructing Christianity with Jean-Luc Nancy*. Preamble by Jean-Luc Nancy.
Emmanuel Falque, *The Metamorphosis of Finitude: An Essay on Birth and Resurrection*. Translated by George Hughes.
Scott M. Campbell, *The Early Heidegger's Philosophy of Life: Facticity, Being, and Language*.
Françoise Dastur, *How Are We to Confront Death? An Introduction to Philosophy*. Translated by Robert Vallier. Foreword by David Farrell Krell.
Christina M. Gschwandtner, *Postmodern Apologetics? Arguments for God in Contemporary Philosophy*.
Ben Morgan, *On Becoming God: Late Medieval Mysticism and the Modern Western Self*.

Neal DeRoo, *Futurity in Phenomenology: Promise and Method in Husserl, Levinas, and Derrida.*

Sarah LaChance Adams and Caroline R. Lundquist, eds., *Coming to Life: Philosophies of Pregnancy, Childbirth, and Mothering.*

Thomas Claviez, ed., *The Conditions of Hospitality: Ethics, Politics, and Aesthetics on the Threshold of the Possible.*

Roland Faber and Jeremy Fackenthal, eds., *Theopoetic Folds: Philosophizing Multifariousness.*

Jean-Luc Marion, *The Essential Writings.* Edited by Kevin Hart.

Adam S. Miller, *Speculative Grace: Bruno Latour and Object-Oriented Theology.* Foreword by Levi R. Bryant.

Jean-Luc Nancy, *Corpus II: Writings on Sexuality.*

David Nowell Smith, *Sounding/Silence: Martin Heidegger at the Limits of Poetics.*

Gregory C. Stallings, Manuel Asensi, and Carl Good, eds., *Material Spirit: Religion and Literature Intranscendent.*

Claude Romano, *Event and Time.* Translated by Stephen E. Lewis.

Frank Chouraqui, *Ambiguity and the Absolute: Nietzsche and Merleau-Ponty on the Question of Truth.*

Noëlle Vahanian, *The Rebellious No: Variations on a Secular Theology of Language.*

Michael Naas, *The End of the World and Other Teachable Moments: Jacques Derrida's Final Seminar.*

Jean-Louis Chrétien, *Under the Gaze of the Bible.* Translated by John Marson Dunaway.

Edward Baring and Peter E. Gordon, eds., *The Trace of God: Derrida and Religion.*

Vanessa Lemm, ed., *Nietzsche and the Becoming of Life.*

Aaron T. Looney, *Vladimir Jankélévitch: The Time of Forgiveness.*

Robert Mugerauer, *Responding to Loss: Heideggerian Reflections on Literature, Architecture, and Film.*